Frontiers of Legal Theory

Frontiers of Legal Theory

RICHARD A. POSNER

HARVARD UNIVERSITY PRESS

Cambridge, Massachusetts
London, England

First Harvard University Press paperback edition, 2004

Library of Congress Cataloging-in-Publication Data

Posner, Richard A.
    Frontiers of legal theory / Richard A. Posner.
        p. cm.
    Includes bibliographical references and index.
    ISBN 0-674-00485-X (cloth)
    ISBN 0-674-01360-3 (pbk.)
    1. Jurisprudence.   2. Sociological jurisprudence.   3. Law—Philosophy.
4. Law and economics.   5. History—Philosophy.   6. Psychology—Philosophy.
I. Title.

K230.P6715 A34 2001
340'.1—dc21   00-050580

Contents

Frontiers of Legal Theory

Introduction

$\mathcal{T}$HE FOCUS of a traditional legal education is practical; it is on how to be an effective lawyer. Emphasis is placed on the parsing of statutes and, of particular importance in a case law system, of judicial opinions; on learning the contours of fundamental legal doctrines; on professional values; and, increasingly, on the acquisition of litigating and negotiating skills. Such an education, followed by practical experience as a lawyer with a good firm or in a good government agency, can form a highly skilled professional, which is to say someone who can "work" the system. But it cannot supply the tools essential for understanding and improving the system, because it cannot cultivate the requisite *external* perspective. It is in recognition of this limitation, of some conspicuous failures of lawyer-engineered legal reform,[1] and of the progress of the social sciences that legal education, and legal thought more generally, have become more interdisciplinary in recent years and as a result (law being an undertheorized field relative to most of the academic fields that might be thought to adjoin or intersect it) more "theoretical." This is not entirely a good thing; a lot of legal theory is vacuous.[2] But not all. Other disciplines have much to contribute

1. For one of the most recent, the performance of the Supreme Court in the key cases that provided the backdrop to the impeachment of President Clinton, see Richard A. Posner, *An Affair of State: The Investigation, Impeachment, and Trial of President Clinton*, ch. 6 (1999).

2. As I argue in Richard A. Posner, *The Problematics of Moral and Legal Theory* (1999). See also Dennis W. Arrow, "'Rich,' 'Textured,' and 'Nuanced': Constitutional 'Scholarship' and Constitutional Messianism at the Millennium," 78 *Texas Law Review* 149 (1999).

1

to the understanding and improvement of law. In this book I examine contributions from economics, history, psychology, epistemology, and statistical inference.

The subject is vast, and my treatment, therefore, necessarily only partial.[3] The emphasis on economics and on the need for more empirical study of law is not a new theme in my work, though I give it some new twists here; but the emphasis on history, on psychology, and on epistemology (by which I mean the critical examination of the truth-finding capacity of the legal process) is new. I draw heavily on previous papers of mine but have revised them in an effort to bring them into a coherent and illuminating relation with each other and to eliminate repetition. I have also updated them—they are not old, but legal theory is a rapidly evolving field—and tried to correct errors, respond to criticisms, and smooth out the prose.

By "legal theory" I mean to exclude both philosophy of law (legal philosophy, or jurisprudence)—which is concerned with the analysis of high-level law-related abstractions such as legal positivism, natural law, legal hermeneutics, legal formalism, and legal realism—and the analysis of legal doctrine, or its synonym, legal reasoning, the core analytical component of adjudication and the practice of law. Legal theory is concerned with the practical problems of law, but it approaches them from the outside, using the tools of other disciplines. It does not consider the internal perspective of the legal professional adequate to the solution even of the practical problems of law.

I realize it is a little late to be trying to appropriate the term "legal theory" for the external analysis of law. The term "theory" has long been used in law as a pretentious term for a litigant's submission ("the plaintiff's theory of the case is that the defendant's conduct amounted to an interference with the plaintiff's contractual rights"), or as a generalization proposed to organize a body of case law ("the theory of the law of torts is that losses should be shifted by law only when the injurer was blameworthy"), or as a purely internal theory of law, a theory ginned up by law professors with little use of insights or methods from

3. Additional treatment will be found in several of my previous books. See, besides those cited in notes 1 and 2 above, *The Problems of Jurisprudence* (1990); *Cardozo: A Study in Reputation* (1990); *Overcoming Law* (1995); *The Federal Courts: Challenge and Reform* (1996); *Law and Legal Theory in England and America* (1996); *Law and Literature* (rev. and enlarged ed. 1998); *Economic Analysis of Law* (5th ed. 1998).

other fields—most constitutional "theory" is of that character. These uses of the word "theory," which amount to equating "theoretical" with systematic, comprehensive, or fundamental, are a tribute to the hold that science has over the modern mind. But as the only approaches to a genuinely scientific conception of law are those that come from other disciplines, such as economics, sociology, and psychology, it is appropriate when speaking of "legal theory" at large to confine the term to theories that come from outside law.

Legal theory so understood is of more recent origin than either legal philosophy or doctrinal analysis. But its roots can be found in the late eighteenth and early nineteenth centuries, in Bentham's utilitarian (essentially, economic) theory of criminal punishment and in Savigny's historicist conception of legal science, which influenced Holmes. Later, Max Weber laid the foundations of a sociological approach to law, which was picked up in the United States by Roscoe Pound and others under the rubric of "sociological jurisprudence." Later still, the legal realist movement of the 1920s and 1930s advocated not only greater psychological realism (Jerome Frank) and economic realism (Karl Llewellyn, William O. Douglas) about the law but also large-scale empirical research as the path of law reform. Legal realism had been anticipated by Bentham, Holmes, and Cardozo, all of whom had, each in his own way, advocated greater use of nonlegal, and, specifically, social scientific, perspectives.

Legal realism failed to deliver on its promises, and by the end of World War II had petered out. The 1950s and particularly the 1960s saw a gradual increase in the intellectual ambitiousness of legal scholarship, but only since about 1970 has legal theory been a major focus of legal thinking. Progress since then has been rapid. The reasons are several. Advances in nonlegal fields—such as economics, game theory, social and political theory, cognitive psychology, and even literary theory—have forged new tools for the study of law, while at the same time the growing complexity of law and society has exposed the poverty of doctrinal analysis as a tool for solving the problems of the legal system. The sheer increase in the number of academic lawyers as a result of a steep rise in the demand for legal services, and hence in the number of lawyers and law students, has played a role too. There are now so many law professors that it is feasible for the theoretically inclined among them to seek an audience for their scholarship among other professors

rather than among practitioners and judges. The opening up of academic law to women, minorities, and political radicals has increased
the market for critical, which generally are external, perspectives on
the legal system. And abundant data on the system that are easily re-
trievable and analyzable are helping to sustain legal theory as a research
program.

Or rather programs. Legal theory is not a single research program.
Its practitioners do not even agree on the meaning of "theory." Some
legal theory is social scientific, some not; some legal theorists emphasize abstract theory, some empirical research, some neither; some legal
theory has a strongly political, even polemical, flavor and some not;
some is primarily descriptive and some heavily normative; some focuses on particular fields of law and some covers a broader span. A
sketch of the principal branches of this ill-defined field may help orient
the reader. I emphasize American law because legal theory is more
highly developed and more influential in the United States than elsewhere. Legal philosophy, in contrast, holds greater sway outside the
United States.

Law and economics, old and new. Rapid increases in recent decades in
the scope and rigor of microeconomics (due partly to the increased incorporation of game theory into economics) have fostered the emergence and continuing growth of a distinct and important subfield of legal theory—economic analysis of law. The leading U.S. law schools
have one or more Ph.D. economists on their faculty. Seven journals (six
American, one European) specialize in the economic analysis of law.
There are several textbooks, a large monographic literature, two ency-
clopedias,[4] and professional associations in the United States, Europe,
and Latin America. Several federal appellate judges are former law and
economics scholars, and most federal, and many state, judges have attended continuing education programs in economic analysis of law.

Economic analysis of law has heuristic, descriptive, and normative
aspects. As a heuristic, it seeks to display underlying unities in legal
doctrines and institutions; in its descriptive mode, it seeks to identify
the economic logic and effects of doctrines and institutions and the
economic causes of legal change; in its normative aspect it advises
judges and other policymakers on the most efficient methods of regu-

---

4. *The New Palgrave Dictionary of Economics and the Law* (Peter Newman ed. 1998); *Encyclopedia of Law and Economics* (Boudewijn Bouckaert and Gerrit de Geest eds. 2000).

lating conduct through law. The range of its subject matter has become wide, indeed all-encompassing. Exploiting advances in the economics of nonmarket behavior, economic analysis of law has expanded far beyond its original focus on antitrust, taxation, public utility regulation, corporate finance, and other areas of explicitly economic regulation. (And within that domain, it has expanded to include such fields as property and contract law.) The "new" economic analysis of law embraces such nonmarket, or quasi-nonmarket, fields of law as tort law, family law, criminal law, free speech, procedure, legislation, public international law, the law of intellectual property, the rules governing the trial and appellate process, environmental law, the administrative process, the regulation of health and safety, the laws forbidding discrimination in employment, and social norms viewed as a source of, an obstacle to, and a substitute for formal law. Economists are extensively employed as expert witnesses in such fields as antitrust and securities regulation, as well as in every type of case—personal-injury cases as well as commercial cases—in which damages have to be calculated.

Economic analysis of law has had its biggest practical impact in fields of explicitly economic regulation, such as antitrust and public utility regulation, where economic analysts have played a significant role in orienting American law in a free-market direction. Increasingly, however, its mark is felt in other areas of law as well, such as environmental law, where tradable emissions rights are a hallmark of the economic approach to the environment; the law of eminent domain, where the increasing judicial concern with "regulatory" takings bears the stamp of the economic analysts of law; and divorce law, where feminist and economic insights have joined to emphasize the economic dimension of household production.

The most ambitious *theoretical* aspect of the economic approach to law has been the proposal of a unified economic theory of law in which law's function is understood to be to facilitate the operation of free markets and, in areas where the costs of market transactions are prohibitive, to "mimic the market" by decreeing the outcome that the market could be expected to produce if market transactions were feasible.[5] It thus has both descriptive, or explanatory, and normative, or reformist, aspects.

---

5. See my *Economic Analysis of Law*, note 3 above, for the fullest elaboration to date of this approach.

The proposal of what might grandly be called *the* economic theory of law builds on a pioneering article by Ronald Coase.[6] The "Coase Theorem" holds that where market transaction costs are zero, the law's initial assignment of rights is irrelevant to efficiency, since if the assignment is inefficient the parties will rectify it by a corrective transaction. There are two important corollaries. The first is that the law, to the extent interested in promoting economic efficiency, should try to minimize transaction costs, for example by defining property rights clearly, by making them readily transferable, and by creating cheap and effective remedies for breach of contract. This sounds simple, but the formulation of efficient rules of property and contract is anything but, as we shall glimpse with reference to property law in Chapter 6.

The second corollary of the Coase Theorem is that where, despite the law's best efforts, market transaction costs remain high, the law should simulate the market's allocation of resources by assigning property rights to the highest-valued users. An example is the fair-use doctrine of copyright law, which allows writers to publish short quotations from a copyrighted work without negotiating with the copyright holder. The costs of such negotiations would usually be prohibitive; if they were not prohibitive, the usual result would be an agreement to permit the quotation, and so the doctrine of fair use brings about the result that the market would bring about if market transactions were feasible.

The economic approach to law plays a central role in this book, as in most of my previous work; it is explained more fully in the first three chapters and applied repeatedly in the succeeding ones.

Legal history. The historical perspective is the oldest, and until recent decades the most commonly employed, external perspective on the legal system. The great antiquity of law, law's notable continuity with its origins (reflected, among other things, in law's archaic terminology), and the emphasis that the American legal system in particular places on old texts—notably the Constitution of 1787—and (along with the other Anglo-American legal systems) on deciding cases in accordance with precedent, make it natural for legal scholars to take a historicist approach, the essence of which is to make both the meaning and the legitimacy of legal doctrines and decisions depend upon their historical pedigree. Although the historicist approach has lost ground in recent

---

6. R. H. Coase, "The Problem of Social Cost," 3 *Journal of Law and Economics* 1 (1960).

decades to other interdisciplinary approaches, what might appear to be an extreme version of it—"originalism"—has achieved notable influence in the Supreme Court and the lower federal courts. The historical approach to law is the subject of Part Two of this book, but I shall argue there that originalism is not best understood as historicist at all, that it is rather an effort to escape from approaches—including the historicist—that whether in theory or in practice license a considerable degree of judicial creativity.

Feminist jurisprudence. The legal profession in all its branches was, until recently, completely dominated by men. Harvard Law School did not admit women as students until the 1950s and the first female U.S. Supreme Court Justice was not appointed until 1981. As a result of the paucity of women in influential positions in the profession and the generally subordinate role of women in the society, the law failed to reflect women's interests concerning, and their perspectives on, a wide range of issues. These issues included the rules of evidence in trials for rape, the sale and display of pornography, sexual harassment in the workplace, gender discrimination in employment and education, rules governing divorce and child custody, legal restrictions on abortion, and workplace accommodations to pregnancy. Beginning in the 1970s, feminist lawyers such as Ruth Bader Ginsburg and Catharine MacKinnon began, through their teaching, writing, litigation, and other professional activities, to achieve significant reforms in the legal treatment of women. The theoretical branch of the woman's law-reform movement is known as "feminist jurisprudence." Liberal feminists, such as Ginsburg, primarily seek equal treatment of women and men. "Difference" feminists, such as Carol Gilligan, believe that masculine jurisprudence is too much oriented to rules, conflict, and rights. Radical feminists are pessimistic about meliorist reforms. MacKinnon, the pioneer of radical feminist jurisprudence (and virtually the inventor of the concept of workplace sexual harassment as a legal wrong), analogizes women to the proletariat in Marxian analysis.

Feminist jurisprudence has influenced a growing body of theoretical work dealing with issues of interest to homosexual men and to lesbians ("gaylaw"), such as the prohibition of homosexual marriage, the exclusion of homosexuals from the U.S. armed forces, other discrimination against homosexuals, and the criminal prohibition of homosexual sodomy, a prohibition that remains on the books in almost half the states.

I have discussed feminist and other sex- and gender-related legal theories at some length in other books,[7] and do not discuss them in this one.

Constitutional theory; law and political theory. The language of the U.S. Constitution is in places both broad and vague, a notable example being the Fourteenth Amendment's guarantees of "due process of law" and "equal protection of the law." The breadth and vagueness of such language, together with the sheer age of most of the Constitution and the dynamism of the society that it seeks to regulate, are invitations to free interpretation. The Supreme Court has often interpreted vague constitutional terms to create rights, such as the right of abortion, that are both remote from the expectations of the Constitution's framers and ratifiers and at odds with democratic majorities in particular states and sometimes in the nation as a whole. The legitimacy of a practice by which a committee of judges can check the power of the democratic majority to implement its preferences in law has long been a staple of debate within the legal profession. A tradition of self-restraint developed from an early article by James Bradley Thayer[8] and enlisted distinguished judicial figures such as Oliver Wendell Holmes, Louis Brandeis, Felix Frankfurter, and Learned Hand, as well as academic notables such as Henry Hart and Herbert Wechsler; Thayer's currently most influential avatar is Supreme Court Justice Antonin Scalia. Wechsler's 1959 article on neutral principles of constitutional law, the *locus classicus* of the restraintist approach, proposed that constitutional law could be stabilized if judges would base their decisions on broad principles.[9] Wechsler criticized *Brown v. Board of Education,* in which the Supreme Court had invalidated racial segregation in public education, on the ground that the only neutral principle applicable to the issue was the principle of freedom of association. He argued that the Court's decision had violated neutrality by implicitly elevating the blacks' freedom to associate with whites over the whites' freedom not to associate with blacks.

7. See Richard A. Posner, *Sex and Reason* (1992); *Overcoming Law,* note 3 above, pt. 4 and ch. 26; *The Problematics of Moral and Legal Theory,* note 2 above, at 314 (index references to "Feminism" and "Homosexuality"). For recent contributions, see Linda R. Hirshman and Jane E. Larson, *Hard Bargains: The Politics of Sex* (1998); William N. Eskridge, Jr., *Gaylaw: Challenging the Apartheid of the Closet* (1999).

8. James B. Thayer, "The Origin and Scope of the American Doctrine of Constitutional Law," 7 *Harvard Law Review* 129 (1893).

9. Herbert Wechsler, "Toward Neutral Principles of Constitutional Law," 73 *Harvard Law Review* 1 (1959).

Wechsler's article touched off an academic debate, which continues, over the proper approach to guide decision in constitutional cases so as to prevent untrammeled discretionary judgments without stifling the powerful impulse to substantive justice evident in *Brown* and other famous "Warren Court" decisions. Landmarks of the debate include Alexander Bickel's proposal (in his book *The Least Dangerous Branch*) to leaven Wechslerian principle with prudential progressivism and John Ely's proposal that the proper role of the courts in constitutional cases is to be "representation reinforcing" and thus to invalidate such obstacles to representative democacy as legislative malapportionment and poll taxes.[10] The liberal thrust of Bickel and Ely and their epigones has been parried by Robert Bork, Scalia, and other advocates of originalism. They reject the idea of a "living Constitution" and would hew to the meaning of the Constitution as it was understood by its framers and ratifiers.

Constitutional theory is heavily normative in its orientation and aim. Almost without exception theorists are much more interested in evaluating existing decisions and providing guidance to how to decide new cases than in explaining, by reference to norms that the theorist may not share, the existing pattern of the case law. Perhaps because of the emotional and political cast of modern constitutional law, constitutional theory as a field has exhibited no tendency toward closure.[11]

Political theorists who interest themselves in issues relating to law go over the same ground (by now the same *old* ground)—the role of deliberation in democratic policymaking, the tradition of civic republicanism, the meaning of American democracy, and the elements of principled judicial policymaking—that preoccupy constitutional theorists. Often they *are* constitutional theorists—so often, indeed, that "law and political theory" is virtually a synonym for constitutional theory. Very different is the approach of those scholars who bring to the analysis of constitutional issues the principles of "public choice" and thus emphasize the role of interest groups in the legislative and judicial processes, the influence of agenda-setting on political and other collective choice, the strategic interactions between different branches of government, and the indeterminacies of voting as a method of aggregating preferences. This, the public-choice branch of constitutional or political the-

10. John Hart Ely, *Democracy and Distrust: A Theory of Judicial Review* (1980).

11. For a recent survey of constitutional theories, see Richard H. Fallon, Jr., "How to Choose a Constitutional Theory," 87 *California Law Review* 535 (1999).

ory, relies heavily on game theory and rational-choice models and can be subsumed under economic analysis of law.

I have discussed constitutional and political theory at length in previous books.[12] In this book I discuss it mainly in Chapters 2–5 and in the second half of this Introduction.

Law and philosophy. Legal philosophy (jurisprudence) does not exhaust the potential applications of philosophy to law. Philosophical themes are prominent in constitutional theory and its twin, law and political theory, and are occasionally encountered not only in normative economic analysis of law, critical legal studies, and other interdisciplinary fields but also in discussions of particular fields of law. These applications define a "law and philosophy" field of legal theory that is distinct from jurisprudence. Kantian and utilitarian political and moral philosophers, and their followers in the legal professoriat, have tried to impose their normative visions on tort law, criminal law, contract law, property law, and other fields or have argued that their philosophical positions are latent in those fields. Epistemologists and philosophers of language have applied their insights to a variety of specific legal issues such as the concept of causation in tort and criminal law, the concepts of intentionality and voluntariness (for example, of a confession to the police) in criminal law, and the scope of statutory interpretation. The epistemological side of law and philosophy plays a role in Part Four of this book; the other branches are discussed at length in other books of mine.[13]

Sociology of law, and the law and society movement. In Europe, sociology of law, which includes criminology, has a long history (Max Weber being the tutelary figure) and continues to be well represented in law faculties, academic journals, the monographic literature, and movements for law reform. The focus of European sociology of law is on the operation and effects of the criminal justice system; the delivery of legal services to the poor; the structure, income, and regulation of the legal profession; how to improve judicial performance; and class and political bias in the judiciary and the profession. Surprisingly, in light of the general hospitality of the American legal academy to legal theory, soci-

12. See, for example, *Overcoming Law*, note 3 above, pt. 2; *The Problematics of Moral and Legal Theory*, note 2 above, at 144–182.

13. See *The Problems of Jurisprudence*, note 3 above; *The Problematics of Moral and Legal Theory*, note 2 above.

ology of law plays a marginal role in American legal theory. Its practitioners are too few to sustain a professional association and journal. To achieve these indicia of an established field of scholarship they have found it necessary to band together with political scientists, anthropologists, and psychologists to form the law and society movement, which has its own professional association and journal. The marginality of sociology of law in the United States is due in part to the failure of criminology to make feasible and credible proposals for dealing with the very high American crime rates, in part to a general malaise of sociology in American higher education,[14] and in part to the rise of forms of legal theory, notably law and economics and feminist jurisprudence, that compete with sociology of law.[15]

Nevertheless, American sociology of law, and "law and society" more broadly, has important strengths. The most important is an emphasis on empirical study of the legal system, an emphasis unmatched by any other field of legal theory. American legal sociologists have made major contributions to the measurement of litigation rates, the international comparison of legal systems, the operation of workaday branches of the legal system such as the divorce and traffic courts, the strategic dimensions of litigation, and the role of race and class in the legal system. Sociology of law played a significant role in a previous book of mine[16] but takes a back seat in this one. Chapter 9, on social norms, addresses a traditionally sociological topic, but my emphasis is on the economics and psychology of norm-directed behavior rather than on the sociological understanding of it.

Law and cognitive psychology; behavioralism. The importance of abnormal psychology in evaluating issues of insanity that arise in criminal trials and civil commitments has long been recognized. New in the era of legal theory is the application of cognitive psychology—the study of the brain's governance of human behavior whether or not "abnormal"—to a variety of topics in law. These topics, many of which I take

14. A malaise due in part to the field's historically leftish flavor, in part (a related point) to its association with many failed policy proposals, and in part to the growing competition of economics, which has expanded to address a number of traditional topics in sociology, only with greater rigor.

15. See Richard A. Posner, "The Sociology of the Sociology of Law: A View from Economics," 2 *European Journal of Law and Economics* 265 (1995).

16. *The Problematics of Moral and Legal Theory*, note 2 above.

up in Part Three and, to a lesser extent, Part Four of this book, include evaluating the testimony of witnesses concerning events in the distant past, measuring distortions in people's evaluation of low-probability risks, assessing the impact of evidence and argument on the thought processes and decisions of jurors, evaluating juries' and judges' decisionmaking procedures in psychologically realistic terms, accounting for the role of emotion in decision-making processes, identifying the mechanisms by which legal and other norms are enforced extralegally, and criticizing the realism of the assumptions made in the economic analysis of law about the rationality of human behavior.

A theme that unifies much though not all of this work—the part that goes by the name "behavioral economics" or "behavioral law and economics" or, the term I prefer because of its brevity, "behavioralism"—is that evolution has produced quirks in the human cognitive apparatus that impede the ability of participants in the legal process to absorb and process essential information. These quirks include the availability heuristic, which is the tendency to give undue weight to vivid, easily recalled facts or impression; hindsight bias, the tendency to exaggerate the inevitability of causal sequences; and the endowment effect, which is the tendency to value what we have because it is ours, regardless of its intrinsic value. Hindsight bias, for example, may lead jurors to infer from the fact that an accident occurred that the injurer should have foreseen and avoided the danger of accident and thus was negligent. The endowment effect may make it difficult to assign rights to the highest-value user (the procedure commended by economic analysis of law) because value becomes a function of whom the right is assigned to. Behavioralists also believe that altruism and a sense of "fairness" play a role in human social behavior that rational-choice theory cannot account for. I argue in Chapter 8 that the rational-choice model is more robust than behavioralists believe, and specifically I show how a model of rational signaling can explain some of the salient empirical results of the behavioral literature.

Law and literature. Since the early 1970s, a number of law professors, a smaller number of literary scholars, and a few academics with training in both fields have been exploring the numerous relations between law and imaginative literature. Works of literature (including some Greek tragedies, several of Shakespeare's plays, and a number of novels and short stories) that depict law have been mined for their jurisprudential relevance. The more practical applications of the field have been concentrated in the areas of interpretation, rhetoric, legal education, and intellectual property. Methods of interpretation developed by literary critics and scholars have been applied to the U.S. Constitution (creating an overlap between constitutional theory and the law and literature movement); methods of evaluating the style and rhetoric of works of literature have been used to criticize judicial opinions; works of literature thought to illustrate ethical principles or provide empathetic insights into the problems of minorities have been recommended for study by law students and judges; and literary scholarship has been used as a source of ideas of originality and creativity that might be used to guide the interpretation of copyright and related laws regulating expressive activity. This is another field of legal theory that I have discussed at length elsewhere[17] and will not take up in this book.

Critical and postmodern legal studies. Also beginning in the early 1970s, a number of legal scholars inspired by both the student movements of the late 1960s and Continental social theory (Marxist, structuralist, and poststructuralist) joined to form the movement which they called critical legal studies. In major part it was a revival of legal realism in an uncompromisingly radical form. The realists had emphasized the political element in law, but without suggesting that it was the only element; and for the most part they advocated nothing more radical than rebuilding legal principles on the findings of value-neutral social science. The critical scholars claimed that law is nothing but politics—and likewise social science (except perhaps Marxist-influenced critical theory), in particular the economic analysis of law, which became a target of these scholars. Their denial of law's objectivity, and the generally nihilistic character of their enterprise and resulting dearth of constructive suggestions, limited the impact of their work both inside and outside the academy; today the critical legal movement is passé except that, like the mother salmon off whose corpse her spawn feeds, it has nurtured three other fields of radical legal theory that continue to exert influence in academic legal circles. They are radical feminist jurisprudence, which emphasizes in the manner of critical legal studies the ideological character of existing legal doctrines and institutions; postmodernist scholarship, which emphasizes the plasticity of the legal sys-

17. See *Law and Literature*, note 3 above.

tem; and critical race theory, which in some versions takes the critique of legal rationality to the point of urging abandonment of the normal canons of scholarship in favor of heeding the "voice of color" sounded by minority legal scholars in autobiographical and other narrative, nonanalytic scholarship. Critical race theory links up with radical feminist jurisprudence in its emphasis on the social construction of race, which is akin to the feminists' emphasis on the social construction of gender. In all three derivative movements the influence of Foucault's extreme social constructionism is apparent. I have discussed these movements at length elsewhere,[18] and mention them only in passing in this book, primarily in Chapter 10.

⌒ THE FOREGOING enumeration of the fields of legal theory is not complete, but the fields omitted from the list tend to have either a narrow focus or few adherents. Examples include a literature that explores the application of Bayesian probability theory to the law of evidence, a literature that applies linguistic theory to the interpretation of legal documents, and a literature that applies evolutionary biology to selected topics mainly in family law and sexual regulation. The first of these fields, however, which could be considered a branch of cognitive psychology or an intersection between psychology and epistemology, figures in the chapters on evidence in Part Four of this book.

Legal theory is here to stay; its successes in illuminating some dark corners of the legal system and pointing the way to constructive changes have been sufficiently numerous to make it an indispensable element of legal thought. But it has proved difficult to assimilate into legal education and the practice of law because of its dependence on fields of learning with which, even today, few lawyers have more than a nodding acquaintance. My hope is to make it more accessible and useful to practitioners, students, judges, and the interdisciplinarians themselves, and to bridge the conventional academic boundaries that have made legal theory sometimes seem a kaleidoscope or even a heap of fragments rather than a unified quest for a better undertanding of the law. The particular areas I examine in this book—economics, history, psychology, epistemology, and quantitative empiricism—may seem lit-

18. Particularly in *Sex and Reason*, note 7 above, and *Overcoming Law*, note 3 above; but see also *The Problematics of Moral and Legal Theory*, note 2 above, at 265–280.

tle related to each other, but we shall see that they overlap and inter-
penetrate, enabling us to glimpse the possibility of legal theory as a
unified field of social science.

We need legal theory above all to help us answer fundamental questions about the legal system, for it is precisely knowledge *about* the system, as distinct from knowing how to navigate *within* the system, that
the lawyer's or law professor's conventional analytic techniques do not
yield. Consider—and this will be the focus of the remainder of this Introduction, a case study of our embarrassing ignorance that legal theory might in time be expected to overcome—the question whether the
power long exercised by the Supreme Court to invalidate federal and
state legislation, and other governmental action, that it considers to violate the Constitution has on the whole had effects that most people
would consider beneficial. The instinctive answer of legal professionals
is "yes," but it is merely instinctive and is now being sharply questioned
by a politically and methodologically diverse group of law professors
and jurists.[19] Some of these doubters have political objections to particular doctrines or decisions and would be happy with judicial review if
they thought the Justices of the Supreme Court were as liberal or conservative (as the case may be) as they. Others, here echoing a note
sounded by Learned Hand,[20] and before him by Jefferson and Lincoln,
among many others, dislike the antidemocratic character of judicial review (as constitutional lawyers call the judicial power to invalidate by

19. See J. M. Balkin and Sanford Levinson, "The Canons of Constitutional Law," 111 *Harvard Law Review* 963 (1998); Michael J. Klarman, "What's So Great about Constitutionalism?" 93 *Northwestern University Law Review* 145 (1998); Klarman, "Constitutional Fetish-
ism and the Clinton Impeachment Debate," 85 *Virginia Law Review* 631 (1999); Richard D.
Parker, *"Here, the People Rule": A Constitutional Populist Manifesto* (1994); Mark Tushnet,
Taking the Constitution away from the Courts (1999); Robert H. Bork, *Slouching towards Gomor-
rah: Modern Liberalism and American Decline* 117–118 (1996) (Bork would not abolish the
power of judicial review outright, but he would weaken it by allowing Congress to override a
judicial decision that invalidated a federal statute); Jeremy Waldron, *Law and Disagreement*
(1999). In addition, David A. Strauss, in an article entitled "The Irrelevance of Constitutional
Amendments," (forthcoming in March 2001 *Harvard Law Review*), makes a powerful argument that even formal amendments to the U.S. Constitution after the founding period have
made little difference to the nation's constitutional order and institutions. If so, it would appear even less likely that judicial decisions interpreting the Constitution, which do not have
the authority of formal amendments, have made a big difference.

20. Who famously said that he would not like to be "ruled by a bevy of Platonic Guardians"
because he would "miss the stimulus of living in a society where I have, at least theoretically,
some part in the direction of public affairs." Learned Hand, *The Bill of Rights* 73–74 (1958).

reference to the Constitution the acts of the other branches of government). Others simply doubt the capacity of judges to exercise the great power of judicial review responsibly. I am concerned not with the grounds or motives of these doubts, but only with the doubters' questioning of the beneficent consequences of the doctrine; for it shows that after two centuries of the distinctive American doctrine of judicial review and many thousands of judicial decisions and countless works of constitutional scholarship, the consequences of the doctrine remain a matter for conjecture.

The doubters argue as follows:

1. Legislators and other officials take the Constitution seriously even when there is no prospect of judicial enforcement. We saw this in the Clinton impeachment. Although courts take a hands-off attitude toward impeachment, allowing Congress to do pretty much anything it wants, Congress was careful not to stray outside the mainstream of arguable interpretations of the relevant constitutional provisions. Imaginative arguments that challenged settled beliefs about the meaning of these provisions, such as the argument that the Senate can convict a president of high crimes and misdemeanors yet decide not to remove him from office, were tacitly ruled out of bounds. To the extent that plausible claims of unconstitutionality can be effective political rhetoric, the Constitution may be self-enforcing.

2. A related point with similar implications is that legislators and other officials are likely to take the Constitution *more* seriously if they can't pass the buck to the courts. They are more likely to be blamed for unconstitutional behavior if there is no mode of correction. For this and other reasons officials have incentives to obey most constitutional provisions; such provisions are "incentive compatible" and so don't need external enforcers.[21]

3. The public may be "turned off" from taking an active interest in the Constitution if constitutional interpretation is the preserve of a judicial mandarinate. Judicial review tells the public that the Constitution is the judges' business, not the people's business. Mark Tushnet distinguishes between a "thick" Constitution, which is to say the entire text with the enormous body of judicial interpretation that it has accreted, and a "thin" Constitution, consisting of a handful of basic

21. Tushnet, note 19 above, ch. 5.

norms, many of them derived from the Declaration of Independence, which isn't even part of the Constitution, technically speaking, and from the preamble to the Constitution.[22] The "thin" Constitution is the one revered by the people, the one that informed the Lincoln–Douglas debates. It is obscured by the judicial elaboration of the thick Constitution—an increasingly impenetrable thicket of rules and jargon, the work of technically proficient but narrow-gauged lawyers in an era of rationality, specialization, and disenchantment.

4. Judicial review is condescending and antipopulist. It casts the Justices of the Supreme Court in the role of regents of a populace assumed incapable of self-government because of its ignorance, its passions and prejudices, and its lack of principle. Life tenure gives the federal judiciary a monarchical air, and is a formula not only for insulation from the passions of the day but also for irresponsibility and highhandedness.

5. Where the Constitution is clear, for example in entitling each state to two senators regardless of population, there is no need for judicial review to determine whether there has been a violation; the violation would be obvious, and (save in an extraordinary crisis) the people indignant. Where the Constitution is unclear, judicial review is likely to be guided by the political and policy preferences of the judges rather than by the Constitution itself. The text is so old, and controversies over its meaning so charged with political significance, that constitutional interpretation in doubtful cases (the only ones likely to be litigated) is bound to be discretionary rather than constrained.

6. Discretionary constitutional lawmaking might be salutary if a committee of unelected lawyers—which is what the Supreme Court is, after all—had the resources for informed lawmaking—for politics raised to the level of statesmanship. But it does not. Constitutional law covers so vast a domain of policy issues—from immigration to education, from poor relief to homosexual rights, from crime to religious liberty—that few Justices can be well informed about a substantial fraction of them. Training in law is not training in lawmaking. Like other lawyers, judges, even of the highest courts, tend to be narrowly professional rather than either statesmanlike or intellectually broad-gauged.

7. And so constitutional decisions, lacking guidance either from the

22. Id. at 9–13.

text of the Constitution or from a body of expert knowledge, are likely to reflect, and so to enact, the prejudices of the social set, the "class," from which Justices of the Supreme Court are drawn—a cultural elite with little claim to be representative of how the average American thinks or feels.

8. Courts lack the tools required to make unpopular constitutional rulings effective. They can outlaw public school segregation, but they cannot prevent parents from enrolling their children in private schools or moving to lily-white neighborhoods; and anyway busing is a highly imperfect remedy for—indeed, may actually accelerate—"white flight." Courts can create new constitutional rights for criminal defendants but they cannot muster the will to forbid legislatures to respond by making sentences more severe or by starving the lawyers for indigent criminal defendants of essential resources or by curtailing the nonconstitutional rights of criminal suspects. Because of limited fact-finding capacity, the courts cannot even monitor compliance with their rules effectively; police who fail to give *Miranda* warnings can testify that they did, and they will usually be believed.

9. Because we have a case law system with the powerful and prestigious U.S. Supreme Court at its apex and because cases, and above all major constitutional cases, are often dramatic and exciting, the institution of judicial review has caused constitutional debate and analysis to focus excessively on the agenda of the Supreme Court. Parts of the Constitution that for one reason or another don't generate much litigation (such as Congress's exclusive right, regularly flouted with impunity, to declare war), and constitutional claims that the Court decisively rejects (such as the claim that the equal protection clause of the Fourteenth Amendment requires equalizing per-pupil expenditures across public school districts), are off the radar screen, however intrinsically important and meritorious they are. Instead of studying issues, constitutional scholars study Supreme Court opinions, even though the Justices—who are just lawyers, remember—are often poorly informed about the issues they decide.

10. The political power that judicial review confers on the courts results in politicizing the process of judicial selection. The federal judiciary would be more professional if it were less powerful and would also be better able to perform its nonconstitutional judicial tasks.

11. The legislative process may be better than courts at dealing with

intractable, fundamental issues of political morality. Jeremy Waldron points out that "the only structures that interest contemporary philosophers of law are the structures of judicial reasoning. They are intoxicated with courts and blinded to almost everything else by the delights of constitutional adjudication."[23] They are so little interested in legislation that they fail to grasp the significance of the fact that legislators do not, at least not routinely, reason their way to "correct" conclusions. Legislators vote. The side that loses is not convinced by the vote that it was wrong; the position it took is not declared illegal, mistaken, or unprincipled; its convictions are unaltered; it merely accepts defeat, perhaps comforting itself with the thought that it may win the next time, or with having obtained some concessions by way of compromise.

A national legislature is designed to embody the full range of opinion in society, and in a society as diverse as that of the United States the range is so wide that the ends don't, as it were, touch. As a result, the selection of representatives by popular election in different districts brings into the halls of the legislature spokesmen for a range of irreconcilable opinions, and invariably what emerges from the cacophony as the legislative product is the product of compromise, polemic, and sheer electoral muscle rather than of a consensus forged by reasoning from common premises and toward common ends. There is little pretense that legislation is the triumph of right over wrong. The legislative process thus is more respectful of disagreement than the judicial and tends therefore to diffuse rather than to focus and inflame the passions aroused when political issues are debated in terms of fundamental right.

Waldron emphasizes the formality of the legislative process—for example, the use of Robert's Rules of Order to structure discussion and voting—and hence its remoteness from "models [of deliberation that are] derived from ordinary conversation" (p. 70). The informality of conversation "tends to be predicated upon the idea that participants share implicit understandings and that their interaction is oriented towards the avoidance of adversarial disagreement and the achievement of consensus" (id.). Legislation is the democratic solution to the problem posed by the fact that in a complex, heterogeneous society people do not agree on ends.

23. Waldron, note 19 above, at 9. Subsequent page references to Waldron's book appear in the text. All italicized words in my quotations from his book are so in the original.

Immediately, anyone accustomed to taking judicial review for granted will perceive a disquieting resemblance between the legislative process described by Waldron and the judicial process. Courts too decide questions by voting and judges' deliberations have their own formality. Judges when deliberating rarely engage in free-form conversation. They speak in a sequence determined by seniority, they are careful not to interrupt each other, and the amount and intensity of discussion generally are inverse to the depth of conviction that each judge brings to the particular question at issue. Even elected judges (as most state judges still are) are not representatives in the same sense as legislators. Yet cases, like legislative proposals, often raise issues on which disagreement, being rooted in differences in fundamental values or life experiences, is unresponsive to the tools of argument that judges bring to the table in lieu of the democratic legitimacy that they lack. If the legislative process is not a satisfactory method of resolving fundamental disagreements, neither (prima facie at least) is the judicial. If the legislative process is a satisfactory method, why do we need judicial review?

John Rawls and others argue for a master theory of justice that a court could employ to resolve disagreements that legislators can only bracket by passing laws that give temporary victory to one side or the other but do not resolve the disagreement by determining which side is "right." But though well aware of the intractable character of disputes over "the good," Rawls fails to draw the corollary that reasonable persons *cannot* "be expected to agree about the proper balance to be assigned in social life to their respective comprehensive conceptions" of the good (p. 152). The same uncertainties that make it impossible to achieve a consensus on the good make it impossible to achieve a consensus on the theory of justice. Not only will deeply religious people refuse to be persuaded that atheists have a superior conception of the good; they will refuse to be persuaded that secular theorists of justice like Rawls have a superior conception of justice. This is true irrespective of whether one believes, with the moral realists, that even the most difficult questions involving moral concepts such as that of justice have right answers. That is an issue of ontology (is there a moral reality?). The critical issue is epistemological; it is how to demonstrate the rightness of one moral beliefs to skeptics. "If moral realism is true, then judges' beliefs clash with legislators' beliefs in moral matters. If realism is false, judges' attitudes clash with legislators' attitudes" (p. 184). "No matter how often or emphatically we deploy words like 'objective,' a claim about what justice *objectively* requires never appears in politics except as someone's view" (p. 199).

Powerful as the challenges to judicial review that I have been examining are, a number of ripostes are possible. I do not mean such tired chestnuts as that judicial review gives the Supreme Court a platform from which to lecture the American people on their civic and moral responsibilities. Appellate courts may be more deliberative bodies than legislatures, but they deliberate with a mindset shaped by lawyers' traditions and experience, producing constitutional norms that may reflect professional bias, for example in favor of elaborate but costly procedural rights. In the hands of judges, constitutional law loses most of its inspirational potential, becoming a jumble of particulars that lacks conceptual or rhetorical unity. (The "thin" Constitution, the Constitution that the judges do *not* enforce, might be a more effective vehicle for instilling a civil religion.) There is little evidence that the people take their moral or ideological cues from the courts.[24]

More persuasive is the argument that the power of judicial review secures the core of the Constitution against infringement. Clear violations are unlikely to be committed or, if committed, to generate appeals all the way up to the Supreme Court. The result is a selection bias: the cases "selected" for decision by the Supreme Court are those on the legal frontier, and so are bound to be dominated by cases to which the Constitution does not speak with clarity, thus licensing judicial discretion. Litigation at the rind provides a bulwark against infringement of the rights in the core.

A further argument is that even if the judges can't get much guidance from the Constitution, their power to invalidate actions of other branches of government protects liberty by decentralizing governmental powers. This argument is closely related to the previous one because both imply that the power of judicial review protects Americans' libery. This is a difficult proposition to test. We cannot rerun history without judicial review and count the infringements of liberty that would have occurred under that hypothetical regime but that under the

24. See, for example, Michael J. Klarman, "The Plessy Era," 1998 *Supreme Court Review* 303, 391–392.

regime of judicial review are deterred. There have been such infringements notwithstanding judicial review and it is plausible that there
would be more without it. But just as a dog will bark loudest at
passersby when he is secure behind a fence, so a legislature is most
likely to pass unconstitutional laws when it knows that the courts will
strike them down. For then without doing any harm the legislators can
still be credited with trying by the interest group that advocated the
law. The example of impeachment suggests that legislatures are reluctant to commit clear violations of the Constitution when there is little
likelihood of judicial rectification unless the public pressure for violating the Constitution is immense, as when Lincoln suspended habeas
corpus or when Congress and state legislatures cracked down on radical speech in the aftermaths of the world wars. Other examples are the
relocation of Japanese-Americans during World War II, the enactment
of gun-control laws in the face of the Second Amendment's right to
bear arms, and the repeated flouting, most recently in the Kosovo campaign, of Congress's exclusive right to declare war. But in such cases, either the courts are ignored, as in the case of Lincoln's refusal to comply
with a writ of habeas corpus issued by Chief Justice Taney, or they
flinch, as in each of the other examples, by interpreting the Constitution loosely or, as in the case of the war power, declaring a constitutional claim nonjusticiable.

Another defense of judicial review is that courts, especially federal
courts, with their unelected, life-tenured judges, do have, despite the
undoubted limitations of their capacities in some respects, important
advantages over ordinary lawmakers. They are insulated from most of
the political pressures that beset elected legislatures and these pressures sometimes reflect selfish or parochial interests, ugly emotion, ignorance, irrational fears, or prejudice. This insulation, together with
the traditions and usages of the bench and the fact that federal judges
are screened for competence and integrity, confers a power of detached
and intelligent reflection on policy issues that is a valuable complement
to the consideration of these issues by the ordinary lawmakers.

Ordinary lawmaking, moreover, has built-in impediments to the effective functioning of democratic government that only the courts may
be able to remove. The clearest example is the reluctance of a malapportioned legislature to reapportion itself; the legislators who benefit from the malapportionment will fight like the devil against reap-

portionment. Officials may seek to entrench themselves with laws forbidding "unfair" criticisms of officials; incumbent legislators may try to prevent challengers from financing their campaigns or securing a place on the ballot; unpopular minorities may lack the political influence to ward off discriminatory legislation; and the sheer inertia of the legislative process—the fact that it is as difficult to repeal a statute as to enact a new one[25]—allows many obsolete laws to remain on the books and cause occasional mischief. Congress's seniority system, combined with Democratic domination of southern politics, gave southern congressmen and senators the power until the 1960s to block civil rights legislation strongly supported by a majority of Americans. The result was a legislative logjam that only the federal courts, wielding the power of judicial review, could break.

John Hart Ely and others, turning the tables on those who argue that judicial review is antidemocratic, claim that judicial review can make government *more* democratic.[26] Jeremy Waldron points out in response that when a democratic issue is settled undemocratically, as by a court wielding the power of judicial review, self-government is diminished even if the court got the issue right. But this response dissolves in the ambiguity of the term "democratic." Suppose Congress voted to confine the franchise to persons having a net worth of at least $1 million. The "democratic" character of the Congress elected under the new, restricted franchise could not be justified by reference to the fact that the restriction had been adopted democratically. There is no widely accepted theory of what specific rules and institutions relating to voting, districting, legislative procedures, legislators' qualifications, frequency of election, and the like are necessary in order for the legislative product to be "democratic." When legislators run in districts rather than at large, the legislature may fail to reflect majority preference, and this quite apart from the effect of interest groups in skewing the democratic process; a majority of voters in a majority of the districts will elect a majority of the legislators, though a majority of a majority can easily be a minority (for example, 60 percent of 60 percent is only 36 percent). And setting aside the question of representation, we must not be starry-eyed about the legislative process. Waldron says it's not an "un-

25. Often it is *more* difficult, because the statute may have created or strengthened an interest group that has a strong interest in the statute's continuing in force.

26. See note 10 above and accompanying text.

holy scramble for personal advantage" (p. 304) but rather "a noisy scenario in which men and women of high spirit argue passionately and vociferously about what rights we have, what justice requires, and what the common good amounts to, motivated in their disagreement not by what's in it for them but by a desire to get it right" (p. 305). This is as unrealistic a picture of the legislative process as is the corresponding roseate view of courts. The truth lies in between these two poles and probably closer to the first. Nor should it be thought self-evident that people of diverse perspectives "are capable of pooling these perspectives to come up with better decisions than any of them could make on their own" (p. 72). That proposition is refuted by the realistic view, implicit in much of what Waldron has to say about the limitations of reason in bridging fundamental disagreements, that deliberation among people who have such disagreements will tend only to entrench their disagreements. We shall note empirical evidence for this in Chapter 11.

Given the arguments *for* judicial review, the theoretical case against it must be judged inconclusive. The issue is empirical, and its empirical resolution has been retarded, in part because of a loss of interest by political scientists in law but in greater part because of the speculative character of counterfactual historicizing (more on this in Chapters 1 and 5). We know what the Supreme Court *has* done, but we do not know what legislatures *would have* done had the Supreme Court disclaimed the power of judicial review. We can make a few pretty good guesses. Official racial segregation of public schools in the South would not have ended as soon if the Court had not decided *Brown v. Board of Education,* although it surely would have ended many years ago. Many state legislatures would no doubt have remained malapportioned to this day had it not been for *Baker v. Carr* and the cases following it. Connecticut and Massachusetts would have retained, for a time anyway, their laws forbidding the sale of contraceptives had it not been for the Court's decisions invaliding the laws. A number of states would still have highly restrictive laws concerning abortion. What these examples have in common, and what enables reliable counterfactual prediction concerning them, is the use of novel constitutional principles to invalidate long-existing laws. When those laws were adopted there had been no basis for thinking them unconstitutional. The legislatures that enacted them were not shielded by judicial review from the consequences of their actions and would not have hesitated to act for fear of being criticized for violating the Constitution. The laws would therefore have been enacted, at the same time and in the same form as they were, even if there had not been a power of judicial review, and—through sheer inertia of the legislative process—they would have lasted longer, in some instances much longer, had the Court not exercised that power to strike them down.

The unclear cases are ones in which legislation was passed in the teeth as it were of the Constitution, such as the federal laws that the Supreme Court struck down forbidding the burning of the American flag. We do not know whether, were there no power of judicial review, Congress would still have passed such constitutionally questionable laws. Opposition within Congress would have been greater had opponents not had a second line of defense—namely, the courts.

One could examine the cases in which judicial review does seem to have made a difference and ask whether, taken all in all, these cases have made the nation better off in some sense on which most of us might agree. The undertaking would be vast, and it would also entail a disquieting, even disorienting shift in focus from legal to practical consequences. *Brown v. Board of Education* was a legal landmark and, on the plane of principle, a triumph of enlightened social policy. But in consequentialist terms the decision was less important, conceivably even marginal. Few schools were desegregated—very little actual enforcement of minority rights of any kind occurred—until the enactment of antidiscrimination legislation in the 1960s. And that legislation appears to have owed much more to the nonlegalistic civil rights movement (a movement of civil *dis*obedience to law) led by Martin Luther King, Jr., than to anything the Supreme Court had done or said. Of course *Brown* may have done something, perhaps much, to encourage southern blacks, and their northern supporters, to take the next step toward equality; but this is conjectural too. Some students of the period believe that the South's angry reaction to *Brown* made northerners more sympathetic to the civil rights movement than they would otherwise have been.[27] If correct, this belief illustrates the workings of the law of unintended consequences—and the more powerful *that* "law" is believed to be, the less confident a court can be that an activist judicial posture is likely to have on balance good consequences. Sporadic judi-

27. Tushnet, note 19 above, at 146.

cial intervention, with the limited tools of social reform available to the courts, in immensely complex social or political contests are bound frequently to have unanticipated consequences. Recent illustrations include the Supreme Court's partial invalidation of federal campaign finance laws[28] to create the paradox that a wealthy person can spend unlimited amounts of money on his own political candidacy but can give only $1,000 to a candidate likely to be far better qualified, and the Court's validation of the independent counsel law,[29] now thankfully expired, which enabled the Clinton impeachment fiasco.

As William Eskridge's book on the treatment of homosexuals in American law shows, their progress toward full citizenship, like that of other unpopular groups, has depended far more on their own efforts and on deep social forces than on constitutional law. The courts have been reluctant to recognize homosexual rights, though by applying the general protections of the law (including constitutional law) to homosexuals they have assisted the cause of equality.[30] The women's movement, too, appears to owe very little to the Supreme Court (or other courts), which did not discover a constitutional right to gender equality until the movement was well under way, and much more to transformations in women's role in society that have technological causes—better contraceptive methods, lower infant mortality, improved household labor-saving devices, and the reduced importance of physical strength in the job market. *Roe v. Wade* doubtless increased the abortion rate, but perhaps not by much—the rate of legal abortions was rising rapidly at the time the case was decided.[31] And the case galvanized the "right to life" movement, which succeeded in preventing federal funding of abortions and intimidating many abortion providers. And, even if *Roe v. Wade* has led to more abortions, no one can say with any confidence whether it is good or bad to have as many abortions as we do.

In periods when constitutional values have been seriously threatened, the Court has tended to take a back seat, and at other times—

---

28. See Buckley v. Valeo, 424 U.S. 1 (1976) (per curiam).

29. See Morrison v. Olson, 487 U.S. 654 (1988), discussed in Posner, note 1 above, at 217–225, 227–230.

30. See Eskridge, note 7 above, ch. 3.

31. Gerald Rosenberg, *The Hollow Hope: Can Courts Bring about Social Change?* 178–180 (1991). Rosenberg is one of the few contemporary political scientists who has conducted a sustained empirical analysis of a major phase of the American legal system.

the present, for example—its constitutional interventions tend to lack theme or coherence. It is possible to view today's Court as strewing random impediments to experimental solutions to social problems, whether the experiment is a prohibition against hate speech and Internet indecency, or a residency requirement intended to staunch the inflow of indigents to states with generous welfare laws, or term limits for Congressmen, or the one-house veto of administrative regulations, or the line-item veto, or requiring prisons and other public bodies to accommodate the practices of religious minorities, or limiting the role of money in political campaigns—all areas where the Supreme Court in the name of the Constitution has thrown spanners into the works. The experiments may be bad but we'll never know if they're snuffed out before the results are known. Perhaps the Justices should ponder Isabel's warning to Angelo in *Measure for Measure* that "it is excellent / To have a giant's strength, but it is tyrannous / To use it like a giant."[32]

The skeptics of judicial review have not "proved" that it is on balance a bad thing, or even that it is not on balance a good thing. What they have demonstrated is how little we know about this important practice of the American legal system—and, by implication, about the system in general. Maybe we need a book like this, which explores the potential of other disciplines, besides law, to help us to understand and improve the legal system.

32. Act II, scene 2, lines 111–114.

~ I
ECONOMICS

~ 1

The Law and Economics Movement: From Bentham to Becker

$\mathcal{T}$HE FOREMOST interdisciplinary field of legal studies is economic analysis of law, or, as it is more commonly referred to, "law and economics." The dean of the Yale Law School, a critic of the law and economics movement, nevertheless calls it "an enormous enlivening force in American legal thought," and says that it "continues and remains the single most influential jurisprudential school in this country."[1] A comprehensive examination of the field is beyond the scope of this book, and anyway can be found elsewhere.[2] What I try to do instead in this chapter is to anchor a brief description of the field by reference to two of its most illustrious progenitors, Jeremy Bentham and (briefly) Gary Becker, whom almost two centuries separate but a shared conception of the breadth of the economic model of human behavior unite; in the next chapter to illustrate how economics can illuminate an area of law that seems particularly remote from economics—namely, freedom of speech; and in the third chapter to take up some of the difficult normative issues that beset the application of economics to law. Other topics in the economic analysis of law are taken up later in the book, for example the economics of possession in Chapter 6 and of procedure in Chapters 11 and 12. Another goal of the present chapter

1. Remarks of Anthony T. Kronman at the Second Driker Forum for Excellence in the Law, 42 *Wayne Law Review* 115, 160 (1995).
2. See Richard A. Posner, *Economic Analysis of Law* (5th ed. 1998).

is to begin to wrestle with the issue of historical causality, which recurs in Part Two of the book; and let me begin with that issue.

The question of Bentham's influence on the law and economics movement is particularly difficult even though it concerns only a tiny slice of Bentham's vast influence on legal thinking and practice.[3] It is difficult because the determination of influence is difficult, especially when the span of time to be considered is great. The law and economics movement, in anything like its present form, began sometime between 1958 and 1973. The first date is the first year that the *Journal of Law and Economics* was published, and the second date is the date of publication of the first edition of my book *Economic Analysis of Law*. Before the launching of the *Journal of Law and Economics*, the law and economics movement could not have been said to exist; after my book was published, its existence could not be denied, though it could be deplored. If one year must be picked for the beginning of the movement, it would be 1968, and for a reason that turns out to be connected, though only loosely, with Bentham. And in 1968 Bentham had been dead for 136 years.

I need to distinguish between two meanings of "influence." One, which I'll call "inspiration," refers to the situation in which (if we are speaking of the influence of a person's ideas) an idea held by one person, call him *A*, is picked up *from A* by *B* and used by *B*. The important thing is that *B* in fact got the idea from *A* rather than discovering it independently or borrowing it from someone whose chain of title does not go back to *A*. The second sense of "influence," which I'll call "cause," refers to the situation in which *B* would not have used the idea had *A* never held it. *B* might have been inspired by *A* in the sense of having gotten the idea from him, and yet it might be that if *A* had never lived *B* would have gotten the same idea from someone else, who would have discovered or invented it had *A* never existed—discovered it later,

3. On which see, for example, *Jeremy Bentham and the Law: A Symposium* (George W. Keeton and Georg Schwarzenberger eds. 1948); Gray L. Dorsey, "The Influence of Benthamism on Law Reform in England," 13 *St. Louis University Law Journal* 11 (1968); Peter J. King, *Utilitarian Jurisprudence in America: The Influence of Bentham and Austin on American Legal Thought in the Nineteenth Century*, chs. 2–5 (1986). I have found only one previous discussion of Bentham's relation to the law and economics movement: Alan Strowel, "Utilitarisme et approche économique dans la théorie du droit: autour de Bentham et de Posner," 18 *Revue interdisciplinaire d'études juridiques* 1 (1987). It is mainly a comparison of Bentham's and my views, and does not discuss his influence.

but before *B*'s time. The longer the interval between *A* and *B*, the likelier this is to happen.

Inspiration is more easily determined than what I'm calling causation, because it does not involve speculation about counterfactuals. It can usually be determined from records or statements by *B* or his acquaintances, or by the sort of internal evidence (striking similarity inexplicable except on the hypothesis of copying) used in many copyright cases to determine whether a later work has copied an earlier one.

The distinction between inspiration and cause, though one might suppose it fundamental to the history profession, is often overlooked by historians, as by the distinguished historian William McNeill in the following passage: if the Assyrian army had conquered Jerusalem in 701 B.C. and deported its inhabitants, "Judaism would have disappeared from the face of the earth and the two daughter religions of Christianity and Islam could not possibly have come into existence. In short, our world would be profoundly different in ways we cannot really imagine."[4] Judaism was an inspiration for Christianity and Islam in the sense that the latter two religions borrowed from it, but it does not follow that had Judaism disappeared in the eighth century or indeed never existed Christianity and Islam in the approximate sense in which we know these religions would not have arisen and developed in essentially the form and at the time that they did. For they emerged as responses to powerful forces and, in religion as in the market, demand tends to evoke supply.

It would be extremely difficult to establish a causal relation between Bentham and an event—the birth of the law and economics movement—that occurred almost a century and a half after his death. But I think he can be shown to be one of the inspirers.

That economics has a relation to law has been known at least since Hobbes's discussion of property in the seventeenth century. Both David Hume and Adam Smith discussed the economic functions of law.[5] As early as the 1930s, a handful of legal fields, mainly antitrust and public utility regulation, that deal explicitly with competition and mo-

---

4. William H. McNeill, "The Greatest Might-Have-Been of All," *New York Review of Books*, Sept. 23, 1999, p. 62.

5. As emphasized in Charles K. Rowley, "Law-and-Economics from the Perspective of Economics," in *The New Palgrave Dictionary of Economics and the Law*, vol. 2, pp. 474, 474–476 (Peter Newman ed. 1998).

nopoly were receiving the sustained attention of leading English and American economists. (Competition and monopoly had received the attention of economists since Adam Smith; hence the qualification "sustained.") And, in retrospect, an economic literature dealing with other fields of law, notably Robert Hale's work on contract law, which also dates from the 1930s, can be identified.[6] But even after the *Journal of Law and Economics* began publication in 1958, a law and economics *movement*, if discernible at all, would have been associated primarily with the study of competition and monopoly, although occasional forays had been made into taxation (Henry Simons) and corporations (Henry Manne), even patents (Arnold Plant); and if one went back to the eighteenth century there was Bentham's largely forgotten utilitarian—essentially, economic—analysis of crime and punishment, of which more shortly. It was not until 1961, when Ronald Coase's article on social cost was published,[7] and at about the same time Guido Calabresi's first article on torts,[8] that an economic theory of the common law could be glimpsed. When in 1968 Gary Becker published his article on crime,[9] reviving and refining Bentham, it began to seem that perhaps no field of law could not be placed under the lens of economics with illuminating results. And sure enough, within a few years papers on the economics of contract law, civil and criminal procedure, property, consumer protection, and other areas new to economists had appeared and the rough shape of the mature field was discernible. Later, books and articles would extend the economic analysis of law into such fields as employment, admiralty, intellectual property, family law, legislation, environmental law, administrative law, conflict of laws, and judicial behavior—and this is only a partial list. The expanded range of economic analysis of law was facilitated by the expanding application of the economist's model of rational choice to nonmarket behavior. Lately

6. See Barbara Fried, *The Progressive Assault on Laissez Faire: Robert Hale and the First Law and Economics Movement* (1998); Ian Ayres, "Discrediting the Free Market," 66 *University of Chicago Law Review* 273 (1999).

7. R. H. Coase, "The Problem of Social Cost," 3 *Journal of Law and Economics* 1 (1960 [but actually published in 1961]).

8. Guido Calabresi, "Some Thoughts on Risk Distribution and the Law of Torts," 70 *Yale Law Journal* 499 (1961).

9. Gary S. Becker, "Crime and Punishment: An Economic Approach," 76 *Journal of Political Economy* 169 (1968), reprinted in *The Esssence of Becker* 463 (Ramón Febrero and Pedro S. Schwartz eds. 1995).

the range and depth of the economic approach to law have been enlarged by developments in game theory, signaling theory, and the economics of nonrational behavior ("behavioral economics"), all of which we'll encounter in later chapters.

The economic analysis of law has both positive (that is, descriptive) and normative aspects. It tries to explain and predict the behavior of participants in the legal system and even the doctrinal, procedural, and institutional structure of the system. But it also tries to improve law by pointing out respects in which existing or proposed laws have unintended or undesirable consequences and by proposing practical reforms. It is not merely an ivory-towered enterprise, especially in the United States, where the law and economics movement has influenced legal reform in such fields as antitrust law, the regulation of public utilities and common carriers, environmental regulation, the calculation of damages in personal injury suits, the regulation of the securities markets, the design of federal sentencing guidelines, methods for dividing property and calculating alimony in divorce cases, and the law governing investment by pension funds and other trustees. The deregulation movement, and the increased respectability of free-market ideology generally, owe something to the law and economics movement.

Noneconomists tend to associate economics with money, capitalism, selfishness, a reductive and unrealistic conception of human motivation and behavior, a formidable mathematical apparatus, and a penchant for cynical, pessimistic, and conservative conclusions. It earned the sobriquet of "the dismal science" because of Thomas Malthus's thesis that famine, war, and sexual abstinence were the only ways in which population and food supply could be equilibrated. The essence of economics is none of these things. The essence is extremely simple, although the simplicity is deceptive. The simple can be subtle, can be counterintuitive; its antithesis is "complicated," not "difficult."

Most economic analysis consists of tracing out the consequences of assuming that people are rational in their social interactions. In the case of the activities that interest the law, these people may be criminals or prosecutors or parties to accidents or taxpayers or tax collectors or striking workers—or even law students. Students treat grades as prices, so that unless the university administration intervenes, unpopular professors, in order to keep up their enrollments, will sometimes compensate students for the low perceived value of the course by giving them higher grades, that is, by raising the price that the professor pays for the student.

I said that the economist's tracing out the consequences of a practice or policy is subtle as well as simple, and here is an example.[10] A "spend-thrift trust" is a common form of trust that does not authorize the trustee to pay out any of the money or other property in the trust to the creditors of the trust's beneficiaries. The law will enforce such a restriction. Yet it has seemed to many students of the law a fraud on creditors; for the trust beneficiary, assuming that his whole wealth is in the spendthrift trust, can borrow all he wants, spend what he borrows, and not be coercible by law to repay the lenders. But economics suggests the opposite conclusion—that, provided the provision preventing creditors from reaching into the trust is not concealed, a spendthrift trust *limits* borrowing by the trust beneficiary, because he can't offer security to the lender; he thus can't make a credible commitment to repay. From here it is but a step to see how increasing the rights of debtors in bankruptcy, far from causing an avalanche of reckless borrowing, could reduce the amount of borrowing, and so the incidence of bankruptcy, by causing lenders to make smaller loans to risky borrowers. So lenders may oppose easy bankruptcy not because they fear there will be more defaults but because they fear a reduction in the volume of loans. (Just imagine how few loans there would be if borrowers had *no* obligation to repay.) Notice also how creditors are as badly hurt by excessively stringent as by excessively lenient bankruptcy rules: if creditors had the legal right, as under ancient Roman law, to carve up a defaulting borrower into as many pieces as there were creditors, the rate of default on loans would be very low but most people would be afraid to borrow. One understands now why loan sharks break the legs of a defaulting borrower, but do not kill him.

This discussion illustrates two closely related advantages of the economic approach to law. First, it offers a neutral standpoint on politically controversial legal topics. Conventional bankruptcy scholars tend to be either pro-debtor or pro-creditor (and so the course in bankruptcy is sometimes called "Debtors' Rights" or "Creditors' Remedies"

10. Based on Posner, note 2 above, at 560–561, and Adam J. Hirsch, "Spendthrift Trusts and Public Policy: Economic and Cognitive Perspectives," 73 *Washington University Law Quarterly* 1 (1995).

rather than just plain "Bankruptcy"). The economist favors neither side, favors only efficiency. Second, the economic approach frequently dissolves contentious antinomies, here by demonstrating the interrelation of debtors' and creditors' interests.

Rationality implies decisionmaking, and people often have to make decisions under conditions of profound uncertainty. Consider the question of how much care a rational person should take to avoid an accident. The accident will occur with probability P and impose a cost that I'll call L, for loss, while eliminating the possibility of such an accident would impose a cost on the potential injurer, a cost that I shall call B (for burden). The cost of avoiding the accident will be less than the expected accident cost (or benefit of avoiding the accident) if B is smaller than L discounted (multiplied) by P, or $B < PL$.[11] In that event, should he fail to take the precaution (perhaps because he does not reckon the cost to the accident victim a cost to him) and the accident occur, he is properly regarded as being at fault. This is the negligence formula announced by Judge Learned Hand in a judicial opinion in 1947[12] but not recognized as an *economic* formula for negligence until many years later. The formula is simple, but its elaboration and application to specific doctrines in the law of torts have generated an immense and illuminating literature. Hand was not an economist, and he proposed the formula to decide a legal case. This is an example of the frequent isomorphism of legal doctrines and economic principles; the latter can often be used to illuminate and refine the former.

Notice that an injurer can be negligent even if the probability of an accident is very low, because B may be low or L high, and even if the cost of avoiding the injury is very high, because P and/or L may be very high. Notice too that B can signify not only the cost to the potential injurer of taking precautions, but also the cost to him of reducing his output or other activity, which is another way of avoiding injuring people. This will give us a clue to the role, or *a* role, of strict liability in the law. If a person kept a tiger in his backyard for self-defense, and the tiger got out and bit a neighbor's head off, it would be a case of a high P and a high L, and also of a high B if the person couldn't have used

11. I abstract from the complications that are introduced by assuming that the potential injurer or potential victim is risk averse or risk preferring, rather than risk neutral.

12. United States v. Carroll Towing Co., 159 F.2d 169 (2d Cir. 1947).

greater care to keep the tiger from getting out. But *B* might be low if viewed as the cost of not having a tiger at all, of substituting another method of self-protection; and in fact this is a case where strict liability is imposed, in order to induce potential injurers to consider making changes in the character or level of their activity.

I have been discussing accidental injuries, but the Hand formula can accommodate deliberate ones as well, simply by the placing of a minus sign in front of *B*. That models the case in which, rather than having to expend resources in order to avoid an injury (positive *B*), the injurer expends resources on inflicting the injury, so that he would actually save resources by not injuring (negative *B*). Since *PL* must always be greater than a negative *B*, it is apparent that deliberate as distinct from accidental injuries should be presumptively unlawful. It is a mite less obvious that deliberate injuries cannot be left entirely to the tort system to deter. The person who expends resources in order to inflict an injury is likely to anticipate a substantial gain, whether pecuniary or nonpecuniary, from succeeding; he is also likely to take measures to avoid detection. On both counts, the optimal sanction for a deliberate injury is likely to be higher than that for an accidental injury. For example, if the prospective injurer anticipates a net gain of *G*, and a probability of being punished of $P < 1$, the sanction must be fixed at $S = G/P$ to equal his expected benefit of injuring and thus make inflicting the injury worthless to him. Many deliberate injurers cannot pay the optimal sanction, and so society has to resort to nonpecuniary sanctions in an effort to impose on the injurer a disutility equal to or greater than the expected utility to him of the injury. Moreover, many deliberate injurers have no assets—this may be why they turned to crime to support themselves—and so the victims of deliberate injuries will often lack an incentive to bring a tort suit. On both counts, then, society needs to have criminal law to back up tort law.

Let me turn to two less familiar uses of economic analysis than explaining the economic rationality of rules and practices. They are simplifying legal analysis, often by breaking down doctrinal boundaries, and challenging the lawyer or judge to defend his values. The first we just glimpsed in relating criminal to tort law, assigning the former a supplementary role; and notice how decision under uncertainty plays a decisive role in both analyses. The uncertainty of the criminal's being caught, like the uncertainty of a careless act's leading to injury, is a critical determinant of the optimal sanction.

Dr. Miles Medical Co. v. John D. Park & Sons Co.[13] involved the legality under antitrust law of a contract by which a supplier of patent medicines forbade his dealers to charge a price for his medicines lower than his suggested retail price; this is the practice known as resale price maintenance. The Supreme Court held the practice illegal, pointing out that it had the same effect as would an agreement among the dealers to fix the price at which they would sell Dr. Miles's medicines—that is, the same effect as a dealers' cartel, which would be a per se violation of antitrust law. But there was another effect, which the Court overlooked. Dealers who are unable to compete in price yet would make money if they could sell more will compete in nonprice dimensions of competition instead, such as stocking more inventory or having better-informed salespeople, in order to attract more customers. If these services are important to the manufacturer's marketing strategy, he can use resale price maintenance to evoke them. For by setting the minimum resale price above the dealer's barebones cost of sale, the manufacturer will be giving dealers an incentive to compete with one another for additional sales by offering customers more service. This competition will transform the profit built into the minimum resale price into enhanced point-of-sale services—which is what the manufacturer wants.

A dealers' cartel would have this effect too; members of the cartel, each of whom would like to increase his sales at the cartel price because that price is by definition above cost, would try to lure customers from other dealers by offering better service. The difference is that in the cartel case the dealer may be providing *more* service than the customer wants; the customer might prefer a lower price with less service. If that is indeed what the customer prefers,[14] the supplier will not engage in resale price maintenance, for if he did he would lose business and profits to a competitor who did not engage in the practice.

My next example may seem unrelated. Critics of the deregulation of the airline industry have pointed out that airline service is in some re-

13. 220 U.S. 373 (1911).

14. More precisely, the marginal customer, but I will not pursue that refinement. See Posner, note 2 above, at 321.

spects inferior to what it was in the days when it was a regulated industry. Planes are more crowded, there is less legroom, the food is poorer.
Gone, for example, are the piano bars from American Airlines' 747s.
This is what economics predicted. The regulated airline industry was a
government-enforced cartel. Prices were kept high and as a result competition was deflected into nonprice competition. When the airlines
had finally competed away all their cartel profits in the form of service
competition, the industry was ripe for deregulation. And when it was
finally deregulated, prices fell and with it the level of service, because
this combination was what the consuming public wanted, as we can infer from the enormous growth in air travel since deregulation.

So we see, and this is the point of the discussion, that resale price
maintenance of patent medicines and the deregulation of airline transportation raise the same economic issue, that of the relation between
price and nonprice competition, even though one involves goods and
the other services, one is old and one is recent, and one involves the judicial interpretation of the antitrust laws and the other legislative reform of common carrier regulation. This is a recurrent experience in
the economic analysis of law. Practices, institutions, and bodies of law
that are wholly unrelated when viewed through the lens of orthodox legal analysis are seen to involve the identical economic issue. Whole
fields of law are interchangeable when viewed through the lens of economics. When I was a law student, the law seemed an assemblage of
completely unrelated rules, procedures, and institutions. Economics
reveals a deep structure of law that has considerable coherence.

Consider the famous tort case of *Eckert v. Long Island R.R.*[15] A man
saw a child on the railroad tracks. A train that was being operated neg-
ligently (that is crucial, as we'll see in a moment) was bearing down.
The man dashed forward, scooped up the child, and tossed the child
to safety, but was himself killed. Should the railroad be held liable to
his estate for its negligence? Or should the rescuer be held to have
assumed the risk? The issue is one of tort law but a helpful way to approach it is in terms of contract. Were the costs of negotiating a contract between the railroad and potential rescuers low, rather than prohibitive because the potential rescuers are not identified, the railroad
might make a contract whereby the rescuer of a person endangered by

15. 43 N.Y. 502 (1871).

its negligence would be compensated if he were killed or injured in the rescue attempt, provided he was acting reasonably. The railroad would be liable under tort law to the victim of its negligence if the person weren't saved, and therefore a would-be rescuer confers an expected benefit on the railroad for which the railroad would presumably be happy to pay if the cost were less than the expected benefit.

It is merely an "expected" benefit for two reasons. The rescuer may have sufficient altruistic motivation to attempt the rescue without any expectation of compensation; and the attempt may fail. In *Eckert* it succeeded. Suppose the child's life was worth as much as the rescuer's, say $1 million (in current dollars); and suppose further that the rescuer had a 10 percent chance of being killed in the course of the rescue and the child a zero chance of surviving if the rescue was unsuccessful. Then, ex ante, which is to say before the outcome of the rescue attempt was known, the railroad would have been eager to make the contract I have described. The net expected benefit to it would have been $900,000, since in nine cases out of ten it would save the full $1 million, the damages judgment to which Eckert's estate would be entitled under the hypothesized facts. It is another example of how decision under uncertainty permeates and gives analytical unity to many different legal questions.

The analytical device of imagining the outcome of costless contracting is a legacy of Coase's famous article on social cost. Recall, from the discussion of the Coase Theorem in the Introduction, that Coase's analysis sets two closely related tasks for law when law is conceived as a method of promoting efficient resource allocation: minimize transaction costs, as by defining property rights clearly and by assigning them to those persons likely to value them the most (so as to minimize the occasions for costly contracting around the law's initial assignment); try when transaction costs are prohibitive to bring about the allocation of resources that would have come about if transaction costs were zero, for that is the efficient allocation.

The importance that the Coase Theorem assigns to the distinction between high- and low-transaction-cost settings illustrates the breaking down of old boundaries by the economic analysis of law, and here is a more exotic illustration: the use of "personality" as an economic organizing principle of a broad swath of the law's concerns. *Webster's Third New International Dictionary* offers several definitions of the word. Personality is "the quality or state of being a person and not an abstraction." It is "the fact of being an individual person." It is "the condition or fact of relating to a particular person." It is "the complex of characteristics that distinguishes a particular individual or individualizes or characterizes him in his relationships with others." It is "the organization of the individual's distinguishing character traits, attitudes, or habits." It is "the social characteristics of commanding notice, admiration, respect, or influence through personal characteristics." Personality thus signifies human individuality and (as in the last definition) a striving for recognition as a separate, distinctive, and admirable individual. When personality is not recognized, we have anonymity. The "author," conceived as a writer who infuses his personality into his writing, is thus to be contrasted with the ghostwriter, who tries (or tried—for the practice is changing) to conceal his personality.

The concept of personality is central to the copyright laws, and to the variant of copyright protection, just now gaining a foothold in American law, that goes by the name of "moral right." Copying can be a way of impairing or appropriating personality; plagiarism and forgery are among the concepts that the law uses to place limits on copying for the sake of protecting personality. Personality figures largely in trademark law as well, once we understand that a firm or other institution can have personality, just like a natural person. A name-brand product has personality; the generic version of the product does not. Personality is also central to the tort right of privacy, especially but not only the branch of the right that goes by the name of the "right of publicity"— the right of a celebrity, for example, to control the use of his or her name or picture for advertising and other commercial purposes. Personality figures, too, in disputes over the ownership of works of art, partly because of the motives for owning art, which include the display of taste and other dimensions of the owner's personality, and partly because of the importance of provenance to the value of a work of art, where provenance usually means the artist's identity.

Over the course of centuries there has been a steady rise in what, but for its unfortunate association with the former communist nations, one might call the "cult of personality." Anonymity in authorship, not only the authorship of books but also that of journal and newspaper articles, and in the creation of works of art, has declined to the point where it is common today for the name of the ghostwriter to appear on the title page under the name of the (nominal) author and for the student notes and comments in law reviews to carry the name of the student (a practice unheard of three decades ago), however heavily the work may have been edited. The *auteur* movement has sought with some success to obtain recognition of a movie's director as the author of the movie, while at the same time, and only superficially inconsistently, the acknowledgment of contributions to a book or other creative project by readers of drafts, by editors, by family members, and by secretaries and other clerical personnel is increasingly the norm and indeed is becoming mandatory in some forms of writing. Works ostensibly of scholarship increasingly include tidbits of autobiography. Name-brand products are a relatively recent development. All these developments are paralleled by an expansion in legal rights to personality.

This movement, a movement in both social practice and in law (with law presumably both reflecting and facilitating the change in practice), is decried on the Left as a manifestation of an ideology of "possessive individualism," an ideology in which achievement is viewed as the product of individual striving rather than of collective effort. On this view, the cult of personality goes hand in hand with the rise of capitalism. This view has an element of truth, but it is more illuminating and precise to relate the growing social and legal recognition of personality to changes in the costs and benefits of personalized versus anonymous production of goods, both tangible and intangible. Three changes are central. The first is in the size of the market. The smaller the market for some product, the easier it is for consumers to identify the producer without an identifying mark, whether that mark is a signature, in the case of a book or a work of art, or a logo in the case of a less "creative" product or service. Modern, typically large, markets are, tellingly, said to be "impersonal." Their impersonality creates a demand for personalizing.

A market may be so small that production for it cannot be financed by consumers; the producers may require private patronage or public subsidy. If consumers are not paying, they will be less interested in identifying the producer. The smaller the market, moreover, the less important it is to motivate producers by enabling them to appropriate a large part of the social benefits of their work. Despite Samuel Johnson's quip that only fools don't write for money, there have always been some talented people who wrote or composed or painted because of the personal satisfaction it gave them rather than because of the pecuniary income that they obtained. If the demand for a class of work is small, the efforts of the self-motivated producers may be sufficient to satisfy it.

The second variable, which is related to the first (the size of the market), is the cost of information about the quality of goods and services. This cost has been increasing for many products because of the increased number of products and producers, increased product variety and complexity, and increased specialization, which reduces the amount of information that consumers have about the design and production of the products they use. (Consumers do not make their own tools any more.) The higher the cost of information, the more difficult it is to evaluate a product and hence the greater is the value of knowing who produced it. More products, in other words, are today what economists call "credence goods"—goods that one buys on the basis of faith in the producer rather than of direct knowledge of the product.[16]

The interaction between the size of the market and the increasing cost of market-related information is illustrated by the increased importance that modern academics attach to issues of priority, originality, volume of published work, citations and other acknowledgment in published work, and plagiarism. Modern academic markets are large, so academics cannot readily create a reputation by word of mouth; they need a visible stamp of personality.

Although the larger the market and the higher the cost of information the greater the benefits of giving legal recognition to the producer's personality, the costs of that recognition must not be ignored. They have largely to do with the collaborative nature of most production, a characteristic that the Romantic emphasis on genius has obscured and that is the third variable in the cultivation and recognition of personality that I want to stress. Most creative work depends heavily, though to a degree that the creator himself may take pains to conceal, on previous work. The more the appropriation of the previous work is burdened by costs of transacting with its creator because he has been given legal rights in that work, the higher will be the cost of creative

16. There is an analogy to Aristotle's concept of the "ethical appeal," which is to say the effort of a speaker to persuade his audience that he is an honest, informed, and trustworthy person. This is an important device of rhetoric, which Aristotle pertinently defined as reasoning about issues that cannot be resolved definitively by appeals to logic or data. Rhetorical persuasion, for Aristotle, is the attempt to sell a credence good.

work in the present and future. This is an example of collaboration between generations but there is also of course much simultaneous collaboration, as in joint authorship and the creation of multimedia works such as opera and film. Here too the effort to give legal protection to the personality of each contributor may create formidable transaction costs.

There is convergence between the economic analysis of personality and the radical critique of personality with its emphasis on the instrumental or constructed, rather than "natural," character of authorship.[17] Every text has a writer; and for simplicity let us consider only texts written by one person. It is a separate question whether that person shall be deemed an "author" and so obtain not only the legal protection of copyright law but also a reputation that will enhance (or diminish) his ability to sell future books, that will engender curiosity about his life and thought, that will create a market for his biography. He may obtain interpretive authority as well—the authority to determine the meaning of what he has written. Conversely, he may be an interpretive construct of that work: all we know about "Homer" is what we can infer from the texts of the *Iliad* and the *Odyssey*.

The answer to whether the writer shall be deemed an author depends on social and legal conventions rather than on the fact of the writer's having written the text in question. Society might be more impressed by the contribution that the printer or binder or illustrator or publisher or even readers had made to a book than by the writer's contribution. Or it might think the writing less important than the ideas written up, which might have come from someone else. Similarly, people might stop thinking that "Rembrandt" was a useful way of categorizing a set of seventeenth-century paintings. And then the price of a "Rembrandt" would not fall when it was discovered to have been painted by someone else, since the painting itself would not be altered by the discovery. That the price does fall, that a "Rembrandt" loses value dramatically when it is discovered to have been painted by some-

17. See, for example, Michel Foucault, "What Is an Author?" in *Textual Strategies: Perspectives in Post-Structuralist Criticism* 141 (Josué V. Harari ed. 1979); *The Construction of Authorship: Textual Appropriation in Law and Literature* (Martha Woodmansee and Peter Jaszi eds. 1994). "Author" need not be limited to the writer of a text, but can include a painter, composer, or other "creative" worker, or for that matter a producer of conventional goods and services.

one else, suggests that Rembrandts are credence goods, perhaps because there is no "objective," no algorithmic, means of determining the
quality of works of art.[18] And here we stumble on the paradox that the
cultivation and recognition of personality is positively correlated with
fads and herd behavior. The uncertainty about quality standards that
leads us to base a judgment of value on the personality that we call
"Rembrandt" rather than on the intrinsic quality of his paintings also
leads us to defer to the valuation of those paintings by other people.

This analysis can help us understand not only the artificiality of
many of the law's doctrinal distinctions but also the porousness of the
boundaries that separate law from other forms of social control (to
glance ahead at Chapter 9, which deals with social norms). Copyright,
trademark, and privacy law are ways of striking the balance between the
benefits and costs of recognizing personality, but so are concepts of
originality and creativity that shape the art market, as well as nonlegal
norms relating to the acknowledgment of influence or assistance.

⌒ LET ME GIVE some examples of the utility of economics in
challenging one's values. My first example is a short article by the well-
known Harvard political theorist Michael Sandel that surprisingly con-
joins approval of baby selling with condemnation of contracts of surrogate motherhood.[19] A doctor named Hicks, practicing medicine in the
rural South during the 1950s and 1960s, had, Sandel reports, "a secret
business selling babies on the side." He was also an abortionist who
sometimes "persuaded young women seeking abortions to carry their
babies to term, thus creating the supply that met the demand of his
childless customers." Sandel believes that the doctor's "black market in
babies" had morally redeeming features but that surrogate motherhood does not. He points out that compared to Dr. Hicks's "homespun
enterprise, commercial surrogacy, a $40 million industry, is big busi-
ness." But Sandel is comparing one seller in a market to an entire mar-

18. See Holger Bonus and Dieter Ronte, "Credibility and Economic Value in the Visual
Arts" (Westfälische Wilhelms-Universität Münster, Volkswirtschaftliche Diskussionsbetrag
Nr. 219, 1995). The phenomenon is not limited to the art market. Discovery that a play attributed to Shakespeare had actually been written by an obscure contemporary of his would,
after a flurry of initial curiosity, lead to a reduction in the number of performances and sales
of the play.

19. Michael Sandel, "The Baby Bazaar," *New Republic*, Oct. 20, 1997, p. 25.

ket, and moreover one seller in an illegal market, where sellers conceal themselves, to an entire legal market. Since there are more than a million abortions a year, the potential for "baby selling," if legalized, to eclipse commercial surrogacy is manifest.

Sandel's principal ground of distinction between baby selling and surrogate motherhood is that surrogacy, unlike what Dr. Hicks did, encourages commercialization. "Dr. Hicks's black market in babies responded to a problem that arose independent of market considerations. He did not encourage the unwed mothers whose babies he sold to become pregnant in the first place." He did not have to. Demand evokes supply. Women who knew there was a market for their baby if they did not want to keep it would tend to use less care to avoid becoming pregnant. No doubt fewer women knew there was a market than would if it were a legal market rather than a black market. But Sandel does not suggest that Dr. Hicks's practice was redeemed by its illegality!

I do not argue that economic analysis should convince opponents of surrogate motherhood to give up their opposition. I do not believe that economics (or any other body of thought, for that matter) can compel a moral judgment.[20] But the opponents may feel pressed by my economic analysis to reconsider their opposition. Maybe they agree with Sandel that what Dr. Hicks did was not immoral even though it was illegal, but with me that Sandel committed an economic error in thinking that what Hicks did was different from what the commercial surrogacy industry is doing and that it makes a difference that he was just one person while the commercial surrogacy industry comprises many persons.

Here is a more complex example of how economic analysis can motivate a rethinking of ethical commitments.[21] The federal pension law, ERISA (the Employee Retirement Income Security Act), requires an employer who establishes a defined-benefits pension plan to allow the employee's rights under the plan to vest after five years. The purpose of this requirement is to correct the abuse that consists in establishing a nonvesting pension plan and then firing an employee on the eve of his retirement.

The economist asked to evaluate this provision in ERISA would

20. That is a major theme of my book *The Problematics of Moral and Legal Theory* (1999), from which my discussion of Sandel and Hicks is drawn. See id. at 87.

21. The discussion that follows is based on Richard A. Posner, *Aging and Old Age* 299–305 (1995).

want to consider first how common this nonvesting scam would be in the absence of the law and whether forbidding it might have bad effects, in particular on the intended beneficiaries, the employees. Before the law was passed (in 1974), a worker who left before retirement age might indeed find himself with a pension benefit worth much less than his contributions and perhaps worth nothing at all. So he had a strong incentive to remain with the same company until he reached retirement age. And the employer had the power to expropriate employees' firm-specific human capital—which is to say the earning power an employee has that is tied to his working for this particular firm, so that he would earn less working for any other firm—by threatening to fire them before their pension rights vested if they insisted on a salary commensurate with their value to the company. One could imagine an employer reducing the employee's wage to a point at which the wage and the pension benefit together would just exceed the employee's wage in his next best job. The year before the employee retired and became eligible for the pension, the wage might be zero or even negative—the employee might be willing to pay to be allowed to work long enough to become entitled to his pension.

I may seem to have made a compelling case for ERISA's vesting provision. Yet empirical study has shown that employers' pension practices were rarely exploitative before ERISA and that the law was mainly motivated by abuses associated with multiemployer pension plans administered by the teamsters and other unions. Terms of retirement, including pension rights, are a matter of contractual negotiation between employer and prospective employee, not a unilateral imposition. Even if a particular employer refused to negotiate separately with each employee, instead offering terms of employment on a take-it-or-leave-it basis, competition among employers would give prospective employees a choice between different wage-benefit packages. The packages offered by some employers would emphasize good retirement or other benefits at the cost of lower wages, while those offered by other employers would emphasize high wages at the cost of less generous or secure retirement or other benefits. Employees would tend to be sorted to employers according to the individual employee's preferences regarding risk and the allocation of consumption over the life cycle.

As for incomplete vesting, by making pension benefits contingent on the employee's remaining with the firm and performing satisfactorily it facilitated the recovery by employers of their investment in their employees' firm-specific human capital. This would be expected to lead to more such investment and hence to higher wages. Incomplete vesting also solved the problem of the employee who, being about to retire, no longer has an incentive to work hard. It solved this problem—what economists call the "last-period problem"—not only with the stick (the threat of discharge before pension rights vested) but also with the carrot, since pension benefits are usually heavily weighted in favor of the employee's wage in his last few years of employment.

The employer's incentive to abuse the power that incomplete vesting conferred on him by reneging on his unwritten contract to deal fairly with his employees was held in check by his concern with preserving a reputation for fair dealing (if he lost that, he would have to pay new employees higher wages) and by the bargaining power that the possession of firm-specific human capital confers on a worker. (If he quit in anger or disgust, or was fired to eliminate his pension benefits, the firm would have to invest in training a green employee to replace him.) In fact, as I have said, before ERISA opportunistic discharges of workers covered by a pension plan were rare; and the statute has had no detectable impact on discharges of covered workers.

But by limiting incomplete vesting, the Act has tended to reduce the control of employers over their older employees. Such a loss of control would be expected to have two bad effects on the employees themselves. The first would be to lead employers to invest less in the employees' firm-specific human capital, and so the employee's productivity and hence wage will be lower. Second, because employers would have a smaller investment in the employees to protect and the employees would have less incentive to perform well (not being faced with a substantial loss of pension benefits if they were fired), employers would be expected to resort more frequently to an explicit or implicit threat of discharge in order to maintain discipline. And third, anything, legal or otherwise, that adds to the cost of employing a worker will cause employers to employ fewer workers or to pay them lower wages, or both.

Even if you agree with my economic analysis, you may feel that on balance it is more important for workers to have secure pension rights or greater autonomy from their employers. But, once again, you will be forced to ask yourself whether your feeling is strong enough to offset an awareness of the consequences brought home by economic analysis, some adverse to the workers themselves, such as lower wages—or even, ironically, *less* secure employment.

I have given two examples of what might be called the "conservative" bias of economics, though a more precise term would be "libertarian," a preference for regulation by markets and other private ordering over regulation by government. But economics aspires to be value neutral, and with some success, for there are a number of liberal practitioners of economic analysis of law, such as Guido Calabresi of Yale and now of the Second Circuit and John Donohue of Stanford. So let me give an example of how economics can throw some cold water on a policy that conservatives favor.[22] Consider statutes that empower the government to designate a building's façade as a landmark; upon designation, the owner cannot alter the façade. An alternative to designation would be the purchase (possibly backed up by the threat of condemnation, subject to payment of just compensation) by the government of an easement in the façade. This is favored by most conservatives. They believe that the government should not be permitted to get things for nothing and in the process impose heavy costs on the owners of property. And so they urge that the principle of just compensation be given maximum play. They would be inclined to argue, these conservatives, that landmark-preservation statutes cause government to designate too many landmarks compared to a regime in which the government must pay the owner of the landmark for the reduction in his property values as a result of his not being allowed to alter the façade.

Actually, it is unclear that fewer landmarks would be designated under the payment approach. The very fact that there is no compensation under the typical landmark-preservation statute means that landmark owners will resist designation by complaining to their congressmen, bringing other pressure to bear on the designating authority, hiring lawyers to find loopholes in the statute, even organizing to obtain defeat or repeal of the legislation. The resistance of taxpayers to paying the taxes necessary to finance a program of buying landmark easements might be less. Government tax and spend programs (agricultural subsidies, for example) are often as or more socially costly than regulatory

22. The discussion that follows is based on Posner, note 2 above, at 66–67, and on Daniel A. Farber, "Economic Analysis and Just Compensation," 12 *International Review of Law and Economics* 125, 131–132 (1992).

programs, the costs being spread so thinly over the taxpaying public that few taxpayers squawk.

Of course a campaign of resistance to landmark designation may be costly compared to a system in which the owner yields quietly to the government's demand, accepting compensation for the surrender of his right. But the aggregate costs may be small if the threat of resistance deters landmark designations.

But might not the government, because it isn't putting its money where its mouth is, designate the "wrong" landmarks, that is, property that would be worth a lot more in an altered state? Possibly, but possibly not. The greater the alternative value, the stronger will be the resistance to the designation. What is true is that the designation approach may cause a reduction in the supply of landmarks; building owners may rush to demolish potential landmark façades in advance of designation. But that is not the nature of the conservatives' objection.

The fallacy in their objection, the objection that the government should be treated like any other purchaser, is the implicit assumption that government *is* an ordinary purchaser and so responds to financial incentives just as a private purchaser would. But the government is not an ordinary purchaser, and in fact it is meaningless to speak of *making* the government pay for the things it wants just like everybody else, when the government *must* resort to coercion to obtain the money it uses to pay for those things.[23] To pay just compensation for a taking, or even to make a voluntary arms' length purchase without any implicit threat of resorting to condemnation if the seller refuses to sell, the government must first take, without any compensation, the necessary funds from the taxpayer. Just compensation entails an anterior act of expropriation.

As these examples illustrate, the basic job of the economist is to remind us of the consequences that noneconomists tend to overlook, consequences that often though not always are adverse or at least costly, of actual or proposed policies and practices. This use of economics ought to be welcomed by lawyers who think it important to dis-

23. This is true even when the government finances its activities by borrowing, or by printing money, since it can do these things only because of its power to tax or, in the case of printing money, the power to force people to treat its money as legal tender. Only when government finances its activities by competitive user fees is it behaving as a private market participant.

cover what the actual consequences of legal doctrines and institutions are, even those doctrines and institutions that have achieved sacred-cow status within the legal profession.

⌒ HAVING SKETCHED the law and economics movement, let me circle back now to the issue of Bentham's influence, beginning first with the inspirational aspect. Here the clearest evidence, it might seem, would be Gary Becker's 1968 crime paper,[24] which has turned out to be a fount of economic writing on crime and its control. Becker's paper contains several citations to the discussion of the economics of crime and punishment in Bentham's *Introduction to the Principles of Morals and Legislation* (1780; expanded ed. 1789).[25] Bentham had made a number of important economic points in the *Introduction:* a person commits a crime only if the pleasure he anticipates from it exceeds the anticipated pain, or in other words only if the expected benefit exceeds the expected cost. To deter crime, therefore, the punishment must impose sufficient pain that when added to any other pain anticipated by the criminal it will exceed the pleasure that he anticipates from the crime. Punishment greater than this should not be imposed, because the result would be to create pain (to the undeterrable criminal) not offset by pleasure (benefits) to the potential victims of crime.[26] The schedule of punishments must be calibrated in such a way that if the criminal has a choice of crimes, he commits the least serious. Fines are a more efficient method of punishment than imprisonment because they confer a benefit as well as impose a detriment. And, as we saw earlier, the less likely the criminal is to be caught, the heavier the punishment must be, to maintain an expected cost great enough to deter.

These points constitute the essential elements of the economic theory of crime and punishment as revived by Becker. Becker and his successors added a great deal, however, even though the core is clearly stated in Bentham's *Introduction.* Of particular importance to the subse-

24. Note 9 above.

25. Becker also cites Sutherland's treatise on criminology, which contains a few references to Bentham but credits Beccaria with having "made the principal application of this doctrine [utilitarianism] to penology." Edwin H. Sutherland, *Principles of Criminology* 52 (5th ed., rev. by Donald R. Cressey 1955).

26. Bentham recognized the vengeful pleasure that punishment can produce, and though he thought it normally outweighed by the pain of the person punished, he acknowledged that in principle it should be considered in deciding on the utility-maximizing punishment.

quent development of the field was Becker's ingenious suggestion that since fines are from a social standpoint a cheaper form of punishment than imprisonment (for one thing, they do not reduce the defendant's output), the optimal punishment will combine a very high fine with a very low probability of actually detecting the crime and thus imposing the fine, since creating a high probability would require adding police and prosecutors and would thus be costly.[27] We do not observe this "optimal" combination very often, however, and the attempt to answer the question why not has led economic analysts of law to explore the factors that place ceilings on the use of fines and on the severity of punishment generally and to consider the economic properties of the second-best solutions to the problem of punishment that the criminal justice system has come up with.

Even though Bentham was a famous economist and the economic character of his analysis of crime and punishment is unmistakable despite the slightly archaic vocabulary, and even though his theory has influenced the design of the criminal justice system in England and the United States, no economist before Becker, so far as I have been able to determine, had expounded an economic theory of crime and crime control. And Becker has told me that when he began thinking about the economics of crime, he was unaware of Bentham's discussion of it. He became aware of it while he was working on his article, but he no longer remembers whether any of the points made there were suggested to him by it, although a few of his citations to Bentham suggest that they may have been.[28] So this turns out to be an uncertain case of Bentham's having inspired the economic analysis of law.

Which makes it an even more doubtful case for arguing that Bentham was a cause of that analysis. Had Bentham written nothing about crime, or for that matter had never been born, probably some other economist before Becker would have invented the economic theory of crime in essentially the same form as Bentham did. Bentham was not, after all, the inventor of utilitarianism; and in retrospect, at least,

27. The expected cost of punishment is (ignoring attitude toward risk) pf, where p is the probability of its imposing and f (for fine) is the severity of the punishment. Since f is a transfer payment from the criminal to the state, its net social cost is very low, perhaps close to zero, and so a punishment scheme that combines a very high f with a very low p is likely to be cheaper than one with the opposite weighting.

28. See *The Essence of Becker*, note 9 above, at 511 nn. 40, 42, 46.

crime seems a natural field for the application of utilitarian ideas—in fact, Bentham's predecessor, Beccaria, an earlier utilitarian, had discussed crime in utilitarian terms, although much less systematically than Bentham.

Yet if an economic theory of crime was somehow "in the air" in the latter part of the eighteenth century, it is remarkable that almost two centuries passed before another economist picked up on it. So there is just a chance that if Bentham had never lived, the economic theory of crime would have had to wait a few more years to become a part of modern law and economics. But it is a small chance, since Becker's economic theory of crime appears to be largely a case of independent discovery.

Bentham wrote on other areas of law besides crime, notably evidence, but it is only with respect to the criminal law that he formulated an economic theory. I suspect the reason was that he was extremely interested in issues of social and political governance, and the criminal law is an important part of that governance. I don't think he realized that tort, contract, and property law are also important parts of the social fabric. He may have been blinded to this by his antipathy to the common law, which he seems to have thought served no function other than to enrich lawyers. Curiously, though, when he wrote, the criminal law was largely a body of common law as well. Holmes had the same blind spot—that is, he recognized the regulatory role of criminal law, but not of tort law—though in his case it did not arise from any antipathy to the common law.

But we must consider whether Bentham's utilitarian theory may have influenced the law and economics movement quite apart from any specific applications by him of utilitarianism to law. This will require distinguishing between utilitarianism as a description of human behavior and utilitarianism as an ethical theory. Utilitarian ideas go back to Aristotle, and utilitarianism as a fundamental ethical principle had been clearly enunciated in the eighteenth century, before Bentham wrote, by Hutcheson, Beccaria, Helvetius, Priestley, Godwin, and others—and, indeed, by Beccaria in virtually the same words as Bentham—"the greatest happiness of the greatest number."[29] What sets Bentham apart

---

29. See H. L. A. Hart, "Bentham and Beccaria," in Hart, *Essays on Bentham: Studies in Jurisprudence and Political Theory* 40 (1982). Beccaria, however, had apparently gotten the phrase from Hutcheson. J. B. Schneewind, *The Invention of Autonomy: A History of Modern Moral Philosophy* 420 (1998).

is the tenacity, even vociferousness, of his insistence on the *universality* of utility calculations in human decisions. As he put it on the first page of the *Introduction to the Principles of Morals and Legislation,* "Nature has placed mankind under the governance of two sovereign masters, *pain* and *pleasure* . . . They govern us in all we do, in all we say, in all we think." Another name for pain, as I have said, is cost; and for pleasure, benefit; so Bentham is claiming that all people, all the time, in all their activities, base their action (and words, and thoughts) on cost-benefit analysis. Bentham spent much of his life reiterating, elaborating, and instantiating this claim.[30]

This claim could be thought the foundation of the economics of nonmarket behavior. A good deal of the economic analysis of law is an application of that economics, because law is primarily a nonmarket institution and one that regulates nonmarket as well as market behavior—the behavior of criminals, prosecutors, accident victims, divorcing couples, testators, religious believers, speakers (as we shall see in the next chapter), and so forth, as well as businessmen, workers, and consumers. Without an economics of nonmarket behavior, the scope of economic analysis of law would be where it was in the 1950s, limited to the legal regulation of explicit markets. Bentham may be taken to have invented nonmarket economics.

His invention lay fallow for almost as long as his theory of crime and punishment. The explanation is a task for the sociology of science. That is, it has to do with why scientists are interested in one set of problems rather than another, and specifically with why nineteenth-century economists, and economists in the first half of the twentieth century as well, took virtually no professional interest in such social phenomena as crime, litigation, the household, discrimination, accidents, and rules of law. (An important exception is the interest taken by A. C. Pigou and Frank Knight in externalities, of which accidents to strangers is a form and one brushed by Pigou.) Maybe they felt they had their hands full trying to understand the market economy, or maybe they felt they lacked good tools, and a metric comparable to money, for studying nonmarket phenomena; there are economists who believe this to this day. At all events, until Gary Becker's Ph.D. disser-

30. Yet the claim itself had been a commonplace before Bentham was born: "Self-love and Reason to one end aspire,/Pain their aversion, Pleasure their desire" (Alexander Pope, *An Essay on Man* [1733], Epistle II, lines 87–88). It was not in the claim itself, but in the relentlessness and ingenuity with which Bentham pushed it, that his originality lay.

tation in the 1950s on the economics of racial discrimination,[31] the promise of Bentham's claim for the universality of the economic model of human behavior had been essentially ignored.[32]

Becker tells me that he was not consciously following in Bentham's footsteps in insisting on the universality of the rational model. He identified Bentham with the normative thesis that there is a moral duty to maximize the greatest happiness of the greatest number rather than with the positive thesis that people act so as to maximize their own utility. Utility maximization had, however, by the time Becker wrote his article on crime, long been a fundamental principle of economics, and though its origins in Bentham had largely been forgotten (probably because it did not become useful to economists until some fifty years after Bentham's death),[33] he deserves credit for having planted the idea.[34]

The handful of economists between Bentham and Becker who claimed that utility maximization was a universal feature of human psychology—of whom the outstanding example is Wicksteed—did not cite Bentham for this proposition,[35] and, more important, did very little with his insight into the possibility of applying economics to nonmarket behavior.[36] Becker's manifesto on behalf of nonmarket economics does mention Bentham, along with Adam Smith and Karl Marx, as precursors,[37] but criticizes Bentham for having been primarily a reformer

31. Published in 1957 as *The Economics of Discrimination*. A second edition was published in 1971.

32. For a striking example, see T. W. Hutchison, "Bentham as an Economist," 66 *Economic Journal* 288 (1956), which completely ignores, as obviously not "economics," Bentham's theory of crime and his belief that people are rational maximizers in all areas of life.

33. George J. Stigler, "The Adoption of the Marginal Utility Theory," in Stigler, *The Economist as Preacher, and Other Essays* 72, 76 (1982).

34. See id. at 78.

35. See Philip H. Wicksteed, *The Common Sense of Political Economy*, vol. 1, ch. 1 (Lionel Robbins ed. 1935) (first published in 1910). As Robbins points out in his Introduction, Wicksteed "insist[ed] that there can be no logical dividing line between the operations of the market and other forms of rational action." Id. at xxii. Yet Robbins does not attribute this idea of Wicksteed's to Bentham; nor does he cite Bentham in the book in which he expounded his own, equally broad conception of economics. Lord Robbins, *An Essay on the Nature and Significance of Economic Science* (3d ed. 1984). Not much significance can be assigned to Wicksteed's failure to cite Bentham, however, as he cited hardly anyone, except Jevons once.

36. Although Chapter 1 of *The Common Sense of Political Economy* contains a lengthy discussion of household production.

37. See Gary S. Becker, *The Economic Approach to Human Behavior*, ch. 1 (1976), reprinted in *The Essence of Becker*, note 9 above, at 7–8, 15 n. 13. He also cites Robbins's broad definition of economics, id. at 14 n. 3 (citing *The Nature and Significance of Economic Science* 16), but notes that Robbins failed to develop its implications. Id. at 14 n. 5.

and having failed to "develop a theory of actual human behavior with many testable implications."[38] And here we glimpse another reason why Bentham's contributions to economics have frequently been overlooked. He does not have a clear identity as an economist; his importance as a philosopher,[39] reformer, and polemicist has tended to overshadow his economic work. Of course, Adam Smith was also a famous philosopher as well as an economist, but Smith wrote a treatise on economics, and Bentham did not. In fact Bentham wrote, or at least published, little of a systematic character.

Still, if the idea of utility maximization as a fundamental element of the human psyche can be traced to Bentham, then the economics of nonmarket behavior can be said to have been influenced by him. And, to repeat, without the economics of nonmarket behavior, the scope of the economic analysis of law would be greatly contracted. But again this is influence in the sense of inspiration. It is unlikely that if Bentham had never lived, utility maximization would never have been discovered or applied to nonmarket behavior, for remember that we are talking about a lag of almost two centuries between the *Introduction* and Becker and that the concept of utility and the philosophy of utilitarianism both predate Bentham.

Two more possible routes of influence between Bentham and the law and economics movement remain to be traced. The first goes through welfare economics and the second through legal realism. The idea not that maximizing utility is what people in fact do but that it is what people, and governments, *should* do—that utility somehow aggregated across persons (in some versions, across all sentient beings) should be the guide to moral and legal duty—is the foundation of economics viewed as a normative discipline, the view I examine in Chapter 3. Bentham can be considered, along with Adam Smith, who was, however, more ambivalent about the ethical significance of economics, the founder of normative economics. This is true even though so influential an early welfare economist as Pigou did not cite Bentham and used the term "total welfare" rather than utility,[40] instead citing

38. Id. at 8. For a similar criticism of Bentham for having overemphasized reform at the expense of positive analysis, see Richard A. Posner, *The Economics of Justice* 33–41 (1981). I do, however, note there the indebtedness of the law and economics movement to Bentham. Id. at 41–42.

39. See Ross Harrison, *Bentham* (1983).

40. A. C. Pigou, *The Economics of Welfare* 12 (4th ed. 1938).

Sidgwick,[41] whose utilitarianism can, however, be traced to Bentham. And because the law is inveterately normative—because law professors, judges, and practitioners are all looking for grounds for evaluating actions and proposing reforms—the fact that economics has a normative dimension was of great importance in the reception of economics into legal thinking. But, once again, while the inspirational influence of Bentham is undeniable, the causal influence is altogether less clear. Had Bentham never lived, it is likely that a normative version of economics oriented toward utility maximization would still have emerged in the almost century and a half between his death and the birth of the law and economics movement.

Legal realism, which we glanced at in the Introduction, is an instantiation of one side of an age-old jurisprudential debate that is fully discernible as early as Plato's dialogue *Gorgias*, where Socrates, here a proto-legal-realist, equates the rhetoricians whom today we would call lawyers with the lowest form of sophist and demagogue. Much later, in the reign of James I in the seventeenth century, the debate would be carried on between Lord Justice Coke and James, the former extolling the "artificial reason of the law," or what today would be called legal reasoning and James wondering why the law should be the preserve of a guild of obscurantist quibblers. Toward the end of the eighteenth century the debate resumed with Blackstone taking Coke's place and Bentham James's. Although Blackstone was not the shameless apologist for the professional status quo that Bentham depicted him as in *A Fragment on Government* (1776), he did praise the common law and emphasize the importance of legal rights. Bentham, in contrast, thought the common law a hopeless muddle, good only for keeping lawyers in fees, and he thought rights talk nonsensical. But he didn't just say these things; he tried to reconstruct the law, proposing for example that the common law be replaced by a simple, readily understandable code that would largely dispense with the need for lawyers. He wanted law to be rebuilt on a scientific basis shaped by the "Greatest Happiness" principle, and the traditions and usages of traditional law discarded.

He was the great debunker of law, and his numerous followers in England, and fewer but still influential followers in America,[42] includ-

41. Id. at 18, 24.
42. See, for example, Jesse S. Reeves, "Jeremy Bentham and American Jurisprudence" 23–26 (Indiana State Bar Association, July 11–12, 1906).

ing the designer of the first important American law code, David Dudley Field, who drafted a code of procedure for New York State, fanned the Benthamite flame of legal reform. Without Benthamite legal skepticism it is hard to imagine Oliver Wendell Holmes writing what turned out to be the manifesto of legal realism—his 1897 essay "The Path of the Law." And without Holmes's involuntary sponsorship it is a little hard to imagine legal realism obtaining quite the hold over the legal imagination that it did in the 1930s—complete with a zeal for codification that reached its zenith in the drafting of the Uniform Commercial Code, which all the states of the United States have adopted.

A more difficult question is whether, without legal realism, Guido Calabresi would have embarked on his project, which has proved fundamental to modern law and economics, of rethinking the law of torts in light of economics. His first article on torts, although it does not explicitly attribute the economic approach that it adopts to legal realism, contains a few faint hints of realist antecedents.[43] Calabresi is a product of the Yale Law School, the bastion of legal realism and still identified with it when he started teaching there in the late 1950s, and the article, as well as his subsequent work, might be thought saturated with the realist spirit.

But I am skeptical (and am reinforced in this skepticism by a conversation on the subject with Calabresi). For legal realism had taken an *anti*-economic approach to tort law. Holmes, surprisingly oblivious to the deterrent effect of tort law, thought that the only proper basis for using that law to shift a loss from the victim of an accident to the injurer was if the injurer was blameworthy and the victim was not.[44] He did not try to impress an economic meaning on the concept of blameworthiness (as Learned Hand was later to do, as we have seen), but instead used "blame" in an intuitive moral sense and derided the idea that an alternative reason for tort liability might be to provide a form of social insurance against the unexpected and often catastrophic losses caused by accidents. He set social scientific analysis of torts off on the wrong foot by directing the attention of advanced legal thinkers, the kind that took their cue from Holmes, away from the concept of tort law as a regulatory regime in which legal sanctions are used to "price"

43. See Calabresi, note 8 above, at 500–501.
44. Oliver Wendell Holmes, Jr., *The Common Law*, lect. 3 (1881).

dangerous behavior and toward a concept emphasizing moralistic notions of blame and collectivist notions of social insurance. The legal realists thought that moralistic considerations were misplaced in regard
to accidental injuries and that Holmes had undervalued the social utility of using tort law to provide social insurance. In the realist era, "economic" thinking about torts became associated with social insurance
rather than with the use of law to optimize risky behavior, which is the
emphasis of the modern economic analysis of torts.

Here then is a break in the path that leads from Bentham to the
modern law and economics movement. We are left with the fact that he
pointed the way toward using economic thinking normatively and that
this was very important to the movement; his remote begetting of legal
realism may have contributed to the law and economics movement not
at all.

The modern economist with whom Bentham is most closely linked
is, we have seen, Gary Becker. Becker's significance for the law and economics movement has been great, though this is not widely recognized
because his article on crime is the only place in his extensive *oeuvre* in
which one can find an extended discussion of law. Since Bentham's economic theory of crime had been forgotten by economists, though in a
diluted form it remained influential in criminology and criminal law,
Becker performed an important service for law and economics simply
by reviving Bentham's theory of crime and dressing it in the language
of modern economics. But Becker's significance for the economic analysis of law goes far beyond crime. Becker, as I have already suggested, is
the great economist of nonmarket economics,[45] which is fundamental
to the economic analysis of law because much of law regulates nonmarket activities. Becker's work on human capital[46] and (as an offshoot
of that work) on employee compensation[47] opened up the field of employment and pension law, areas of growing importance in law, to economic analysis, as we saw earlier in reference to ERISA. His work on

45. See, for example, Gary S. Becker, "Nobel Lecture: The Economic Way of Looking at
Behavior," 101 *Journal of Political Economy* 385 (1993).
46. See Gary S. Becker, *Human Capital: A Theoretical and Empirical Analysis, with Special Reference to Education* (3d ed. 1993).
47. Gary S. Becker and George J. Stigler, "Law Enforcement, Malfeasance, and Compensation of Enforcers," 3 *Journal of Legal Studies* 1 (1974). Becker wrote the part of the article
that deals with employee compensation.

the economics of racial discrimination did the same for discrimination law, as did his work on the economics of the family[48] for family law.[49] These are now thriving subfields of economic analysis of law. More important, by demonstrating the feasibility and fruitfulness of applying economics to activities remote from the conventional "economic" subject matter of the discipline, he encouraged others to expand the domain of nonmarket economics to the point where few areas of law are now beyond the reach of economic analysis.

Becker's work can help us see the limitations of Bentham's approach. Bentham proclaimed the universality of what in modern terminology would be called cost-benefit analysis, but a manifesto is not a research program. What Bentham failed to show, with the exception of his treatise on crime and punishment, was how the model that he had propounded of people as rational actors in all departments of activity could be used to explain or regulate behavior.

48. See Gary S. Becker, *A Treatise on the Family* (enlarged ed. 1991).

49. Becker also contributed to the law and economics movement through personal influence on students and colleagues, including myself. See Richard A. Posner, "Gary Becker's Contributions to Law and Economics," 22 *Journal of Legal Studies* 211 (1993); Victor R. Fuchs, "Gary S. Becker: Ideas about Facts," *Journal of Economic Perspectives*, Spring 1994, pp. 183, 190.

~ 2

The Speech Market

$\mathcal{I}$N THE INTRODUCTION, I pointed to constitutional law as a conspicuous example of our ignorance about the consequences of legal rules. Economics, we now know, is the science of the consequences of human behavior, and so perhaps we can make some progress toward understanding the consequences of constitutional law by examining that law through the lens of economics. In this chapter I examine this possibility with reference to the free-speech clause of the First Amendment. Such an inquiry involves taking an instrumental approach to freedom of speech, an approach in which freedom is valued only insofar as it promotes specified goals, such as political stability, economic prosperity, and personal happiness.[1] This is to be contrasted with the moral approach, in which freedom of speech is valued as a corollary to or implication of a proper moral conception of persons, for example that they are to be regarded as self-directing beings and therefore should be entitled both to express their ideas and opinions and to

1. See Richard A. Posner, *Economic Analysis of Law*, ch. 27 (5th ed. 1998); Posner, "Free Speech in an Economic Perspective," 20 *Suffolk University Law Review* 1 (1986); Daniel A. Farber, "Free Speech without Romance: Public Choice and the First Amendment," 105 *Harvard Law Review* 554 (1991); Eric Rasmusen, "The Economics of Desecration: Flag Burning and Related Activities," 27 *Journal of Legal Studies* 245 (1998). The approach is criticized in Peter J. Hammer, Note, "Free Speech and the 'Acid Bath': An Evaluation and Critique of Judge Richard Posner's Economic Interpretation of the First Amendment," 87 *Michigan Law Review* 499 (1988).

receive any ideas or opinions that might facilitate their realizing their potential as free, rational choosers.[2] The moral approach thus assigns an intrinsic value to speech, though not necessarily one that can't be overridden by other values. Like other moral theories it seems to me, and not only to me, spongy and arbitrary.[3] Moral theory is no more likely to resolve free-speech issues than theology is to resolve disputes arising under the First Amendment's religion clauses.

Mill in *On Liberty* fused the two approaches, the instrumental (or economic) and the moral, arguing that freedom of thought and expression was essential to the production of true and useful ideas but also to enabling the individual to develop his full potential for its own sake. The fusion suggests that there may not be much practical difference between the two approaches. The instrumental (pragmatic, economic) approach, however, skirts contentious moral and ideological issues and enables freedom of speech to be analyzed fruitfully by reference to whatever goals one wishes to specify—fruitfully because it is so much easier to reason about means to given ends than about the ends themselves. And because the First Amendment uses the term "freedom of speech or of the press"[4] without defining it, because the preconstitutional history of the term is murky, and because the judicial decisions construing it do not compose a harmonious pattern either across time or across the different subfields of free-speech law, the legal conception of freedom of speech is mutable and contestable and so may take its shape from the practical considerations that the instrumental approach brings into view and may change as those considerations change.

Indeed, although not commanded by the First Amendment, the instrumental approach has a respectable constitutional pedigree. The

2. See, for example, Thomas Scanlon, "A Theory of Freedom of Expression," 1 *Philosophy and Public Affairs* 204 (1972). Does this mean that if, as in much Nazi and Communist speechifying, the speaker is urging the audience to despoil other people for the audience's benefit, suppressing the speech would impair the autonomy of the audience in some censurable way? Why should an audience be thought to have a moral entitlement to receive such information and encouragement?

3. For a forceful criticism from within philosophy, see Joshua Cohen, "Freedom of Expression," 22 *Philosophy and Public Affairs* 207 (1993). Although Cohen claims to accept a mixture of intrinsic and instrumental justifications for free speech, id. at 230, his intrinsic justification—basically, that people like to express their opinions, see id. at 224–225—I would call extrinsic: it is free speech as an argument in the individual's utility function.

4. I use "freedom of speech" to refer to both; a better term might be "freedom of expression."

case that first put the constitutional protection of free speech on the map—*Schenck v. United States*[5]—took an instrumental approach. After the United States entered World War I, Charles Schenck, the general secretary of the Socialist Party, arranged for the distribution of 15,000 leaflets to draftees, denouncing the war and urging opposition to the draft. The leaflets did not advocate illegal measures, such as refusing to serve, but Schenck conceded that a reasonable jury could have found that the intent of the mailing had been to "influence [persons subject to the draft] to obstruct the carrying of it out."[6] In an opinion by Justice Holmes, the Supreme Court upheld the convictions. "In ordinary times," Holmes wrote, the Socialist Party might have had a First Amendment right to distribute these leaflets. "But the character of every act depends upon the circumstances in which it is done. The most stringent protection of free speech would not protect a man in falsely shouting fire in a theater, and causing a panic."[7] Speech may therefore be suppressed when "the words used are used in such circumstances and are of such a nature as to create a clear and present danger that they will bring about the substantive evils that Congress has a right to prevent."[8] With the country at war, Congress had a legitimate and indeed urgent interest in preventing the recruitment of soldiers from being obstructed and Schenck's conduct had both the intent and a tendency to obstruct that recruitment.

In the case of falsely shouting fire in a crowded theater, the harm caused by speech is immediate, palpable, grave, and nearly certain to occur. In the case of mailing antiwar propaganda to draftees, the harm (obstruction of recruitment) may be great if it occurs, but it is less certain to occur than in the case of shouting fire in the crowded theater; the *probabilistic* character of most types of harm caused by speech is salient in the draft case. Holmes's "clear and present danger" test requires that the probability be high (though not necessarily as high as in the fire case) and the harm imminent; stated differently, the *danger* of harm must be great. An economist would say that to quantify an uncertain harm you must discount (multiply) the harm if it occurs by the probability of its occurrence. The greater that probability, the greater

5. 249 U.S. 47 (1919).
6. Id. at 51.
7. Id. at 52.
8. Id.

is the expected harm and therefore the greater the justification for preventing or punishing the speech that creates the danger.[9] And the probability is greater the clearer (that is, more certain) and more immediate
the danger is. The economist would add that the *magnitude* of the harm
if it occurs is also relevant, for it is the magnitude that is discounted to
determine the expected harm. I shall have to return to this vital point,
which Holmes's formula overlooks though it may be implicit in the
contrast he draws between wartime and ordinary times.

Immediacy has an additional significance again illustrated by falsely
shouting fire in a crowded theater: the more immediate the harm
brought about by the speech, the less feasible it is to rely on competition among speakers and on other sources of information to avert the
harm without need for public intervention. In economic terms, "market failure"[10] is more likely when dangerous speech occurs in circumstances in which counterspeech, a form of competition that protects
the interests of the audience in much the same way that competition in
ordinary markets protects consumers, is infeasible. It does not follow
that speech should be regulable *only* when the harm is immediate—as
in "without a showing of likely, immediate, and grave harm, government cannot regulate political speech."[11] Such a position would deny
the existence of a trade-off between immediacy and gravity, as would
requiring that the harm be *both* likely and grave. If it is grave enough,
it should be regulable even though unlikely, and if likely enough, it
should be regulable even though not particularly grave, though both
judgments depend on the circumstances. Recall a similar point made
with reference to Hand's negligence formula in Chapter 1.

The possibility of recasting the instrumental approach in specifically
economic terms was suggested by Holmes's use, in a dissent written
just months after *Schenck*, of the market metaphor for freedom of
speech. He said that an idea is true (more precisely, as close to true as it
is possible for us to come) only if it prevails in competition with other

9. This formulation is explicit in Learned Hand's restatement of the clear and present danger test in United States v. Dennis, 183 F.2d 201, 212 (2d Cir. 1950), aff'd, 341 U.S. 494
(1951). Its resemblance to Hand's negligence formula, discussed in the preceding chapter,
should be apparent.

10. The sources of market failure in speech markets are emphasized in Albert Breton and
Ronald Wintrobe, "Freedom of Speech vs. Efficient Regulation in Markets for Ideas," 17
Journal of Economic Behavior and Organization 217 (1992).

11. Cass R. Sunstein, *Democracy and the Problem of Free Speech* 122 (1993).

ideas in the marketplace of ideas.[12] Hence government disserves truth by suppressing competition in ideas. In thus identifying a benefit of freedom of speech, Holmes, who in *Schenck* had discussed just the costs of free speech, in the dissent in *Abrams* can be seen sketching in the other side of the cost-benefit algorithm.[13] The different emphases are natural because in the earlier case Holmes was rejecting the First Amendment claim and in the later one urging its acceptance. In both cases extreme leftists were agitating against U.S. participation in World War I, though the specific goal in *Abrams* was to discourage sending troops to Russia to oppose the Bolsheviks, who had just made peace with Germany; but there was an important difference. The defendants in *Schenck* were actually trying to obstruct the draft, by mailing leaflets to draftees. The defendants in *Abrams* were distributing the leaflets at large; although some draftees and munitions workers may have been recipients, no evidence was presented that the defendants had tried to get the leaflets into the hands of either group.[14] Thus the danger of an actual obstruction of the war effort was less in *Abrams*.

Holmes's two opinions contain the germ of the economic approach to freedom of speech. But only the germ. The analysis of the costs of speech is incomplete in *Schenck* because Holmes focused only on the probability of harm if the speech is allowed and not on the magnitude of the harm if it occurs; he was looking only at one determinant of the expected cost of free speech. And the *Abrams* dissent does not examine the possibility, an implicit premise of *Schenck*, that competition between ideas will not always yield truth—in *Schenck*, the truth that the draftees ought to fight, and in the theater hypothetical the truth that there is no fire. Indeed, it may be doubted whether "truth" was even involved in *Schenck*. The concern was not that the defendants in that case were lying; it was that they were imperiling an important national proj-

12. Abrams v. United States, 250 U.S. 616, 630 (1919). Holmes owed this point to Charles Sanders Peirce and, before him, to John Stuart Mill. See David S. Bogen, "The Free Speech Metamorphosis of Mr. Justice Holmes," 11 *Hofstra Law Review* 97, 120, 188 (1982).

13. In treating Holmes's *Schenck* and *Abrams* opinions as complementary, I depart from the more common view, well argued in David M. Rabban, *Free Speech in Its Forgotten Years* 280–282, 324–325, 346–355 (1997), that they are inconsistent. Rabban bases his view in part on passages in the *Schenck* opinion that seem to undercut the speech-protective thrust of "clear and present danger." The consistency of the two opinions is argued in Bogen, note 12 above.

14. See Richard Polenberg, *Fighting Faiths: The* Abrams *Case, the Supreme Court, and Free Speech* 104 (1987).

ect—the analogy is to disseminating a truthful formula for making poison gas. These are cases in which competition in ideas is undesired even or perhaps especially if it produces truth.

Can the approach introduced by Holmes be generalized and made operational? It can be formalized, though that is not the same thing. If the benefits of challenged speech are given by B; the costs (a fire, desertion, riot, rebellion, and so forth) if the speech is allowed by H (for harm) or O (for offensiveness);[15] the probability that the cost will actually materialize if the speech is allowed by p; the rate at which future costs or benefits are discounted to the present by d (like p a number between 0 and 1); the number of years (or other unit of time) between when the speech takes place and the harm from it materializes is likely to occur if the speech is allowed by n; and the cost of administering a regulation banning the speech by A, then the speech should be allowed if but only if

$$(1) \qquad B \geq pH/(1 + d)^n + O - A$$

That is, the speech should be allowed if but only if its benefits equal or exceed its costs discounted by their probability and by their futurity, and reduced by the costs of administering a ban.

The reason the administrative costs (A) must be subtracted from the costs of the speech is that if the speech is permitted, the costs of administering a prohibition of it are saved.[16] That is why the larger A is (as well as the smaller p, H, and O are and the larger d and n are), the more likely it is that the benefits of the speech exceed its costs. Another way to see this is to rewrite inequality (1) as: ban the speech if but only if

$$(2) \qquad pH/(1 + d)^n + O \geq B + A$$

—that is, if but only if the expected costs of the speech exceed the sum of the benefits of the speech and the costs of administering a prohibition of it—the ban has to cover its costs to be cost-justified. Granted,

---

15. The reason for distinguishing between harm and offensiveness will become clear in a moment.

16. Suppose the benefits of the speech are 50, the costs 70, but the costs of banning it 40. Although the costs of the speech exceed its benefits, outlawing the speech would not be a profitable social project, because the costs of outlawing it—50, the benefits forgone, plus 40, the costs of outlawing it—would exceed the benefits of outlawry, those benefits being only 70, the costs of the speech that would be eliminated.

the implicit assumption that administering a *protection* of free speech is costless is unrealistic. But all that matters for the analysis is that the administrative cost of prohibition exceed the administrative cost of protection; A can be viewed as the first cost minus the second.

Alternatively, let x be the degree of strictness with which potentially harmful or dangerous speech is regulated; the larger x is, the less freedom of speech there is. If C represents the net social costs of suppressing some given category of speech, then

(3) $C(x) = A(x) + B(x) - (pH/(1 + d)^n + O)(x)$

The net costs of suppression are greater the greater the administrative costs and the benefits of the speech suppressed, and are smaller the more harmful or offensive the speech. The net costs are minimized by differentiating C with respect to x and setting the result equal to zero, which yields

(4) $A_x + B_x = - (pH/(1 + d)^n + O)_x$

where the subscripts denote derivatives. In words, optimal strictness is attained when one more turn of the strictness screw would add more to the cost of regulation and the impairment of speech values than it would reduce harm and/or offensiveness.

I offer these formulas as a heuristic, a way of framing and thinking about the regulation of speech, rather than as an algorithm for use by judges. The problems of operationalizing the instrumental approach to free speech are formidable because of the indeterminacies that pervade the field. We just don't know a great deal about the social consequences of various degrees of freedom of speech.

To demonstrate the formulas' heuristic value requires further consideration of two of the variables—B, the benefits of speech, and O, offensiveness. B need have nothing to do with the promotion of social or scientific progress or of political freedom or stability; aesthetic or even sexual pleasure is as genuine a benefit as democracy or truth, though it need not be as great a benefit. Also, B can take a negative value. That is, some restrictions on speech actually promote speech. Consider the following variant of *Arkansas Educational Television Commission v. Forbes*.[17] A publicly owned television station wishes to sponsor a debate among presidential candidates. The problem is that there are (let us say) ten

17. 523 U.S. 666 (1998).

such candidates, all but two from fringe parties such as the vegetarians and the socialists. If to avoid restricting speech the station invites all the candidates to participate in the debate, the time available to the frontrunners will be drastically curtailed. Yet if only because the fringe candidates have no chance of winning, what the frontrunners have to say is probably more valuable to the audience than what the fringe candidates have to say.[18] A debate limited to frontrunners may generate a larger and more attentive audience, as well as give the members of the audience more helpful information about the issues and candidates. Restricting the opportunity of the fringe candidates to speak may thus increase the speech benefits of the debate overall.

As for *O*, offensiveness: if a person shouts "Fire!" in a crowded theater (when there is no fire—and maybe when there is!) and causes a panic in which other patrons are trampled, there is undeniable harm. And likewise if a sale of pornography results in a rape that would not have occurred had the sale not taken place. But what about the indignation that wells up out of the mere knowledge that pornography is being sold or atheism or socialism being propagated? Is that any different from any other disutility? John Stuart Mill thought it was. He distinguished between self-regarding and other-regarding acts, the latter referring to acts that have tangible effects on other people, the former to acts that affect other people, if at all, only through the knowledge that the acts are taking place (a confusing terminology). Mill's example of harm from self-regarding acts was the outrage that English peope felt at knowing that polygamy was being practiced openly in Utah, thousands of miles away.[19] He thought that such a harm, such a "cost," should have no weight in moral or legal judgments. But a cost is a cost whether it is the result of actually seeing (for example, seeing a man exposing his genitals as a result of having been aroused by pornography) or just reading about (for example, reading about the arousal effects of pornography). Although it is likely to be greater in the first case,[20] the fact that a harm is mediated by thought or recollection, rather than be-

18. Probably, not certainly. Major parties can originate as fringe parties, fringe parties can contribute ideas that are later picked up by major parties, and fringe candidates can become major candidates—all points illustrated, by the way, by the rise of Hitler and the Nazi Party. Such illustrations are pertinent as reminders that political free speech is not an unalloyed blessing.

19. See John Stuart Mill, *On Liberty*, ch. 4 (1859).

20. Because of the "availability heuristic," discussed in subsequent chapters.

ing the product of an immediate sense impression, need have no significance in itself.

The "clear and present danger" test is not designed for regulations
based on offensiveness; for the injury caused by offensive speech is not
deferred or probabilistic, but immediate and certain. That is why, unlike the costs that I denote by H (for harm), inequalities (1) and (2) treat
offensiveness (O) as a present and certain rather than future and hypothetical cost. In Holmes's day the right of government to repress offensive speech of a sexual character was so much taken for granted that he
felt no need to develop a free-speech test broad enough to encompass
offensive as well as dangerous speech, though there is a sense, of
course, in which the pamphlets in *Abrams* and *Schenck* were, whether or
not actually dangerous, "offensive" to patriotic sentiment.

The formulas do not refer explicitly to the government's *motivation*
in suppressing particular speech. For example, it might be to stifle criticism of government officials, impose ideological uniformity, or prevent
opposition candidates from competing on equal terms. Tests based on
motivation are often unsatisfactory, because motivations are easily concealed. They usually have to be inferred from consequences, and a test
that focuses on consequences invites us to cut out the middleman, as it
were. A law forbidding criticism of legislators would be bad under my
approach because its costs would exceed any reasonable estimate of its
benefits; nothing would be added by observing that the motivation for
the law was probably selfish.

If (a big if) the benefits and costs of free speech could be estimated,
the approach I am exploring could not be brushed aside as obviously
incompatible with the traditions of First Amendment analysis. A cost-
benefit approach, however alien to the characteristically high-flown
rhetoric of free-speech opinions, is implicit in the majority opinion in
Schenck and the dissent in *Abrams*, and both opinions long ago attained
canonical status in free-speech law. It is not the only approach the
courts have used;[21] and it may lack the rhetorical elevation characteristic of the discourse of freedom of speech from Milton to Meiklejohn.
But there is no more eloquent an opinion in the history of American
law than Holmes's dissent in *Abrams*. Nor would the suggested ap-

---

21. Notably, in Brandenburg v. Ohio, 395 U.S. 444 (1969) (per curiam), the Supreme
Court adopted an extremely narrow version of the "clear and present danger" test, cutting
back on the economic test adopted in Learned Hand's opinion in *Dennis*.

proach knock freedom of speech off the perch that it occupies by virtue of being classified by the Supreme Court as a "preferred" liberty. Ordinary legislation doesn't have to pass a cost-benefit test to comply with the Constitution, and much of it could not get within miles of passing such a test. But under the cost-benefit approach to freedom of speech, legislative or other governmental action that restricts speech is permitted only if the benefits of the restriction can be shown, with some degree of confidence, to exceed the costs.

The law of freedom of speech is already to some extent isomorphic with the economic approach. Consider the elaborate jurisprudence of "fora."[22] The courts distinguish among traditional public forums, designated public forums, limited public forums, and nonpublic forums. The first class consists mainly of public streets, sidewalks, and parks, which have traditionally been available for public assembly and demonstrations. The second consists of publicly owned sites that while not traditionally dedicated to expressive purposes the government has decided to throw open for them. The third (often treated in the cases as part of the second) consists of public sites configured for a specific type of expression, for example a publicly owned theater. The fourth includes all other public property, some of which might be suitable for expressive activity (for example, the streets and sidewalks on a military base or the concourse of an airport) but none of which is intended for such activity. In categories one and two the government can regulate only the time, place, and manner of the speech; in category three it can confine the type of speech to the type for which the facility is designed; in four it can limit speech as it wishes, provided it maintains neutrality among competing points of view (this proviso applies to the other three categories as well, of course).

These distinctions make a rough kind of economic sense. The traditional and the designated public forums can be used for expressive activities without great cost, provided that restrictions to prevent crowding are imposed, and these are permitted. The limited-purpose forum would not be viable if the limitation could not be imposed; imagine

---

22. Summarized in many places, for example Perry Education Association v. Perry Local Educators' Association, 460 U.S. 37, 45–46 (1983). The archaic use of the Latin plural lends a spurious air of erudition to this jurisprudence. For a recent application of the public forum concept, see Chicago Acorn v. Metropolitan Pier and Exposition Authority, 150 F.3d 695 (7th Cir. 1998).

what it would do to a theater if the management had to allow it to be used for demonstrations, political rallies, picketing, and like activities. This is another case, like *Forbes*, in which restricting speech can actually promote speech.[23] Finally, the business of government could hardly be conducted if *any* piece of public property that was physically suitable for demonstrations or other expressive activities could be commandeered for such purposes.

Another value of the economic approach, besides its making practical sense out of some esoteric legal distinctions, is that it invites attention—Holmes was helpfully explicit about this in *Schenck*—to the context of the speech that is sought to be suppressed: war versus peace, the crowded versus the empty theater. Attention to context can help dispel the provincialism and anachronism that lead many modern students of freedom of speech to denounce restrictions imposed by societies very different from that of the United States today. This country is so rich, powerful, secure, and politically stable, and its people are so well informed by historical and international standards and have such easy access to divergent points of view, that allowing anyone to say whatever he pleases is, with very few exceptions, simply not dangerous. This has not always been, and still is not everywhere, true, and so the economist is neither surprised by nor necessarily critical of the fact that freedom of speech has not always and everywhere been understood as capaciously as it is today in this country.

Modern thinking about free speech is colored by the hindsight fallacy. Knowing with the wisdom of hindsight that socialist agitation never posed a real threat to the country (though this was not known at the time), free-speech scholars tend to dismiss the concerns expressed by Holmes in the *Schenck* opinion. Yet many of the same people who criticize *Schenck* and *Dennis* are fearful about free speech on the Internet. The breadth of protection that the law accords to speech is a function not of moral insight but of the perceived harmlessness of the protected speech.

Speech may be harmless yet deeply offensive. But if, as seems to be the case (the issue is explored further in Chapter 9), norms are losing their grip on the behavior of Americans—if we are increasingly a law-

---

23. Still another example is copyright law, which by limiting copying increases the financial incentives to create intellectual property.

governed society of individuals rather than a norm-governed society of sodalities—then indignation at people who flout norms is unlikely to reach a pitch of intensity great enough to mobilize the forces of government. Orthodoxy and offensiveness are the two sides of the same coin; if very little is orthodox, very little is likely to be highly offensive to a national majority. Most Americans are somewhat religious, somewhat egalitarian, and even somewhat straitlaced; but many are not and most of those that are tend to be only weakly so.[24] They are pretty hard to shock. Because there is considerably more homogeneity at the local and even the state level, the pressures for suppression are stronger at these levels. With suppression likelier though the consequences less grave, the net expected cost of suppression may be no less at the local than at the national level. If so, this provides a practical reason for the Supreme Court's decision to apply the full force of the free-speech clause of the First Amendment to state and local action, through a by no means inevitable interpretation of the Fourteenth Amendment.

An approach that makes costs and benefits its centerpiece is vulnerable to criticism if the costs or benefits are highly uncertain. As, of course, they are in the case of the regulation of speech. What the much-ridiculed history of censorship shows is not that censorship is always and everywhere a mistaken policy but that censors are rarely able to determine the truth or other value of dangerous or offensive speech. (The ridicule is misplaced, though, because most censorship is concerned with danger rather than with falsity.) The inherent difficulty of determining truth by the methods employed by censors is compounded by the fact that false claims and mistaken theories can have considerable social value. They not only (as Mill stressed in Chapter 2 of *On Liberty*) stimulate the defenders of truth to think harder about their views, articulate them more persuasively, and support them with more evidence; they bring to light sources of disaffection or misunderstanding that may require corrective action. Both points are illustrated by "hate speech" and verbal harassment generally (for example, verbal sexual harassment, not involving either threats or solicitations, in the workplace). To the extent that hate speech is knitted out of misconceptions about the objects of hatred, such as blacks and homosexuals, al-

---

24. In Chapter 9, I inquire critically into what exactly it means to say that Americans are "highly religious," or "the most religious" people of the Western world.

lowing it to be vented forces the advocates of these groups to go beyond pious exhortations to equality and unconvincing denials of social
pathologies associated with the groups (such as criminal violence in the
case of blacks and sexually transmitted disease in the case of male homosexuals). It also enables the government to identify the sources of
ignorance and resentment that motivate the hate speakers and to take
steps to remove the sources. It is a separate and difficult question, to
which I return later in this chapter, whether and to what extent the
costs of hate speech to the missions of universities and employers justify repression of such speech. The present point is only that such
speech should not be assumed to be barren of social benefits even if it
has little or even no truth value, just as harmful or offensive speech cannot be assumed to be socially beneficial just because it is true.

A subtler benefit of tolerating hateful speech lies in preventing the
speaker from signaling his conviction by being willing to be imprisoned or otherwise punished for his beliefs. Lenity is the antidote to
martyrdom. Tolerating inflammatory speech may thus lower rather
than raise the temperature of public debate by making it more difficult
for speakers to prove that they are in deadly earnest about what they
are saying. Consider that literally inflammatory form of expression, the
burning of the nation's flag. The force of the gesture is greatly weakened if, as the Supreme Court has held, a person cannot be punished
for burning the flag. The cheaper talk is, the less credible it is; tolera-
tion keeps it cheap. Of course, it might be a good thing or a bad thing
to eliminate martyrdom; this is an example of the indeterminacies that
plague the analysis of free-speech issues.

It might seem that while estimating the benefits of speech on a case-
by-case method may not be feasible, a categorial approach may be. The
approach, very popular among commentators on free speech, involves
the creation of a hierarchy in which, for example, political and scientific speech receives the most protection on the ground either that it is
the most valuable from a social standpoint or that (in the case of political speech) it is more central to the concerns that animated the framers
and ratifiers of the First Amendment. Commercial advertising receives
less protection, along with art and entertainment, including pornography. Criminal threats and solicitations receive no protection.

The categorial approach works nicely with the last category. If the
only purpose and likely effect of a speech is to engender uncontro-

versially criminal activity, then the speech is demonstrably worthless—the left-hand side of inequality (1) is zero. The only issue is whether the costs of the speech exceed the costs of prohibiting it, that is, whether the right-hand side of the inequality is positive. What made the Communist cases, such as *Dennis*, difficult was that the Communist Party U.S.A. was both the conspiratorial agent of a hostile foreign government and a source of interesting ideas about the economy, social classes, racism, foreign policy, and other important social phenomena.

Within the broad range of types of speech that confer some lawful benefits, however, the hierarchizing approach fails, because it confuses total with marginal benefits. It might be worse from an overall social standpoint to ban all political speech than to ban all art;[25] but that is not the choice that confronts a board of censors or other tribunal asked to ban a particular speech, whether it is a commercial ad, a violent television program, a graphic lesbian novel, or a topless nightclub show. Even if political speech is socially more valuable than the novel, a tract advocating genocide might have less social value than a resolutely non-political novel by Henry Miller, even if some of the pleasure that readers take in a Miller novel derives from its pornographic elements. It is no answer that the government cannot be trusted to permit criticism of itself. The government cannot be trusted, period. It is likely to suppress any speech that is radically unpopular, whether political, religious, commercial, or aesthetic, with consequences unrelated to any hierarchy of speech values. (Another way to put this is that government is the groups that support it.) Spain, Portugal, and Italy probably did more harm to the long-run welfare of their people by suppressing (or condoning the Church's suppression of) scientific freedom in the early modern period than by suppressing political freedom.[26] The people who want to privilege political speech are often people who simply think that politics is the most important activity that people engage in.

A better argument for giving a special dollop of protection to political speech is related to the "voter's paradox," that is, the puzzle of why anyone votes in political elections, given that the probability that the election will be decided by one vote is vanishingly small. Many people

25. That is, from the standpoint of *our* society. It is by no means clear that every society would or should prioritize the political in this way. Consider Renaissance Italy, for a plausible counterexample.

26. I take up the relation between prosperity and political liberty in the next chapter.

do vote, but because the private value of voting is slight, the incentive to invest in becoming well informed about the issues in the election is also slight. The private demand for political ideas being weak, it makes sense to try to minimize the legal costs of producing such ideas by giving such production a broad legal privilege.

If estimating the benefits of speech by the methods of law is infeasible, the focus of a cost-benefit approach has to be on the costs of speech. They sometimes are demonstrably zero or even negative. Consider *Posadas de Puerto Rico Associates v. Tourism Company of Puerto Rico.*[27] The case holds that Puerto Rico, since it could constitutionally have banned all gambling, had not violated the First Amendment by forbidding the advertising in Puerto Rico (but not outside of it) of casino gambling, which the government of Puerto Rico had legalized. The Court's decision makes little sense to an economist even if advertising is considered to be generally less deserving of legal protection than political speech.[28] The ostensible purpose of the ban on advertising was to reduce the lure of gambling to residents of Puerto Rico[29] (a purpose not inconsistent with legalizing casino gambling, for that might have been done simply in recognition of the futility of trying to suppress it). The ban may have had some effect along that line. But at the same time it reduced the advertising costs of the casinos. This reduction should lead them to reduce their prices—which in turn would make gambling more attractive than before the ban. The ban thus was likely to deprive consumers of valuable information without reducing any of the unwanted side effects of gambling addiction (such as bankruptcy, penury, embezzlement, or suicide); it may even have increased them.

Sometimes the social costs of harmful or offensive speech can be minimized without significantly curtailing its benefits, and sometimes, as I noted earlier, the regulation of speech may actually enhance those benefits. Such cases place little strain on the judicial capacity to conduct or evaluate cost-benefit analyses. Limiting the number of participants in a televised debate, preventing demonstrators from blocking traffic, allowing the prohibition of false advertising, and providing legal

27. 478 U.S. 328 (1985).

28. See Fred S. McChesney, "De-*Bates* and Re-*Bates:* The Supreme Court's Latest Commercial Speech Cases," 5 *Supreme Court Economic Review* 81, 102–105 (1997).

29. By allowing the casinos to advertise out of state, Puerto Rico showed that it cared nothing about corrupting nonresidents!

remedies against copying and defamation are examples. A law requiring all pornographic bookstores to relocate to a "red light" district reduces the costs associated with pornography yet at the same time preserves the essential benefits that pornography might be thought to confer. A law banning pornography would reduce the costs even more, but, to the extent enforced, might eliminate most of the benefits (and likewise copyright and defamation laws so strict that they prevented any use of other people's ideas without their consent and any criticism of people's behavior). And such a law would be much more costly to enforce. These points are related to my earlier point about the importance of evaluating the costs and benefits of particular forms of speech at the margin.

Costs of law enforcement are an underemphasized objection to the radical feminist program for curbing pornography. The antipornography ordinance drafted by Andrea Dworkin and Catharine MacKinnon[30] required proof that the manufacture or sale of pornography by the defendant had harmed the plaintiff. The costs of such an evidentiary inquiry, especially the error costs, would be very high, because it is extremely difficult to determine the causal relation between exposure to pornography and particular acts. A more comprehensive prohibition of pornography, one that dispensed with proof of harm, would be even more costly to administer, as experience with efforts to stamp out other moral offenses have shown. The costs of the vast and intrusive enforcement efforts necessary to make such a prohibition effective would swamp the cost savings from dispensing with proof of harm.

Given these costs and the infeasibility of measuring the benefits of pornography (though the gross benefits could be proxied by the total revenues of the pornography industry—if only that figure were known), estimating the overall social costs of pornography becomes critical. Some of these costs, notably those resulting from the occasional exploitation and abuse of models and actresses employed to make pictorial pornography, are the artifacts of the formal illegality of "hard core" pornography, which deprives the models and actresses of

---

30. The ordinance entitled anyone harmed by the sale of materials that graphically depicted the subordination of women to men to bring a civil suit against the seller. The ordinance, adopted by Indianapolis, was held unconstitutional in American Booksellers Association, Inc. v. Hudnut, 771 F.2d 323 (7th Cir. 1985), aff'd without opinion, 475 U.S. 1001 (1986).

the usual contractual and legal protections that workers and producers enjoy.[31] The principal cost of which feminists complain—namely, the tendency of pornography to perpetuate inaccurate and offensive stereotypes about female sexuality or even to incite men to rape or otherwise abuse, degrade, or disvalue women—has yet to be established.[32]

Conservative opponents of pornography tend to emphasize not the harms but the offensiveness of pornography. But like most self-regarding harms in Mill's sense, this offensiveness is very difficult to measure in even the roughest terms. And it is doubtful whether much weight should be placed on offensiveness as a basis for restricting freedom of speech. Offensiveness is often a by-product of challenging the values and beliefs that are important to people, and these challenges are an important part of the market in ideas and opinions. People get upset when their way of life is challenged, yet that upset may be the beginning of doubt and may lead eventually to salutary change. Think of all the currently conventional ideas and opinions that were deeply offensive when first voiced. Maybe a condition of being allowed to hear and utter ideas that may challenge *other* people's values and beliefs should be the willingness to extend the same right to others and thus to agree that offensiveness will not be a permissible ground for punishing expression. Pornography is a case in point. Today a *bête noire* of radical feminists, historically it was been associated with challenges to political authority[33] and indeed with feminism.[34]

This analysis suggests a qualification to my earlier point that self-regarding acts in Mill's sense are costs, just as other-regarding acts are. The point reflects a static analysis, and ignores dynamic consequences, the very consequences Mill emphasized. Allowing maximum freedom

31. The use of children is not an effect of illegality, but it could be forbidden without a general ban on pornography. Presumably child pornography that does not involve the use of children, for example purely verbal child pornography (the novel *Lolita*, or the movie when either it is bowdlerized or Lolita is played by an adult actress), should be treated the same as other forms of pornography, in the absence of evidence that child pornography incites child molestation, as distinct from providing masturbation aids to pedophiles. But this is abstracting from offensiveness, an alternative ground for prohibiting pornography.

32. See, for example, Paul R. Abramson and Steven D. Pinkerton, *With Pleasure: Thoughts on the Nature of Human Sexuality* 188–190 (1995); Richard A. Posner, *Overcoming Law* 361–362 (1995).

33. See, for example, Robert Darnton, *The Forbidden Best-Sellers of Pre-Revolutionary France*, ch. 3 (1995).

34. Id. at 114.

of speech, notwithstanding the offense likely to result, may maximize social progress; if so, the benefits are likely to outweigh the offensiveness cost, which is in any event likely to be modest. Bashing in a person's skull is likely to be both more costly to the person and less beneficial in its long-run consequences. There is an economic basis for differentiating as Mill did between self-regarding and other-regarding acts, after all.

But "offensiveness" is not a homogeneous phenomenon. In the case of public or workplace display of pornography, part of the audience is involuntary, consisting of women offended by it. In a discreet private sale of pornography, in contrast, the aim is to please the consumer, not to insult, intimidate, or embarrass anybody. Such a sale can harm a woman only if the buyer of the pornography is incited by it to mistreat her. The effect is indirect, and has not been shown to be substantial. And women who work in a place in which pornography is displayed are compensated for having to put up with it, in the practical economic sense that wages reflect the amenities or disamenities of a job as well as the worker's productivity. Other things being equal (an essential qualification, obviously), the more dangerous, dirty, unhealthful, strenous, uncomfortable, unpleasant, or demeaning the workplace, the higher the wage.[35]

In the case of both pornography and hate speech, and the "political correctness" movement more broadly, the advocacy of regulation has little to do with demonstrable harms or even offensiveness. It has rather to do with an ideological project—in fact with the same project, that of denying or occluding the existence of deep-seated differences between groups (in particular men and women, and blacks and whites). Hate speakers are vociferous deniers of equality, and pornography caters primarily to a specifically male interest in women as sexual playthings for men rather than as persons in their own right who are inherently no different from men except in reproductive anatomy. (Primarily, not exclusively; there is pornography directed to women and to homosexuals of both sexes, and much pornography "advocates" sexual pleasure for women as well as for men, and even sexual equality.) Insofar as campaigns for the regulation of hate speech and pornography

35. See Gertrud M. Fremling and Richard A. Posner, "Status Signaling and the Law, with Particular Application to Sexual Harassment," 147 *University of Pennsylvania Law Review* 1069, 1088–1093 (1999).

have the purpose and effect of correcting ideological or political "error," giving these campaigns the backing of the law interferes arbitrarily with the market in ideas and opinions.

Some politically or ideologically motivated intervention in the speech market takes the form not of suppression of rebrobated speech but of subsidization of counterspeech, whether it is advocating safe driving, safe sex, or patriotic values, or providing financial support to political campaigns. This is governmental interference with the market in ideas and opinions, and it involves the coercion of those taxpayers who disagree with the position that the subsidy supports and do not want their money used to propagate it. But subsidization and prohibition are not symmetrical in their effects. A given dollar expenditure by government will have a bigger effect if devoted to enforcing a prohibition rather than to financing counterspeech. Advertising is both very expensive and likely to be ineffectual when urging behavior contrary to the self-interest of the audience. The second point shows the futility of counterspeech directed, for example, against pornography or against violence in movies; people who enjoy these things will not be moved by advertisements that tell them not to enjoy them. Antismoking advertising that emphasizes the health effects of smoking is more likely to be effective, because it appeals to the self-interest of the audience, than advertising designed merely to make consumers of pornography feel guilty or "dirty."

Antiabortion advertising presents an intermediate case. The audience consists of people who have choices—whether they are women who are already pregnant, the parents of teenage girls, or girls or women deciding whether to have sex and if so whether and what type of contraception to employ. These choices involve a complex interweaving of considerations of self-interest with altruistic concerns. If the choices are finely balanced, public propaganda may tip the balance in some cases. Compare, however, the government's spending $100 million on an antiabortion advertising campaign and the same amount of money prosecuting people who advocate abortion. In the latter case abortion advocacy would be driven to a very low level, and as a result the number of abortions would fall, though a partial offset would be that abortions would be cheaper because abortion clinics would perforce be economizing on advertising, as in the case of Puerto Rico's regulation of casino advertising. The effect of spending $100 million on advertisements denouncing abortion would be less if only because, since the government's antiabortion advertisements would be in addition to privately financed such ads, the latter would decline. The *incremental* contribution of the private advertisements to the formation of public opinion would be reduced with the government in the picture. So the net increment in antiabortion advertising might be slight. And the government advertisements would give their audience information that to a large extent it already had, with or without advertising—information balanced, moreover, and to that extent offset, by pro-choice advertising. In short, dollar for dollar the subsidy approach would have less impact on the market in ideas and opinions than the regulatory approach, making it less problematic from the standpoint of preserving the freedom of that market—though not entirely unproblematic, since it would force taxpayers to pay for propaganda in support of causes that they might abhor, which would be a source of disutility to these taxpayers.

Governmental efforts to correct "unsound" beliefs should be distinguished from governmental speech in support of core governmental functions, such as national defense. The government can hardly be faulted for trying to recruit soldiers by appeals to their patriotism, even if pacifists are offended. When the government is a legitimate participant in labor or other markets, it should have the same rights as other participants to advertise. And when it is exercising a traditional regulatory responsibility, such as combating epidemics, it should be permitted to use advocacy as one of its tools, and thus for example to advocate monogamy and safe sex in order to reduce the incidence of AIDS.

Two forms of regulation—for example, the banning of pornography and the confinement of pornographic bookstores to specified districts within a city—may differ in their costs yet both flunk a cost-benefit test because the benefits exceed either set of costs, or pass because the benefits were smaller than either set of costs. Unfortunately those benefits are often underestimated because of an asymmetry in the salience or reckonability of the costs and the benefits of speech. If a speech touches off a riot, the costs are palpable but the benefits in promoting truth or happiness are not—they are diffuse and indirect and almost impossible to demonstrate by the methods of litigation. An alternative to trying to weigh them is to confine regulation to cases in which the harm inflicted by the speech is *manifestly* great in relation to the amount or value of speech suppressed—in other words, to place a heavy thumb on the cost-benefit scale.

But that approach engenders decisions that strike many people as doctrinaire and foolish. Almost all the "soft core" pornographic magazines and films that pass constitutional muster, along with neo-Nazi ravings that are even more securely within the protection of the Constitution as it is currently interpreted, seem to have no greater social value than a speechless consumer product such as a cap pistol or a sex toy. Yet if I'm right that the benefits of speech are not demonstrable by the methods of litigation, the approach of deeming the benefits great even in the dubious examples that I've just given may make strategic sense. An analogy will help to show this. The U.S. defense strategy during the Cold War was a forward defense. Our front line was the Elbe, not the Potomac. The choice between a forward and a close-in defense involves trade-offs. The forward defense is more costly, and the forward-defense line, because it is nearer the enemy forces, is more likely to be overrun. But the forward defense allows a defense in depth, reducing the likelihood that the home front will be penetrated. If the home front is very difficult to defend, the case for the forward defense becomes compelling. Similarly, rather than defending just the right to say and write things that have some plausible social value, the courts, by following a "deeming the benefits great" approach, defend the right to say and write utterly worthless and deeply offensive things as well. The fight goes on at these outer pickets; it is costly because the claim of free speech is weak because overextended; and sometimes the claim is defeated. But the home front is secure, the enemy having dissipated its strength in penetrating the outer bulwarks. And this is vital because if the battle shifted to the home front, and the courts had to defend the value of, say, allowing people to read *The Bell Curve* or *The Case for Same-Sex Marriage*, they would find it difficult to establish the social value of these or any other books against arguments that the first is poison to race relations and the second undermines morality.[36]

36. Vincent Blasi, in his article "The Pathological Perspective and the First Amendment," 85 *Columbia Law Review* 449 (1985), discusses a related issue: what is the best type of free-speech doctrine to develop in periods in which free speech is not under great stress if the main concern of free-speech law is to plug the dike in periods (such as the Red Scare after World War I or the McCarthyite period after World War II) when free speech is under great stress?

The forward strategy that I have described helps to place in proper perspective the claim by Stanley Fish that "'free speech' is just the name we give to verbal behavior that serves the substantive agendas we wish to advance."[37] The judges, he says, protect the "speech they want heard" and regulate "the speech they want silenced."[38] At one level this is true. Freedom of speech is not absolute. It is relative to social conditions. It had a narrower scope for Blackstone than it has for us, and it would take careful historical inquiry to substantiate a claim that he had too narrow a conception of it even for his time. People can still be punished for disseminating obscenity, for revealing military or trade secrets, for defamation, for inciting riots, for copyright and trademark infringement, for plagiarism, for threats, for perjury, for false advertising and other misrepresentations, for certain types of verbal abuse, for exchanging information in the hope of facilitating price fixing, for talking back to prison guards, for revealing confidences of various sorts, for certain forms of picketing and aggressive solicitation, for invasion of privacy, for indecorous behavior in courthouses, for publicly criticizing one's employer on matters not deemed to be of public concern, for irresponsible or offensive broadcasting, even for using loudspeakers. But there is a difference between free-speech doctrine that is shaped and constrained by broadly political considerations and judicial decision making that has no theoretical coherence, let alone decisionmaking shaped by preference for or aversion to the character or content of particular speech. Most of the "speech" that survives legal challenge in the United States—not just the neo-Nazi ravings and the pornography that does not cross the line to obscenity but also blasphemous art, government documents containing diplomatic secrets (the Pentagon Papers, for example), flag-burnings, picketing, and cross-burnings—offend the mostly conservative, mostly middle-aged and elderly persons who, as judges, insist that the government allow such displays.

Fish himself acknowledges that judicial decisionmaking in the free-speech area is not *completely* ad hoc in discussing a parody published in *Hustler* magazine and held constitutionally protected by the Supreme Court, in which Jerry Falwell, the fundamentalist religious leader, is

---

37. Stanley Fish, *There's No Such Thing as Free Speech, and It's a Good Thing, Too* 102 (1994). The discussion that follows draws on Richard A. Posner, *The Problematics of Moral and Legal Theory* 277–279 (1999).

38. Fish, note 37 above, at 110.

represented as having sexual intercourse with his mother in an out-
house.[39] The Court's inability to draw a line that would permit the
suppression of so intellectually barren and gratuitously repulsive a
personal attack draws a pointed remark from Fish about the judiciary's
"self-imposed incapacity to make distinctions that would seem perfectly obvious to any well-informed teenager."[40] That incapacity
sounds like the opposite of ad hoc political decisionmaking—sounds, in
fact, like a judicial commitment to the strategy of the forward defense.

    In commending that strategy and thus the desirability of keeping the
government's hands off the speech market, I may seem to be assuming
that this market can be counted on to operate efficiently as long as the
government keeps hands off. Actually, there are reasons to doubt that
the speech market will operate efficiently: it is difficult to establish
property rights in information; there are deep uncertainties of both a
practical and a philosophical nature concerning the feasibility of determining by competition or anything else the value (for example, the
truth, fruitfulness, or beauty) of particular ideas, opinions, works of art,
or other intellectual or expressive work; and the "market in ideas" is
frequently metaphorical rather than literal because (this is related to
the first point) speech often is neither bought nor sold. The possibility
that markets in ideas may fail to internalize externalities is shown by
such unexceptionable interventions as punishing a person who shouts
"Fire!" in a crowded theater, knowing there is no fire.

    These markets may also fail by producing "goods" that have no net
value, such as the totalitarian ideologies that wrought such extraordinary havoc during much of the twentieth century. Even today Americans are awash in superstitious and erroneous, even preposterous, beliefs, in part because of sensationalistic and inaccurate "news" media;
many members of the intelligentsia are dupes of absurd ideas peddled
by radical postmodernists; and there is a staggering amount of trash
culture, both popular and highbrow. Markets in ideas are often undone
by prohibitive information costs, which makes it difficult to retain a robust confidence in the truth- and beauty-producing properties of these
markets.

    Holmes was a skeptic—which in economic terms is someone who

<hr>

39. Hustler Magazine, Inc. v. Falwell, 485 U.S. 46 (1988).
40. Fish, note 37 above, at 132.

thinks information costs are *really* high—yet he was not lukewarm in his attitude toward freedom of speech. Quite the contrary—and it was on skepticism that he based his belief in the desirability of leaving the market of ideas largely unregulated. The very thing that makes this market inefficient—the extremely high costs of information—makes the regulation of them inefficient. If consumers can't sort out truth from falsity, or beauty from ugliness, in the wares produced in these markets, how likely is it that censors, judges, or juries can? Moreover, the difficulty that the producer of ideas is likely to encounter in trying to capture the social benefits of his output will make him exaggeratedly sensitive to expected-punishment costs. The unpopular speaker bears the full costs of punishment, while the benefits of the speech may be long deferred and thus enjoyed largely by other persons. The law has responded to this problem (a problem of what the economist calls "external benefits") in a variety of ways. One is by denying a privilege to republish defamatory material without being liable for defamation. If only the original publisher were liable, newspapers and other new sources would be even more reluctant than they are now to risk publishing defamatory material, because they would know that their competitors could republish it without bearing any of the expected liability costs of defamation.

This analysis supplies a reason independent of any value judgment for giving commercial speech less than average constitutional protection but hate speech full protection. Commercial speech is robust not because business is politically powerful, which it sometimes is and sometimes isn't, but because the commercial speaker normally expects to recoup the full economic value of his speech in the form of higher product prices or a greater output. It is doubtful that commercial speech should get any greater constitutional protection than commercial activity generally. In contrast, hate speech is fragile because the costs are concentrated but the benefits diffused. The student who is expelled from school for expressing racial antagonism bears all the costs of his speaking out but captures little of the social benefits (if any) of giving vent to his opinion.

All this would be of little importance had Plato been correct in thinking that all truth was discoverable by experts. We permit censorship when we trust expert opinion to generate "true knowledge," as in the regulation by the Food and Drug Administration of claims con-

cerning the safety and efficacy of drugs; the regulation of the truthfulness of advertising and labeling by the Federal Trade Commission; and
the determination of truth in defamation cases. Censorship in these areas has been defended as a desirable form of paternalism—"epistemic
paternalism."[41] The defense is all right, but the term is not apt. All that
is involved is delegation to expert, neutral, and basically trustworthy
bodies of responsibility for making definitive factual or other determinations that a private citizen does not have the time or the training to
make. Most of our knowledge is secondhand, acquired by simple acceptance of the testimony of people, often experts, whom we have de-
cent reasons to credit.[42]

Unfortunately, the truth of political and even many scientific ideas,
and even more plainly the beauty or delight of works of art or literature, cannot be determined reliably by forensic processes or government
experts, and so cannot be delegated to judges, bureaucrats, or experts.
Truth and beauty must be left to the competitive struggle and the test
of time to "determine"—but only tentatively, always subject to revision.
Once this is granted, the censor is disarmed, since competition and the
test of time are not methods that he can use to carry out his duties.

The test of time links Holmes's skepticism to his strong defense of
free speech. An extreme skeptic would doubt that censorship was an
impediment to the discovery of truth, because he would doubt that
there was truth to discover; the only objection to censorship would be
the costs, which are often (though not always, as I emphasized in discussing pornography) modest, of administering the censorship program. Holmes wasn't that kind of skeptic, at least in *Abrams*. What he
said there was not that truth is undeterminable but rather that it is
determinable only through competition and so requires freedom of
speech and is killed by censorship. A corollary is that where the determination of truth does not require a competitive process, as in many
advertising and defamation cases, the case for censorship is much
stronger.

~ So far I have been discussing mainly old issues of freedom of
speech. I now want to consider what the instrumental approach may be

41. Alvin I. Goldman, "Epistemic Paternalism: Communication Control in Law and Society," 88 *Journal of Philosophy* 113 (1991).

42. As argued in C. A. J. Coady's important book *Testimony: A Philosophical Study* (1992),
which I discuss in Chapter 10.

able to contribute to the resolution of three of the newer issues: hate-speech codes;[43] the regulation of campaign financing; and the regulation of the Internet.

Hate-speech codes. I noted one objection to hate-speech codes already —that they deprive the government of valuable information about the disaffection of people harmed or offended by affirmative action, multiculturalism, and political correctness. They also put the government's thumb on one pan of the balance of opinion about equality. This is true even when the hate-speech code is racially neutral, so that a black student can be punished for calling a white student a honkey. There is a current of opinion in the black community—it is associated with the movement known as Afrocentrism—that whites are inferior to blacks. This is silly, but it is not the government's business to punish people for denying racial equality. It is after all only a dogma, and a recent one, that the races and the sexes and the nationalities and ethnic groups and so forth are equal to one another; and to punish people for challenging it is as objectionable as punishing people for advocating communism or laissez-faire.

It is true that the most carefully drafted of the hate-speech codes are limited to "fighting words," a category of speech that the Supreme Court has long held to be excepted from the protections of the First Amendment.[44] Fighting words are defined as words likely to incite a breach of the peace. This is a perverse definition. It enlarges the legal rights of violence-prone, thin-skinned people and so encourages people to cultivate a reputation for hypersensitivity. By focusing on audience reaction it condones a kind of "heckler's veto," which the Supreme Court has properly rejected as a basis for restricting freedom of speech.[45] It discriminates against the inarticulate, putting the hate-speech codes into conflict with the desire of the same liberals who support these codes to increase the access of marginal groups to the mar-

43. The censorship of hate speech should be distinguished from the punishment of hate crimes, which I take up in Chapter 7. For a good discussion of the First Amendment issues raised by efforts to suppress hate speech, see James Weinstein, *Hate Speech, Pornography, and the Radical Attack on Free Speech Doctrine* (1999).

44. See Cantwell v. Connecticut, 310 U.S. 296 (1940).

45. Forsyth County v. Nationalist Movement, 505 U.S. 123, 133–135 (1992). Not only can the government not ban the unpopular speaker, it cannot charge him for the added cost of providing him with police protection. If it could, this would encourage the hecklers, who would hope to make the cost of protection as high as possible in order to bring financial pressure to bear on the speaker.

ket of ideas.[46] And in adopting a norm of decorum it reveals a misunderstanding of the character of expressive activity. An abstract painting is not less expressive than an essay on the historical roots of the First Amendment. Neither, for that matter, is a political assassination. Discursive prose represents a tiny fraction of the expressive activity that has shaped history. Political assassinations are punished not because they do not contribute to the market in ideas and opinions—often they do contribute, sometimes crucially—but because of their costs. It is only on the score of cost that it is rational to distinguish among the various genres of expressive activity, and not on the score of verbal articulateness.

The issue of what to do about hate-speech codes can, however, be finessed by a reminder that the First Amendment is limited to state action. If a private university wants to have such a code there is nothing in the Constitution to prevent it. It is, to be sure, a considerable mystery why government is in the business of owning and operating colleges and universities in the first place. The mystery is not public support of education, but public operation. Many students at private universities receive public money in one way or another; but the universities are still private. If government got out of the business of operating universities, the issue of hate-speech codes, like that of affirmative action, would be removed from the constitutional agenda altogether.

This discussion illustrates the general point that strict enforcement of the free-speech clause creates an incentive for privatization of governmental activities. By "going private" an enterprise can escape the costs of compliance with legal directives that bind only government. This is not necessarily an evasion of the First Amendment and hence a threat to freedom. Private enterprises have different, and often healthier, incentives than public ones, and less power.

This point casts a shadow on proposals to require the government to throw open more of its property to advocacy.[47] Such a requirement will accelerate the trend toward privatization. Suppose the courts decided that airports and schools should be deemed public forums available for all types of advocacy—marches and other demonstrations, soapbox oratory, aggressive solicitation. Nothing in principle requires that air-

---

46. See, for example, Cohen, note 3 above, at 245–248 (fair access), 250–257 (hate speech).

47. See, for example, id. at 247. Privatization of public colleges and universities would cut the other way.

ports or schools be public property; there is a growing private-school movement in this country; and airport privatization is a likely eventual step in air transportation anyway. The more that courts pile costs on public enterprises in the name of free speech, the *less* governmentally protected free speech there will be in the long run if the costs tip the balance in favor of privatization.

Campaign financing regulation. Despite some public subsidies and some restrictions on the size of individual contributions to campaigns, the American system of campaign financing is extremely porous and is widely and probably correctly believed to constitute a thinly disguised system of quasi-bribes of elected officials; at the very least, it tilts the playing field very steeply toward the wealthy and the well organized, who have an advantage in raising large sums of money from individuals limited by the federal campaign financing law to contributing $1,000 per candidate. These consequences are entrenched by the Supreme Court's interpretation of the First Amendment as permitting *that* limitation on campaign spending but forbidding, as an infringement of free speech, the placing of legal limits on overall campaign spending, on an individual's right to buy political advertising with his own or family money, and on the right of an individual who, or organization that, is "independent" of the candidate to advertise with respect to campaign issues (that is, there is an unlimited right to make "soft money" donations).[48] The system magnifies the effect of interest groups and, of course, the wealthy on public policy—interest groups because by definition they can overcome the usual obstacles to cooperation and so raise sums of money disproportionately greater than what can be raised from the members of diffuse, unorganized groups that may be much larger and so democratically entitled to greater weight in the formulation of public policy. While facilitating speech by the wealthy and by interest groups, the present system is said to distort the market in ideas by drowning out the speech of the unorganized and the impecunious. The exercise of freedom of political speech has limited practical significance without access to the mass media, and such access requires resources that only a fraction, constituting a nonrandom sample, of the population commands. This point is related to my earlier observation, in discussing government speech, about the high cost of advertising.

48. Buckley v. Valeo, 424 U.S. 1 (1976) (per curiam).

With these points conceded, it would be rather odd to say to an ad-
mirer of President and Mrs. Clinton that "you should not buy 1,000
copies of *It Takes a Village* to distribute free of charge, as this would
enable you to 'speak' with a louder voice than a person who could not
afford such a purchase." This example makes it easy to see that restricting "soft money" donations really would be an infringement of freedom of speech and so would require a convincing demonstration of the
harms caused by such speech. The harms are elusive. Individuals or
groups that have more than the average amount of money have always
had more than the average ability to spend money on trying to influence public opinion. We do not consider such inequality a compelling
reason for limiting free speech. Somehow the market in ideas seems robust to inequalities of expenditures by the producers and consumers in
this market. Consistent with my earlier discussion of government subsidies of the speech market, the elasticity of public opinion to expenditures on shaping that opinion seems very low. Is the public policy of the
nation worse because interest groups use campaign expenditures to try
to influence policy and wealthy people use their wealth to try to get
elected to office? This has not been shown, although I suspect that
most of the people who advocate limits on campaign spending believe
that if money played a smaller role in the electoral process the public
policies they favor would be more likely to be adopted. The contributions are very small in relation to the resources of the contributors, and
so do not burden business greatly.[49] So far as appears, the contributions
buy access and modest influence, at best, and often just offset the contributions to competing candidates rather than causing substantial distortions in the markets in which the contributors operate.[50]

It has been suggested that the problem of quasi-bribery could be
solved by requiring that campaign donations be anonymous.[51] But

49. They are also extremely small in relation to the scale of modern government. See John
R. Lott, Jr., "A Simple Explanation for Why Campaign Expenditures Are Increasing: The
Government Is Getting Bigger" 43 *Journal of Law and Economics* 359 (2000).

50. See Steven D. Levitt, "Congressional Campaign Finance Reform" *Journal of Economic
Perspectives*, Winter 1995, pp. 183, 190–192; Stephen G. Bronars and John R. Lott, Jr., "Do
Campaign Donations Alter How a Politician Votes? Or, Do Donors Support Candidates
Who Value the Same Things That They Do?" 40 *Journal of Law and Economics* 317 (1997).

51. See Ian Ayres and Jeremy Bulow, "The Donation Booth: Mandating Donor Anonymity
to Disrupt the Market for Political Influence," 50 *Stanford Law Review* 837 (1998).

there would be an information cost: the identity of a donor is a clue to
the likely policies of the donee should he be elected—a valuable clue if
the donor has better information about the candidate than the average
voter has. (So it might be better to *forbid* anonymous donations!) What
is more, to the extent that campaign donations really are quasi-bribes,
the incentive to make them would be greatly reduced if they were
anonymous.

Limiting campaign expenditures may create its own distortion of the
market in ideas by making it harder to challenge incumbents. To get a
foothold in a market, a new product has to be advertised more heavily
than the existing products, which are already familiar to consumers. A
limit on the amount that could be spent to advertise a product would
thus reduce competition in product markets, and the same possibility
looms when campaign expenditures are capped. Yet spending limits
may actually hurt incumbents more than challengers because incumbents generally are able to raise more money—a natural advantage that
spending limits would blunt. Empirical evidence is mixed, but seems
on balance not to support the claim that spending limits would help
rather than (as seems more intuitive) hurt incumbents.[52] Another possibility, however, is that a reduction in campaign contributions, by reducing publicity about the political process, would actually strengthen
interest-group politics by reducing both the amount of scrutiny that
interest groups receive and the already-weak incentive of politicians to
pay close attention to the policy views of ordinary voters.

To those who think it immoral that the wealthy and the organized
should have advantages in the political arena, the argument just
sketched will carry no conviction. But to the economist, the morality of
our oligarchic system of political financing is neither here nor there;
the issue is the consequences of changing it. Of course, any noninstru-
mental issue can be "instrumentalized" by a suitable positing of ends. If
the end were equality of influence, strict limits on campaign financing
could be defended as instruments to that end. Some critics of campaign
financing would posit such an end, but it would be basically a *façon de
parler*. Equality, especially in so specialized, even esoteric, a domain as
campaign finance, is too abstract to count as an end for an instrumen-
talist thinker, who will insist that the proponent of equality in cam-

52. See Levitt, note 50 above, at 188–190.

paign finance explain what tangible good is supposed to come out of such equality. Will Americans be happier if campaign spending is limited? Will the poor be better off? Will there be less crime, less discrimination, or even less pollution? Will government be bigger, smaller, better, worse?

If there is a problem of campaign finance, it has been exacerbated by the Supreme Court's response to legislative efforts to regulate it. To couple upholding the $1,000 limit on individual contributions with invalidating all limits on self-spending gave an arbitrary boost to wealthy individuals. If A is wealthy and has strong views on public policy but no political skills, and B is not wealthy and shares A's views and has political skills, A cannot give B the money that A would spend on himself if he ran for office. What sense does that make? The limitation on individual campaign contributions has other perverse effects as well. It confers an arbitrary advantage on candidates who have the support of large businesses that have many affluent executives, since these businesses can easily generate a large pot of money for the candidate. It makes fund raising a much more time-consuming chore for candidates (thus discouraging many able people from running for political office) by requiring the candidate to raise money at retail, rather than allowing him to rely on a relatively small number of large donors. And it arbitrarily favors unions, which contribute money from union dues, deducted by the employers from the workers' paychecks, to political campaigns. Although the worker has a right to be excused from having his paycheck reduced by the proportion of the dues allocable to the union's political activities, inertia favors the union; companies have no corresponding right to take money out of their employees' wages for political uses.

Regulation of the Internet. Free speech on the Internet has aroused concern on basically four grounds. First it is argued that the Internet facilitates the anonymous dissemination and receipt of indecent material, notably child pornography. Second that it lacks all quality control and therefore promotes the dissemination of inaccurate and misleading information, which by a kind of Gresham's Law will obliterate truthful information; it is argued, for example, that unscrupulous, unsupervised Internet journalists "force" the respectable media to report unsubstantiated rumors. Third it is argued that because the Internet gives people unmediated access to huge potential audiences for their speech, it magnifies the potential harm caused by irresponsible speech. Fourth the Internet is said to foment antisocial behavior by enabling perverts and extremists to find their soulmates more easily.

The fourth point is particularly interesting. People who have weird ideas tend to keep these ideas to themselves, fearing ostracism if they express them and perhaps doubting the validity of their ideas for want of any reinforcement by other people; isolation destroys self-confidence in most people. Once eccentrics discover in Internet chat rooms and Web sites that hundreds or thousands of other people think the same way they do, they become emboldened not only to express their ideas but also to act upon them, their self-confidence bolstered by membership in a community of believers. But governmental efforts to close chat rooms and Web sites that attract dangerous or unstable people would have the side effect of censoring potentially socially valuable but unconventional communication. And since chat rooms are open to all, including government agents, society can protect itself by governmental monitoring of these rooms. A weak government can be undermined by free speech, but a strong government can be strengthened by it because it enables government to keep tabs on potential threats.

The first and second grounds for concern about free speech on the Internet involve transitory features of the new medium. There are a variety of technological and regulatory techniques for preventing the dissemination of illegal materials and shielding nonconsenting consumers from them;[53] and private demand for screening for accuracy will eventually result in equipping the Internet with quality controls as effective as those of the traditional media. The third ground—the potentially greater magnitude of harmful speech carried by the Internet because of the potentially greater size of the audience for individuals whose speech is too harmful or offensive to get through the gateways of the conventional media—is the most worrisome. A nut who couldn't get a newspaper to publish any of his letters to it can reach thousands or even millions of people over the Internet at virtually a zero cost. But this is a problem that the instrumental approach copes with automatically. The social cost of a speech is a function not only of its harmful or offensive character but also of the size of its audience; it is worse to shout "Fire!" (at least when there is no fire, and sometimes when there is one) in a large crowded theater than in a small one.

Another consideration is that the Internet is a method of circum-

53. See Lawrence Lessig, *Code and Other Laws of Cyberspace* (1999).

venting private censorship. Private censorship, which sometimes reaches oppressive dimensions in the "respectable" mass media, is both a part of and an impediment to the market in ideas and opinions. Without any private censorship, the volume of speech would increase to the level of unintelligible cacophony; but with it, important ideas, information, and insights are often suppressed. The market depends on selectivity and gatekeepers, but can also be undermined by such things. The Internet is among other things a safety valve.

~ 3

Normative Law and Economics: From Utilitarianism to Pragmatism

$\mathcal{E}$CONOMICS HAS ALWAYS been closely allied to social reform. From Adam Smith's advocacy of free trade, to Bentham's criticism of usury laws, to Keynes's advocacy of deficit spending in depressions, to Milton Friedman's advocacy of monetarism, a volunteer army, and a negative income tax, economists have thought it natural to translate their diagnoses of economic pathologies into prescriptions for cure. They have rarely thought it necessary to construct a bridge between "is" and "ought"—that is, to lay philosophical foundations for the use of economics as a normative rather than merely a positive science. The branch of economics that addresses the issue of the normativity of economics rigorously, "welfare economics," although it has engaged the attention of a number of distinguished economists, such as Paul Samuelson and Amartya Sen, has always been rather peripheral to the discipline, in almost the way that medical ethics is peripheral to medicine. Economists can get away with being casual about the normativity of their subject because they can usually appeal to a generally accepted goal, such as maximizing the value of output, rather than having to defend the goal. By showing how a change in economic policy or arrangements would advance us toward that goal, they can make a normative statement without having to defend their fundamental premises. They can keep debate at the technical level where reasoning is over means rather than ends. They can demonstrate, for example, that cartelization results in a reduction in the value of output, and since maximizing that value is a generally accepted goal of a commercial society, their demonstration provides, without more, a prima facie case for prohibiting cartels.

The qualification "prima facie" is important. Opponents of proposals for economic reform are quick to posit competing goals to that of efficiency or value maximization. This is especially the case when economists get into areas that are not traditionally economic, which happens often in economic analysis of law. To say that an area is not traditionally regarded as "economic" is to say that suggestions for orienting it toward efficiency or other economic values are likely to jar, because it is assumed that noneconomic values dominate issues that are not explicitly economic. And then what is the economist to do? Can he say more than that he's shown that policy X would increase efficiency but that he can't speak to its ultimate merit?

Not without hitching economic values to some more comprehensive source or concept of value, and historically, as we glimpsed in discussing Bentham in Chapter 1, that meant hitching economic science to utilitarian philosophy. Modern economics makes heavy use of utilitarian terminology, in such key expressions as "expected utility," "marginal utility," and "utility maximization," but in practice is rarely utilitarian in any rigorous sense. To go back to the cartel example, while it is true that a cartel reduces the value of output, it also transfers wealth from consumers to producers, and if producers happen to obtain much more utility from money than consumers do, the cartel could increase aggregate utility by more than the loss of utility caused by the fall in the value of output. Modern economics has given up on trying to measure utility, because such measurement requires information about people's preferences and emotions that seems unobtainable.[1] The historical linkage between economics and utilitarianism thus has largely been severed. The practical significance of utility in modern economics is mostly limited to attitudes toward risk, which can drive a wedge between wealth and a broader sense of value that economists call "utility";

1. Some economists say that comparing different people's utility is "meaningless," but they are wrong. Parents, for example, are constantly making guesses, often pretty good ones, about the relative effect on their utility and their children's utility of transferring money to the children. This is a general feature of altruism, and altruism both within and outside the family is common.

a risk-averse person, for example, will by definition value a 10 percent chance of obtaining $100 at less than a certainty of receiving $10, even though the chance and the certainty would be valued equally by a person who was indifferent to risk.

It turns out, moreover, that utilitarianism is not a reliable guide to social policy, all measurement problems to one side.[2] The basic reasons are threefold. First, few people actually believe—and there is no way to prove them wrong—that maximizing happiness, or contentment, or joy, or preference satisfaction, or the excess of pleasure over pain, or some other version of utility is or should be one's object in life. Happiness is important to most people, but it isn't everything. How many of us would be willing to take a pill that would put us into a blissfully happy dreamlike trance for the rest of our lives, even if we were absolutely convinced of the safety and efficacy of the pill and the trance? Even today, when science has brought close to reality many of the technological marvels that Aldous Huxley in *Brave New World* (1932) projected 600 years into the future—feel-good drugs (his *soma* is our Prozac), comprehensive cosmetic surgery, elimination of the ills of old age, the divorce of reproduction from sex, consumerism, and so forth —most of us would side with "Mr. Savage" in rejecting the Utopian lives of the "normals."

Second, by aggregating utility across persons, utilitarianism treats people as cells in the overall social organism rather than as individuals. This is the source of the familiar barbarisms of utilitarian ethics, such as the deliberate sacrifice of innocents to maximize the total amount of happiness in the society (or the world, or the universe), or the "utility monster" whose capacity for sadistic pleasure so far exceeds the capacity of his victims to experience pain that utility is maximized by allowing him to commit rape and murder. Defenders of utilitarianism seek to deflect such criticisms by pointing out that lack of trust in officials would defeat any effort to empower the state to attempt to maximize utility on an individual basis. They show that the only regime that would be utility maximizing in the real world would be a form of rule utilitarianism that limited the power of government and so would rule out, for example, the kind of authoritarian regime, well-intentioned

2. The literature on the relation between economics and utilitarianism is vast. For a useful anthology, see *Ethics, Rationality, and Economic Behaviour* (Francesco Farina, Frank Hahn, and Stefano Vannucci eds. 1996).

but sinister (a techno-futuristic version of the reign of the Grand Inquisitor described in *The Brothers Karamazov*), depicted in Huxley's novel. But practical objections to the logical implications of utilitarianism miss the point. The logic itself is repulsive. Even if we assume away all the problems of implementation, and contemplate the result—the inducement of blissful trances by utterly benign, democratically responsive officials—we still don't like it.

Third, utilitarianism has no boundary principles, except possibly sentience. Peter Singer, the leading philosophical advocate of animal liberation, is a utilitarian.[3] Animals feel pain, and even more clearly do foreigners, so that utilitarianism collides with powerful intuitions that our social obligations are greater to the people of our own society than to outsiders and greater to human beings than to (other) animals.

Some of the objections to utilitarianism can be elided by substituting wealth for utility as the maximand. "Wealth" is to be understood in this context not in strictly monetary terms but rather as the summation of all the valued objects, both tangible and intangible, in society, weighted by the prices they would command if they were to be traded in markets. In other words, the market transaction is taken as paradigmatic of morally appropriate action. This view, though anathema to anyone who retains even residual socialist sympathies in this era of triumphalist capitalism, can be defended (though how successfully remains to be seen) by reference to notions both of express and of implied consent. If A sells B his stamp collection for $1,000, this implies that the stamp collection is worth less than $1,000 to A and more than $1,000 to B. Let us suppose that it is worth $900 to A (that is, he would have thought himself better off at any price above that) and $1,200 to B (the most he would have paid for it). The transaction is wealth maximizing because before it took place A had something worth $900 to him and B had $1,000 in cash, while afterward A has $1,000 and B has something worth $1,200 to him; so aggregate wealth has increased by $300 ($1,000 + $1,200 − $1,000 + $900). The increase in wealth has been brought about by consent rather than coercion; and provided that the transaction has no third-party effects, it has made two people better off and no one worse off. It thus is the product of free, unanimous choice.

Wealth maximization mitigates the problems that I listed earlier

3. See Peter Singer, *Animal Liberation* (rev. ed. 1990).

with utility maximization. Value is easier to measure than utility; no position is taken on what people want or should want, such as happiness; the scope of permissible coercion is less (though, as we are about to see, not zero) because the right to act on one's desires is limited by willingness to pay (*B* can't grab *A*'s stamp collection just because it gives him more pleasure than it gives *A*); noneconomic values such as freedom and autonomy are preserved; and the boundary problem is solved because the community is defined as those who have money to back their desires.

Serious problems remain, however, though the fundamental objection to wealth maximization as an ethical norm is not, as might be supposed, that most transactions have third-party effects and that the economy cannot be organized on a purely voluntarist basis. It is true that coercion is indispensable to preventing a number of serious market failures and, in the form of taxation, to financing the coercive measures needed to prevent those market failures. But it is possible to design methods of regulation that bring about the approximate results that the free market would bring about when, as in the example of the sale of the stamp collection, transaction costs do not prevent a market from functioning. Much economic analysis of law is directed at suggesting "market mimicking" forms of regulation to deal with monopoly, externalities, and other conditions that prevent the market from working well because they cannot feasibly be contracted around.[4]

The fundamental objection to wealth maximization as an ethical norm is not inoperability, but the dependence of market outcomes on the distribution of wealth. *A* may have valued his stamp collection at only $900, and *B* have valued it at $1,200, not because *A* loves stamps less than *B*—he may love them much more—and not because there is any appealing concept of desert to which *B* might appeal to validate his claim to be able to buy the collection at the price. *A* may simply be destitute and have to sell his stamp collection in order to eat, and *B*, while not passionate about stamps—while indeed, let us assume, indifferent

4. As Coase's classic article on social cost (cited in the Introduction) showed, if transaction costs are low the market will internalize externalities. Similarly, if transaction costs in a monopoly setting are low the victims of the monopoly will pay the monopolist to expand his output to the competitive level. There will still be a transfer of wealth to the monopolist, but, at least as a first approximation, the allocation of resources will be efficient because the output of the monopolized market will be the same as it would be under competition.

to them—wishes to diversify his enormous wealth by holding a variety of collectibles. These circumstances are not at all inconsistent with the sale's making both *A* and *B* better off; on the contrary, they explain *why* it makes both better off. But they sap the moral foundations of a social system oriented to wealth maximization. For after the paradise of optimality is attained, and all society's institutions have been brought into conformity with the requirements of wealth maximization and so consist of free markets supplemented by market-mimicking governmental interventions, the pattern of consumption and production will be strictly derivative from an underlying distribution of wealth. If that distribution is unjust, the pattern of economic activities derived from it will not have a strong claim to be regarded as just either. And insofar as the distribution of wealth is itself largely determined by the market, the justice of the market cannot be derived from some independent notion of the just distribution.

There is another indeterminacy at work, moreover: when a good is a large part of the wealth of an individual, the wealth maximizing allocation of the good may be indeterminate. If *A* and *B* each have only $100, and the question is whether some good is worth more to one of them than to the other, the answer may depend on who receives it and in that case the criterion of wealth maximization cannot be used to determine who shall receive it. If the good is worth $200 and is given to *A*, *A* will value it more than *B* because *B* will not be willing (if only because unable) to pay more for it; but if instead it is given to *B*, *B* will value it more because *A* will not be able to afford to buy it from *B*.

Some of these problems can be bracketed—the one just mentioned by observing that it makes the criterion of wealth maximization unusable only in cases in which the good to be allocated is a large part of the wealth of the contenders for it. The argument that common law decisionmaking should be guided by that criterion does not require taking a position on its ultimate merits. Provided that wealth is a genuine social value, though not necessarily the only or even the principal such value, that it is one that judges are in a good position to promote, and that issues of economic equality are more efficiently or legitimately addressed by other organs of government, there is no compelling normative objection to using it to guide the common law. We might even think it Pareto efficient, a more powerful normative criterion than wealth maximizing. A state of affairs is Pareto optimal if it cannot be changed without making at least one person worse off, and it is Pareto superior to another state of affairs if it makes at least one person better off and no one worse off. In either case the criterion, essentially, is unanimity, and the outcome of a unanimous choice has considerable moral appeal. If common law shaped by wealth maximization has the attractive features that I think it does, it might command almost unanimous consent ex ante if there were a mechanism for eliciting that consent.

Although economists cannot generate or validate a theory of distributive justice, they can make some descriptive points that might help other social theorists come up with or defend such a theory. Most obviously the economist can point out that income and wealth[5] are unevenly distributed in our society (just how unevenly we shall be considering shortly)—though the economist will quickly add that much of the inequality reflects choice—I would be wealthier had I not accepted an appointment as a judge many years ago—including the choice of what amount of financial risk to assume. This degree of inequality satisfies the Pareto criteria. Much inequality reflects the different stages of the life cycle, a pretty neutral determinant. Much reflects character and effort, but here we get into deep water, because these are products to a great extent (maybe entirely, to one who disbelieves in free will) of a "natural lottery"—differences in innate characteristics, including brains, energy, and a predisposition to good health, rather than of choice.

Much of the inequality of wealth must be conceded to reflect sheer luck even if one's natural endowment of character and intelligence is considered an entitlement rather than a product of the random sorting of the genes. There is the luck of being born in a wealthy rather than a poor country, the luck of being a beneficiary or casualty of unpredictable shifts in consumer demands and labor markets, the luck of inheritance, the luck of the financial markets, the luck of whom you know, and the luck of your parents' ability and willingness to invest in your human capital. Determinists think that it's all luck, that deservedness has nothing to do with how rich or poor anyone is.

A point that reinforces skepticism about the justice of the income distribution, and that has received less attention than it should, is that a

---

5. Income is the flow, wealth the stock; since each can be converted into the other, I use them essentially interchangeably.

market system tends to *magnify* differences in innate ability, driving a wedge between the natural lottery and income. The cause is the "superstar" phenomenon.[6] Consider two concert pianists, one (*A*) slightly better than the other (*B*). Suppose that most of the income of a concert pianist nowadays derives not from performing or teaching but from recording. Since recordings of the same piece of music are close substitutes, a consumer has no reason to buy recordings made by *B* rather than those made by *A* unless there is a significant difference in price, and there need not be; even if *A* receives a higher royalty from his contract with the record company than *B* could command, the added cost to the record company may be offset by the economies of a larger output. *A* may thus end up with a very substantial income from recording and *B* with a zero income from it, though *A* may be only a 2 percent better pianist and the difference in quality may be discernible by only a small percentage of the music-loving public. There need be nothing "unjust" in the difference in income between the two pianists; but neither can it be confidently referred to the difference in their quality, so disproportionate is it to that difference. It illustrates the moral *arbitrariness* of many of the wealth differences among individuals. A system of wealth maximization ratifies and perfects an essentially arbitrary distribution of wealth.

The justification for such a system, if there is one, is not ethical but pragmatic. And there is a pragmatic justification. This can be argued in two ways, one specific and one general. The specific involves rebutting the claim, a recurrent one in debates over wealth maximization as a social goal, that a high degree of economic inequality, as in the present-day United States, is politically destabilizing. The general involves rebutting the criticisms of cost-benefit analysis, viewed as the operational method of wealth maximization.

Concerning the effect of economic inequality on political stability, I must define some terms. "Political stability" could just mean, narrowly and negatively, the absence of civil wars, of coups (successful or attempted), of frequent constitutional changes (for example, a change from dictatorship to democracy), and of rampant domestic political terrorism, corruption, and expropriation.[7] But this would fail to distin-

6. See Sherwin Rosen, "The Economics of Superstars," 71 *American Economic Review* 845 (1981).

7. See John Londregan and Keith Poole, "The Seizure of Executive Power and Economic Growth: Some Additional Evidence," in *Political Economy, Growth, and Business Cycles* 51 (Alex

guish stability from repression. Authoritarian regimes may suppress the symptoms of political instability—for example, mass demonstrations against the regime—through intimidation; but we have plenty of recent experience with the sudden collapse of authoritarian regimes that had looked very strong, very stable, even unshakable. Like fixed versus flexible exchange rates, authoritarian government conceals rather than eliminates political instability. The only reliably stable regimes are those in which the symptoms of political unrest are absent *despite* those symptoms' not being forcibly suppressed. The purely symptomatic measures of stability must therefore be supplemented with measures of political liberty; we shall see that measures of political stability are indeed positively correlated with measures of political liberty.

Economic inequality is as difficult to define or measure as political stability. The inequality of *measured* income across households, individuals, percentiles of the population, social classes, or other standard aggregates used in economic and other social scientific research is, as I have suggested already, a crude proxy for real economic inequality. But as long as we focus on *changes* in equality of income over time, or *differences* in the degree of equality across nations, income equality may be a satisfactory even though not ideal proxy for real economic equality. It enables us to say, not that the United States is a nation characterized by "too much" inequality of income, but that there is more economic inequality in the United States today than there was fifteen years ago or that there is more economic inequality in the United States than in Japan or Sweden.

Economic inequality in the wealthy nations declined pretty steadily after the 1920s and especially after 1945,[8] but it has risen since 1980.[9]

Cukierman, Zvi Hercowitz, and Leonardo Leiderman eds. 1992), emphasizing coups and constitutional changes. I put "rampant" before "domestic political terrorism" because occasional political assassinations, and even so dramatic a domestic terrorist episode as the bombing of the U.S. federal building in Oklahoma City on April 19, 1995, are not destabilizing.

8. Hartmut Kaelble and Mark Thomas, "Introduction," in *Income Distribution in Historical Perspective* 1, 55–56 (Y. S. Brenner, H. Kaelble, and M. Thomas eds. 1991).

9. For the developed countries, see Peter Gottschalk and Timothy M. Smeeding, "Cross-National Comparisons of Earnings and Income Inequality," 35 *Journal of Economic Literature* 633, 636 (1997); for the United States in particular, see, for example, Frank Levy and Richard J. Murnane, "U.S. Earnings Levels and Earnings Inequality: A Review of Recent Trends and Proposed Explanations," 30 *Journal of Economic Literature* 1333, 1371–1372 (1992); Richard B. Freeman and Lawrence F. Katz, "Rising Wage Inequality: The United States vs. Other

In the developing as distinct from the developed world, consistent with a thesis propounded by Simon Kuznets, rising *levels* of income are associated with rising *inequality* of incomes.[10] So, in general, economic inequality seems to be rising in all but poor, stagnant nations. Among the wealthy nations the United States and Switzerland appear to have the most unequal income distributions; Sweden, Norway, and Germany the most equal.[11]

Measuring the effect of income and the income distribution on the political system is complicated by the two-way character of the causal path that connects incomes with politics. When there is great income inequality in a democracy, the median voter has a strong incentive to support heavily progressive taxes, since the opportunities for redistribution from the wealthy to the nonwealthy will be great. The more equal the distribution of income, the less the median voter will have to gain from such taxes because the less income the wealthy will have to be taxed away. We might therefore expect, and there is some evidence,[12] that incomes are more equal in democratic than in nondemo-

Advanced Countries," in *Working under Different Rules* 2, 29 (Richard B. Freeman ed. 1994); Isaac Shapiro and Robert Greenstein, "The Widening Income Gulf" (Center on Budget and Policy Priorities, Sept. 4, 1999); Frank Levy, *The New Dollars and Dreams: American Incomes and Economic Change* 2 (1998). The latest official U.S. statistics on income distribution are for 1997 and show no significant differences from the figures from the early 1990s on which I mainly rely. U.S. Bureau of the Census, Current Population Reports, P60–P200, *Money Income in the United States: 1997* xi–xiii (1998). So perhaps the rise in inequality in the United States has leveled off, though this may be the temporary result of an unusually low unemployment rate. Lawrence Mishel, Jared Bernstein, and John Schmitt, *The State of Working America 1998–99* 49–56 (1999), presents evidence that inequality continued to increase throughout the 1990s, albeit at a lower rate than in the 1980s.

10. Kaelblee and Thomas, note 8 above, at 9–10, 42–47. Contrary evidence is presented in Jae Won Lee and Suk Mo Koo, "Trade-Off between Economic Growth and Economic Equality: A Re-Evaluation," in *The Theory of Income and Wealth Distribution* 155 (Y. S. Brenner, J. P. G. Reijnders, and A. H. G. M. Spithoven eds. 1988).

11. John A. Bishop, John P. Formby, and W. James Smith, "International Comparisons of Income Inequality: Tests for Lorenz Dominance across Nine Countries," 58 *Economica* 461 (1991). The other three countries in their study—Australia, Canada, and the United Kingdom—were intermediate between the United States and Switzerland at one end and Sweden, Norway, and Germany at the other. For more recent data, consistent with those of the study just cited except that Australia has become more unequal than Switzerland, see "For Richer, for Poorer," *Economist*, Nov. 5, 1994, p. 19. A somewhat different ranking system producing broadly similar results can be found in Gottschalk and Smeeding, note 9 above, at 662–663.

12. Alberto Alesina and Dani Rodrik, "Distribution, Political Conflict, and Economic Growth: A Simple Theory and Some Empirical Evidence," in *Political Economy, Growth, and*

cratic nations (where "democracy" is defined not just formally, but in terms of actual behavior such as voter turnout)[13] as a consequence of the political system. If democracy is correlated with political stability because of the correlations between democracy and political liberty and between political liberty and political stability, income equality may be an effect rather than a cause of political stability.

A median-voter model of democratic politics is a terrible oversimplification, however. It ignores the role of interest groups in the political process and important institutional limitations on the operation of the democratic principle. As a result of the efforts of interest groups, many public expenditures, for example on elite educational institutions such as the University of California at Berkeley, benefit high-income persons disproportionately. So though it is frequently asserted that after-tax incomes are more equally distributed than pre-tax incomes, the latter may be the wrong baseline. Incomes might be more equally distributed if taxes were lower and government smaller.

Successful democracies, moreover, invariably are liberal states, because pure, direct, plebiscitary democracy—democracy with no legal or institutional checks on majority rule—is bound to unravel into dictatorship. The modern welfare state is more democratic and less liberal than nineteenth-century advocates of laissez-faire would have thought optimal, but it typically allows considerable occupational freedom and almost complete personal freedom, as well as a reasonably broad scope for private enterprise, implying recognition and protection of property rights, though less than laissez-faire liberals would like. The net effect of these liberties on the income distribution cannot be predicted. But

---

Business Cycles 23 (Alex Cukierman, Zvi Hercowitz, and Leonardo Leiderman eds. 1992). See also Edward N. Muller, "Democracy, Economic Development, and Income Inequality," 53 *American Sociological Review* 50, 65 (1988); Gerald W. Scully, *Constitutional Environments and Economic Growth*, ch. 8 (1992); Steven Stack, "The Political Economy of Income Inequality: A Comparative Analysis," 13 *Canadian Journal of Political Science/Revue canadienne de science politique* 273 (1980). Notice that redistributive taxation will reduce pre-tax as well as post-tax income inequality, as high-income people reallocate their energies and investments to endeavors that escape tax. For example, tax-free municipal bonds are more attractive to high-income earners the higher the marginal income tax rate, but the yield on such bonds is lower than the yield on taxable bonds as a consequence of the demand by investors in high tax brackets for tax-free income.

13. An ambiguous indicator, however, since repressive governments may compel citizens to vote—one way. Kenneth A. Bollen, "Political Democracy: Conceptual and Measurement Traps," 25 *Studies in Comparative International Development* 7, 8 (1990).

they certainly complicate democratic efforts to bring about equality of incomes through taxation and other coercive measures.

These points help explain how the income distribution within a liberal democratic regime may, in particular historical circumstances, such as those of the wealthy democratic countries today, tend toward inequality. The computer having finally come into its own, the demand for highly skilled labor to operate computers and related products of advanced technology has increased. At the same time, the demand for low-skilled and unskilled labor, especially in manufacturing, where computers, robots, and other forms of capital have proved effective substitutes, has fallen, in part as a result of increasingly intense international competition in manufactured goods. The resulting shift from manufacturing to services in the developed countries is a shift to forms of work in which the low-skilled or unskilled tend to receive low wages and the highly educated very high wages. Deregulation in a variety of industries has placed downward pressure on wages. Marginal tax rates have fallen too. The combined effect of these and other developments, including changes in family structure, has been to widen the income distribution.[14]

Moreover, when mental ability rather than physical strength, courage, and stamina becomes the decisive element in productivity, income may tend to become more highly correlated with IQ, and the distribution of IQs is highly unequal.[15] Any such tendency for the income distribution to follow the IQ distribution is likely to be augmented by the

14. See, for example, H. Naci Mocan, "Structural Unemployment, Cyclical Unemployment, and Income Inequality," 81 *Review of Economics and Statistics* 122 (1999); John A. Bishop, John P. Formby, and W. James Smith, "Demographic Change and Income Inequality in the United States, 1976–1989," 64 *Southern Economic Journal* 34 (1997); Gordon W. Green, Jr., John Coder, and Paul Ryscavage, "International Comparisons of Earnings Inequality for Men in the 1980's," in *Aspects of Distribution of Wealth and Income* 57, 71 (Dimitri B. Papadimitriou ed. 1994); Kevin M. Murphy and Finis Welch, "The Structure of Wages," 107 *Quarterly Journal of Economics* 285 (1992); and for a thorough review of the possibilities, Gottschalk and Smeeding, note 9 above, at 646–651. The shift from high-paying manufacturing to low-paying service jobs is in part illusory, however. Some of the high pay in manufacturing was and is merely compensation for the physical danger and other disamenities of such work, rather than a pure return to productivity. If a clerk and a coal miner are paid the same wage, the former is actually receiving a higher income. This is another example of the pitfalls of using income inequality to measure real economic inequality.

15. Linda S. Gottfredson, "What Do We Know about Intelligence?" *American Scholar*, Winter 1996, p. 15.

breakdown of traditional caste or caste-like barriers to occupational mobility, barriers that drive a wedge between intelligence and reward. (Critics of affirmative action describe it as an effort to recreate caste barriers to full competition in labor markets.) And with the decline of arranged marriage and of taboos against interracial or interethnic marriage, prospective marriage partners can be expected to be sorted more by "real" similarities, including intelligence.[16] IQ has a significant heritable component, so the implication of more perfect assortative mating is that the IQ distribution, and possibly therefore incomes as well, will widen in future generations—especially since a high IQ is likely to have a bigger effect on an individual's productivity than physical strength, and so tend to widen income inequality. Physical strength just increases the individual's own productivity, while mental acuity may enable increases in the productivity of others (for example, the high-IQ-individual's employees or clients), for which the high-IQ individual will earn a large premium. The high incomes of professional athletes are only an apparent counterexample. These athletes earn large returns because television enables them in effect to "resell" their output to millions of customers, achieving a multiplier effect comparable to that of the high-IQ individual who multiplies his productivity by leading others. It is the "superstar" phenomenon again.

These examples show that public or private measures that promote equality of opportunity can actually reduce equality of results, and specifically equality of incomes. Although society can intervene to alter the distribution of income by its tax and fiscal policies, the heavy political as well as economic costs are increasingly recognized and the people who would be harmed directly by them (the wealthy) are adept at orchestrating an effective political opposition. Mill was mistaken in thinking that while government could do little to increase the aggregate wealth of society, it had a free hand in deciding upon the distribution of that wealth across the population.[17]

Should we fear that a growing inequality of incomes will create a restive, potentially destabilizing underclass, who though democratically

16. On the tendency to "assortative" mating—likes mating with likes—see, for example, Gary S. Becker, *A Treatise on the Family*, ch. 4 (enlarged ed. 1991).

17. John Stuart Mill, *Principles of Political Economy* 200 (W. J. Ashley ed. 1926). In fairness to Mill, his conception of government was remote from that of late-twentieth-century democratic government.

impotent because too alienated to participate in voting and other civic activities are potential recruits for violent protest movements?[18] I think not. In countries in which the vast majority of the population is reasonably well off, and thus able and willing to finance a formidably large and powerful apparatus for the maintenance of public order, an underclass has no significant political leverage or opportunities. There is always the danger that the apparatus will become so powerful as to get out of hand, oppress law-abiding citizens, by doing so undermine the regime's legitimacy, and so eventually destabilize the regime. One theory of revolutionary action is that such action will provoke the government into adopting radically unpopular, though effective, methods of suppression, such as torture and collective punishment. But wealthy countries can afford the costly methods of law enforcement that preserve civil liberties, eschewing torture and collective punishment—which are cheap because they economize on the costs of investigation—and the censorship of dissident views.

If this is right, we can expect the income *level*—a society's average or median income—to affect political stability even though the income *distribution* may not. And for the further reason that if the mass of the people is very poor, there will be few defenders of the existing regime against a putsch. Being badly off, the people are likely to feel (though often wrongly) that they have nothing to lose from a change in the system of government. Hence, "Almost any reasonable theory of freedom would predict a positive correlation between freedom and real income. On the demand side, freedom must be considered a luxury good so that the resources devoted to the attainment of individual freedom are likely to be greater when per capita income is high. On the supply side, it is undoubtedly more costly to repress a wealthy person than a poor person and the need to do so is probably less acute."[19]

18. As argued, for example, in Rebecca M. Blank, "Changes in Inequality and Unemployment over the 1980s," 8 *Journal of Population Economics* 1, 14 (1995). See also Paul S. Sarbanes, "Growing Inequality as an Issue for Economic Policy, in *Aspects of Distribution of Wealth and Income*, note 14 above, at 168 ("the growing inequality of wealth and income is a real danger and threat to our society").

19. John F. O. Bilson, "Civil Liberty—An Econometric Investigation," 35 *Kyklos* 94, 103 (1982). Bilson finds just such a positive correlation between income and political freedom. Id. at 107. See also Bryan T. Johnson, "Comparing Economic Freedom and Political Freedom," in Bryan T. Johnson, Kim R. Holmes, and Melanie Kirkpatrick, *1996 Index of Economic Freedom* 29 (1996).

The point about "resources devoted to the attainment of individual freedom" parallels my point about the resources necessary for a system of internal controls that does not incite revolutionary action, while the point that the need to repress a wealthy person is less acute parallels my point about the greater stake of a well-off person in the preservation of the existing system of government. The implication is that unless the distribution of income is skewed in a particular way—a tiny upper tail and a huge lower tail—a high average income, even though it is unequally distributed and there is a sizable permanent underclass, will ensure stability. Moreover, when average income is rising, the incomes of the poor may be rising even if the income distribution is becoming more unequal. If people use their own experience as their benchmark for measuring how they are doing, rather than the experience of people who live in circumstances remote from theirs, the widening of the income distribution is unlikely to exacerbate whatever resentments the people in the lowest decile feel toward those above them in the income distribution.

We must not confuse income inequality with poverty. Indeed, if measures such as progressive taxation that reduce the inequality of income also reduce economic growth—for example by deflecting socially valuable resources into sterile activities like tax avoidance, or by discouraging economic risk taking—and thus retard the growth of the average income of the population, poverty and inequality may actually be negatively correlated. There may be fewer poor people in a society that does *not* attempt to make the distribution of income more equal than in one that does. This possibility is masked by the fact that the United States has at once a very high average income, many poor people, and a distribution of income that is more unequal than that of other developed nations.[20] Yet one of the reasons for this inequality—the large number of recent immigrants—is consistent with a negative correlation between poverty and inequality. If a high average income is more likely in a nation that is tolerant of income inequalities, an immigrant may sense greater economic opportunity in the United States than in his country of origin even though the transition to his new life will be a painful one. The more that careers are open to talents regardless of national origin, the more attractive a nation will be to immigrants, while

20. See Gottschalk and Smeeding, note 9 above, at 644.

that very openness may result in a highly unequal distribution of income as people are sorted into the different income classes in accordance with attributes of intelligence and character that vary widely among persons, and as first-generation immigrants work for low wages to make up for their lack of the language and other skills that are highly valued in the workplace. Moreover, nations strongly committed to equality are bound to limit immigration lest they be flooded with poor people looking for an immediate, and (thanks to the generous safety net of an egalitarian society) guaranteed, improvement in their economic status.

The other side of this coin is that a polity that in quest of equality depresses average earnings will drive many of its most productive citizens to emigrate to areas of better economic opportunity. This apparently has been a consequence of the egalitarian policies of the widely admired socialist government of the Indian state of Kerala,[21] just as earlier it was a consequence of the very heavy marginal income tax rates in England, Sweden, and other social democracies.

Even if the issue of inequality is decoupled from that of poverty— even if efforts to ameliorate inequality are likely to increase poverty—it is possible to be concerned that a gradual drift toward an ever more unequal distribution of income will fray the bonds of political community, eventually undermining political stability.[22] We are to imagine a situation in which the distance between the lower middle class and the upper class keeps growing, in which at one end of the income distribution a relative handful of highly intelligent men and women—made healthy and beautiful by fitness programs, cosmetic surgery, genetic engineering, and preventive health care—pull down huge salaries enabling them to live in luxurious sequestered communities and pass down their advantages to their descendants by direct bequests, by genetic bequests through assortative mating, and by gifts of expensive schooling, while just above the poverty line labor millions of modestly endowed individuals at modest wages in jobs that confer no prestige or security and yield few intrinsic satisfactions, living restricted and relatively unhealthy lives among their own kind. The inhabitants of the two classes

21. Jean Drèze and Amartya Sen, *India Economic Development and Social Opportunity* 198 (1995).

22. As argued in Michael Lind, *The Next American Nation: The New Nationalism and the Fourth American Revolution* (1995).

may become so different in values, outlook, intelligence, interests, aspirations, education, style of living, and even physical appearance (height, figure, apparent age), and so segregated except in the most superficial workplace encounters, that they will not be able to understand or empathize with one another, to "pull together" on national projects.

This sketch is overdrawn even if intermediate income groups are ignored. (Each income group will touch another at either end, so that even if the highest group has very little in common with the lowest a line of indirect communication will be established via the intermediate groups.) For it overlooks the rise in the average income. Twenty years from now, when the mean income of the American people may well have risen by 50 percent (in real terms), the people in the bottom decile will be much better off than they are today. They will be healthier, live longer, travel more, know more things, have broader horizons, and probably be more tolerant and easygoing.[23] Even if people who today make \$1 million a year will twenty years from now earn \$3 million, they will not be three times as fit, healthy, educated, and so on as they now are. There is diminishing marginal utility of money.

Indeed, though these are glorious days for wealthy people, the gap between the wealthiest people and the people just above the poverty line is smaller than it was in eighteenth-century England, when the rich lived in magnificent mansions attended by armies of servants and the average ordinary man was a farm laborer. The English example suggests that there is no determinate threshold of economic inequality above which a society breaks apart. Even if *some* fellow feeling is a precondition of willingness to accept the outcomes of democratic choice, it may be so little as to be unaffected by even huge differences in incomes. New York City is remarkable among other things for the immense inequality of incomes of its residents, residents who include at one end some of the wealthiest people in the world, people who literally are billionaires, and at the other end desperately poor people who beg for a living and sleep on sidewalks. The billionaires and the other wealthy people are served by a huge army of lower-middle-class taxi drivers, kitchen employees, servants, clerks, newsvendors, and police-

---

23. Cf. Edward J. Rickert, "Authoritarianism and Economic Threat: Implications for Political Behavior," 19 *Political Psychology* 707, 717 (1998).

men, who commute long distances from the outer boroughs of the city. There is an upper middle class of lawyers and stockbrokers, a bohemian class, a multitude of immigrants legal and illegal, students, criminals, an underclass, and a vast mosaic of ethnic and religious groups. Yet with all this incredible heterogeneity, New York City is a stable community. Of course it is stabilized in part by being included within larger polities, the State of New York and more important the United States. Yet it illustrates the possibility of basically peaceable and cooperative if not quite harmonious and certainly not placid coexistence among people scattered across an enormous spectrum of incomes.

Another point—the one that famously attracted the scorn of Anatole France—is that a democratic society recognizes the political equality of its citizens by granting them extensive rights: the right to vote, the right to stand for election, the right to speak freely, to be free from certain kinds of discrimination, and so on. Even if the economic value of these rights is proportional to pecuniary income or wealth, to the extent that they have value even to people of modest incomes they increase the self-respect and self-esteem (the sense of personal "worth") of all citizens and so make the absence of income equality less stigmatizing, less degrading. At the same time, however, an ideology of political equality may promote an "every man a king" attitude that leads people to question the legitimacy of differences in income: if I'm as good as the next guy, why does he have 400 times my income?

I have not yet considered the bearing on the analysis of economic inequality of either envy or equity. The two concepts are more alike than they seem. Envy is negative altruism: if I am envious of a wealthier person, the implication is that my happiness would increase if the person lost his wealth, because then my envy, a source of disutility, would be abated. People who would like to see greater equality of incomes do not justify their preference in terms of envy. They say that a more equal distribution of incomes would be more just. But if there were no envy, and if I am right that efforts to equalize the distribution of incomes (which should not be confused with efforts to reduce poverty) would reduce average incomes, what would be gained by such efforts? In any event, the envy factor is automatically taken into account in a democratic society. Should the distribution of income get too far out of line with the preferences of a large bloc of voters, the politicians will respond and laws will be passed that reduce, or at least mask, the inequality. This is one reason for believing that societies in which people are free to express their resentments both directly and through voting are likely to be more stable than repressive societies.

I differ from John Rawls in not thinking envy entirely a bad thing.[24] It is, in a curious way, a form of social cement, enabling us to identify empathetically with others who are unlike us, to feel their joys—albeit as our pains—and their pains, albeit as our joys. The opposite of envy is altruism, but the mean between envy and altruism is indifference to others. In any event, in a society in which the system of property and contract rights is sufficiently robust to make it difficult to alleviate one's envy by making the better off worse off, envy is a goad to effort and success—effort to rise above others, but not to push the others down. Rawls acknowledges the existence of "benign envy," which he calls "emulation."[25] But he does not consider the possibility that a society that protects people against assaultive, defamatory, or otherwise aggressive acts by the envious will channel bad envy into good. He overlooks this possibility because he believes that envy and emulation are different feelings rather than the same feeling differently acted upon. Envy is tinctured with hostility, emulation with admiration. But the envious will be stimulated by their envy to constructive effort, just like the emulators, if the constructive path is made easier than the destructive by the political and economic arrangements of the society. Kant, of whom Rawls is a distinguished follower, thought "enviously competitive vanity" one of the essential spurs to man's developing his natural capacities.[26]

If envy depends on empathy, it may be more acute when differences in income are small than when they are large, because it is easier to empathize, whether positively or negatively, with people who are like us. Certainly the behavior of academics suggests that envy is not a function of large differences in incomes. Tocqueville opined that "greater equality tends to produce envious comparisons: as they become more equal individuals find their inequality harder and harder to bear."[27] To the ex-

---

24. John Rawls, *A Theory of Justice* 530–541 (1971).

25. Id. at 533.

26. Immanuel Kant, "Idea for a Universal History with a Cosmopolitan Purpose," in *Kant: Political Writings* 41, 45 (Hans Reiss ed., 2d ed. 1991).

27. Raymond Boudon, "The Logic of Relative Frustration," in *Rationality and Revolution* 245 (M. Taylor ed. 1988).

tent that the goad of envy fails to bring about equality, and the political fabric is too weak to contain securely the destructive impulses of envy, inequality may be destabilizing. But if Tocqueville is right, more inequality may be *less* destabilizing than less inequality.

The broader point is that it is not the degree to which income is unequally distributed across the population, but the ethical or emotional response to that degree of inequality,[28] that determines the political consequences of inequality. A strong social commitment to equality of opportunity, as in the United States, may dampen feelings of envy (without dampening efforts to get ahead) by making wealth seem more a consequence of personal desert, or luck, or other virtuous or innocent conditions and less a ratification and reward of exploitation, discrimination, or other injustices. If so, then maximizing equality of opportunity may alleviate the pressures for redistribution at the same time that, for the reasons I explained earlier, it makes the distribution of income more unequal. Yet equality of opportunity may exacerbate envy precisely by making outcomes seem the result of luck rather than of desert (especially if, as in Rawls, even genetic endowments are regarded as a product of luck), and therefore arbitrary, or by underscoring differences in ability and thereby humiliating the losers in the competition to demonstrate superiority. It is an empirical question, therefore, how equality affects envy and self-esteem and hence political stability. Evidence presented by Sam Peltzman that equality precedes and facilitates the redistributive state suggests that envy of the rich is not the motive force of egalitarian policies.[29]

This discussion has implications for the question how far the law should go in protecting property rights. On the one hand, a robust protection of those rights will make an economic system operate more efficiently, resulting in higher average incomes and greater economic opportunities. On the other hand, if that protection is pushed to the point at which redistributive measures such as progressive taxation are deemed unconstitutional or otherwise forbidden because they impinge on property rights, inequality of incomes may grow to the point at

28. On the difference, see Peter van Wijck, "Equity and Equality in East and West," 47 *Kyklos* 531, 543 (1994) (table 4).

29. Sam Peltzman, "The Growth of Government," 23 *Journal of Law and Economics* 209 (1980).

which envy demands redress, but the safety valve that is the democratic process will be closed and political stability may therefore be endangered. We want a political process supple enough to respond to demands for equality when those demands, whether rooted in envy or in some other emotion or principle, become exigent. The advantage of democracy as a political system is its ability to mediate between equality and stability.

～ I HAVE HYPOTHESIZED a positive correlation between political stability and average incomes—basically because the citizens of a wealthy country have a big stake in political stability and can afford to employ "civilized" repressive measures that do not breed widespread resentment of the wealthy—but no correlation between political stability and equality of incomes. I have now to test the hypothesis. This is done in Table 3.1. Measures of political stability in the narrowest sense—measures such as the risk of expropriation, the "coup count," and the frequency of extraconstitutional changes of regime—together with measures of political liberty—commitment to the rule of law and a "freedom rating" based on civil liberties and political rights—are regressed on a measure of income equality (the ratio of the income of the poorest 20 percent of households to the income of the richest 20 percent),[30] on the average income in the society, and on changes in that income (which might be thought destabilizing). Because the countries aggregated in the table differ from each other in many respects other than income that are potentially relevant to political stability, I also include regional dummy variables and allow the error terms to have different variances in different countries.[31]

The table is in two parts. Part A reports the regressions in which the dependent variables are ratings. In these regressions, the larger the de-

30. This is not a sophisticated measure of income inequality, but there are insufficient data to construct sophisticated measures, such as the Gini coefficient, for enough of the years and countries in the sample. An alternative to the ratio of richest to poorest quintiles would be separate variables for the poorest and for the richest, but the alternative procedure would be more cumbersome, less intuitive, and yield similar results.

31. For a fuller discussion of the data and methodology used in Tables 3.1 and 3.2, including summary statistics and definitions of the dependent variables, see the Statistical Appendix in Richard A. Posner, "Equality, Wealth, and Political Stability," 13 *Journal of Law, Economics, and Organization* 344, 354–364 (1997).

pendent variable, the "better" (for example, a higher value for risk of expropriation means that the risk is less). In Part B, which reports the regressions in which the dependent variables are counts of events (such as the number of coup d'états), the larger the dependent variable, the "worse" (for example, the more coup d'états). The specifications differ slightly for the two sets of regressions; the details are available from me on request.

The sign of the coefficient of the income-equality variable is statistically significant at the conventional 5 percent level (indicated by a t statistic with an absolute value greater than 1.96) in only two of the regressions. In one of them—deaths from political violence—the sign is negative, indicating that greater income equality is correlated with reduced levels of political violence. But in the other—the freedom rating—greater income equality is correlated with less freedom. Taken as a whole, these regressions do not suggest that reducing economic inequality is likely to increase political stability. To test my earlier conjecture that *extreme* inequalities in income might be politically destabilizing, I replaced (in an unpublished set of regressions) the equality variable in Table 3.1 with the square of that variable, the effect being to increase the spread between the most and the least equal distributions of income. The adjusted equality variable, like the unadjusted, failed to attain statistical significance.

The *level* of income has a highly statistically significant effect in five of the equations. And in all but one of the eight equations, the sign is as predicted: political stability is enhanced by high average income. The exception—the positive and significant sign of the the protest-demonstrations variable—is only apparent. Stable societies are able to tolerate such demonstrations, which are likely to be viewed as destabilizing, and therefore severely repressed, in unstable or illiberal societies.

Finally, the sign of the coefficient of the change-in-income variable is statistically significant in four of the eight regressions. In the statistically significant regressions, the rate of economic growth in the previous five years is associated with fewer deaths from political violence, fewer protest demonstrations, and less risk of expropriation, but, surprisingly, with a lower freedom rating.

These results imply that level of income, and less strongly growth in income, are positively correlated with political stability and that equality of income is uncorrelated with it. The significance of these results,

Table 3.1 Regressions of political stability on real average income, growth in real average income, income equality, and region (t statistic in parentheses)

A. Regressions with political stability ratings

Dependent variables (N = number of observations)	Independent variables								
	Income equality (percent) (lagged by one year)[a]	GDP/capita (log) (lagged by one year)[b]	Five-year growth in GDP/capita (percent)	Africa	North America, Europe, and Australasia	Asia	Latin America	Constant	Log-likelihood
Risk of expropriation (−5 to +5) (N = 303)	−0.0025 (−0.267)	0.0002 (6.281)	0.0277 (11.693)	0.3325 (2.002)	1.5767 (4.288)	0.2174 (0.883)	0.2681 (1.182)	0.4523 (2.013)	1.335
Corruption in government (−6 to +6) (N = 311)	−0.0143 (−1.369)	0.0003 (5.716)	0.0016 (0.897)	0.7774 (2.939)	2.2192 (4.335)	−0.9950 (−2.296)	−0.8921 (−3.596)	−0.7595 (−2.872)	77.002
Rule of law (−6 to +6) (N = 320)	−0.0324 (−2.170)	0.0002 (5.067)	0.0018 (0.712)	0.0487 (0.272)	5.1139 (11.884)	−0.1056 (−0.294)	0.4295 (1.820)	−1.4349 (−4.595)	−7.747
Freedom rating (−6 to +6) (N = 462)	−0.0065 (−0.477)	0.0003 (8.024)	0.0142 (−10.291)	−0.3447 (−1.208)	3.6232 (8.292)	1.1647 (3.214)	3.1498 (7.427)	−1.7465 (−4.973)	−114.551

Table 3.1 (continued)

B. Regressions with empirical political stability measures

Dependent variables (N = number of observations)	Independent variables								R-squared
	Income equality (percent) (lagged by one year)[a]	GDP/capita (log) (lagged by one year)[b]	Five-year growth in GDP/capita	Africa	North America, Europe, and Austral-asia	Asia	Latin America	Middle East	
Protests/capita (log) (N = 567)	−0.0080 (−0.353)	0.3890 (2.081)	−0.0132 (−2.848)	−2.1296 (−1.642)	−1.3678 (−0.793)	−1.2896 (−0.880)	−2.3667 (−1.561)	−1.5217 (−1.156)	0.60
Deaths from political violence/capita (log) (N = 567)	−0.0719 (−2.898)	−0.2809 (−1.321)	−0.0352 (−3.470)	4.5078 (2.731)	0.0119 (0.316)	6.2167 (3.637)	4.3061 (2.525)	5.1298 (2.735)	0.47
Irregular executive transfers (log) (N = 567)	−0.0002 (−0.163)	−0.0162 (−1.677)	−0.0002 (−0.891)	0.1402 (2.000)	0.1570 (1.770)	0.1710 (2.082)	0.1834 (2.099)	0.1528 (1.805)	0.05
Coup d'états (log) (N = 683)	−0.0001 (−0.087)	−0.0147 (−1.791)	−0.0003 (−0.835)	0.1131 (1.872)	0.1425 (1.764)	0.1386 (1.856)	0.1783 (2.352)	0.1385 (1.795)	0.05

a. Share of income held by poorest 20% of households expressed as a percentage of the share of income held by richest 20% of households.
b. Real GDP per capita in constant 1985 dollars (chain index).

however, is limited.[32] International economic data, especially for the poorer nations, tend to be unreliable; political data are often both unreliable and subjective. But the results of my study do cast doubt on the proposition that income equality is a key to political stability, while at the same time providing support for the proposition that high average incomes promote political stability.

An important question is the direction of causality. Could political stability be the cause of high and growing average income, rather than the result? The use of lagged independent variables suggests not, but two-staged least squares regressions (not reported) run on my data do not enable me to reject the hypothesis that political stability does foster high and growing average income. The causal process probably is two-way, since a stable, rights-enforcing political environment encourages investment in both physical and human capital, as is suggested by an economic literature that finds a positive correlation between political stability and economic growth.[33]

I mentioned earlier that the various measures of political stability tend to be positively correlated. Table 3.2 tests this suggestion by calculating correlation coefficients for the dependent variables in the previous table. The numbers in parentheses indicate the probability that the correlation coefficient is actually zero, that is, that the variables are not correlated with each other. As expected, the variables are for the most part strongly correlated, and with the predicted sign. Thus, expropriation risk is strongly positively correlated with corruption in gov-

---

32. Two regression analyses using different independent variables and data from my own find a significant positive relation between income inequality and political violence. Cliff Brown and Terry Boswell, "Ethnic Conflict and Political Violence: A Cross-National Analysis," 25 *Journal of Political and Military Sociology* 111 (1997); Edward N. Muller and Mitchell A. Seligson, "Inequality and Insurgency," 81 *American Political Science Review* 425 (1987).

33. See, for example, Robert J. Barro, "Economic Growth in a Cross Section of Countries," 101 *Quarterly Journal of Economics* 407, 437 (1991). See also Roger C. Kormendi and Philip G. Meguire, "Macroeconomic Determinants of Growth: Cross-Country Evidence," 16 *Journal of Monetary Economics* 141, 156 (1985); Kevin B. Grier and Gordon Tullock, "An Empirical Analysis of Cross National Economic Growth, 1951–80," 24 *Journal of Monetary Economics* 259, 271–273 (1989). And see Adam Przeworski and Fernando Limongi, "Political Regimes and Economic Growth," 7 *Journal of Economic Perspectives*, Summer 1993, pp. 51–69, for a highly critical review of the economic literature relating political regimes to economic growth. It should be emphasized that because rights are not costless, their overprotection can reduce national wealth, especially in a poor country. Stephen Holmes and Cass R. Sunstein, *The Cost of Rights* (1998); Richard A. Posner, "The Costs of Enforcing Legal Rights," *East European Constitutional Review*, Summer 1995, p. 71.

Table 3.2 Correlations of proxies for political community (significance level in parentheses, with number of observations below it)

	Risk of expropriation	Corruption in government	Rule of law	Freedom rating	Protests per capita (log)	Deaths from political violence per capita (log)	Irregular executive transfers (log)	Coup d'états (log)
Risk of expropriation	1.0000 1,672							
Corruption in government	0.6274 (0.000) 1,672	1.0000 1,712						
Rule of law	0.7865 (0.000) 1,672	0.7379 (0.000) 1,712	1.0000 1,712					
Freedom rating	0.5337 (0.000) 1,408	0.5146 (0.000) 1,428	0.5466 (0.000) 1,428	1.0000 2,099				
Protests per capita (log)	0.0560 (0.653) 67	0.3051 (0.004) 87	0.2466 (0.021) 87	0.2633 (0.000) 705	1.0000 2,739			
Deaths from political violence per capita (log)	0.0000 (1.000) 67	0.0000 (1.000) 87	0.0000 (1.000) 87	0.0275 (0.466) 705	0.2759 (0.000) 2,739	1.0000 2,739		
Irregular executive transfers (log)	-0.1021 (0.411) 67	-0.1879 (0.081) 87	-0.1206 (0.266) 87	-0.0870 (0.021) 705	0.0843 (0.000) 2,739	0.2039 (0.000) 2,739	1.0000 2,739	
Coup d'états (log)	-0.1118 (0.006) 595	-0.1437 (0.000) 635	-0.1633 (0.000) 635	-0.0859 (0.003) 1,173	0.0610 (0.002) 2,532	0.1695 (0.000) 2,532	0.6200 (0.000) 2,532	1.0000 3,229

ernment and strongly negatively correlated with the rule of law and freedom variables; corruption is strongly negatively correlated with the rule of law; coup d'états are negatively correlated with the rule of law and strongly positively correlated with irregular executive transfers; and so on.

I move now from political stability (and its relation to equality) to cost-benefit analysis. The term has a variety of meanings and uses. At the highest level of generality, which we encounter in Amartya Sen's paper for a conference on cost-benefit analysis,[34] it is virtually synonymous with the normative use of economics. At the other end of the scale of generality, the term denotes the use of the criterion of wealth maximization to evaluate government projects, such as the building of a dam or the procurement of a weapons system; government grants, such as grants for medical research; and government regulations, including not only administrative regulations dealing with health, the environment, and other heavily regulated activities but also statutes and common law doctrines and decisions. But cost-benefit analysis has positive as well as normative utility. That is, it can be used to explain and predict some government decisions, especially decisions that are relatively insulated from the operation of interest-group politics.

Along a different axis of definition, cost-benefit analysis can refer to a method of pure evaluation, conducted without regard to the possible use of its results in a decision; to an input into decision, with the decision maker free to reject the results of the analysis on the basis of other considerations; or to the exclusive method of decision. When used in the last sense, as in my advocacy of the use of cost-benefit analysis to guide common law decisionmaking, the criterion of wealth maximization (if that is the criterion of the cost-benefit analysis used) must be defended. But when cost-benefit analysis is merely an input into decision, and even more clearly when it is a pure exercise in scholarship, there is no need to insist on its adequacy as a normative principle, provided that wealth is accepted to be *a* social value, even if not the only social value. I think that even Sen, who is more skeptical about free markets than I, agrees that it is (see p. 947) and that Henry Richardson,[35] who is even more skeptical about free markets than Sen, also agrees. And, to repeat an earlier point, to the extent that distributive

---

34. Amartya Sen, "The Discipline of Cost-Benefit Analysis," 29 *Journal of Legal Studies* 931 (2000).

35. Henry S. Richardson, "The Stupidity of the Cost-Benefit Standard," 29 *Journal of Legal Studies* 971 (2000).

justice can be shown to be the proper business of some other branch of government or policy instrument (for example, redistributive taxation and spending), and that ignoring distributive considerations in the particular domain of decisionmaking that is under consideration will not have systematic and substantive distributive consequences, it is possible to set distributive considerations to one side and use the wealth-maximization approach with a good conscience.

In a paper at the same conference, John Broome challenges the proposition that wealth maximization is a social good with the example of a forced uncompensated transfer of a table from a poor person to a rich person. He is right that allowing such a transfer would not improve social welfare in any intelligible sense. But it would not be wealth maximizing, either, when one considers the incentive effects, on rich and poor alike, of allowing such transfers, compared to the alternative of forcing the rich person to transact with the poor person. The typical project or policy to which cost-benefit analysis guided by the criterion of wealth maximization is applied does not have the features that makes Broome's example unpalatable. The example helps show, however, why willingness to accept rather than willingness to pay should be the measure of value when the policy whose costs and benefits of which are being measured takes away property rights, as in the case of the table, or where farmland will be flooded as a result of the building of a dam. A willingness-to-accept requirement better protects property rights, which have an important economizing role in a market economy.

Other conference papers, by Robert Hahn, Lewis Kornhauser, Cass Sunstein, and Kip Viscusi[36] are primarily concerned with defending cost-benefit analysis against its critics. Robert Frank, Barry Adler, and Eric Posner[37] wish to alter it in significant ways, while in the papers by Broome, Martha Nussbaum, and Richardson[38] doubt about the validity

36. Robert W. Hahn, "State and Federal Regulatory Reform: A Comparative Analysis," 29 *Journal of Legal Studies* 873 (2000); Lewis A. Kornhauser, "On Justifying Cost-Benefit Analysis," 29 *Journal of Legal Studies* 1037 (2000); Cass R. Sunstein, "Cognition and Cost-Benefit Analysis," 29 *Journal of Legal Studies* 1059 (2000); W. Kip Viscusi, "Risk Equity," 29 *Journal of Legal Studies* 843 (2000).

37. Robert H. Frank, "Why Is Cost-Benefit Analysis So Controversial?" 29 *Journal of Legal Studies* 913 (2000); Matthew D. Adler and Eric A. Posner, "Implementing Cost-Benefit Analysis When Preferences Are Distorted," 29 *Journal of Legal Studies* 1105 (2000).

38. John Broome, "Cost-Benefit Analysis and Population," 29 *Journal of Legal Studies* 953 (2000); Martha C. Nussbaum, "The Costs of Tragedy: Some Moral Limits of Cost-Benefit Analysis," 29 *Journal of Legal Studies* 1005 (2000); Richardson, note 35 above.

and utility of cost-benefit analysis is the dominant chord. Sen's paper seems perfectly balanced between the second and third groups, and I discuss it last.

We shall make some interesting discoveries in working through these papers. The first is how well cost-benefit analysis passes the pragmatic test by so often turning out to serve well whatever goals we happen to have. If, for example, we are particularly interested in the welfare of minority groups, we should ask whether cost-benefit analysis serves or disserves their interests—and we shall find, on the evidence of Viscusi's paper, that it serves them well. We shall see, too, that the utility of cost-benefit analysis as a decision rule is a function of the degree to which a particular type of governmental decision process is insulated from political influence, and many such processes are so insulated, to a greater or less degree. We shall also see that the supporters of cost-benefit analysis have made a persuasive pragmatic case, focused principally on risk regulation, that cost-benefit analysis can improve the quality of governmental decisionmaking. Sunstein puts this point well, saying that cost-benefit analysis is "best taken as [a] pragmatic instrument, agnostic on the deep issues and designed to assist people in making complex judgments where multiple goods are involved" (p. 1077). He argues that its practical value is especially great because of cognitive quirks that he believes make it difficult for people to think straight and therefore require the kind of rational discipline that cost-benefit analysis imposes on decisions. Sen also refers approvingly to the disciplinary benefit of insisting on explicitness in valuation. When cost-benefit analysis is applied to the regulation of risks to health and safety by different federal regulatory agencies, bizarre anomalies are uncovered that no one would defend.

Finally, we'll see that those papers that accept the essential validity of cost-benefit analysis but seek to improve its normative flavor by modifying or even rejecting the use of the criterion of wealth maximization to orient it gain less in normative plausibility than they lose in complication and uncertainty. Better to accept that cost-benefit analysis cannot be the only decision rule used by government and that it can have value when used as an input into decision, as the risk-regulation studies show. So used it compels the decision maker to confront the costs of a proposed course of action,[39] and perhaps that is as much as can be asked

---

39. "Cost-benefit analysis was intended from the beginning as a strategy for limiting the play of politics in public investment decisions." Theodore M. Porter, *The Pursuit of Objectivity*

in a democratic society. If agency staff, taxpayer, and voter all know—thanks to cost-benefit analysis—that a project under consideration will save sixteen sea otters at a cost of $1 million apiece, and the government goes ahead, I would have no basis for criticism.

None of the papers that considers cost-benefit analysis an unacceptable procedure to apply to the issues in which the author is most interested suggests a superior alternative for evaluating public policies. I doubt that any of them would favor an *uninformed* political judgment. Cost-benefit analysis is inescapable across a wide range of policy decisions.[40]

Hahn's paper might be thought pessimistic about the practical utility of cost-benefit analysis I've just been stressing. He finds that the trend toward requiring cost-benefit analysis at the state level has achieved little in the way of more efficient regulation. He remarks that "more than half (57%) of the federal government's regulations would fail a strict benefit-cost test using the government's own [dubious, self-serving] numbers" (pp. 892–893; footnote omitted), and that "a reallocation of mandated expenditures toward regulations with the highest payoff to society could save as many as 60,000 more lives a year at no additional cost" (p. 893; footnote omitted). These are shocking figures, at least if one suppresses the heartless thought that not all those 60,000 lives may be worth saving. The successes for cost-benefit analysis that Hahn recites, of which my favorite are the repeal of one regulation barring hearses from certain (I assume scenic) parkways and another, a regulation of school signs adopted at the suggestion of a schoolchild, are undoubtedly modest. Politics, and no doubt (though Hahn does not emphasize this) bureaucratic inertia and self-seeking, have proved major impediments to cost-benefit analysis at all levels of government.

As significant as the failures of cost-benefit analysis, however, is how

---

in Science and Public Life 189 (1995). He is discussing the use of cost-benefit analysis by the U.S. Army Corps of Engineers, which began using such analysis on proposals for dams, harbors, and other public works in the 1920s.

40. "Those who oppose the use of benefit-cost analysis of course, are seldom completely faithful to their 'health-only' creed. They talk about economic feasibility rather than cost; they countenance lax enforcement; they create exemptions for special classes of polluters; they encourage—indeed, sometimes even demand—delay, lest the consequences of their general policy become too apparent." R. Shep Melnick, "The Politics of Benefit-Cost Analysis," in *Valuing Health Risks, Costs, and Benefits for Environmental Decision Making: Report of a Conference* 23, 25 (P. Brett Hammond and Rob Coppock eds. 1990) (footnote omitted).

fashionable the technique has become at all levels of government. The theoretical objections to cost-benefit analysis have crumbled at the practical level and retreated to the academy. The spread of cost-benefit analysis, even when it takes the form merely of lip service to the principles of efficiency, confirms an international trend toward free markets. Cost-benefit analysis is an effort to introduce market principles into government, or to induce goverment to simulate market outcomes, or in short to make government more like business. There is an ideology of free markets; it has some influence on specific governmental decisions; and the growing popularity of cost-benefit analysis is both an effect, and to a small degree a cause, of this ideology.

Hahn may underestimate the degree to which foolish administrative decisions are undone in the compliance phase of administrative proceedings or circumvented by adroit exploitation of loopholes by the regulated firms. He also overlooks the significance of judicial review of administrative action in keeping the cost-benefit analyses conducted by government agencies honest. When regulations are based on cost-benefit analysis however inept or tendentious, persons subject to them are armed in challenging them in court to point out the respects in which the the government's cost-benefit analysis was unreasonable and their own superior. It is more difficult to challenge a regulation that rests entirely on nebulous equity grounds.

Kornhauser makes the essential pragmatic defense of cost-benefit analysis—that it "often seem[s] to improve the quality of decisions" (p. 1038)—and reinforces it with a useful distinction between evaluating cost-benefit analysis by reference to a global moral criterion and evaluating it by reference to the feasible alternatives. The latter is surely the preferable approach. It is no help to be told that cost-benefit analysis violates some moral desideratum, if there is no feasible alternative method of dealing with a problem or if the only feasible alternatives yield results that even moral philosophers would think worse.

But I am troubled by Kornhauser's discussion of the value of life. He makes an important point, which I'll come back to, that cost-benefit analysis doesn't really attempt to value lives. But he defends it with an example that he claims, I believe mistakenly, shows that "cost-benefit analysis does not even provide a unique valuation of the value of the life [of] an individual who smokes" (p. 1051). He points out correctly that smokers need not be indifferent among three policies each of which is expected to reduce the expected number of deaths from lung cancer by one-half—making cigarettes safer, reducing the number of smokers, and reducing the lethality of lung cancer. He infers from this that there is no unique value of life even for smokers. But it is not the value of life that varies in these examples; it is the other consequences of smoking. In the first example, the smoker gets to have his cake and eat it, while in the second he loses whatever utility he obtains from smoking and in the third he incurs the cost of lung cancer, though it is a lower cost because he has a better chance of surviving.

What Kornhauser should have said about the value of life is that cost-benefit analysis values risks, not lives; the "value of life" that cost-benefit analysts refer to is just a mathematical transformation. Suppose that it is discovered by studying people's behavior that the average person would be willing to incur a maximum cost of $1 to avoid the one in one million chance of being killed by some hazard that a proposed project would eliminate. And suppose that 2 million persons are at risk from this hazard and that the proposed project (which for simplicity I'll assume has no other benefits) will cost $3 million. Since each of the persons benefited (in an expected sense) by the policy would pay only $1 to avoid the hazard, for a total of $2 million, the benefits are less than the costs. Another way to put this is that the life-saving project can be expected to save the lives of only two people, each of whom "values his life" at "only" $1 million ($1/.000001), and so the total benefits are only $2 million and are less than the costs. As I said, this is just an arithmetical transformation of an analysis that values risks rather than lives.

Broome offers an example that illustrates the pitfalls of attempting to value lives rather than risks. Two projects each of which will result in the death of one person have the same cost (assuming all their other costs are the same), he argues, even if the death in the first project is the result of imposing a one-in-a-million risk of death on each of a million people and the death in the second project is the result of imposing a one-in-a-thousand risk of death on each of a thousand people. The cost is the same in an ex post sense, but evaluating the projects ex ante requires consideration of the ex ante costs, and they are not the same. The second project is more costly ex ante, because people are much more reluctant (plausibly more than a thousand times as reluctant) to be subjected to the higher risk. If the million would pay less in the aggregate to avert the risk to them than the thousand would pay to avert the risk to *them,* the second project is more costly.

Sunstein's paper strikingly inverts one of the standard criticisms of cost-benefit analysis, and of economic thinking more generally: that it undervalues "soft" variables. These critics argue that people give too much weight to factors that can be quantified, and if so this is a good illustration of the availability heuristic in action. Sunstein argues that cost-benefit analysis can be used to combat that heuristic and promote rationality in public policy. In so arguing, however, he risks circularity, since if the cognitive quirks that concern him infect market behavior, the prices on which cost-benefit analysis is based will not be a dependable tool for disciplining thought.

Another problem is that some of the "quirks" actually are rational, such as that people think better when they are given a context rather than asked to solve a problem in isolation. And preference reversal comes about not because people are inconsistent but because when they are prodded to recall information that helps them deal with the problem of valuation they give better answers. Likewise it is rational to be more afraid of novel risks, such as that of nuclear power, than of old ones, such as pollution caused by the burning of coal, since when a risk is novel its mean and variance are difficult to estimate. When some new horror occurs, like the first mass shooting of schoolchildren by fellow students, there is a natural concern that this may be the beginning of a trend rather than an isolated occurrence; in the particular example there is also a concern with the possibility of imitation, another legitimate source of alarm.

Some of Sunstein's examples can be analyzed in simpler terms than he uses. For example, I don't think the concept of "voluntariness" is necessary or useful for explaining our different reactions to investing in the reduction of deaths in sky-diving accidents compared to deaths in childbirth. In the former but not the latter case, we realize that a low-cost measure of saving lives is for sky divers to switch to safer sports, whereas we do not think that the cheapest way of avoiding deaths in childbirth is a zero birthrate. Students of strict liability have made this point in distinguishing between changes in activity or activity level, as distinguished from changes in care levels, as methods of accident avoidance; sometimes the cheapest method is to abandon the dangerous activity. Similarly, an important economic consideration in choosing a level of protection against assassination of public officials is that they are much more likely to be attacked than the average person, so we may be able to dispense with dread as the explanatory variable.

Sunstein hedges on whether to accept or combat misperceptions in determining costs and benefits. If property values will plummet because of an irrational fear of contagion from patients in a hospital, should that count as a cost in deciding where to locate the hospital? On the one hand, to accept the market's irrational valuation reduces the advantage of cost-benefit analysis that he stresses, which is that it promotes more rational thinking. If the hospital is built, and neighbors do not become infected, irrational fears of contagion will tend to dissipate. On the other hand, the costs to people of their irrational fears are real costs in the sense of making them unequivocally worse off. Thus, in the example given, the decline in property values is a tangible cost, and incidentally one that will be incurred by property owners who do not have irrational fears (but it is a benefit to fearless buyers of their property). In principle the best solution to the dilemma is Adler-Posner's— weight the irrational fears if but only if they are unlikely ever to be dissipated. For in that case, overriding the fears will not produce Sunstein's hoped-for benefit of getting people to think straighter. But this solution both is difficult to implement, because it is often unclear whether a fear is irrational, and does nothing to prevent the loss in property values that irrational fears can generate. I am not much troubled by the second point, however, because the values will be restored once the irrational fears dissipate. The winners and losers will be different people but that is a purely distibutional concern, which I exclude from my conception of a proper cost-benefit analysis.

Viscusi distinguishes among "heterogeneity in individual riskiness, heterogeneity in individual willingness to incur risks, and differences in preferences for activities that pose risks" (p. 847). In the first category he places the higher death rates of men than of women from accidents and homicides. But these examples belong in the second category, differential willingness to incur risks. Men don't get killed in accidents, or get murdered, because they are clumsy or weak, but because they engage in riskier activities than women do, on average. Viscusi's typology also leaves out an important fourth category of heterogeneity in the individual valuation of risk, that of a pure taste for danger. Dangerous sports, and dangerous occupations such as fighting fires, are valued by their participants in part for the danger, the confronting of which en-hances the participant's sense of self-worth.

Viscusi is too cavalier in recommending the dissemination of infor-mation about health and safety hazards by government in order to dis-pel misinformation that drives a wedge between subjective and objec-tive costs (or irrational and rational fears). Such a program will often lack credibility because government policies are known to be subject to political influence. And (recurring to a point I made in the preceding chapter) it may depress private efforts to disseminate the information by reducing the incremental information effect of those efforts once the government program is in effect; as a result, the net increase in in-formation may be slight. Information is also costly to absorb, so that flooding the public with information about hazards may cause people to become less well-informed about some other and equally important matter. And informing the public about a subset of hazards may cause people to underestimate the significance of other hazards, thinking that if they were substantial the government would inform the public about those hazards as well.

Viscusi devotes too little attention to the issues involved in measures for saving elderly lives.[41] It is too simple to say that "efforts that save very little in terms of life expectancy divert resources from programs that could have a major life expectancy effect" (p. 859). The assump-tion that saving the life of a fifty-year-old must be more beneficial than saving the life of an eighty-year-old because the former will normally have a longer life expectancy may seem obvious; but if the usual ex ante perspective is taken, it may not be correct. People's valuation of their remaining life generally does not decline with age. For at no age do most people consider themselves to have any good alternatives to liv-ing, and so they will spend as much to gain a few years of life as to gain many, because the expenditure has (to exaggerate slightly) no opportu-nity cost to them even if they are not protected against financial risk by private or social insurance.

But when the issue is not curing a disease of the elderly but merely reducing risk, willingness to pay may indeed be inverse to age, as Viscusi assumes, since the older you are, the smaller the expected bene-fit of reducing the risk. A further support for his conclusion that we

41. See Richard A. Posner, *Aging and Old Age* 109–110, 270–272 (1995).

should reallocate resources from saving the old to saving the young is that saving an old person is a disease subsidy. Diseases compete to kill people, so if you save a person from one disease you increase the likelihood of his being killed by another. The older the person, the more vigorous the competition and the less it is dampened by eliminating one of the competitors. That is why, for example, a complete elimination of cancer would have only a modest effect on longevity. Most cancer victims are old, and if they are spared by cancer it increases the opportunities for the other diseases of the old. A related point is that saving an old person increases his expected medical costs and that altering the age composition of a society can have substantial although not necessarily bad consequences of both an economic and a political character.

Viscusi raises but lets drop the difficult question of whether to discount consequences for future populations, asking, "Should risks [that will materialize] at least 100,000 years from now merit the same concern as risks to current populations?" (p. 865). One argument against giving them the same concern and thus for discounting is that people are so likely to be much wealthier in the distant future as a result of continued scientific progress, and, specifically, to be much better able to eliminate risks to safety and health, that for us to devote our resources now to heading off those risks would produce a grave maldistribution of wealth across time. The decisive argument, however, is that we cannot project risks 100,000 years in advance.

Robert Frank offers a variant of Viscusi's "100,000 years from now" conundrum. He sympathizes with the view that "if failure to adopt more stringent air quality standards today means that respiratory illnesses will be more common a generation from now, those illnesses should receive roughly the same weight as if they were to occur today" (p. 916). But because a generation from now most respiratory illnesses will probably be easily and cheaply curable and therefore less costly than today, some discounting is warranted.

Frank places great weight on income as a positional good, arguing that "measuring the social value of a consumption good by summing what individuals spend on it is similar to measuring the social value of military armaments by summing the amounts that individual nations spend on them" (p. 923). In other words, striving to increase one's income is a move in an arms race, which is a zero-sum game. If people use consumption goods to signal desired traits such as neatness, respect, and dignity, a general increase in the income level may result in substituting more costly goods as signals with no gain in information. But there are reasons to doubt that this is the principal effect of higher incomes. First, relative income is important as a signal of how well one is doing. If your boss is paying you a lot less than someone who does similar work, something is wrong, unless you have decided to substitute nonpecuniary for pecuniary income. Evening out all incomes would deprive people of a great deal of information about their status and prospects.

Second, relative income is important in bidding for scarce goods. One's ability to buy a fine painting, for example, depends more on one's relative than on one's absolute income. Frank may be misinterpreting the result of the survey that asked graduate students whether they would rather earn $50,000 when others were earning $25,000 or $100,000 when others were earning $200,00 and found that a majority preferred the first state. If average personal income were half of what it is today, other than as the consequence of some catastrophe such as another Great Depression or a major war, prices would probably also be half what they are today, so that the $50,000 earner in the first state would be as well off as the $100,000 earner in the second state, which means better off in terms of my first two points. My point about the *informational* significance of relative income may explain the second finding in the survey, that the students were much less interested in relative vacation time than in relative income. The length of one's vacation is an ambiguous indicator of "how one is doing"; a longer vacation may just indicate that one has an undemanding job.

A striving for income-conferred status has desirable incentive effects, at least in a well-ordered society, that may explain much of America's prosperity. This is just my earlier point about the social benefits of envy. If you can assuage your envy only by working harder and so catching up with the people you envy, society as a whole will benefit to the extent you're not able to capture the entire social product of your harder work as private product. Vying for higher incomes is not a zero-sum game.

Barry Adler and Eric Posner wish to modify cost-benefit analysis in order to accommodate some of the common criticisms of it. In effect they want to align it more closely with its utilitarian foundations. My own view is that perceptions of the shortcomings of cost-benefit analysis should not affect how that analysis conducted, though they should sometimes affect how it is used; here the distinction between cost-benefit analysis as a method of evaluation and as a decision rule becomes critical. The difference between complicating cost-benefit analysis in order to align it more closely with its desideratum, and keeping it simple while acknowledging its normative incompleteness, is like the difference in accounting between what goes in the text, and affects the bottom line directly, and what goes in the footnotes, reflecting subjective judgments that if introduced into the income statement and balance sheet proper would make their interpretation opaque.

At the same time, I am puzzled by the decision by Adler and Posner to exclude moral commitments, even when monetizable, in calculating the benefits or costs of a policy. I understand the difference between acting from a sense of duty and acting to increase one's happiness. But in cases in which the cost of not being able to fulfill a duty can be monetized, why exclude it? Suppose someone who does not expect to benefit from preserving the existing number of species nevertheless believes, perhaps as a matter of religious conviction, that it is wrong to allow a species to become extinct as a consequence of human activity; and he backs up his conviction with his money by making charitable contributions from which his implicit, and positive, valuation of species preservation can be inferred and even monetized with adequate objectivity to be incorporated into a cost-benefit analysis. Arguably, at least (the counterargument is made by Sen, and I'll come to it later), such a person incurs a real cost if a policy measure causes the extinction of a species, and it is not a sufficient reason for excluding this cost from the cost-benefit analysis of the measure that it falls outside Adler and Posner's definition of overall well-being.

The deeper problem is that what the contingent values used in environmental cost-benefit analysis measure are not well described, for the most part, as moral commitments having the curious properties that trouble the authors. People can love wild animals or wilderness and want them to be preserved without either feeling a moral commitment to them or wanting to meet them, as it were. The enjoyment of these things is a type of consumption activity that is distinguishable from keeping pets or a garden only by the greater difficulty of measuring the value of the enjoyment. There is no difference in principle, and hence no paradox in asserting that a person's utility would be reduced more by the extinction of the striped cheetah than by a flood that damaged the person's carpet. The problem is measurement, as with the principle advocated by Adler-Posner that uninformed (plus adaptive) preferences should be excluded when one is confident that the preferences would change as a result of the policy's being adopted. I agree with them that it would be infeasible to weight costs or benefits by the marginal utility of income. But this is not because interpersonal comparison of utilities is unsound in principle; it is because the measurement problem is insoluble and if overcome still would result in a bottom line that was a confusing mixture of efficiency and equitable considerations.

I disagree with their suggestion that government agencies should "ignore morally objectionable preferences when preferences violate widespread, uncontroversial intuitions about morally proper behavior" (p. 1143). This may be correct as a matter of decisionmaking but it is dubious as a matter of evaluation. As between two equally effective drug-treatment programs, costing the same amount, one of which gave drug addicts the same pleasure that they had derived from an illegal drug and the other of which did not, the first would be preferable from a utilitarian standpoint.

Let me turn now to the three severe critics of cost-benefit analysis—Broome, Nussbaum, and Richardson. Broome says that because cost-benefit analysis is a method of evaluation (though it can also be a decision rule), "it needs to be founded on a theory of value" (p. 954). This is a play on words ("value"–"valuation"). Cost-benefit analysis need be "founded" on nothing deeper or more rigorous than a showing that it has consequences that we like. The most important contribution of cost-benefit analysis in recent years has been to demonstrate, in the writings of Stephen Breyer, Viscusi, Sunstein, and others, that federal regulation of hazards to safety and health is a crazy-quilt and in particular that many of the regulations are bad *because* they flunk a cost-benefit test. This is increasingly accepted and reform is progressing, albeit haltingly, even though the analysts in this field have implicitly rejected Broome's claim that "to do cost-benefit analysis properly, we need a theory about the goodness of a life" (p. 958).

It does not help Broome's case that he is unable to come up with such a theory, though his attempt to do so is interesting. He argues that on the one hand bringing or not bringing a person into existence does not make the person better off or worse off than he would otherwise have been, because he would not have *been* otherwise. There is no other state with which to compare the person's state of existence, so adding one more person to a society (by birth, not immigration) cannot be said to create more benefits than costs, or more costs than benefits, excluding effects on other people. But on the other hand we can imagine this person being added to two different societies and (this is the only relevant difference) his being better off in one than in the other. The society in which he is better off will have, therefore, a higher level of overall utility than the other and so is to be preferred—which means that the bringing of a new person into existence *can* create additional benefits. Broome shows that this is a genuine paradox. But this will not surprise anyone who has eavesdropped on the debate over whether average or total utility should be the utilitarian maximand. It is absurd to think that we should immiserate ourselves to create a vastly increased human (and perhaps animal) population that will have a greater total utility though average utility is low. But it is equally absurd to think that we should destroy a large part of the population (in a way they wouldn't notice, so they would suffer no pain) if that would maximize average utility.

These paradoxes of utilitarianism reflect one of the fundamental and seemingly insoluble problems of that philosophy, its inability to specify the community whose utility is to be maximized. Should it be just the living? Should it be just human beings? Just Americans? Should it include fetuses? The human population 10,000 years from now? Sentient animals? These questions are not answerable, at least within utilitarianism and probably not at all. But I will make one suggestion. Suppose that adding 1,000 people to society would have no effect on the welfare of the existing population; there would be no congestion or other negative externalities (or for that matter positive externalities). But suppose further that each of these 1,000 people, though their lives would be "mediocre" in Broome's term, would none of them want to commit suicide; that is (I am setting aside any religious scruples or other costs to suicide), each of them would derive a positive utility from being born. Then the addition of the 1,000 people would be Pareto efficient, which, as we have seen, is a strong normative principle. Average utility would be less (assuming the average life of the members of the existing population was above the "mediocre" level), but total utility would be greater and no person would be worse off. To the extent that any concrete issue of population policy approximates this example, we should be able to make a relatively uncontroversial normative judgment in favor of the unborn when they do not impose negative externalities.

Broome uses the problem of global warming as a vehicle for speculating about the welfare effects of adding population. He makes the mistake of claiming that by killing people through flooding, global warming will reduce the future population "because some of the people it kills would later have had children" (p. 969). This assumes that the number of children a person has is fixed, rather than being a matter of choice. The assumption is false and has led in other contexts to such erroneous predictions as that the number of births is reduced by the number of abortions. The reduction in births is smaller because abortion is in part a matter of the timing of births rather than the number of births. If a woman wants to have two children, aborting her first pregnancy is unlikely to induce her to have only one child. And likewise, if many people are killed in floods, other people may decide to have more children. A couple who loses a child in a flood may decide to have another child, which they would not have had if the child had lived; here the analogy to abortion (or, even better, to miscarriage) is very close. And by raising the ratio of land to people, the killing floods may increase the incomes of the survivors, and this may (or may not) increase the number of children that the survivors decide to have.

Since it is wholly uncertain how many people global warming will kill, and since the effect of an increased death rate on future populations is uncertain, and since the benefits and costs associated with larger or smaller future populations are uncertain even apart from the paradox explored by Broome, I should think the proper approach to cost-benefit analysis of global warming would be simply to ignore population effects, as in Fankhauser's careful study, which finds substantial social costs of global warming without considering population effects.[42] I wonder whether Broome would agree with Fankhauser's approach or would suggest that cost-benefit analyses of global warming not be conducted at all, and if so what mode of analysis or response he would suggest instead for dealing with global warming.

42. Samuel Fankhauser, *Valuing Climate Change: The Economics of the Greenhouse* (1995). Earlier cost-benefit analyses of global warming are summarized in id. at 121–123.

Nussbaum's paper is concerned with tragedy and tragic choice. She illustrates these terms with reference both to Sophocles' play *Antigone* and to her own difficulties as a junior faculty member in balancing professional and family obligations. Her conception of tragedy is best seen in the implicit comparison of herself to Antigone; her minor tragedy[43] has a happy ending and she suggests that if only Thebes had adopted something like the religion clauses of our First Amendment, Sophocles' play (or rather the legend on which it is based) could have had a happy ending too. This notion of tragedy seems to me both too broad and too shallow. Nussbaum exaggerates the tragic domain even when she says, a little more plausibly than in her own case, that "not to have the freedom of speech . . . is always a tragedy" (p. 1023). Was it a tragedy that Shakespeare wrote plays in a society in which the theater was heavily censored?

The real point of tragedy, both as a literary genre and as a concept distinct from that of the hard or painful choice—a point well illustrated, as it happens, by *Antigone*—is to show that some conflicts cannot be solved. They do not yield to cost-benefit analysis however generously construed; they are genuine no-win situations. Creon is ruling Thebes in succession to the disgraced and exiled, but charismatic, Oedipus. One of Oedipus's sons, Eteocles, is the commander of Thebes's army. The other son, Polynices, revolts against Creon and Thebes. In the ensuing battle, both Eteocles, heroic defender of the city, and Polynices, the traitor, the rebel, are killed. Creon gives Eteocles a hero's funeral but orders that Polynices be left unburied, to be food for vultures. This is a terrible punishment in Greek mythology, and Antigone, Oedipus's daughter and thus the sister of the slain brothers, disobeys Creon's order and buries Polynices. Having specified capital punishment for anyone who disobeyed the order, Creon orders Antigone executed. He believes it essential to the preservation of civic order that the traitor be treated in death in a fashion that differentiates him from the loyal brother and that the traitor's sister who disobeyed his order be punished for that disobedience. Otherwise his authority would erode and the civic values that he personifies (including the rule of law) would be subordinated to the potentially subversive religious and familial values personified by Antigone. She believes, in contrast,

---

43. I do not mean to belittle the tensions and pressures that women experience in trying to balance a job with motherhood, but merely to suggest that it cannot be equated to Antigone's situation, which resulted in her being executed.

that those values have transcendent significance. There is no *via media* between these two value systems; that is what makes the play a tragedy rather than a plea for working out compromises.

Nussbaum would annul tragedy by "imagin[ing] what a world would be like that did not confront people with such choices" (p. 1013). She dreams of a world in which all conflicts, all public conflicts anyway, are resolved by balancing the competing interests, or, as we might say, comparing the costs and the benefits. Such a conception of what is possible to achieve in the way of resolving conflicts should make her friendlier to cost-benefit analysis than she is. She does not reject it but she qualifies it to the point where its utility as a tool for public policy is greatly diminished. For example, she argues that in the case of basic constitutional rights the costs of infringement should not be subject to being offset by benefits, because they are wrongs that no citizen should be required to bear. But constitutional rights are to a large extent determined by a balancing of costs and benefits. Think of the limitations on the constitutional right of freedom of speech discussed in Chapter 2. And cost-benefit analysis is unavoidable when the question is how many resources to devote to the enforcement of a constitutional right.

The heaviest thumb that she wants placed on the cost-benefit balance is a "tragedy tax" designed to reflect the special indignation that particular costs should engender in the analyst. I shall explain my disagreement with this suggestion with the help of an example she gives of girls' education in the Third World. We now know a lot about the return to investments in human capital and we can use that information to conduct cost-benefit analyses of proposals to expand education in poor countries. We can compare the benefits of adding a year of high school for boys to, say, the benefits of adding two years of elementary education for girls, in societies in which boys are favored in education. (I'll assume for simplicity that the costs are the same.) Suppose the economy of the country is such that quite apart from any religious or customary inhibitions on the employment of women (because I want also to abstract from concerns with irrational and adaptive preferences), women's opportunities in the job market are meager. The reason might be the infeasibility of child-care arrangements that would enable women to work full time in the market. In such a case, the added education for girls might be less productive than that for boys. Or might not, for one would have to consider the increased productivity of children (when they become adults), which might be considerable, if their "stay at home" mothers were educated, as well as benefits from a reduced birth rate, a likely consequence of a higher female education level. These are very difficult calculations, but not impossible.

After conducting such a cost-benefit analysis and finding as one might (though I doubt it) that giving the boys the extra education would be more valuable than giving extra education to the girls, the decision maker might still decide that equality was more important than the benefits in greater productivity. But at least he would know what would have to be given up in order to achieve the desired equality. To inject the "tragedy tax" into the cost-benefit analysis would disguise the cost of equality.

Henry Richardson offers two worthwhile observations about cost-benefit analysis. The first is that it won't by itself pick out the projects or policies to be evaluated or compared. The second is that *explicit* cost-benefit analysis is not required for all rational decisions. These points establish valid limits to the utility of the analysis. But they don't make it "stupid" (his characterization of cost-benefit analysis). Often a project or policy is a given and the only task remaining is to compare it with doing nothing. And if the project or policy is complex, the kind of seat-of-the-pants reasoning that we often quite satisfactorily employ in everyday life may yield results that no one wants.

Richardson overlooks the distinction between evaluation and decision. He thinks cost-benefit analysis a stupid decision procedure yet implicitly commends it as a method of evaluation and indeed as an input into decision by saying, "I in no way mean to downgrade the importance of collecting information about the benefits and costs of alternative proposals. To the contrary, this is the first step in any intelligent process of deliberation" (p. 973). But collecting that information *is* what is meant by cost-benefit analysis as an evaluative tool, indeed as anything less than the exclusive decision rule. It is not the equality or inequality sign that marks analysis as cost-benefit but the collection and display of costs and benefits. If the analyst finds that the benefits of some project would be $10 million and the costs $12 million, the analysis is complete; he doesn't have to add, "And therefore the costs exceed the benefits."

Richardson points out that a consideration of alternative ways of achieving a given end may lead us to change that end, a possibility that he claims cost-benefit analysis precludes. We might wish to be clothed, and therefore consider alternative means of clothing; but "if the only available covering was poison ivy, I, for one, would feel justified in going naked" (p. 979; footnote omitted). But this is not a problem for cost-benefit analysis. The method of covering that produces the greatest surplus of benefits over costs in his example is, obviously, nudity. Nudity produces zero benefits, but zero benefits are greater than negative benefits, which is what poison ivy, the only alternative to nudity, produces. (Likewise, burning down one's house to cook pork produces negative benefits compared to the alternative of simply going without cooked pork, though the balance would change if starvation loomed.) Alternatively, the analyst's goal is misspecified: not, what is the best covering, but what choice with regard to covering is best. In the division of intellectual labor, the cost-benefit analyst may not be the one who adds alternatives or respecifies goals. But his analysis may still produce information that leads someone else in the decision-making chain to modify the original design of the analysis.

A better example of the limitations of cost-benefit analysis than the poison-ivy example, but one that is subject to the same response that I gave to it, is the case in which the maximand is hopelessly vague ("I want to be a success"). Before embarking on a cost-benefit analysis in such a case, the analyst will ask whoever commissioned the analysis for clarification. No one denies that discussion and deliberation may help a person get a better fix on what the costs or benefits of a proposal are, or what alternative proposals ought to be considered. If anything, the example of the vague maximand points up an additional advantage of cost-benefit analysis. The inability to conduct such an analysis without greater specification of the maximand may induce reflection on its vagueness, leading the analyst to seek further guidance from the decision maker and thus in turn stimulating the latter to engage in deliberation over ends.

A related point is that in the process of implementing a means toward some end, one may discover that the means is an end in itself, as when one studies ballet to improve one's posture and discovers that one loves it as an art form. This point is the same as that of Sunstein and others concerning the proper design of cost-benefit analysis in the face of uninformed preferences; had the ballet dancer known how much he would enjoy the ballet lessons, he would have attached a greater benefit to the lessons than merely better posture. This is a legitimate point, but it merely identifies a problem of information, which would plague any decision rule

Denver had to decide whether to equip its police with hollow-point bullets. Richardson (in an interesting discussion omitted from his published paper) says he does not understand how such a question could be answered by cost-benefit analysis. The answer is straightforward. Hollow-point bullets are more effective than ordinary bullets in stopping an assailant, though likely to injure him more seriously; and they are less likely to ricochet and hit a bystander. The benefits of such bullets thus lie in reducing the number of injuries to the police and to bystanders by armed criminals and in increasing the expected cost of crime to criminals, while the costs consist in more serious injuries to some criminals (but the overall costs to criminals may be lower if there are fewer crimes) and also to innocent people mistakenly shot by the police under suspicion of being criminals. All these costs and benefits are calculable—along, of course, with the cost of the bullets themselves. There is no need to distinguish in the analysis between innocent and guilty lives. Injuries are costly even when the injured person is a criminal, though in that case there may be offsetting benefits in preventing or deterring crime. Those benefits should be taken into account, but so should the injuries, a source of cost. Another cost is the zero-sum arms race that may ensue from the adoption of hollow-point bullets by the police: the criminal community may respond by arming itself more heavily, though at a cost that may have a desirable effect in reducing the amount of crime. Consideration of this point might lead in turn to considering the alternative of equipping police in high-crime areas with body armor rather than making police bullets more lethal.

Sen discusses the principles and pitfalls of cost-benefit analysis[44] but (with one exception) not actual cost-benefit analyses, and so it is difficult to tell how often he thinks it goes wrong. He mentions as an alternative approach to assessing cost-benefit analysis a "bottom-up" approach in which the actual practice of cost-benefit analysis is examined and a critique evolved from that examination. I wish he had followed that approach, because it is impossible to tell from his discussion of principles how he would like to alter the practice, and it is the practice

---

44. The subject of an immense literature. See, for good introductions, *Cost-Benefit Analysis* (Richard Layard and Stephen Glaister ed., 2d ed. 1994); Robert Sugden and Alan Williams, *The Principles of Practical Cost-Benefit Analysis* (1978).

that I am interested in. But toward the end of the paper he does finally get concrete, raising a powerful objection to measuring environmental values by asking people what they would pay to save a member of an endangered species, say, when the purchase of that good is not in fact an option for the person questioned. To put Sen's objection in the simplest possible form, we do not *buy* endangered species, the way we buy toothpaste, and so while asking a person what he would pay for a tube of toothpaste will elicit a meaningful answer, asking him what an endangered species is worth to him will not; the weird answers that these surveys elicit may reflect not a cognitive quirk, as behavioralists believe (see Chapter 8), but the remoteness of the inquiry from the real-world settings in which people encounter the price system. The question, then, which Sen however does not address, is what to do. (So his paper has an analogous trajectory to Broome's.) One possibility is to limit cost-benefit analysis to the market consequences of the proposed policy (an environmental-protective policy, I'll assume) and leave to the political process a determination of whether the net costs (if the costs exceed the benefits) override the pressures brought to bear by environmental groups. As a preliminary to assessing this possibility, someone could compare the environmental evaluations that are elicited in the questionable surveys with the rankings of environmental projects implicit in the lobbying activities of the leading environmental groups. Though worthless as "prices," these valuations may indicate the intensity of emotion that becomes translated into and can be measured by the amount and intensity of political advocacy by environmentalists.

~ II
HISTORY

～ 4

Law's Dependence on the Past

$\mathcal{L}$AW IS THE MOST historically oriented—more bluntly
the most backward-looking, the most "past-dependent"—of the pro-
fessions. It venerates tradition, precedent, pedigree, ritual, custom, ancient practices, ancient texts, archaic terminology, maturity, wisdom,
seniority, gerontocracy, and interpretation conceived of as a method of
recovering history. It is suspicious of innovation, discontinuities, "para-
digm shifts," and the energy and brashness of youth. These ingrained
attitudes are obstacles to those like me who would like to reorient law
in a more scientific, economic, and pragmatic direction. But, by the
same token, pragmatic jurisprudence must come to terms with history.
Where better, then, to begin my discussion of the historicist approach
to law than with Nietzsche's great essay on history?[1] It is at once a powerful, albeit oblique, challenge to that approach and a founding document of pragmatism.

We must first distinguish the *study* of history, and thus history as a
way of relating to, interpreting, or explaining the past (*Geschichte*), from

---

1. Friedrich Nietzsche, "On the Uses and Disadvantages of History for Life," in Nietzsche,
Untimely Meditations 57 (R. J. Hollingdale trans. 1983). The essay was first published in 1874.
Page references to it appear in the text of this chapter. I have found only one previous discussion of Nietzsche's essay in the legal literature: Donald P. Boyle, Jr., Note, "Philosophy, History, and Judging," 30 *William and Mary Law Review* 181, 185–189 (1988).

history as simply events, chronology, or record of the past (*Historie*).[2] It is history in the first sense that is Nietzsche's target. He does not deny that there are knowable facts about things that happened in the past; he is not a postmodernist crazy. But the sum of those facts, devoid of analysis, interpretation, or causal ascriptions, is not what we mean by historical understanding, and such understanding is elusive. Yet Nietzsche is not, at least in the essay that I am considering, an *epistemic* skeptic about either type of history. He does not deny that we can know that Napoleon Bonaparte abdicated for the second time in 1815, or even that we can know that Napoleon did (or did not) accelerate the emergence of German nationalism.[3] He is skeptical about the social rather than the truth value of *Geschichte*. He audaciously contends that the quest for historical understanding can have a debilitating effect on meeting the challenges of the present and the future.

There is a lot to his point for students of the law to ponder, but only with respect to the use of history to guide law. I am not such a philistine as to want to disparage the study of legal history for its own sake. Curiosity about the past is natural, and the law has a long and fascinating history. But the disinterested study of legal history is as rare as it is unexceptionable. Apart from the patient work of a relative handful of professional legal historians—work that is painstaking, time-consuming,

2. The distinction is well articulated in Carl L. Becker, "Everyman His Own Historian," 37 *American Historical Review* 221 (1932); C. A. J. Coady, *Testimony: A Philosophical Study* 233–236 (1992) (distinguishing between historical facts, on the one hand, and historical theory, or scientific history—"an imaginative reconstruction of the past" [id. at 235]—on the other); and Lionel Gossman, *Between History and Literature*, ch. 9 (1990) (distinguishing between historical research and historical interpretation). Coady takes sharp issue (see Coady, above, ch. 13) with Collingwood's skepticism about historical facts. See R. G. Collingwood, *The Idea of History* (1970). *Historie* corresponds to the quest for truth at the level of the trial court, and it may be that rather similar methods and problems attend both the historical and the adjudicative quest for factual truth, as suggested by the philosophical discourse on "testimony," well illustrated by Coady's book, which treats of both quests and which I return to in Part Four of this book.

3. The idea that historical theories are a legitimate species of scientific theory is strongly argued in Murray G. Murphey, *Philosophical Foundations of Historical Knowledge*, ch. 7 (1994). This is not to deny the *practical* indeterminacy of much historical theorizing; I give examples later. On the general question of skepticism about historical knowledge, see Arthur C. Danto, *Narration and Knowledge* (1985). And for a powerful empirical demonstration that historical fact is recoverable even when it concerns episodes that arouse intense political passions, see Alan B. Spitzer, *Historical Truth and Lies about the Past: Reflections on Dewey, Dreyfus, de Man, and Reagan* (1996).

long-incubated, and consequently small in quantity—most legal writing about history is done by judges, who are of course not legal historians, and by law professors, who are at best amateur legal historians. This work is normative in aim and thus invites consideration of its practical social value, which is the concern of Nietzsche's essay.

His critique of the study of history is organized around three points. The first is that the academic study of history, the attempt to reconstruct the past with scrupulous accuracy—the *wie es eigentlich gewesen ist* ("how it really was") school of Leopold von Ranke and his followers, against which Nietzsche was writing—is disillusioning, and we need illusions to achieve anything. "Historical verification always brings to light so much that is false, crude, inhuman, absurd, violent that the mood of pious illusion in which alone anything that wants to live can live necessarily crumbles away" (p. 95). People who have a potential for greatness need "a monumentalistic conception of the past," from which they learn that "the greatness that once existed was in any event once *possible* and may thus be possible again" (p. 69). "One giant calls to another across the desert intervals of time and, undisturbed by the excited chattering dwarfs who creep about beneath them, the exalted spirit-dialogue goes on" (p. 111). This conception of history is to be contrasted with the "idolatry of the factual" (p. 105), in which every event in history is determined—is a link in an inexorable chain of causes and effects—a view that excludes the possibility of human freedom and creativity. Ironically, the type of historical sense that Nietzsche deplores is nowhere better illustrated than in the work of his epigone Michel Foucault, who, for example in his history of criminal punishment since the eighteenth century,[4] finds nothing of greatness or even progress but only an ever more insidious weaving of the sinews of power, a portrait of human helplessness. Such a method of doing history breeds a cynicism that is quietistic, even paralyzing.

Nietzsche's second criticism of the historical sense, which is only superficially inconsistent with the first, is that it breeds complacency by making us think we are better people than our forebears. We might call

4. Michel Foucault, *Discipline and Punish: The Birth of the Prison* (1977). Yet Foucault's historical method derives from Nietzsche, specifically the "genealogical" methodology of *On the Genealogy of Morals.* See Brian Leiter, "What Is 'Genealogy' and What Is the *Genealogy?*" in Leiter, *Nietzsche on Morality* (forthcoming). The *Genealogy* was written many years after the essay on history; I briefly consider the relation between the two in the next chapter.

this "datism" and illustrate it by the current left-wing criticisms of Aristotle for misogyny and Jefferson for owning, perhaps even fathering, slaves. History, Nietzsche observes, "leads an age to imagine that it possesses the rarest of virtues, justice, to a greater degree than any other age" (p. 83). The concept of moral progress, which is definitionally historicist, invariably makes us look good in comparison to our predecessors because it is assessed from the standpoint of the present; it is our values that determine what is to count as progress. The naive think that "to write in accord with the views of their age is the same thing as being just"; hence "their task is to adapt the past to contemporary triviality" (p. 90).

The relation to the first criticism is that both the sense of paralysis and the sense of progress come from the same thing, the fact that "every past is worthy to be condemned" (p. 76). Some people react to the horrors and follies of the past with despair and others with complacency; neither mindset is conducive to a wholehearted, energetic, and optimistic address to current problems.

We might call the first criticism a criticism of history as belittling the past and the second a criticism of history as glorifying the present. Nietzsche's third criticism of the historical sense—call it belittling the present—is his most interesting and least developed. It was developed further by Max Weber, who in this respect is another of Nietzsche's epigones; and in relation to literary creativity by Harold Bloom. It is that a lively consciousness of the past induces a sense of belatedness. It makes us feel like "latecomers," living "in the old age of mankind" (pp. 83, 109), and to old age "there pertains an appropriate senile occupation, that of looking back, of reckoning up, of closing accounts, of seeking consolation through remembering what has been, in short historical culture" (p. 109). This point is related to the first criticism and despite appearances is not inconsistent with the second (that the study of history induces complacency). We may think we've made moral progress and of course economic, scientific, and technological progress as well, but we cannot imagine ourselves on a plane with Jesus, Socrates, the Buddha, and the other great moral innovators of the past. And where we have made unquestionable progress it is due largely to specialization. We cannot imagine a scientist of today having the same breadth of achievement as a Newton, or an economist having the breadth of an Adam Smith, or a biologist who could have as revolutionary an impact as Darwin. We cannot imagine a conqueror on the scale of Alexander the Great, or a military genius to equal Napoleon, or that there will ever be a Chief Justice of the United States to rival John Marshall.[5]

These pessimistic predictions could reflect just a lack of imagination; Nietzsche is far from endorsing the feeling of belatedness that an immersion in history creates. In fact since 1874 a number of giants (a category that includes monsters as well as geniuses and saints) have crossed the world stage, including Freud, Yeats, Einstein, Wittgenstein, Lenin, Hitler, Ghandi, Churchill, Kafka, Weber, Holmes, Joyce, Stravinsky, and Picasso. It does seem, however, that the scope and possibility of genius, of greatness, of true individualism and breathtaking individual achievement, diminish, and a sense of belatedness becomes marked, as greater and greater areas of human life are brought under the rule of rationality by the trend to specialization (division of labor), to bureaucratic (as distinct from charismatic or tyrannical) governance, and to universal education, media-induced sophistication, the automation of many tasks formerly requiring human skills, the increasing success of natural and social science in addressing social and personal problems rationally and systematically, and (as part of the advance of science and technology) improved therapeutic intervention to correct physical and mental defects and normalize abnormal personalities. Earlier generations, including generations far earlier than Nietzsche's, had a sense of belatedness; you can find it in Hesiod, in Homer's generation. But modern conditions make it more plausible than ever before.

The sense of belatedness has an undercurrent of complacency as well as of defeatism, which relates the third of Nietzsche's criticisms of the historical sense to the second. If humanity has reached a collective old age, this means that it has experienced maturity—has, in other words, peaked—and so there is a temptation to equate humankind's current "miserable condition" to "a completion of world-history . . . so that for Hegel the climax and terminus of the world-process coincided with his own existence in Berlin" (p. 104). Yet what we think of as civilization is only about 5,000 years old. For all we know, there may be a thousand, a

5. Holmes seems to have had a sense of belatedness in relation to Marshall. See Oliver Wendell Holmes, "John Marshall," in *The Essential Holmes: Selections from the Letters, Speeches, Judicial Opinions, and Other Writings of Oliver Wendell Holmes, Jr.* 206 (Richard A. Posner ed. 1992).

hundred thousand, or even a million or more epochs of that length before homo sapiens departs the scene (perhaps for other planets). So in
a curious sense, the historical perspective, the perspective that makes us
feel like latecomers, distorts a proper sense of where we are in history.

The third criticism may seem to be in tension with the first and second in targeting a form of monumentalistic historicism in which the
greatness of the past is highlighted—a form that might seem the very
opposite of the belittling historicism that is the target of the other criticisms. But the tension dissolves when we recognize that the type of
monumentalistic history decried in the third criticism is the type that
belittles the present, which is as debilitating as belittling the past. The
Lilliputian historians deprive the present generation of needed models
of achievement (those giants calling to each other over the desert intervals of time) or breed a contemptuous attitude toward the past, while
the belittling monumentalizers "do not desire to see new greatness
emerge: their means of preventing it is to say 'Behold, greatness already exists!' . . . They act as though their motto were: let the dead bury
the living" (p. 72).

Nietzsche does not argue that the study of history has no possible
value. This is apparent from his commending the type of monumentalistic history that exhibits to the present achievable models from the
past. That is history "in the service of the future and the present and
not for the weakening of the present or for depriving a vigorous future
of its roots" (p. 77). It is thus history "in the service of life . . . The study
of history is something salutary and fruitful for the future only as the
attendant of a mighty new current of life, of an evolving culture for example, that is to say only when it is dominated and directed by a higher
force and does not itself dominate and direct" (p. 67). The study of history should be oriented toward enlarging our "plastic power," which is
"the capacity to develop out of oneself in one's own way, to transform
and incorporate into oneself what is past and foreign, to heal wounds,
to replace what has been lost, to recreate broken moulds" (p. 62). In
short, "history belongs above all to the man of deeds and power, to him
who fights a great fight, who needs models, teachers, comforters and
cannot find them among his contemporaries" (p. 67). Still, if a certain
kind of history is bad for you, a certain kind of forgetfulness must
be good for you: this is the most arresting implication of the essay.
Mythmaking through selective remembrance and selective forgetting
is Nietzsche's conception of socially worthwhile history.

Nietzsche's criticisms of the study of history are psychological in character: too much history, or history of the wrong kind (psychologically wrong, not inaccurate—Nietzsche does not value accuracy for its own sake),[6] fans emotions that impede achievement. Any doubt that Nietzsche was on to something has been dispelled by events in Yugoslavia; the Serbian preoccupation with history, and in particular with the (possibly mythical) Battle of Kosovo between the Turks and the Serbs in 1389, is bad for the Serbs, as well as for their neighbors. The Serbs could do with a dose of forgetting.

There is also reason to be concerned about untoward *cognitive* consequences of studying history, though Nietzsche barely hints at them. Historical knowledge takes up space in the brain, leaving less room for other intellectual material. It is not useless knowledge, at least if its emotional effects are put to one side; it provides a stock of precedents that can be used to solve current problems. But precedents provide *good* solutions to current problems only if the present resembles the past very closely. If it does not, then a person who "only repeats what he has heard, learns what is already known, imitates what already exists" (p. 123) will not be able to solve any of these problems. History provides a template for framing and "sizing" contemporary problems; but the template may prove to be a straitjacket. The use of historical analogies ("another Munich") is full of pitfalls.[7] Hence the adage that the only lesson of history is that there are no lessons of history.

We should not expect Nietzsche's criticisms to be fully applicable to the law's use of history. Nietzsche was preoccupied with the concept of genius;[8] and his criticisms of the historical approach seem motivated primarily by a sense of the incompatibility of genius with a certain kind

6. "History in the service of life can never be scientific history." Werner Dannhauser, "Introduction to 'History in the Service and Disservice of Life,'" in Friedrich Nietzsche, *Unmodern Observations* 73, 79 (1990).

7. An example at once more recent and less familiar is how the "template" of the Battle of the Bulge contributed to the failure of the American military command in Vietnam to take adequate measures in preparation for the 1968 Tet offensive. The command believed that the enemy was on the ropes and might, like the Germans in 1944, launch a desperate offensive; but the fact that the German offensive had failed and that Germany had been utterly defeated within months bred complacency about the likely consequences of such an offensive by the North Vietnamese. James J. Wirtz, *The Tet Offensive: Intelligence Failure in War* 129–132 (1991).

8. The notion that in the nineteenth century "genius" was a career, and one to which Nietzsche aspired, is argued in Carl Pletsch, *Young Nietzsche: Becoming a Genius* (1991).

of historical knowledge or sense. The essay does two things, however, that bear importantly on law. It opens up the question whether the historical sense is an unalloyed blessing (and thus whether, for example, Santayana's aphorism that those who forget history are condemned to repeat it is the truism that it is usually taken to be); it problematizes what had been taken for granted. And it invites us to think of historical inquiry and the historical sense as instruments rather than things of intrinsic value oriented exclusively to truth. Truth is a good, but there are other goods, which forgetting or even forging the historical record might promote. As Nietzsche says elsewhere, "there exist very salutary and productive errors."[9] This is heady stuff—fresh and bracing. It is also irresponsible. To endorse a purely instrumental approach to history writing could be thought a license for rewriting history, the sort of thing that the Soviet Union did and that Orwell parodied in *Nineteen Eighty-Four*. But even the excesses in Nietzsche's essay on history are helpful for an understanding of law, because they illuminate a parallel instrumental conception of history writing by judges and other legal professionals. Judges rewrite history, like commissars.

Extreme versions of a tendency to make, or at least pretend to make, the past rule the present in law are found in Blackstone, who thought the aim of the common law of England should be to revive the customary law of *Anglo-Saxon* England,[10] which is to say the law of a regime that had been extinguished 700 years earlier; and in Savigny, the founder of the historical school of jurisprudence, who as we shall see in Chapter 6 thought the study of Roman law the key to improving modern law. But Blackstone's version (or Savigny's) is just that—an extreme. It isn't *fundamentally* different from the belief held by a great many modern American lawyers, judges, and law professors that the answers to modern questions of constitutional law can be found in the text or background of the Constitution, a documentary palimpsest most of which was drafted more than two centuries ago.

A moment's thought will suggest another possibility, however—that the ostensible use of history whether by Blackstone or Savigny or the Justices of the U.S. Supreme Court is not a sign of thralldom to history

9. Friedrich Nietzsche, "David Strauss, the Confessor and Writer," in *Untimely Meditations*, note 1 above, at 3.

10. See, for example, William Blackstone, *Commentaries on the Laws of England*, vol. 4, p. 413 (1769); Thomas A. Green, "Introduction," in id., vol. 4, pp. iii, xii.

but of the opposite, of bending history to the service of life, Nietzsche-fashion. Neither Blackstone nor a modern judge (or shadow-judge law professor) is comfortable saying, "This is what the law ought to be to-day, whatever it was yesterday, because we have new problems and need new solutions."[11] That is the kind of thing a politician might say but it doesn't sound like the utterance of a legal professional, as it has nothing of the esoteric or the arcane about it. The professional wants to say, "I can employ my special skills to find the already existing solution to the new (or new-seeming) problem, in authoritative decisions made centuries ago."[12] This claim is an illusion, as legal realists and critics of lawyers' history like to point out.[13]

Think of the sexual privacy cases, which culminate in *Roe v. Wade.* The first of them, *Griswold v. Connecticut,*[14] was decided in 1965, a century after the Fourteenth Amendment that furnished its ostensible ground was adopted. A robust, enforceable, constitutional right of free speech barely existed before the 1950s, and yet it is supposed to have been promulgated in 1789, when the First Amendment was ratified. Much of what passes for constitutional law is a modern construct, but it is defended by reference to ancient (as Americans measure historical time) texts to which it is tenuously and often only opportunistically linked. But though its ancientness is an illusion, Nietzsche teaches us that historical illusions can be empowering, can free us from the dead

11. Cf. Carl E. Schorske, *Thinking with History: Explorations in the Passage to Modernism* 88 (1998): "[W]hen men produce revolutionary changes, they screen themselves from their own frightening innovations by dressing themselves in the cultural clothing of a past to be restored."

12. This is very much the spirit of Savigny's opposition to the codification of law. He described pre-code law, particularly Roman law, as "the scientific element, properly so termed, whereby our calling acquires a scientific character." Friedrich Carl von Savigny, *Of the Vocation of Our Age for Legislation and Jurisprudence* 163 (Abraham Hayward trans. 1831). See Chapter 6.

13. See, for example, Alfred H. Kelly, "Clio and the Court: An Illicit Love Affair," 1965 *Supreme Court Review* 119; Martin S. Flaherty, "History 'Lite' in Modern American Constitutionalism," 95 *Columbia Law Review* 523 (1995); Laura Kalman, "Border Patrol: Reflections on the Turn to History in Legal Scholarship," 66 *Fordham Law Review* 87 (1997); Barry Friedman and Scott B. Smith, "The Sedimentary Constitution," 147 *University of Pennsylvania Law Review* 1 (1998). For a recent study that casts great doubt on a key orthodoxy of constitutional lawyers' history—the impact of Madison's constitutional theory on the drafting and ratification of the Constitution—see Larry D. Kramer, "Madison's Audience," 112 *Harvard Law Review* 611 (1999).

14. 381 U.S. 479 (1965).

hand of the past. The legal profession's use of history is a disguise that allows the profession to innovate without breaching judicial etiquette, which deplores both novelty and a frank acknowledgement of judicial discretion and likes to pretend that decisions by nonelected judges can be legitimated by being shown to have democratic roots in some past legislative or constitutional enactment. Since the most convincing deceptions are those rooted in self-deception (because then the deceiver is not in danger of giving himself away), one is not surprised that many lawyers and judges think of law as the application to the present of the lessons of the past as reflected in statutes, reported decisions, and other materials created in the past to govern the future. Yet the truth is that, for the most part, these past settlements of disputes frame and limit, but do not dictate, the outcome of today's cases.

The law's rhetorical use of history that I have been describing is entwined with the idolatry of the past that is a conspicuous feature of conventional legal thought. A backward-looking orientation invites the criticism that the dead should not be allowed to rule the living, and one way to rebut the criticism is to argue that our ancestors had a freshness of insight or power of thought that is denied to us moderns; they are our betters and we should be content to be in thrall to them.

It is remarkable how an essentially deceptive conception of the law's relation to the past can be maintained year after year, decade after decade, century after century. Most Americans continue to take for granted that the Supreme Court's constitutional decisions, even in the area of sexual and reproductive liberty, are in some meaningful sense rooted in the Constitution itself. Probably most legal professionals, even, believe this, though perhaps their belief is that morally dubious form of quasi-belief that Sartre called "bad faith." In the rhetoric of constitutional law, Nietzsche's illusionistic concept of historical writing holds sway. The judges invoke the authority of the ancient texts, deify the framers (great calling to great over the desert intervals of time), and in short create a fictive history in service of a contemporary, pragmatic project. Most professors of constitutional law, even such "theorists" as Ronald Dworkin, cheer them on, though sometimes opposing their own fictive history to that of the judges. So firmly is the mask in place that even disinterested critics of the Supreme Court's historical sense are more likely to call for better history than for no history. The result is to marginalize their criticism by making it seem an argument in a technical dispute over details of historiography.

Dworkin is no "originalist," in the sense of someone who believes that modern constitutional issues should be decided by reference to the meanings that the words of the Constitution bore in the eighteenth century or to the mental horizons of the framers. Nor is Frank Michelman or Cass Sunstein. But as Laura Kalman points out, Sunstein and Michelman, like Dworkin, think it important to construct a historical pedigree for their desired constitutional interpretations; they want "to imbue the past with prescriptive authority."[15] But, Kalman argues, it is a constructed rather than a found past. "The republican revivalists [Michelman and Sunstein] appropriated historians for advocacy purposes, permitting the present to overwhelm the past."[16] They employ "the rhetoric of originalism."[17] Kalman considers this rhetoric an indispensable condition of judicial innovation, given our legal culture. Maybe so (though I express some skepticism about this later); and maybe the academics are just trying to speak a language that judges will understand rather than fooling themselves that they are doing history. But let us be clear that what they are doing is indeed rhetoric, and not historiography. Later I argue that, paradoxical as this may seem, real originalists are *less* historicist than many antioriginalists—originalism is a *response* to historicism.

Kalman thinks that constitutional theorists "see through" their own historicism. Whether they do or not is of little moment, but I worry that some judges fool themselves into thinking that history really does deliver the solutions to even the most consequential legal issues and thus allows them always to duck the really difficult question—the soundness of the solutions as a matter of public policy. I think that some at least of the Justices of the Supreme Court would be hesitant to expand states' rights in the name of the Constitution if they realized that constitutional history provided no guidance to resolving such issues as whether the Eleventh Amendment (which merely forbids a citizen of one state to sue another state in federal court) codifies a far-reaching doctrine of state sovereign immunity even from suits based on federal law.

Not in constitutional doctrine or outcomes, but in a number of other respects, the law *is* in thrall to history, and not merely as a matter of judicial psychology. This point can be made perspicuous with the aid of

15. Kalman, note 13 above, at 103.
16. Id. at 107.
17. Id. at 124.

the economists' concept of *path dependence*, which means that where you end up may depend on where you start out from, even if, were it not for having started where you did, a different end point would be better. The best-known although possibly spurious example in the economic literature concerns the typewriter keyboard. According to the economic historian Paul David, the keyboard was designed to limit typing speed in order to prevent constant jamming of the keys. The jamming problem disappeared with the advent of electric typewriters and word processing yet we are stuck with the old keyboard because the costs of reaching agreement among manufacturers on a new keyboard and of "retooling" the millions of people who were trained on and have become habituated to the old one are prohibitive.[18] We can thus expect to observe path dependence when transition costs are high relative to the benefits of change, and they tend to be high when transition requires a high degree of coordination. Stated differently, even if there are large positive benefits to a change, they may be swamped by the costs of altering the status quo if the alteration requires a large number of people or institutions to change their behavior more or less at once. Consider what is involved in, for example, changing a nation's language from, say, Spanish to English, or changing the width of railroad tracks, or switching a nation's drivers from driving on the left to driving on the right.

David's minor premise, that the conventional keyboard is inefficient, has been subjected to searing criticism as part of a larger questioning of the empirical significance of path dependence.[19] I don't want to get into those issues; whatever the situation in competitive markets, where there are powerful incentives for efficiency, there can be little doubt

18. See Paul A. David, "Clio and the Economics of QWERTY," 75 *American Economic Review Papers and Proceedings* 332 (May 1985). For a general analysis of the economics of path dependence, see Stanley M. Besen and Joseph Farrell, "Choosing How to Compete: Strategies and Tactics in Standardization," *Journal of Economic Perspectives*, Spring 1994, p. 117.

19. See S. J. Liebowitz and Stephen E. Margolis, "The Fable of the Keys," 22 *Journal of Law and Economics* 1 (1990); Liebowitz and Margolis, "Path Dependence, Lock-In, and History," 11 *Journal of Law, Economics, and Organization* 205 (1995). Leibowitz and Margolis take an extreme position, denying the existence of path dependence in software markets (despite the value of compatibility between computers and the costs of switching from one computer system to another), in their recent book *Winners, Losers and Microsoft* (1999). For a more mainline economic discussion of path dependence, see Lucian Arye Bebchuk and Mark J. Roe, "A Theory of Path Dependence in Corporate Ownership and Governance," 52 *Stanford Law Review* 127 (1999).

that path dependence is an important phenomenon in law.[20] Some evidence of this is that the convergence of legal systems is much slower than the convergence of technology and economic institutions. For example, the laws and legal institutions of the different states of the United States differ more than the economic practices and institutions of the states do. The differences are still greater and more mysterious in a cross-country comparison, even when comparison is confined to countries whose economic and political systems, and levels of education and income, are similar to ours. It is hard to believe that the heavy use of the civil jury in the United States is unrelated to differences between English and Continental public administration that go back to the Middle Ages.[21] It is unlikely that if we were starting from scratch we would make the right to trial by jury turn on whether the plaintiff was seeking damages or an injunction—a distinction rooted in the historical accident that England developed two separate court systems for the two types of relief—or that statutes of limitations would vary as much as they do across states,[22] or that the level of detail in American law would be as great as it is, or that there would be as many procedural differences as there are between tort suits and breach of contract suits (since many wrongs can be pleaded under either heading—and *analytically* tort and contract are interchangeable).[23] The modern law is full of vestiges of early law. If we were starting from scratch, we could design and (even with due regard for political pressures) would adopt a more efficient system. This implies that there must be formidable obstacles to changing the existing one.

The law's obeisance to the past at the expense of the present and the future thus need not be attributed to a mystical, perhaps quasi-religious, veneration of ancient ways. It could just reflect transition costs,

20. Cf. Larry Kramer, "Fidelity to History—and through It," 65 *Fordham Law Review* 1627, 1640–1641 (1997), making a similar point. But Kramer attaches normative significance to it, and I do not. For more on path dependence, see Chapter 9.

21. See, for example, James Bradley Thayer, *A Preliminary Treatise on Evidence at the Common Law: Development of Trial by Jury* 2–3 (1896). Although the civil jury may be a more efficient institution than its critics believe, as I shall argue in Chapter 11, the extent to which it is used today may owe much to factors unrelated to efficiency, such as the Seventh Amendment to the U.S. Constitution, which guarantees the right to jury trial in civil cases at law if the stakes exceed $20—with no adjustment for the inflation that has occurred since 1789!

22. See *National Survey of State Laws* 94–104, 392–404 (Richard A. Leiter ed., 2d ed. 1997).

23. See, for example, Richard A. Posner, *Economic Analysis of Law*, ch. 8 (5th ed. 1998).

though here they arise not from a coordination problem, as in the type-writer keyboard example, but from problems of information. Judges, and legal professionals in general, may be so bereft of good sources of information for deciding novel cases or reforming the institutions of the law to conform to social changes that their most efficient method of deciding cases and resolving issues of institutional design is to follow, or at least be strongly constrained by, precedent, as is brought out in Dworkin's analogy of the common law to the writing of a chain novel.[24] The more heavily the judges rely on precedent, the more likely is current doctrine to be determined by history rather than by current needs. Legislators are not formally constrained by precedent but their ability to innovate is limited by the inertia that is built into the legislative process, especially at the federal level in the United States. By creating an essentially tricameral legislature (the Senate, the House, and the president with his veto power), the Constitution makes it difficult to enact statutory law; but once enacted, it is, by the same token, difficult to change, because the legislative procedures for amending an existing statute are the same as those for promulgating a brand-new statute. The Constitution, being difficult to amend, is itself a potent source of path dependence, in the provisions that do not lend themselves to *aggiornamento* through interpretation.

Path dependence is a less serious problem at the doctrinal than at the institutional level of the law. By rejecting strict stare decisis, American judges have empowered themselves to alter doctrine to keep abreast of changing circumstances. As a result, the structure of common law doctrine (broadly understood as doctrine forged in the process of deciding cases, whether or not they are "common law" cases in the technical legal sense) seems on the whole pretty efficient.[25] Generally worded provisions of statutes, constitutions, and contracts allow judges to mold them to current needs and values. Guido Calabresi has proposed that courts be allowed to "overrule" archaic statutes as if they were obsolete precedents,[26] and it is possible to argue that courts are already doing this, only calling what they do "interpretation." The law also fights off the dead hand of the past directly by refusing to enforce some of the limitations that the makers of wills attempt to impose on their bequests

24. See Ronald Dworkin, *Law's Empire* 228–238 (1986).
25. See Posner, note 23, esp. pt. 2 ("The Common Law").
26. See Guido Calabresi, *A Common Law for the Age of Statutes* (1982).

and by the closely related *cy pres* doctrine, which allows charitable foundations to circumvent some of the conditions in the instrument creating the foundation, for example allowing the March of Dimes Foundation to reallocate its resources from polio to lung diseases when the polio vaccine largely eradicated polio. But even at the institutional level, the legal system has proved resourceful in seeking to lift the dead hand of the past. The Seventh Amendment is immovable, but by shrinking the size of the civil jury (from the traditional twelve to six) and by expanded use of summary judgment to take cases away from juries and by subtle pressures to substitute bench trials for jury trials, the federal judicial system has curtailed and domesticated the originally intended operation of the amendment.

Path dependence in law resembles another important concept, that of law's autonomy. To the extent that a practice or field, whether it be music, mathematics, or law, is autonomous, developing in accordance with its internal laws, its "program," its "DNA," its current state will bear an organic relation to its previous states. Many legal thinkers have aspired to make law an autonomous discipline in this sense. It is a questionable aspiration and my own view is that law is better regarded as a servant of social need,[27] a conception that severs the law from any inherent dependence on its past.

There is a big difference between relying on the past either because we lack good information about how to cope with the present and future or because legal innovation involves heavy transitional costs—the problem just discussed of path dependence—and treating the past as normative, as when Paul Kahn, whom we meet in the next chapter, says that legal arguments "begin from a commitment to the past,"[28] and that "the rule of law is for us the manner in which the authoritative character of the past appears,"[29] or when Anthony Kronman says that "the past is, for lawyers and judges, a repository not just of information but of value, with the power to confer legitimacy on actions in the present," and "the past deserves to be respected merely because it is the past,"[30]

27. See, for example, Richard A. Posner, *The Problematics of Moral and Legal Theory* (1999).

28. Paul W. Kahn, *The Cultural Study of Law: Reconstructing Legal Scholarship* 43 (1999).

29. Id. at 44. "We can imagine a policy science that is wholly unbounded by the past, but it is not law's rule." Id. at 45 (footnote omitted).

30. Anthony T. Kronman, "Precedent and Tradition," 99 *Yale Law Journal* 1029, 1032, 1039 (1990).

or when Ronald Dworkin says that "the past must be allowed some special power of its own in court, contrary to the pragmatist's claim that it must not."[31] Why *must*? A possible answer is that justice demands that like cases be treated alike, and the happenstance that one case was decided long ago and the other is a current case does not sever the likeness. Fair enough; but it is not pastness that must on this view be allowed a special power; it is likeness. The only significance of pastness is to remind us that the fact that a case was decided a year ago or a century ago does not in and of itself entitle a court deciding a current case to ignore it. The court must have a reason to ignore it, just as it must have a reason to ignore any plausible potential source of guidance to deciding the present case.

Another possible answer to the "must" question is that events in the past can create commitments for the future. Contracts in which performance is to occur over time are the most obvious example. Constitutions and statutes can be thought of as kinds of contract and a judge-made rule might be conceived of as a promise to the community to decide future cases in conformity with the rule. But these are at best analogies. The sense in which today's Americans "consented" to the provisions of the Constitution and of statutes is highly attenuated in comparison to the consent that attends the signing of a contract, and the rejection of rigid stare decisis makes judge-made rules revocable, attenuating the reliance that they invite and receive. Reliance interests are, though, an example of a commitment that past practices or pronouncements can create; and quite apart from specific reliance there is a general value in a kind of social or political inertia that takes certain issues off the agenda, such as how many senators each state should have. It is often more important that something be settled than that it be settled just right. To reject historical piety is not to endorse a restless experimentation with political and legal institutions. It is merely to reject piety—but in law that is not a mean accomplishment.

A look into history will often bring to light information relevant to dealing with the present and the future. But when this happens, it is the information itself that should shape our response to current problems, rather than the past as such; the past is just a data source. If the only reason that can be given for deciding one way rather than another is

31. Dworkin, note 24 above, at 167.

that this is how it was done in the past, it is a feeble reason though good enough if there is no reason to change. The database conception of history is now fairly well understood in relation to judges' use of "legislative history," the background out of which a statute or a constitutional provision emerges. What an influential member or committee of the legislature said about the meaning of a bill that was later enacted, or what were the historical events out of which the bill welled, are data that may be helpful in determining the meaning of the enactment. This history is not normative, but just a convenient body of relevant data.

Commitment, reliance, information, even inertia are reasons for standing by decisions made in the past. But to call the past itself normative is a mystification. It might be an indispensable mystification if the general public believed it, because then the legitimacy of judicial decisions might depend upon the judges' accepting the yoke of history. The general public believes something *like* this, that decisions must be "rooted" in authoritative sources of law, but is pretty casual about the sources. Uninterested in and uninformed about history, the public is unlikely to demand that modern cases be decided consistently with ancient texts and precedents. Otherwise Robert Bork would have been confirmed as a Supreme Court Justice.

Dworkin himself makes no claims to be a historian, and so in practice as opposed to preaching treats the past in just the opportunistic way commended by Nietzsche, rarely looking farther into the past than the Warren Court for benchmarks by which to evaluate current decisions.[32] The benchmarks are arbitrary. They are an artifact of the choice of which historical period is to count as normative, a choice determined by Dworkin's politics. The history of the Supreme Court is one of cyclicity rather than progress—cycles of innovation and retrenchment, of liberal thrust and conservative parry, conservative thrust and liberal parry. Disinterested judicial historiography would enforce the lesson of cynicism that Nietzsche found so debilitating. Maybe that is why we have so little such historiography.

Another bad reason to embrace a historically oriented jurisprudence is a belief that the quality of the people who make law, mainly judges

---

32. That Dworkin's talk about keeping faith with the past does no actual work in his constitutional jurisprudence is argued in Michael W. McConnell, "The Importance of Humility in Judicial Review: A Comment on Ronald Dworkin's 'Moral Reading' of the Constitution," 65 *Fordham Law Review* 1269 (1997).

and legislators, has declined. This is a typical "golden age" fallacy (the type of monumentalistic history-writing, criticized by Nietzsche, that belittles the present)—that the world is going to hell in a handbasket—and is as tenacious as it is naive. It reflects the aging process, which sheds a golden glow over our youth (the nostalgia fallacy, we might call it); selection bias, which leads us to compare the best of the past with the average of the present because time has not yet sorted the best of the present from the average; related to both, a tendency to hero worship that requires a temporally distant hero to make worshipfulness a remotely plausible attitude; and, in recent times, the growth of specialization, which makes us feel smaller than our predecessors. Correcting for these factors that give us a distorted sense of the past, a sense that belittles the present, we would realize that the framers of the Constitution, and outstanding judges such as John Marshall, Holmes, Brandeis, Cardozo, Jackson, and Hand, were, with the exception of Holmes, who had world-class philosophical and literary talents, and Madison, who had penetrating political insights, merely very able lawyers. (Some recent candidates for deification, such as Earl Warren, William Brennan, and Harry Blackmun, are not uniformly acknowledged to have been even that.) There are many equally able lawyers today; if the nation decided it wanted a new Constitution, there would be no shortage of competent drafters. And even if the lawyers and judges of the fabled past were abler than the current crop, they knew so much less than we about conditions today that it is ludicrous to accord them a mystical power over the present. A more plausible view is not that they were abler but that they rose to the occasion presented by the unusual circumstances in which they found themselves. Crisis brings out the best (or the worst) in people. Harry Truman and even Abraham Lincoln might have been commonplace presidents under present conditions.

Any votary of deciding modern constitutional cases in conformity with the "original intent" of the framers or ratifiers is thus making a mistake if his ground is that the juvenescence of the United States was the golden age of legal thought. The only good reason for originalism is pragmatic and has to do with wanting to curtail judicial discretion and thus to transfer political power from judges to legislators, including the framers and ratifiers of constitutional provisions and amendments. (The bad reason, because it is question-begging, is that judicial decisions lack legitimacy if they are the product of an exercise of judicial discretion; the question begged is the validity of the conception of legitimacy that compels this conclusion.) It may not be a *very* good reason, for there are other ways of limiting judicial discretion besides trying to tether judges to a time line. But what I want to emphasize is that criticisms of originalism as bad history miss the point of originalism. The point is to curb judicial discretion by adopting a mechanical method of interpretation, one essentially lexicographical and algorithmic rather than historicist.

I have suggested that a policy of generally adhering to precedent, that is, of deciding cases in the same way that like cases have been decided previously, both economizes on judges' and lawyers' time and enables the decided cases to serve as guides to persons who want to avoid being sued. The policy need have nothing to do with a veneration of the past unless it is pushed to the point at which judges, like foreign-policy makers preoccupied with historical analogies (a form of precedent), prefer strained analogies to acknowledging the need to deal with novel issues without the crutch of precedent. Almost everyone would agree that a historical analogy cannot be used as a cookie cutter that will stamp out the answer to a current issue of policy. This is easy to see because history never repeats itself exactly. At best the historical analogy furnishes a lesson that may be applicable to a current problem. In the case of legal precedent, the cookie-cutter method will sometimes work; some cases are undeniably identical in all conceivably relevant respects to previously decided cases. But when they are merely "analogous," there is no metric of similarity that will enable a later case to be decided by reference to an earlier one, just as there is no metric of similarity that would have enabled Lyndon Johnson to figure out whether abandoning South Vietnam to its fate would have been "another Munich."

Historical analogies are causal; the Munich accord is used to show that if we act in a certain way, the same dire outcome will follow. Legal precedent is normative: the new case is to be decided the same way as the former one because they are relevantly alike. But the pitfalls are similar. Notions of likeness are vague. The valid use of either type of analogy, the historical or the legal, is to extract a principle, or consideration, which can then be used to illuminate a subsequent event or case. In neither case, then, is history normative; it is merely a source of potentially useful data.

In the case of history, arguments from analogy are plagued by the difficulty of evaluating counterfactual historical assertions.[33] We glimpsed this difficulty in the Introduction, in asking what the consequences have been of the Supreme Court's exercise of the power of judicial review of statutes, and in Chapter 1, in asking what influence Bentham had on the law and economics movement. We cannot rerun history without the Munich accord (or judicial review, or Bentham) and see what would have happened. To assess a historical counterfactual, we need a historical law,[34] such as that appeasement invites further aggression; if we are confident that the law is sound (a confidence hard to come by in historical inquiry, however), we can predict the consequences of an act of appeasement, such as the Munich accord. But not otherwise. Similarly, to make a legal argument from analogy requires the legal analyst to extract a principle from the prior cases that covers the current case.[35] The prior cases, as such, are not normative, any more than history is.

Decision by precedent has implications for the optimal age of judges.[36] The older one gets, the more one lives in the past. A very young person has little to draw on in his past by way of resources for coping with the present, but his powers of imagination and ratiocination are at their peak. An old person has waning powers of imagination and ratiocination but a rich store of recollections to use as templates— as "precedents" in almost a literal sense—for solving new problems by comparing them with old ones. The young person can always read about the past, but what a person takes away from what he reads depends critically on what he brings to his reading. The past is less vivid to one who reads about it than to one who has lived it.

33. Professional historians acknowledge this problem. See, for example, Peter Novick, *That Noble Dream: The "Objectivity Question" and the American Historical Profession* (1988).

34. Fred Wilson, *Laws and Other Worlds: A Humean Account of Laws and Counterfactuals* 72–89 (1986). For an example of how economic theory can be used to test a counterfactual historical assertion, see Raymond Dacey, "The Role of Economic Theory in Supporting Counterfactual Arguments," 35 *Philosophy and Phenomenological Research* 402 (1975). And for an example from game theory, see Bruce Bueno de Mesquita, "Counterfactuals and International Affairs: Some Insights from Game Theory," in *Counterfactual Thought Experiments in World Politics: Logical, Methodological, and Psychological Perspectives* 211 (Philip E. Tetlock and Aaron Belkin eds. 1996). I do not deny the existence or discoverability of genuine historical laws, but merely emphasize the difficulty and uncertainty of the undertaking.

35. Richard A. Posner, *The Problems of Jurisprudence* 86–100 (1990).

36. Richard A. Posner, *Aging and Old Age*, ch. 8 (1995).

It is probably no accident that the average age of judges is lower in Continental legal systems than in common law jurisdictions. The proximate cause of the difference is that Continental judiciaries are career judiciaries; people enter them shortly after they get their law degree, while in common law systems judges generally are lateral entries from practice or teaching. Continental adjudication is more formalistic, more "logical," than Anglo-American adjudication, and there is, concomitantly, less emphasis on adherence to precedents. Because logic is more a tool of the young for solving problems and precedent more a tool of the old, we should not be surprised to find younger judges in a legal system that emphasizes logic and older judges in one that emphasizes precedent. I acknowledge, however, the possibility that the causation is the reverse of what I've described—that it is the character of the Anglo-American judicial career that is responsible for the less formalistic character of Anglo-American adjudication.

The historically oriented judge that I have been describing—this elderly chap who wants to decide cases in a way that will display their pedigree, their continuity with earlier cases, statutes, or constitutional provisions—may seem poles apart from the pragmatic judge, who wants to decide cases in the way that will best promote, within the constraints of the judicial role, the goals of society. He uses history as a resource but does not venerate the past or believe that it ought to have a "special power" over the present. As Holmes memorably remarked, "It is revolting to have no better reason for a rule of law than that so it was laid down in the time of Henry IV."[37] Yet the two types of judge may not be as different as they seem. I said earlier that history provides a useful mask for decisions reached on other grounds. I add here that it is almost always a mask, because of the indeterminacy of most historical inquiries of the sort that might be thought to bear on legal decision-making; and behind the mask may be a pragmatist.

All this is not to say that the facts of history lie beyond our ken, that the historically oriented judge is therefore an impossibility. Even though we cannot (except in astronomy) actually observe events that occurred in the past, we can have enormous confidence in many facts about them, for example that George Washington was the first president of the United States or that France was defeated in the Franco-

37. Holmes, "The Path of the Law," in *The Essential Holmes*, note 5 above, at 160, 170.

Prussian war.[38] But it is not facts to which judges and law professors appeal when they are arguing about the interpretation and application of constitutional and statutory provisions and previous judicial decisions. History in the narrow sense of what happened does not reveal meaning. It might tell us what certain words in the U.S. Constitution meant in the 1780s, or what the provenance of certain constitutional provisions was, or what someone said about their meaning at the time; but there is an unbridgeable gap between uninterpreted historical data, on the one hand, and claims about the meaning of constitutional provisions in cases decided today, on the other. The sorts of claim that judges and law professors like to make about history are simply not verifiable, because they depend not on facts but on disagreements about the interpretive process itself. We know for example that the framers and most of the ratifiers of the Fourteenth Amendment did not regard blacks as the social or intellectual equals of whites, but we don't know what to make of this bit of historical lore when the issue is whether the amendment's equal protection clause forbids public school segregation.

There are two problems here, not one. The first is the elusiveness of historical Truth. By that I mean not the truth of facts that compose a simple narrative or chronology, or even of statistical inferences from historical data, but the truth of causal and evaluative assertions about history. The second problem, which arises when the issue is the meaning of some historical event or document, and thus an interpretive issue, is the indeterminacy of the choice of an interpretive approach. When one law professor says that the equal protection clause is about securing the basic political equality of blacks and another that it is about creating an evolving, generative concept of equality, their disagreement is over interpretive theory and cannot be resolved by a deeper or better study of history. History might reveal the interpretive presuppositions of the drafters or ratifiers of an enactment, but it would not reveal the weight that a modern interpreter should give to those presuppositions.

No doubt there are situations in which a knowledge of history, and not just the history of a doctrine, is important in legal decisionmaking.

---

38. These are examples of the robustness of "testimony" (in the philosophical sense) as a source of knowledge, the theme of Chapter 10 of this book.

In interpreting the term "high Crimes and Misdemeanors" in Article II of the Constitution, for example, we may not want to stop with the eighteenth-century meaning of the term and with the discussion of it in the constitutional convention, but we will probably want to start there; otherwise we may stumble badly over the word "misdemeanor," which today means a minor crime but which then had a much broader signification.[39] Even less problematic is the use of history that Holmes himself most fancied, that of showing that a modern doctrine is just a historical vestige, and so ought to be discarded; or the use of history to shoot down the ignorant historicism found in too many judicial opinions.[40] These are examples of historiography as therapy, which corresponds to the therapeutic use of analytic philosophy—its use against fallacious invocations of philosophy, as opposed to its "constructive" use, the dream of many philosophers.

Even the limited uses in law of the study of history that I have just been describing depend upon the existence of a consensus among professional historians, or at least a lack of controversy (because there are historical questions in law that have never attracted the interest of professional historians, maybe because the answers were obvious) among them. When professional historians reasonably disagree about the answer to a historical question that bears upon a legal case, the judges must find another method than history of resolving the case, for they are not competent to umpire historical disputes. And because they're not, inevitably they pick the side of the historical dispute that coincides with their preferences based on different grounds altogether, if they are determined to cast their decision in historical terms.

Sophisticated originalists know all this. They don't want to substi-

---

39. For example, Johnson's dictionary defines it as "offence; ill behaviour; [or] something less than an atrocious crime." Samuel Johnson, *A Dictionary of the English Language* (1755). See Richard A. Posner, *An Affair of State: The Investigation, Impeachment, and Trial of President Clinton*, ch. 3 (1999).

40. For an example picked almost at random, consider United States v. Curtiss-Wright Export Corp., 299 U.S. 304, 316–318 (1936), where the Supreme Court said that the war power of Congress differs from the commerce power in not having been among the sovereign powers of the states before the Constitution was promulgated. Charles A. Lofgren, a professional historian, in his article "United States v. Curtiss-Wright Export Corporation: An Historical Reassessment," 83 *Yale Law Journal* 1, 32 (1973), pronounced the historical discussion in *Curtiss-Wright* "shockingly inaccurate." I do not believe that his evaluation has been questioned. See generally Jack L. Goldsmith, "Federal Courts, Foreign Affairs, and Federalism," 83 *Virginia Law Review* 1617, 1660 and n. 184 (1997).

tute amateurish inconclusive debates over history for professional but inconclusive debates over policy or values. They want, or at least ought to want (for they often yield to the temptation of doing what legal historians with proper derision call "law office history"),[41] a narrowly focused inquiry into precise and answerable questions of historical meaning of specific words and sentences, coupled with a list of "canons of construction" that will enable those historical meanings to be brought to bear on contemporary issues.

The originalists of the present day, such as Justice Scalia, are reacting to the exercise of free-wheeling judicial discretion by the courts during the era of Earl Warren and, to only a slightly lesser extent, of his successor, Warren Burger. Not that their practice is consistent; I am speaking only of their preachment. The originalists want or at least say they want to minimize judicial discretion, and they have devised a kind of algorithmic mechanism for doing so. The historicists in law want no such thing. They mainly want to forge a historical pedigree for their preferred positions in order to deflect charges of judicial creativity. Richard Fallon has it backwards when he suggests that disingenuous rhetoric is inherent in pragmatic adjudication.[42] A pragmatist might or might not adopt a formalist rhetoric, historicist or otherwise; but the adoption of a historicist rhetoric is a sure sign that the judge is not disclosing the true springs of decision.

41. For examples of highly debatable historical excursus by originalist judges, see Plout v. Spendthrift Farms, Inc., 514 U.S. 211, 219–225 (1995); Michael H. v. Gerald D., 491 U.S. 110, 128 n. 6 (1989) (plurality opinion); United States v. Lopez, 514 U.S. 549, 584 (1995) (concurring opinion).

42. Richard H. Fallon, Jr., "How to Choose a Constitutional Theory," 87 *California Law Review* 535, 574 (1999). Fallon says that "by inviting judges to act on their personal views of what would make the future better, pragmatism would authorize judicial behavior that offends both rule-of-law and democratic values." But pragmatism does not license decision according to *personal* views, which would be mere willfulness; rather, it asks the judge to focus on the social consequences of his decisions. Fallon acknowledges that the pragmatist might want judges to consider rule-of-law and democratic values, but infers from this that "pragmatist judges might therefore follow established rules except where it would be very costly to do so, and they might write disingenuous opinions purporting to accept the authority of past decisions even when they were setting out in new directions that they thought better for the future." But why would they feel constrained to write disingenuous opinions? Why could they not say, as judges frequently say, that an existing rule must bend to take account of changed or special circumstances? The references in Fallon's discussion of pragmatic adjudication indicate that he derives his conception of it not from anything that pragmatists have written but rather from Ronald Dworkin's tendentious characterizations.

Originalism is thus, in a queer but I think valid sense, a response to the difficulty of resolving contested historical issues rather than a school of historical jurisprudence. But those who are not much drawn to originalism, and must cast about for some other alternative to history as the method of resolving cases, are open to the criticism that the difficulty of getting history right is relevant only if there is a *simple* alternative. If the alternative is policy analysis, as some pragmatists would be inclined to answer, this may seem to be jumping from the frying pan into the fire—substituting for one indeterminate inquiry another equally indeterminate one. But in grappling with issues of policy the judge is at least dealing with something that matters, and he can hope to make some progress and reduce error. Moreover, he is facilitating the correction of errors by refusing to hide behind a claim to possess an arcane methodology impenetrable to "mere" policy makers and other noninitiates. And perfection in historical inquiry, even if attainable, would answer one objection to historical inquiry but leave unanswered the more basic one: why *should* the past rule the present?

~ 5

Historicism in Legal Scholarship:
Ackerman and Kahn

$\mathcal{I}$ HAVE BEEN DISCUSSING the risks of historicism for adjudication. It poses risks for legal scholarship as well, as I shall argue
with reference to one of the most ambitious historicist efforts of current legal scholarship—Bruce Ackerman's effort to prove that Article V
of the U.S. Constitution does not provide the exclusive method of
amending the Constitution[1]—and with the effort of his colleague Paul
Kahn to encourage a strongly historicist "cultural" mode of studying
law. I shall suggest despite my own misgivings that Nietzsche might
have looked approvingly on Ackerman's method; and I shall note
Kahn's debt to Nietzsche's "genealogical" approach to history.

Article V creates a procedure, or rather two procedures, for amending the Constitution. The first requires that each house of Congress
approve a proposed amendment by a two-thirds vote and that three-
fourths of the states then ratify the proposal. The second requires Congress upon the application of the legislatures of three-fourths of the
states to convene a constitutional convention; any amendment proposed by the convention must, as under the first procedure, be ratified
by three-fourths of the states. The second procedure has never been
used. The original Constitution was promulgated by a convention and

---

1. This is a major aim of Bruce Ackerman's projected trilogy, *We the People*, of which two
volumes have been published. See Ackerman, *We the People*, vol. 1: *Foundations* (1991), vol. 2:
Transformations (1998). I focus here on the second.

then ratified by the states, but of course it was not a convention summoned pursuant to Article V, which did not yet exist.

As evidence that the Constitution can be amended without complying with Article V, Ackerman cites the amendments adopted after the Civil War—the Thirteenth through Fifteenth Amendments. He says that their adoption violated Article V in a variety of ways, but what his argument boils down to is that the victorious North rammed the amendments down the throat of an unwilling South. Without that coercion, the amendments would not have been ratified, at least as soon as they were, by the required three-fourths of the states. Ackerman further argues that the Constitution was amended completely outside the precincts of Article V during the New Deal, when no formal amendments were made except the ones, irrelevant to his thesis, abolishing Prohibition and moving up the date on which the president takes office, after being elected, from March to January. The New Deal "amendments" that count for Ackerman are decisions by the Supreme Court that expanded federal power over the economy and shifted the emphasis in constitutional liberty from the economic sphere to the political and the personal spheres. He does not consider the absence of formal constitutional text a critical difference between the Reconstruction and New Deal amendments. The significance of the Reconstruction amendments lies not in what they said—lies not, that is, in the enacted text—but in what they symbolized: a fundamental shift of power from the states to the federal government.

Ackerman's precedent for the usurpative-seeming amendment processes of Reconstruction and the New Deal is the adoption of the original Constitution. The framers exceeded their terms of reference from the Continental Congress, which had authorized the convening of a constitutional convention to amend the Articles of Confederation. The Articles required that amendments be unanimous, despite which the convention specified that the new Constitution, displacing (thus radically "amending") the Articles of Confederation, would take effect upon ratification by nine of the thirteen states (though it would bind only the ratifying states). Ackerman believes that in all three instances compliance with the legally prescribed requirements for amendment would have taken too long. He concludes that as a consequence of the informal amendments, the United States has had not one but three constitutional regimes. We live not under the 1787 Constitution as amended and interpreted but under the 1787 Constitution, a Reconstruction Constitution, and a New Deal Constitution, all irregularly promulgated but nevertheless valid.

Ackerman is not alone in believing that the "Constitution" we live under today bears only a modest resemblance to the document drafted more than 200 ago. But he does not regard this situation, as others do, as the consequence of misinterpretations, judicial willfulness, and a felt need to adapt the written Constitution to social change through a process—namely, judicial interpretation—less cumbersome than the amendment process. He regards the divergence between the original and today's "Constitution" as the consequence of what he claims is the dualist nature of American politics. Most of the time, Americans are apathetic about politics. This is the time of "ordinary politics"—a sordid, at best uninspiring business of interest-group politics, logrolling, lobbying, quasi-bribery, misrepresentations, and general selfishness. But in times of crisis people become attentive and involved. The policies that emerge during these periods of heightened public attention to political issues constitute a higher order of lawmaking to which the courts and other agencies of government are obliged to defer until the next upheaval yields a comparably authentic expression of the popular will. It would thus be *unconstitutional* for the Supreme Court to overrule the leading decisions of the New Deal era, even if those decisions were erroneous interpretations of either the original Constitution or the Reconstruction amendments; those decisions are constitutional amendments.

Ackerman seeks to rehabilitate—though not to resurrect—a host of decisions by the Supreme Court that have seemed either erroneous or at least questionable to most constitutional scholars. These decisions include *Lochner*[2] (striking down a state maximum-hours law), *Adkins*[3] (striking down a federal child-labor law), *Radford*[4] (striking down a federal debtors-relief law), *Griswold*[5] (striking down a state law prohibiting the use of contraceptives by married couples), and *Roe*.[6] Ackerman argues that the first three decisions appropriately honored the libertarian

2. Lochner v. New York, 198 U.S. 45 (1905).
3. Adkins v. Children's Hospital, 261 U.S. 525 (1923).
4. Louisville Joint Stock Land Bank v. Radford, 295 U.S. 555 (1935).
5. Griswold v. Connecticut, 381 U.S. 479 (1965).
6. Roe v. Wade, 410 U.S. 113 (1973).

premises of the Reconstruction amendments. For, he claims, those amendments were intended to protect "free labor" not only by outlawing slavery but also by preventing governmental interference with employment contracts. The last two decisions, *Griswold* and *Roe*, honored (he argues) the personal-libertarian premises of the New Deal "amendments." He thus challenges the conventional history of constitutional law, which denies that the Constitution has been amended as extensively as he believes, attributes overruled decisions such as *Plessy*[7] and *Lochner* to prejudice, error, or class bias rather than to supersession by constitutional amendment, and honors the dissenters in such cases (such as the first Justice Harlan, Holmes, and Brandeis) rather than the authors of the majority opinions.

Ackerman believes that Ronald Reagan, and more recently Newt Gingrich, attempted to launch an extratextual amendment process aimed at overruling the New Deal "amendments" but that Reagan was thwarted when his nomination of Robert Bork to the Supreme Court failed of Senate confirmation and Gingrich when Clinton was re-elected president.

What I have described so far is the academic counterpart to the type of normative historicizing, described in the previous chapter, in which judges engage when they try to enlist history on their side. Ackerman is trying to give a historical pedigree to a normative conception, in his case a conception of the proper way to amend the Constitution. There is much to be said against both the pedigree and the conception. The procedures specified in Article V for amending the Constitution are obviously designed to make amending difficult. They would fail to do so if alternative, less demanding procedures could be employed by Congress or the Supreme Court to bring about the same result. Even if the alternative procedures were no less demanding, but merely different, they would be problematic because they would inject a high degree of uncertainty into constitutional politics. Supporters and opponents of proposed legislation, or of proposed judicial interpretations by the Supreme Court, could never be entirely sure whether they were jousting over "mere" legislation or "mere" judicial interpretations—or over amendments to the Constitution. Congress would not know when it was entitled to legislate in the ordinary way and when it must use Arti-

---

7. Plessy v. Ferguson, 163 U.S. 537 (1896).

cle V or, if it wanted to amend the Constitution without recourse to
Article V, how to proceed. If Congress tried to overrule a decision of
the Supreme Court by ordinary legislation, the Court could thwart
Congress by declaring the decision to have constitutional stature. So
Ackerman's approach would alter the balance of power between Congress and the courts, with unpredictable results; but the more basic
objection is that it would wreak havoc with a central feature of the constitutional design—a procedure for amending the Constitution that
would be clear, exclusive, and rarely employed.

Another objection to the approach is that it carves the states out of
the amending process. Whereas Article V assigns a central role to the
states, empowering one more than one-quarter of them to veto any
amendment, Ackerman proposes to allow the Constitution to be
amended without the states' having any say at all.

The deepest objection is that an approach that treats the structural
features of the Constitution as optional cannot logically be limited to
Article V. The approach implies that Congress or the president (or perhaps the courts) might add to the federal government a third house of
Congress, a dictator who would give orders to the president, a court
empowered to review decisions by state courts on matters of state law,
or a separate mode of impeaching and removing the president—for
none of these additions is expressly forbidden by the Constitution. If
Article V is not a limitation on congressional power, why should any of
the other provisions that establish the structure of the federal government be treated as a limitation?

Ackerman's approach *makes* Article V inadequate, rather than revealing and curing its inadequacy. If judges did not enforce extratextual
amendments—if, for example, they had not held much of the early
New Deal legislation unconstitutional because (on Ackerman's interpretation of what the Supreme Court was doing—and rightly doing) it
infringed the extratextual Reconstruction amendments—there would
be little need for recourse to Article V and hence little pressure to circumvent it. The New Deal legislation would have been upheld (most
of it, anyway), and so Roosevelt wouldn't have had to try to coerce the
Supreme Court by proposing his Court-packing plan. Ackerman pro-
liferates constitutional amendments. His Constitution is longer than
anyone else's, and the more provisions a Constitution has, the easier
the amending process must be made in order to prevent governmental
paralysis.

Strict adherence to Article V as the exclusive mode of amending the Constitution would not, as Ackerman argues, have required the Court to invalidate the Reconstruction amendments. The Court could have taken—in fact has taken—the position that Congress has the final say on when an amendment shall be deemed adopted and in force.[8] The Court based this decision on the "political question" doctrine, which the Court invented and occasionally applies when necessary to avoid massive intrusions into the operations of other branches of government. Legal formalists may decry such prudential abstentions, but Ackerman is not a formalist and never makes clear why he considers the political-question route an unsatisfactory means of legitimizing the Reconstruction amendments, though he might argue that the doctrine avoids rather than resolves the issue of legality.

Nor is it clear that the Reconstruction amendments were the product of "coercion" in a pejorative sense of the term. The Civil War began with an unprovoked attack by South Carolina on Fort Sumter. The national government was entitled to defend itself, the occupation of an enemy's territories is a lawful outcome of a lawful war, and hence the military governments installed by the national government at the conclusion of the Civil War were lawful and could have required the congressional delegation of each of the occupied states to vote for the proposed amendments and could have then, when Congress adopted them by the requisite supermajority and sent them to the states, compelled the population to vote to ratify them. So it is far from clear that the Reconstruction amendments violated Article V. Nor could the original Constitution have violated it. Two of the three struts of Ackerman's historical analysis collapse. The third, the idea that a number of judicial decisions during the New Deal era have constitutional status, is the least plausible because of the absence of any textual "handle" corresponding to the original Constitution or the Reconstruction amendments.

Ackerman's conception of how the U.S. Constitution is and should be amended both is a bad conception as a matter of policy and (though this is something that does not trouble me) has no real historical pedigree. But I also want to emphasize how remote his conception of history is from the conception of history as a collection of data, and how damaging that remoteness is to his project of using history to guide law.

8. Coleman v. Miller, 307 U.S. 433 (1939).

In its abstractness and interpretive ambitiousness, his historicist theory of constitution amending would place upon the courts the unsupportable burden of identifying constitutional "moments" and determining which aspects of them should be deemed of constitutional dignity. The burden would rest on the critics of the courts as well. The conformity of a judicial decision to the text or background or purpose of particular constitutional provisions, or to past decisions interpreting those provisions, or to sensible public policy, or to other values, would be irrelevant to an evaluation of the decision's soundness. The only relevant conformity would be to some past *Zeitgeist.*

The difficulty of this style of historicizing is shown by Ackerman's attempt at it. He is playing in his own sandbox, yet playing badly. Key decisions of the Supreme Court refute him. In cases like *Plessy v. Ferguson* the Supreme Court refused to recognize liberty of contract; this suggests, contrary to Ackerman's argument, that the Court was not enforcing some extratextual Reconstruction amendment that guaranteed such liberty against curtailment by the states. The Supreme Court left the Jim Crow laws of the southern states, laws that were an affront to federal power, starkly alone during the entire period of the "Reconstruction Constitution" that in Ackerman's view decisively strengthened federal power over the states.

Cases like *Brown v. Board of Education*[9] and *Griswold v. Connecticut* cannot be attributed to the New Deal "amendments"; neither public school education nor sexual liberty was an interest of the New Deal. Ackerman's interpretation of the Bork nomination as an effort to repeal the New Deal "amendments" is groundless too. Had Reagan been able to fill up the Supreme Court with Borks and Scalias, *Roe v. Wade* might have been overruled, affirmative action declared unconstitutional, prayer allowed in public schools, the constitutional rights of criminal defendants further curtailed, and the power of the federal government over the states reduced. Only the last item on this agenda—which at this writing a less conservative Supreme Court is nevertheless pursuing vigorously—would have brushed up against New Deal legislation, and then only lightly. Indeed, the net effect of the overrulings by a Bork-Scalia Court would be to return constitutional law to where it was when FDR died! Neither Bork nor Scalia believes that *Lochner,*

9. 347 U.S. 483 (1954).

Adkins, or any of the other decisions that created the Reconstruction Constitution were correctly decided. Neither believes in constitution-alizing economic rights à la Richard Epstein, who believes that *Lochner* was correctly decided and that much of the New Deal was unconstitutional.

Ackerman particularly wishes to establish the similarity of the three constitutional moments that he has identified to each other and their dissimilarity to the failed fourth moment of Reagan and Gingrich. This exercise in historical analogy-making carries Ackerman deep into the archives. The body of primary and secondary materials relevant to an understanding of the three historical periods that Ackerman studies is vast; only a historian can evaluate Ackerman's selection from and interpretation of it.[10] Ackerman is not a historian, and historical research is only a part of his academic work. History, like most academic fields, is increasingly specialized. The more specialized a field, the greater the disadvantage of the nonspecialist; the more "amateurism" becomes a danger and a deserved reproach.[11]

No one will deny the ingenuity of the historical parallels that Ackerman draws. He matches the Reconstruction Act of 1867, which he treats as having amended Article V of the Constitution by conditioning the readmission of the southern states' senators and congressman to Congress upon those states' voting to ratify the Fourteenth Amendment, with Article VII of the Constitution, which had diluted the unanimity requirement of the Articles of Confederation. He matches the radical Republicans who controlled Congress during Reconstruction to Franklin Roosevelt, and matches Andrew Johnson— the border-state president who was Lincoln's successor and opposed

10. For assessments (both critical and admiring) of Ackerman's project by professional historians and others, see "Symposium: Moments of Change: Transformations in American Constitutionalism," 108 *Yale Law Journal* 1917 (1999); Colin Gordon, Book Review, "Rethinking the New Deal," 98 *Columbia Law Review* 2029 (1998); Larry Kramer, "What's a Constitution for Anyway? Of History and Theory, Bruce Ackerman and the New Deal," 46 *Case Western Reserve Law Review* 885 (1996); Michael J. Klarman, "Constitutional Fact/Constitutional Fiction: A Critique of Bruce Ackerman's Theory of Constitutional Moments," 44 *Stanford Law Review* 759 (1992).

11. This point cuts both ways, as shown by the failure of professional historians to have contributed construcively to the debate over the impeachment of President Clinton. See Richard A. Posner, *An Affair of State: The Investigation, Impeachment, and Trial of President Clinton* 234–237 (1999).

the radical Republicans—to the Supreme Court that tried (at first with some success) to thwart the New Deal. For Ackerman, the fact that these powerful efforts to prevent the "enactment" of the irregular amendments (coerced, in the case of the Reconstruction amendments, and nontextual, in the case of the New Deal amendments) failed—that the current of reform was able to overcome such resistance—proves the strength of the popular will and thus verifies the existence of true constitutional moments. More, it shows that the failure of regular enactment in the Reconstruction and New Deal eras was a trivial detail, on a par with a misspelling in a judicial commission. Had President Johnson not flinched during the trial of his impeachment, he would have been convicted, removed from office, and replaced by a radical; had Secretary of State Seward refused to proclaim the adoption of the Fourteenth Amendment, Congress would have overridden him; and had the Supreme Court in 1937 not abandoned its opposition to the New Deal, Roosevelt's Court-packing plan would have been enacted.

I don't know whether these or any of the other counterfactual claims or "alternative histories" with which Ackerman's book is studded are true. (The one about Johnson is the most plausible.) That is for professional historians to say, if they can. My guess is they'll say it is impossible to speculate responsibly about such counterfactuals, posed by Ackerman, as Lincoln's having survived his second term or Roosevelt's having failed to survive his first term, enabling John Nance Garner to become president and play Andrew Johnson's role in resisting a radical Congress. No "laws" of history predict the outcomes of these counterfactuals.

Even if all the "what if" questions could be answered, it would not follow that, as Ackerman believes, judges should dispense with the formalities of enactment by attempting to answer counterfactual questions about recent or contemporary controversies. The logic of his approach is that if a court were confident that some law would be passed by Congress and signed by the president, but for some irrelevant reason (maybe just an oversight by the clerical staff in one of the houses of Congress, or a filibuster on an unrelated issue) it was not enacted, the court could go ahead and enforce it as if it had been enacted. Formalist readers of Ackerman may come away with their faith strengthened, and pragmatists may be forced to acknowledge that formalism has a legitimately pragmatic role to play in law. The statute under which Seward acted, requiring the secretary of state to certify as valid a constitutional amendment when it has been ratified by the requisite number of states, begins to be a rather appealing formality; Ackerman calls the certification "a legalistic piece of paper."[12]

Ackerman's effort to identify three constitutional "moments"—three peaks in U.S. history—and consign the rest of our history to the plains is excessively schematic. He ignores such other plausible candidates for moments of heightened public attention to political matters as the War of Independence, which produced the Declaration of Independence (by Lincoln always treated as one of the founding documents of the American "Constitution")[13] and the Articles of Confederation; the first few decades under the Constitution, with the tug of war between the Federalists (including John Marshall) and the Jeffersonian Republicans over whether the national government would be effective; the presidency of Andrew Jackson, which inaugurated populist democracy; and the Progressive era, embracing the presidencies of Theodore Roosevelt, Taft, and Wilson, which gave us trust-busting, the Federal Reserve Act, the national park system, and the independent civil service.

The second volume of Ackerman's trilogy ends with a radical proposal for amending Article V—extraconstitutionally of course. The proposal is to empower the president, upon being reelected, to propose constitutional amendments that would be placed on the ballot at the next two presidential elections and if passed would become formal amendments to the Constitution. In other words, a president popular enough to be reelected would be empowered to sponsor two referenda spaced four years apart, and concordance of the results of the referenda would make the proposals part of the Constitution. The proposal would be embodied in a statute which would provide that it would take effect if proposed by a second-term president and passed by a two-thirds majority of Congress and then supported by the voters at the next two presidential elections. In other words, like the original Constitution, the statute would prescribe its own mode of becoming an enactment that would have the force of a constitutional amendment.

The motive behind this proposal is obscure, as it is not addressed to the historical events that provide Ackerman's evidence for its needful-

12. Ackerman, *Transformations*, note 1 above, at 154.
13. Recall the discussion of the "thin Constitution" in the Introduction.

ness. It is irrelevant to the founding; and as for Reconstruction, a proposal for constitutional amendments could not have been made under
the procedure advocated by Ackerman until 1872, when Grant was reelected, or adopted until 1880, by which time Reconstruction was over
and no Reconstruction amendment could have passed. The New Deal
amendments could not have been made until 1936, when Roosevelt
was reelected, or adopted until 1944, when the Second World War was
in full flow and the New Deal largely forgotten. The proposal is addressed to problems that have not arisen and may never arise, while
failing to address the problems that give rise to it.

The disjunction between the history that Ackerman narrates (or creates) and the proposal for policy change in which his historicizing cul-
minates is a further indication that he does not see history as a source of
data that may cast warning and other lights on the problems of today,
in the way for example that the economic crisis between the election
and inauguration of Franklin Roosevelt suggested the need to compress the presidential lame-duck period. The crises that Ackerman re-
counts were overcome *more* satisfactorily than they would have been
had his proposal been in effect, because his proposal requires a longer
period of time for implementing reform than would have been feasible.
Rather, Ackerman sees history in its interpretive as distinct from its factual sense as the appropriate method of legitimizing a radical proposal:
the proposal is okay because something like it was used in the past. The
pragmatic social reformer will not be happy with such an approach. He
is less interested in whether a radical proposal has a pedigree, let alone
an invented one, than in whether its benefits outweigh its costs. He
would prefer Ackerman to concentrate on that question, the answer to
which is more dubious than he assumes, rather than to build historical
sand castles.

Ackerman does not believe that the past is normative or want to return us to the original understanding of the Constitution-amending
process. His aim is to make his radical proposal seem natural by presenting historical analogies to it and desirable by identifying historical
crises that might have been averted had something like his proposal
been in effect. But these are just other ways than those of Blackstone or
Savigny or their many successors in which lawyers' historicizing is
marked as rhetorical rather than scientific in a way that Nietzsche's critique of the study of history can help us to understand—and maybe to

forgive. Nietzsche, we recall, commended the use of history by "the man of deeds and power, . . . him who fights a great fight, who needs models, teachers, comforters and cannot find them among his contemporaries." We might think of Ackerman as reaching back to the great men of the past for models and teachers in his work of overcoming the limitations of Article V. If the Constitution has been amended extratextually in the past and if the nation would have been better off if this had been recognized, maybe the Constitution can and should be amended extratextually in the future. History reveals possibilities and by doing so emboldens us to consider changes in our current methods. An exercise in selective remembrance and selective forgetting, Ackerman's project may come closer than that of other legal historicists to satisfying Nietzschean criteria for constructive engagement with history. This conclusion may, however, merely reinforce the doubts I expressed in the preceding chapter about the normative significance of the constructive aspect of Nietzsche's essay.

Consider the type of history that Nietzsche himself did, notably in *On the Genealogy of Morals*. Though the *Genealogy* purports to be a history of morality, it is unlike anything a professional historian would write—or, rather, would have written before the profession's recent rediscovery, in the spirit of Nietzsche, that "history can be redescribed as a discourse that is fundamentally rhetorical, and that representing the past takes place through the creation of powerful, persuasive images which can be best understood as created objects, models, metaphors or proposals about reality."[14] The *Genealogy* is edifying rather than scientific history. It is an argument that is in the form of a historical narrative for the sake of vividness, rather than an attempt to "get right" the events in history. It is historicizing in the service of life, and in like manner we might consider Ackerman's trilogy to be the service—at least the attempted service—of life.

Yet looking backward is an odd stance for those who believe we should be forward-looking. Nietzsche would say, or Holmes or perhaps Ackerman, that a certain kind of looking backward, a skeptical, debunking looking backward, can liberate us from thralldom to tradition and thus clear the decks for a forward-looking approach. I think it

14. Hans Kellner, "Introduction: Describing Redescriptions," in *A New Philosophy of History* 1, 2 (Frank Ankersmit and Hans Kellner eds. 1995). See generally Hayden White, *Metahistory: The Historical Imagination in Nineteenth-Century Europe* (1973).

largely did this for Holmes, but not for Nietzsche, for Ackerman, or for our leading contemporary philosopher of pragmatism, Richard Rorty. Nietzsche is nostalgic for the world of the pre-Socratic philosophers and tragedians; Ackerman for the New Deal; and Rorty, another New Deal nostalgist, for the often violent struggles by organized labor that culminated in the Wagner Act.[15] These are reactionary stances, celebrating movements and outlooks that, whatever their value in their time, have no value for ours.

⌐◡   PAUL KAHN, also a law professor at Yale, has written a manifesto for what he claims to be a new (indeed newly invented, by him) and better form of legal study, the *cultural* study of law.[16] He wants law professors to stop doing what they are doing and take up this new genre. Cultural studies are all the vogue in the academy today; it was inevitable in this age of interdisciplinary legal scholarship that someone would try to bring the law within its domain. Kahn's is not the first effort to do so,[17] but it is the most thoroughgoing. His particular version of cultural studies is strongly historicist and indebted to Nietzsche; on both counts, though it has a closer affinity to anthropology than to history, it comes within the scope of this part of the book.

Kahn believes that legal scholars are obsessed with projects of law reform, are indeed inveterately normative, and that this makes them participants in the legal system rather than observers of it. Even legal theory is what Kahn calls "auto-theorizing"; it is theorizing in the very terms given by the law. He thinks we need a type of scholarship that

15. This is the strongly marked theme of the later chapters of his book *Philosophy and Social Hope* (1999). See id., pts. 4 and 5.

16. Paul W. Kahn, *The Cultural Study of Law: Reconstructing Legal Scholarship*. (1999). Page references to his book appear in the text of this chapter.

17. A colleague of his at Yale, Jack Balkin, has, along with James Boyd White of the University of Michigan, a strong claim to be acknowledged as a founder of the cultural study of law; but neither one's claim is acknowledged and only Balkin is cited, and then only in a footnote on a peripheral point. Kahn mentions the critical legal studies movement, but only as a failed effort at legal reform. It is that but it is also an effort to view the rule of law from the outside as "myth"—a noxious myth, which it is not to Kahn, but that is a detail. The idea that judges internalize the rule of law because adherence to it is a rule of the "game," the game of judging, that they have decided to play is not new either. Kahn does not discuss previous works of cultural anthropology of law, by lawyers and anthropologists such as Karl Llewellyn, Simon Roberts, and John Comaroff, or the anthropological and sociological literature that has been produced by the Law and Society movement, or the rousing attacks on the normativity of legal scholarship by law professors Pierre Schlag and Paul Campos.

will approach the legal system from the outside, without any commitment to the validity of the system's presuppositions, just as a cultural anthropologist studies the belief system of a primitive tribe without normative commitments. Beliefs rather than institutions, procedures, professionals, or particular rules are central to law. They are summarized in the concept of the "rule of law," the central tenet and aspiration of the American legal ideology.

The cultural student of law is to proceed first by breaking up this concept into its constituent beliefs and then by subjecting each of them to the methodologies that Kahn calls "genealogy" (in the Nietzschean or Foucaldian sense)—hence the importance of a certain kind of historicizing to his project—and "architecture." The first is concerned with the historical origins and evolution of the belief, the second with its relations to other beliefs. Both are to be guided by assumptions designed to purge considerations of normativity from the study of law. These assumptions are, in particular, that law is not a failed or incomplete effort to achieve something else (that is, law is to be viewed as autonomous rather than instrumental); that it is not a product of rational design; that it is not to be evaluated by reference to any idea of progress; and that the lawful is inseparable from the unlawful—the criminal is as much a product of the rule of law as the judge, and likewise the judicial decision that is denounced as "lawless" by a dissenting judge.

Much of what he says is persuasive, for example that legal "theory has substantially failed to separate itself from practice" (p. 7)—that even the airiest theorists, whose proposals for legal reform are thoroughly impractical, assume that "reform is the appropriate end of [their] scholarship" (id.). "Legal scholars are not studying law, they are doing it" (p. 27). This is not just an accident of how lawyers are trained and law professors recruited. It is inherent in legal ideology itself, which places law at the intersection of reason and will (by "will" he means, in a democratic society, popular consent). Because reason is thus "a fundamental value internal to the legal order . . . , legal study unavoidably becomes a program for the reform of law" (p. 18). Here I begin to lose him:

1. It is not legal ideology that causes theory to collapse into practice, but the fact that legal training, which is the primary training of law professors, is primarily normative; lawyers are trained to make arguments designed to sway courts.

2. Kahn has run together two quite different distinctions: that be-

tween positive and normative analysis (the former explanatory, the latter reformist) and that between viewing a practice from an internal and from an external perspective (the lawyer's view of law versus the anthropologist's). A lawyer can try to understand law without trying to improve it, and a nonlawyer can urge changes in law.

3. "Reform," in the sense of altering either the physical or the social environment, is a central project of most social and natural science; it is not some peculiar deformity of legal scholarship.

4. Kahn exaggerates the normative emphasis of that scholarship, great as it is. And it is great. Normative scholarship employing the same categories and methods of the judge or legislator is the dominant form of legal scholarship today as always. In the influential jurisprudence of Ronald Dworkin, as Kahn shrewdly observes, "the reform of law through its reasoned elaboration is a part of what the *law already is*" (p. 21; emphasis in original). Dworkin is a votary of natural law; for him bad law is no law. But Kahn ignores a large body of scholarship in economics, sociology, and political science, much of it done in law schools and by law professors, that views the law in terms different from those of the law itself—that views it, in short, from an external perspective. (That is, indeed, the project of this book.) Much of this scholarship is normative, but not all is. Some of it seeks to understand rather than to change the law—to understand it for example as an instrument for promoting efficiency or doing corrective justice or maintaining social peace, without worrying whether it might be a better instrument to whatever end has been identified. Little of this scholarship has the densely descriptive character of cultural anthropology, but it is genuinely positive and it bears on Kahn's project of shifting the emphasis of legal scholarship from normative to positive analysis.

At some level Kahn must be aware of this point because in his concluding chapter, without retracting anything said earlier, he invokes a literature in political science (exemplified by Gerald Rosenberg's book *The Hollow Hope*, which I cited in the Introduction) that has demonstrated the frequent ineffectuality of legal interventions in social problems, such as racial discrimination in schools. ("Judicial decisions are not what they seem. Their claims are often vastly disproportionate to their effects" [p. 128].) Kahn aptly observes that "courts can draw our attention to the aberrational, i.e., to remnants of social practices that we have otherwise abandoned, but they cannot make us other than we are" (p. 130). But he seems not to realize that the literature that shows this is a species of positive (as distinct from normative) external critique that is yet not the cultural study of law. Because of this oversight he embraces a false antithesis: internal critique in the manner of Dworkin versus the cultural study of law.

He might be able to deflect this criticism by redefining his subject as the study (both external and positive) of the rule of law rather than of the law. The "rule of law" is a complex of beliefs that legal professionals explicitly and ordinary citizens implicitly hold about the nature of legality. Although this complex has been studied from external perspectives that owe nothing to cultural anthropology, it invites, like any other body of myth, the attention of the cultural anthropologist. To call *our* ideology a "myth" (even to call it an "ideology"), or as Kahn sometimes does a "fiction" (without meaning that it is necessarily false), will grate on some of his readers. But he is right that it is possible to study a body of beliefs without assessing their truth value—for example, to study the Aztec belief in the efficacy of human sacrifice, or the Catholic belief in the eucharist, without asking whether these beliefs, these "myths," are true. It is difficult to do this when the beliefs are our own, such as our belief in the rule of law as a cornerstone of a liberal polity, but it is not impossible. "A cultural approach sees that all of law's texts are works of fiction. Each sustains an imaginative world by representing it as our world" (p. 126). One of these fictions is law's efficacy in bringing about social change; recent decisions by the Supreme Court that appear to be shifting power from the federal government to the states are merely an episode in America's age-old "romance of the local" (p. 131).

How much to invest in a study of these "fictions" is a critical question. Kahn wants a massive redirection of legal scholarship from its present concerns to the cultural study of the rule of law, but he is not clear about the payoff to be anticipated. His book is not itself a cultural study of law but merely a prolegomenon to such a study, though it is peppered with specific claims of which the following are examples:

Our concept of the rule of law contains traces of the Old Testament's concept of "the linear history of the nation of Israel" (p. 46; footnote omitted), which established "the authority of the origin" (id.). Law "takes up and redeploys [this] religious conception of history" (p. 48). In the redeployment, "revolution replaces revelation" (id.). Hence "law's origin is characterized by a radical otherness" (p. 49), namely the American Revolution as codified in the Constitution. American law starts with the Revolution and the promulgation of the Constitution and must constantly return to these events for strength. This is Kahn's principal historicist claim. It echoes the historicism of Ackerman, who describes his project of constitutional history as "aim[ing] to place the revolutionary experience of the American People at the center of constitutional thought."[18]

The concept of the rule of law, culturally viewed, has, Kahn argues, a strong territorial component. This is connected to the "will" element of the law (remember that law is for Kahn the intersection of will and reason). Jurisdiction, which both establishes and limits legal authority, being indeed the condition of that authority, is a vital element of the rule of law and a fundamentally territorial concept, like property, which it resembles. Yet jurisdiction plays no role, according to Kahn, in liberal theory, which in consequence "seems to move inexorably toward world government" (p. 58). For Kahn this demonstrates the tension between the idea of global law based on world government and the concept of the rule of law; the first does not grow smoothly out of the second, because it lacks borders.

The rule of law, Kahn continues, is an argument rather than a fact. Before a case is decided, a lawyer may accuse his opponent of advocating a "lawless" result, a result that cannot be justified in terms of the law. A dissenting judge may denounce the majority in similar terms. But the decision once rendered becomes a precedent to which the loser and the dissenter owe the same duty of obedience they would to a decision with which they agreed. "After the decision, to fail to follow that precedent itself becomes the rule of men" rather than the rule of law (p. 68).

The law devalues action; this is related to its being backward-looking. "An event is *legal* when it appears as an instance of an already established rule" (p. 71; emphasis in original). "What matters to the legal perception is not what is done but that there was a legally established power to do it" (p. 75). This leads to the paradox that while the Constitution may appear to be the basis for the judicial assertion of power to

18. Bruce Ackerman, "Revolution on a Human Scale," 108 *Yale Law Journal* 2279, 2280 (1999).

invalidate statutes, it is really the judicial assertion of the power that has created "the permanent Constitution" (p. 77). Because of that power, we are constantly being forced back to a text written in 1787 and having to acknowledge its continuing validity as law; we become ruled by the past. This is a further illustration of the historicist cast of Kahn's approach.

The disenfranchisement of criminals affirms our commitment "to law's rule as our political culture" (p. 82) by depriving the criminal of a political voice. It is the same affirmation that judges make when (as a few do) they refuse to exercise their right to vote lest that mark them as political beings and thus blur the line between law and politics.

In the nineteenth century there was a lot of talk about a "science of law," but the discrediting of Social Darwinism, a "science" that had influenced a conservative Supreme Court, and the rise of policy sciences and the administrative agency conceived as a "scientific" organ of government, caused a migration of scientific aspiration from the courts to the agencies. "The American lawyer's reluctance to rely upon claims for a science of law is a remnant of this genealogy" (p. 117).

The "politics of victimization" (p. 85), what is more familiarly called "identity politics," undermines the rule of law by depicting people as victims of law imposed by outsiders rather than as makers of law, thus entitling them to claim special rights that operate to separate them still further from the community.

There is some truth in all these claims, but less than Kahn believes. He overstates his thesis. He tries to relate almost every legal phenomenon to the concept and supporting practices of the rule of law. He argues that we imprison a higher fraction of our population than any other civilized nation in order to demonstrate the depth of our commitment to the rule of law—though the other civilized nations think us lawless to vest so much discretion in our prosecutors to overlook offenses. The North fought the Civil War, he argues, not to save the Union but to preserve the rule of law, though slavery was legal and the Dred Scott decision, which held that the federal government could not prevent the extension of slavery to the terrories, was the authoritative declaration of the nation's highest court, while Lincoln's suspension of habeas corpus was unconstitutional. The rehabilitative goal of imprisonment has faded, Kahn believes, not because it has proved unattainable but because it alters law in the direction of therapy, while revenge is forbidden not because it is an inefficient and destructive method of keeping order but "in order to make possible the assertion of legal meanings . . . The victim becomes the occasion for an affirmation of the rule's meaning, rather than the source of meaning of the criminal act" (p. 97). In fact, reciprocity, both positive and negative, remains an important method by which compliance with legal and other social norms is obtained, as we shall see in Chapter 9.

Kahn speculates that the emergence of a legal norm prohibiting genocide may have increased rather than, as one might have expected, reduced, or left unchanged, the incidence of genocide. Announcing a prohibition stimulates interest in the prohibited conduct. He claims that the military strategy of "mutually assured destruction" (that is, of having enough nuclear weapons and secure launchers to be able to retaliate massively after a massive first strike) is not a deterrent strategy but instead a remnant "of the mystical corpus of the state in the contemporary imagination. The king's body had a kind of infinite or incomparable value. This remains true of the body of the state under law's rule . . . Rather than lose political identity, the state announces its willingness to destroy itself entirely" (pp. 61–62).

These are examples of a rather perverse unwillingness to seek functional explanations for social practices. All such practices—oddly in a culture in which the social sciences flourish and pragmatism is the reigning ideology—are, Kahn implies, the product of myth, not of rational design. (They could be both, in the sense of having myth at their root yet surviving because they are discovered to serve important social needs.) He exaggerates the explanatory power of a purely cultural study of the rule of law. He also fails to lay out a research program to guide that study. What remains to be done, and how is it to be done? He will not persuade many law professors to retool as cultural anthropologists without indicating what tools they need, what materials to use them on, and what they are likely to produce. Fledgling anthropologists immerse themselves in a tribal society for several years as a critical stage in their training. The obvious parallel in the cultural study of law would be a dose of legal practice; and yet that dose (especially when it takes the form of a Supreme Court clerkship, which has indeed warped many a scholarly career) is likely to make it more difficult for the student to escape the internal perspective. The observations that Kahn offers about the rule of law appear to owe little to any particular body of theory or any empirical methodology; and he never indicates what might refute them. Nor does he make an argument for why law schools, which are professional schools that charge a very high tuition, should support a form of scholarship that he does not contend has any value for lawyers. Why is it not a fitter subject for professional anthropologists, who are busy looking for new systems of belief to study now that cultures uncontaminated by Western influence have disappeared?

The most curious feature of Kahn's book, illustrating the difficulty that legal scholars face in adopting an external perspective, is his belief that the rule of law is a uniquely American phenomenon caused by the fact that the nation was created by a revolution followed shortly by a written constitution designed to memorialize that revolution. "Americans believe they created themselves first through a violent, revolutionary break with an inherited, unjust, monarchic order and then through a positive act of popular lawmaking [the Constitution]" (p. 9). But this is false, because "Americans" were called, and called themselves, "Americans" before the Revolution, and, more important, because modern Americans do not, in thinking about law, attach the weight to the Revolution and the Constitution that Kahn thinks they do. We celebrate Independence Day, not the day on which the Constitution was ratified. Kahn is describing his own belief system, not that of the American people; and likewise when he says that "the rule of law begins when man steps into the place previously held by God" (p. 16; footnote omitted) and that this happened for us with the birth of the nation.

He could use a dose of forgetting; he has the American Revolution, and revolution in general, too much on the brain. He calls revolution "the source and underlying truth of law" (p. 121); "without revolution, law does not begin" (p. 69). That is absurd. The concept of the rule of law, in approximately the form in which it is held in the United States today, was clearly articulated by Aristotle (who, unlike Plato and Socrates, is not mentioned in Kahn's book). Its core is treating like cases alike and abstracting from the personal qualities of the parties to a legal dispute (justice as the blind goddess). Kahn sometimes discusses the rule of law in these terms—for example, he says that "virtuous citizens are not entitled to win their lawsuits on the basis of character alone" (p. 79). But he thinks the concept of the rule of law some American specialty; actually it is the common property of all Western (and today of many non-Western) societies, notably England, which does not have a written constitution, just as Athens in the fourth century B.C., when Aristotle wrote, did not have a written constitution.

Kahn calls Senate confirmation hearings for federal judges an important "rite of transformation" of the private citizen into "a representation of the law" (pp. 84–85), but English judges are not confirmed, let alone after public hearings. Kahn calls the tomb of the unknown soldier a substitute for a monument to the king; in America "everyone is king," so "each citizen can become a focal point through which the whole of the state appears" (p. 62). But the tomb of the unknown soldier is (I believe) an English invention, motivated by the number of unidentifiable dead in the First World War, an invention we copied; and England was and is a monarchy. Americans do place a heavier emphasis on their legal rights than most other peoples. But this may simply reflect the fact that the United States is such a heterogeneous society that law must do the work that in other societies is done by informal norms enforced by static, homogenous local communities and close-knit families.

Kahn commits an illuminating error when he says that the U.S. Supreme Court "has the ultimate authority to say what the law is" (p. 50), the Court being the bridge between the nation's origins and the nation's laws, which Kahn thinks must always be tethered to the Revolution and Constitution. The Supreme Court does not have the ultimate authority to say what the law is. It has, though even this is contested in some quarters, the ultimate authority to say only what *federal* law is. Most American law is still state law, and ultimate authority to pronounce on state law lies with the supreme court of each state. These courts were not ordained by and do not owe their authority to the Constitution. So Kahn himself, champion though he is of studying law from an external perspective, cannot get outside his internal perspective as a constitutional lawyer. The book is provincial in other ways as well. For example, in arguing that liberal theory leads inexorably to world government, Kahn ignores what liberal philosophers from Kant to Rawls have actually said about the importance of the nation state to liberalism.

Law is a practice in which texts figure largely; myths and fictions are the stock in trade of literary critics; and there is a thriving interdisciplinary movement (not mentioned by Kahn) called "law and literature." One might have expected Kahn to examine the rule of law under the lens of literature or rhetoric. He does not, though there are places in the book where he seems on the verge of doing so, as when he describes the invalidation of legislation by judicial interpretation of the Constitution as a species of "irony" because the legislation is rendered nonlaw, "merely an ironic play at law" (p. 76), by the decision. Or when he says that courts, again when invalidating legislation on constitutional grounds, "juxtapose the permanent will of the popular sovereign, expressed in the act of constitutional ratification, to the mere popular will of a transient legislative majority" (p. 13), and thus speak with the voice of "the People" (p. 79).

Kahn's touch in his glancing encounters with law's rhetoric is not sure, as when he refers to Justice Holmes as having "capture[d] for himself the paradigmatic image of the American judge" (p. 101). Holmes is noteworthy for having written in what I have called (following Robert Penn Warren) the "impure" style—the style of "straight talk" that eschews the hieratic impersonal tone and inflated political-theoretic fictions that Kahn considers inherent in the culture of the rule of law.[19] And while Kahn is correct that some judges use "the first person plural to establish identity over the Court's entire past," as when they say "'In such and such a case, *we* held . . .'" (p. 113; emphasis in original)—perhaps before the writer was born—other judges shudder at the usage. The judicial "we" does not *always* refer "to a single, transgenerational, communal self" (id.).

Kahn does not inquire whether the traditional rule-of-law rhetoric that indeed permeates lawspeak is an organic, or as I suspect an accidental and readily dispensable, element of our legal ideology. The web of beliefs that for Kahn is constitutive of the rule of law may be a rhetorical dress that we could discard without damaging the law. Most Americans, and indeed most legal professionals in their reflective moments, understand that the law plays an essentially pragmatic role in social governance. They understand that its success in this role depends on a degree of adherence to such rule of law virtues as impartiality, impersonality, publicity, and predictability. But they don't think of their commitment to the rule of law as something that "defines" themselves as Americans. They do not consider the Revolution, the Constitution, or the Supreme Court central in their lives. They would find

19. Richard A. Posner, *Law and Literature* 288–293 (rev. and enlarged ed. 1998).

unintelligible the Kahn-like statement by three Supreme Court Justices that Americans' "belief in themselves" as "people who aspire to
live according to the rule of law" is "not readily separable from their
understanding of the Supreme Court."[20] Americans' identity is not
constituted by the ideology of the rule of law in the way in which the
identity of a deeply religious person might be constituted by his creed.
Law is not our civic religion; freedom, work, wealth, and religion are.
The inflatedness of traditional judicial rhetoric is matched in Kahn's
book by an inflation of the symbolic and psychological aspects of a law
and a deflation of its functional aspects. The rule of law is both more
and less than myth.

20. Planned Parenthood of Southeastern Pennsylvania v. Casey, 505 U.S. 833, 868 (1992).

~ 6

Savigny, Holmes, and the Law and Economics of Possession

$\mathcal{F}$RIEDRICH CARL VON SAVIGNY (1779–1862), whom I mentioned in passing in Chapter 4, was the founder of the historical school of jurisprudence, and as such claims attention in a discussion of the historical approach to law. He was long regarded as one of the most important figures in the history of legal thought, and throughout the nineteenth century enjoyed enormous international prestige. Today, in America at any rate, he is barely a name.[1] Despite my criticisms in previous chapters of historicism in law, I believe that we do lose something when we forget our intellectual ancestors so thoroughly. I shall try to demonstrate this by approaching Savigny from the direction of Oliver Wendell Holmes's book *The Common Law*, which criticizes the influential theory of possession expounded in Savigny's 1803 book *Das Recht des Besitzes* and in doing so paves the way for a modern economic analysis of possession. I focus on Savigny's theory of possession, rather than on any of the other fields of law that he discussed, because it is the only part of his work that Holmes discusses other than in passing. The disagreement between these two great legal thinkers over the law of possession also brings into view the question of Savigny's method, which is quintessentially historicist and the contribution for which he is (or,

---

1. As of November 1999, the *Social Sciences Citation Index* recorded only 180 journal citations to Savigny since 1972, an average of only about six a year.

more accurately, was) famous. Savigny and Holmes had not only or mainly different theories of possession; they had different conceptions of legal theory, of how to "do" law, and specifically of the proper role of history in law.

I said that Savigny's prestige in the nineteenth century was international and immense and now I add that this was as true in the Anglo-American legal world as it was elsewhere. The reason both for his former celebrity and for his present obscurity has to do with his "take" on law, which can be summarized in the following connected propositions and provides the background to Holmes's disagreements with him:[2]

1. It is a mistake to try to codify a nation's laws; codification stunts and distorts the growth of law. It is especially foolish to borrow another nation's code, and thus for a German state to borrow the *Code Napoléon*.[3]

2. The authentic law of every nation, including the Germany of Savigny's time, a cultural rather than a political entity, is the law that has evolved from the nation's aboriginal "folk spirit" (*Volksgeist*) or "common consciousness of the people" (*der allgemeine Volksbewusstein*) in much the same way that a nation's language is an organic development from ancient origins rather than the product of rational design, of a "code."[4]

---

2. For helpful discussions in English of Savigny's approach to law, see John P. Dawson, *The Oracles of the Law* 450–458 (1968); William Ewald, "Comparative Jurisprudence (I): What Was It Like to Try a Rat?" 143 *University of Pennsylvania Law Review* 1889, 2012–2043 (1995); Susan Gaylord Gale, "A Very German Legal Science: Savigny and the Historical School," 18 *Stanford Journal of International Law* 123 (1982); Herrmann Kantorowicz, "Savigny and the Historical School of Law," 1937 *Law Quarterly Review* 326; Edwin W. Patterson, "Historical and Evolutionary Theories of Law," 51 *Columbia Law Review* 681, 686–690 (1951); Mathias Reimann, "Nineteenth Century German Legal Science," 31 *Boston College Law Review* 837, 851–858 (1990); James Q. Whitman, *The Legacy of Roman Law in the German Romantic Era: Historical Vision and Legal Change* (1990); "Savigny in Modern Comparative Perspective" (Symposium Issue), 37 *American Journal of Comparative Law* 1 (1989). For a brief biography, see James E. G. de Montmorency, "Friedrich Carl von Savigny," in *Great Jurists of the World* 561 (John Macdonell and Edward Manson eds. 1914).

3. See Friedrich Carl von Savigny, *On the Vocation of Our Age for Legislation and Jurisprudence* (Abraham Hayward trans. 1831).

4. Id., ch. 2; Friedrich Carl von Savigny, *System of the Modern Roman Law*, vol. 1, pp. 12–17 (William Holloway trans. 1867). A computer language is an example of a language created by the application of rational principles rather than organically evolved. Esperanto is an intermediate example. Savigny's organicist conception of law has antecedents in Montesquieu and Burke, as argued in Peter Stein, *Legal Evolution: The Story of an Idea* 57–59 (1980).

3. To recover the authentic law, therefore, requires historical study. The focus of study should be Roman law. It is the common law (in the sense of the nonlegislated law) of Europe,[5] and its principles are thus the *Ur* law of Germany. The task of legal theory is to recover those principles and discard later accretions not necessitated by present conditions, the later accretions being for the most part barnacles.

4. Once the original Roman principles are grasped in their purity, the resolution of legal disputes should proceed by deduction. Legal analysis properly is deductive ("formalist") rather than inductive, casuistic, social scientific, or political. Granted that the Roman jurists of the creative period of Roman law were themselves casuists, the principles that guided their work have now to be extracted and made the foundation of a logical system of legal doctrine.[6] Savigny's own analogy of law to language is suggestive of formalism; language is a system of rules that you can't get away with violating by invoking social policies.

5. The leading role in formulating the law should be played not by legislators or judges but by law professors,[7] who alone have the time, training, and aptitudes necessary for the recovery of the law's authentic principles and the adaptation of those principles to modern needs. Universities are the supreme court of German private law.

It is easy to see why only the first of these propositions would resonate with American lawyers and jurists in the nineteenth century and why none would today. And so an initial question is why Savigny was highly regarded by American legal thinkers in the nineteenth century. Part of the answer is the admiration that educated Americans felt then for German universities, which were the best in the world. Part is the nationalistic character of Savigny's conception of law (a nationalism

5. Savigny, note 4 above, vol. 1, p. 3. Unless otherwise indicated, however, I shall use the term "common law" to refer to the Anglo-American common law.

6. "The German Romanists [including Savigny] were not interested in tracing the way in which Roman law had been adapted to serve the needs of contemporary society . . . They wanted to reveal the inherent theoretical structure that was implicit in the [Roman] texts." Peter Stein, *Roman Law in European History* 119 (1999).

7. See Savigny, note 4 above, vol. 1, pp. 36–40; Savigny, note 3 above, at 149–151. Savigny was himself a law professor, first at Marburg, where he wrote his treatise on possession (it was his doctoral thesis), and then at Berlin, where until the Revolution of 1848 he occupied high judicial and other posts in the Prussian government while continuing as an academic. His political conservatism led to his removal from his governmental posts when, in the wake of the failed but frightening revolution, the Prussian king decided to give his government a more liberal appearance.

blurred, however, by the transnational character of Roman law); the nineteenth century, especially its second half, witnessed the rapid growth of nationalism in both countries. His appeal to American lawyers may also have been due to the fact that he academified or "scientized" law.[8] At a time when the academic study of law in America was in a primitive state, this move was bound to be welcome to law professors and other legal intellectuals regardless of the applicability of his specific methods and results to American law. Savigny placed at the forefront of legal reform the need to achieve an academic or theoretical understanding of law by historical research, a mission more congenial to law's theoreticians than to its practitioners. He laid out an ambitious research program calculated to keep squads of professors busy for many years. But when the program was completed and Roman law well understood, the historical school, as the approach of Savigny and his epigones came to be known, faded. It no longer provided a research program, the sine qua non of a successful school of academic thought.

Now that American universities have caught up with their European counterparts and now that law has become a secure part of university education and research, Savigny's project of making law a respectable academic subject—indeed, in remaking it into "legal science" (*Rechtswissenschaft*)—has become irrelevant to the American legal community. That leaves the five propositions I listed earlier, none of which is especially relevant to American concerns. Codification is a nonissue in modern American law. Our law is too vast in extent and varied in content, the grip of the case law system too tight, for our law to be brought under the rule of a single code or even a handful of like codes. Codification has proceeded, as it could only proceed, piecemeal—we have a federal criminal code, federal rules of civil and criminal procedure and of evidence, a Bankruptcy Code, and a Uniform Commercial Code governing sales, negotiable instruments, secured transactions, and other commercial subjects, and a number of other codes as well. There is no felt need to codify core common law subjects, such as torts, contracts (though the Uniform Commercial Code codifies a portion of the field of contracts), agency, and property (except intellectual property). Savigny's opposition to codification has no present relevance even in

8. This ground of admiration for Savigny is explicit in Joseph H. Beale, Jr., "The Development of Jurisprudence during the Past Century," 18 *Harvard Law Review* 271, 283 (1905).

Germany, which in defiance of Savigny's followers adopted a comprehensive code in 1900—a code that, incidentally, jettisoned many of his
key ideas about possession.

As for the *Volksgeist*, such a concept can have little significance for a
nation such as the United States, a nation of immigrants from many
different countries. The nation's founders frayed the threads that
bound it to the *Ur* law, which was English, by splitting with Great Britain, the "mother" country. In any event, for us the *Ur* law was never
Roman law. Britain began moving away from Roman law early in its
post-Roman history.[9] There are traces of Roman law in American legal
thought,[10] not least in the law of possession. But we have become oblivious to them; Roman law is a subject virtually unstudied in American
law schools. Savigny's project of recovering the legal principles that
are authentically in tune with the *Volksgeist* by studying the history of
Roman law is incomprehensible to all but a tiny handful of modern
American legal thinkers.[11] This incomprehension, moreover, is part of
a larger "presentist" orientation, very much in the American grain, that
marginalizes historical inquiry as a method of assisting in the solution
of current problems and in providing guidance for the future. Nothing earlier than the Constitution is authoritative for most American
lawyers and judges. We have seen that when American lawyers and
judges, and even law professors, invoke history, it is usually for rhetorical effect.

As for trying to deduce legal solutions from fundamental principles,
most American lawyers and jurists deride that as "formalism." We are
casuists and pragmatists, proceeding in the decision of actual cases and
in the formulation of our legal generalizations from the bottom up
rather than from the top down, that is, proceeding from the facts of
specific disputes and from specific social policies, often of a utilitarian
cast, rather than from general principles whether historically or other-

9. Though it has been argued that "Roman law itself is closer to the common law than is
any modern codified system based on Roman law." Peter Stein, "Roman Law and English Jurisprudence Yesterday and Today," in Stein, *The Character and Influence of the Roman Civil
Law: Historical Essays* 151, 165 (1988).

10. See, for example, "The Attraction of the Civil Law in Post-Revolutionary America," in
Stein, note 9 above, at 411.

11. Among influential writers on American law at the present time, only Richard Epstein
regularly harks back to Roman law for ideas. See, for example, Richard A. Epstein, *Principles
for a Free Society: Reconciling Individual Liberty with the Common Good* 258–259 (1998).

wise derived. Our legal system remains a case law system, one administered by judges who place more weight on precedent and on their own intuitions of policy than on the treatises of law professors. Indeed, in recent years those professors, especially at the most prestigious universities, have grown ever farther apart from the practical side of the profession. The idea of appealing a judicial decision to a law school— an actual practice in Savigny's time and place—is unthinkable in our system.

America's rejection of Savigny was announced in 1881 by Oliver Wendell Holmes, Jr. The two chapters in *The Common Law* that deal with possession[12] are the two in which Holmes discusses "German theories" of law, and I have not discovered a sustained discussion of German legal theory anywhere else in Holmes's *oeuvre*. The German theoretician whom Holmes discusses most in those lectures is Savigny. Holmes groups him with other German thinkers, including Kant and Hegel, as arguing that in the eyes of the law possession requires that the would-be possessor intend to hold the property as an owner rather than recognizing the superior title of another person, so that in providing possessory remedies to lessees, bailees, and others who lack such an intention, modern law sacrifices principle to convenience. Holmes responds that he

> cannot see what is left of a principle which avows itself inconsistent with convenience and the actual course of legislation. The first call of a theory of law is that it should fit the facts. It must explain the observed course of legislation. And as it is pretty certain that men will make laws which seem to them convenient without troubling themselves very much what principles are encountered by their legislation, a principle which defies convenience is likely to wait some time before it finds itself permanently realized.[13]

And yet *The Common Law* could be thought—has in fact been thought—a project much like Savigny's of "deriving fundamental principles to guide the present from a study of the past."[14] One of Holmes's

12. Lecture V ("The Bailee at Common Law") and Lecture VI ("Possession and Ownership").

13. Oliver Wendell Holmes, Jr., *The Common Law* 211 (1881); see also id at 207, 218–219 (1881).

14. G. Edward White, *Justice Oliver Wendell Holmes: Law and the Inner Self* 193 (1993).

criticisms of the German theorists, signally including Savigny, is that they "have known no other system than the Roman,"[15] and he sets out to prove that the Anglo-American law of possession derives not from Roman law but rather from pre-Roman German law. Thus, just like Savigny and the other jurists of the historical school, Holmes uses historical inquiry to excavate and refine the principles of law. The focus of the inquiry is different—Roman in Savigny's case, Germanic (ironically) in Holmes's—and the principles recovered by historical inquiry are also different, as we are about to see. But these seem almost details. Holmes's very challenge to the "universal authority" of Savigny's theory of possession[16] could be thought a tacit endorsement of the concept of the *Volksgeist:* a different *Volk* can be expected to have a different *Geist.* Which means that Holmes shared with Savigny a rejection of natural law; law cannot be excogitated from a universal moral code. And the erudition of *The Common Law,* which is an academic work rather than a handbook for practitioners, marks it as a contribution to *Rechtswissenschaft.*[17] Savigny's influence on Henry Maine has been noted,[18] and Maine's *Ancient Law* (1861) influenced Holmes. Holmes had, therefore, a (characteristically unacknowledged) debt to Savigny.[19]

But the differences between the approaches of the two are profound. Although Savigny's treatise is entitled "The Law of Possession," its actual subject, except for its brief last section devoted mainly to ecclesiastical law, is the *Roman* law of possession. Not until a third of the way through the treatise is the possibility of a discrepancy between Roman and modern law, and the consequent need of modifying the former to make it serviceable for the present day, acknowledged.[20] But the modifications discussed are minor. This is remarkable. Savigny was writing in the nineteenth century. Justinian had lived in the sixth century, and the legal rules collected under his auspices were most of them much older. But Savigny believed that the principles of ancient law were ser-

---

15. Holmes, note 13 above, at 168.

16. Id. at 206.

17. Holmes was appointed a professor of the Harvard Law School on the strength of *The Common Law.*

18. Stein, note 4 above, at 89–90.

19. White, note 14 above, at 149.

20. "If a theory of Possession lays claims to be of any use in practice, it must subjoin to the views of the Roman lawyers those modifications under which the above views obtain practical validity amongst us at the present day." *Von Savigny's Treatise on Possession, Sixth Edition* 134 (Erskine Perry ed. 1848).

viceable in modernity, and so his work was largely completed when he discovered those principles. Holmes was interested in the process of change itself, in how the ancient principles had evolved into a greatly altered body of modern law. The motor of evolution was convenience, or policy. "The substance of the law at any given time pretty nearly corresponds, so far as it goes, with what is then understood to be convenient; but its form and machinery, and the degree to which it is able to work out desired results, depend very much upon its past . . . The old form receives a new content, and in time even the form modifies itself to fit the meaning which it has received."[21] Pragmatic and forward-looking, Holmes was content with this process; he had no desire to return the law to an earlier period of its development.

The difference between Savigny and Holmes with regard to history is obscured by the fact that the concept of possession existed in something like its modern form in ancient law; it is not an artifact of modernity. It is undoubtedly the earliest form or precursor of property, itself an ancient notion. The "problem" of possession, the source of its enduring fascination as much to the Romans, Savigny, and Holmes as to ourselves, is precisely its relation to property. On the one hand, possession seems an incident of property, or ownership; on the other hand, nonowners frequently are "in possession" of land or other things of value and owners are frequently out of possession. Moreover, the law in Roman times as today granted remedies to possessors as well as to owners, and sometimes to possessors against owners (as in the acquisition of title by prescription, that is, by lapse of time) and to owners against possessors. Possessory remedies were often simpler than ownership remedies; this was as true of the Roman interdicts as of the English action in ejectment—a formally possessory action used commonly to prove title to real property—or trover, the counterpart to ejectment for personal property. So even owners might seek the former. Sorting out these relations was and remains a challenging intellectual exercise.

For Savigny, possession was the conjunction of two facts: physical power over a thing, and an intention to own it in the sense, factual rather than legal, of being allowed to use it, with no limitation of time, exclusively for your own benefit (*animus domini*). If you had that power and that intention, you had possession. (And so a thief could obtain

21. Holmes, note 13 above, at 1–2, 5.

possession.) This would entitle you to a remedy against anyone who interfered with your possession unless he had a claim to possession that the law regarded as superior, which the owner might (if the possessor was not the owner) or might not.

From this definition much followed. Consider the first element, power. If you buy goods that are in a locked warehouse, you do not obtain possession in Savigny's sense until you get the keys. You possess your domestic animals, because they're in your physical power. But you do not possess wild animals until you trap or kill them unless the animal has *animus revertendi*, that is, the habit of returning, which makes him like a domestic animal (the common law makes the same distinction); it's as if he were on a long leash.

The implication of the power component of Savigny's definition is that possession, as distinct from use, which is often shared, can never be joint. If you can act with reference to a thing only with the concurrence of someone else, it follows that you don't have physical dominion. A further implication is that separate parts of a whole cannot be separately possessed: the house and the soil it rests on, the arm and head of a statue, a carriage and its wheel, two stories of the same house. In the case of land, however, because it is divisible without destroying an organic unity (boundaries are arbitrary), Savigny is willing to allow shared possession. To have a one-third interest in a parcel of land is enough like owning a smaller parcel carved out from the larger one to be treated the same way, since if the land were to be divided into three separate parcels, each owner would have exclusive control over his parcel. Likewise, buried treasure is severable from the land above it because it can be removed without *necessarily* disturbing the land—the clearest case would be if the treasure was found by a contractor whom the landowner had hired to dig a well. The buried treasure and the land are not an organic unity, like the parts of the statue or the house and the land that the house is sitting on. Living before the age of the trailer park, Savigny evidently could not imagine moving a house.

The notion of physical power as a condition of possession is problematic in the case of land. One does not take possession of land in the same sense in which one might take possession of a wad of cash, a carriage, or even a house, unless one fences the land, which Savigny does not require as a condition of possession. All he requires is *presence* on the land (conjoined, of course, with *animus domini*). But because presence is an ambiguous sign of taking control, the would-be possessor must give notice of his possessory intent (his "adverse possession," as we would say) if someone else already possesses the land.

Once possession is obtained, the exertion of physical power that was necessary to obtaining it often will cease. You don't remain on your land all the time, and in fact you may have leased it to someone else and so are never there; and you leave your carriage on the street, where it is out of your control. Savigny does not treat these cases as cases of abandonment, which would deprive the owner of his possessory rights and remedies. But he requires, for possession to continue, that "there must always be a possibility of *reproducing* the immediate condition which has been described as the foundation of acquisition."[22] He makes an exception, as already noted, for land, where possession cannot be lost until the existing possessor is notified that someone is seeking to wrest possession from him. But someone who loses a good ceases to possess it; the finder obtains possession, provided that he intends to keep it for his own use rather than return it to the owner or the previous possessor.

The second element of Savigny's definition of possession—the requirement of *animus domini*—also has important and sometimes startling implications. Two in particular require note. The first is that a bailee, tenant, or other custodian or occupier who has, as is usually the case of such holders, no intention of becoming the owner cannot be said to possess the thing held or occupied. The second implication is that you cannot possess something you don't realize you control, because then the *animus domini* is missing.

The idea that a tenant does not possess the leased premises seems both odd and impractical. Savigny explains that the tenant can always call on his landlord to defend the tenant's rights. But this seems roundabout,[23] as well as inconsistent with Savigny's recognition that a "hirer" (someone who has the use of a thing by virtue of a contract with the

22. *Von Savigny's Treatise on Possession*, note 20 above, at 265 (emphasis in original).

23. The landlord might not care, for example, whether the tenant was dispossessed, however wrongfully, by a creditor who promised to continue paying the rent. The tenant would have to sue the landlord for the cost of being dispossessed and the landlord presumably would then turn around and sue the creditor as the primary wrongdoer. This is a circuitous method of dealing with wrongful dispossession—unless the tenant hasn't taken possession yet. Under the so-called English rule, if when the lease begins the previous tenant remains in possession the landlord has a duty to oust him.

owner), a pledge creditor (a lender who holds the borrower's property as a kind of hostage to ensure repayment), and a "fructuary" (someone who has a right to the fruits or other income of land or goods) all have a right of possession if the right is granted to them by the owner.

Such grants confer what Savigny calls derivative possession. He regards such cases as anomalous because the derivative possessor lacks *animus domini*, but he is willing to accept "an anomaly founded on practical grounds,"[24] most clearly in the case of the pledge creditor: if the borrower could dispossess the creditor, the purpose of the pledge would be defeated. In the case of the hirer or the fructuary, Savigny argues that after creating such a relationship the owner might have sold the land to someone not interested in coming to the rescue of the person in possession. In that event, requiring that person—the hirer or fructuary—to appeal to the owner for help would be unavailing. So these holders are given possessory remedies. The reasoning is sound but seems equally applicable to tenancy. Still, it shows Savigny willing to allow, to some extent anyway, practical need to trump *elegantia juris* or even fidelity to Roman legal principles. He acknowledges explicitly that "merely theoretic considerations must give way to the actual wants of daily life."[25]

His emphasis on the acquisition of rights by prescription was apparently intended to foster the gradual extinction of feudal rights. Thus he was, in his own way, an agrarian reformer.[26] Emphasis on possession as the basis of property rights—Savigny's consistent emphasis—has itself unmistakable antifeudal overtones because the distinctively feudal rights (to services and support) are nonpossessory. And because possession, especially in Savigny's conception of it, is active, exertional, his emphasis on it could be taken as an implicit criticism of a rentier economy based on inherited wealth. But the theme of social reform is a muted one in Savigny's treatise. He is reluctant to allow fidelity to legal principle to be overridden by pragmatic considerations, for "even this

24. *Von Savigny's Treatise on Possession*, note 20 above, at 95. See also id. at 91.

25. Id. at 404.

26. Whitman, note 2 above, at 183–186; Stein, note 6 above, at 119–120. The acquisition of rights by passage of time implies their possible extinction by passage of time; and when Savigny wrote *Das Recht des Besitzes* many feudal obligations had fallen into disuse, especially in the wake of the French incursions into Germany that followed the French Revolution. See id., ch. 5.

latter practical interest [that is, the actual wants of daily life] undoubtedly gains nothing by a procedure . . . [that] renders all fixed principles
uncertain."[27]

⌣ WHEN WE TURN to the chapters on possession in *The Common Law* we may at first think the differences between Holmes and
Savigny largely technical, and wonder therefore at Holmes's hostility
toward the German school. Holmes agrees with Savigny that possession requires physical power over the object possessed (and more
power to gain than to continue in possession), conjoined with a certain
intent. Only for Holmes the requisite intent is merely the intent to exclude others (except the owner, unless the owner has transferred possession) from interfering with one's use. This explains the common law
right of the bailee to obtain a possessory remedy against someone who
wrongfully deprives him of the bailed good. Holmes discusses a case in
which the plaintiff had entrusted a safe to the defendant to sell for him.
The defendant found some banknotes, evidently the plaintiff's, in a
crevice in the safe. The plaintiff demanded the money back. Holmes
argues that he was entitled to get it back; contrary to Savigny's view, the
plaintiff had not abandoned the notes, even though, being unaware of
them (or at least of their presence in the safe), he could not be said to
have *animus domini* with regard to them. In short, Holmes severs possession from ownership; the former, and the rights that go with it, need
have nothing to do with any claim of ownership.

There are other differences between Holmes's theory of possession
on the one hand and that of Savigny and his followers on the other—
differences greater, incidentally, than the differences between the actual German and Anglo-American law of possession in the nineteenth
century and especially today.[28] Notably, Holmes rejects Savigny's claim
that the possibility of reproducing the physical power used to obtain
possession is a condition of retaining it. He gives the example of a person who has left a purse of gold in his country house and is now a hundred miles away, in prison, and "the only person within twenty miles
[of the house] is a thoroughly equipped burglar at his front door, who
has seen the purse through a window and who intends forthwith to en-

27. *Von Savigny's Treatise on Possession*, note 20 above, at 404.
28. See James Gordley and Ugo Mattei, "Protecting Possession," 44 *American Journal of
Comparative Law* 293 (1996).

ter and take it."[29] Holmes thinks it weird to regard the owner of the purse as losing possession to the burglar before the burglar takes the purse. But he thinks this result is entailed by Savigny's theory because the owner has lost the ability to reproduce the exercise of physical power that got him the purse in the first place (Holmes assumes that he had found it) and the burglar has acquired the ability to exercise exclusive control over it.

Holmes's definition of possession encounters anomalies, just like Savigny's. For example, at common law, which is to Holmes as Roman law is to Savigny—the body of principles that is to be reclaimed, clarified, purified, and expounded—an employee who steals his employer's goods is a thief. That is, he is treated as having taken the goods from the employer's possession, even though, under Holmes's definition of possession, the employee had possession because he had physical dominion over them coupled with the intent to exclude all others from using them. (A similar example that he discusses is that of a tavern customer who steals the plate on which the food is served him.) Holmes considers this rule a pure historical vestige, reflecting the fact that slaves, the historical antecedents of employees, had no legal standing and so could not be regarded as possessors.

So far there is nothing to suggest a methodological cleavage between Savigny and Holmes. That cleavage is to be found not in particular rules and outcomes but in a difference in attitudes toward theory and history. Holmes does not challenge Savigny's or other German jurists' interpretations of Roman law. But he does not believe that Roman law is the actual source of German legal theory, and in particular of Savigny's theory of possession. He thinks that the source is philosophy, particularly the philosophy of Kant and Hegel (though in fact Savigny was hostile to Hegel's legal theory).[30] According to that philosophy, Holmes tells us, "possession is to be protected because a man by taking possession of an object has brought it within the sphere of his will . . . Possession is the objective realization of free will."[31] The idea that *animus domini* is an element of possession—the idea that principally distinguishes Savigny's theory of possession from Holmes's at the oper-

29. Holmes, note 13 above, at 237.

30. The identification of Savigny with Kant rests on stronger grounds. See Ewald, note 2 above, at 1935–1938.

31. Holmes, note 13 above, at 207.

ational level—thus takes its origin, in Holmes's view, not from Roman law (though Holmes thought it consistent with that law) and not from convenience, policy, or "the actual wants of daily life," but instead from German ethical philosophy.[32]

For Holmes, this was a tainted origin. He was a moral skeptic who despised ethical philosophy and believed that a clear understanding of law required a clean separation between legal and moral duty and between legal and moral terminology. He may have misunderstood Savigny. The concept of the *Volksgeist* (which does not appear in the treatise on possession, however) expresses a historical rather than a rationalistic conception of law and to that extent should have been congenial to Holmes—who instead repeatedly denounces Savigny and his followers for their "universalist" pretensions.[33] But the attitudes of the two men toward history are indeed crucially different, almost opposite. Savigny's is reverential; legal history has a "holier duty to perform" than merely "guard[ing] our minds against the narrowing influence of the present," and that is to keep up "a lively connection with the primitive state of the people . . . The loss of this connection must take away from every people the best part of its spiritual life."[34] Holmes's attitude toward history, like Nietzsche's, is critical. For Savigny, the best legal thinkers were the Roman jurists, and the task of modern law is to recover the principles that animated Roman legal thought. For Holmes, the best legal thought is modern, because only a modern thinker can come to grips with modern problems. History provides a repertoire of concepts and procedures that can be drawn upon to deal with modern problems. To that extent it is a resource and a help. But it is also a drag, because of the legal profession's methodological conservatism, which by positing a duty of continuity with the past retards adaptation to the needs of the present. Holmes's dismissing as a historical vestige the rule that an employee does not "possess" goods that his employer entrusts to him is thus a characteristic move for Holmes. He is a legal paleontologist, identifying doctrines and practices that exist in modern law not because they are functional but because the struggle for survival that powers evolution has somehow failed to weed them out.

If, moreover, as Holmes emphasizes, "the proximate ground of law

32. "Roman law comes in to fortify principle with precedent." Id. at 209.
33. Id. at 167–168, 206.
34. Savigny, note 3 above, at 136.

must be empirical," that is, if "law, being a practical thing, must found itself on actual forces,"[35] we can expect variations in legal rules that cannot be referred to any general principle. Holmes illustrates with the different rules known to him for obtaining legal possession of whales. Under one rule, if the first whaler to strike the whale with his harpoon cannot hold on, he has no right to the whale if it is eventually killed by another; under another rule, he is entitled to half the whale; and under another to the whole provided that the point of the harpoon remains in the whale, even though the line has been cut. Notice that the latter two rules are exceptions to the common law principle, which is similar to the Roman law principle expounded by Savigny, that to gain possession of a wild animal you must actually capture it.

Although Holmes makes clear his belief that law should be shaped to serve the practical needs of the present, he does not take the next step; he does not evaluate particular rules and decisions by that criterion. Like Savigny, he focuses on the inner logic of the law of possession rather than on its conformity to social need. The only explanation that he gives for his crucial move of rejecting the requirement of *animus domini* in favor of requiring only an intent to exclude is that legal duties precede legal rights. The law of possession creates a duty not to interfere with the possessor's exclusive use of the thing possessed; the duty gives rise to a corresponding right to enjoin or otherwise prevent, or obtain redress for, such interference; therefore the only intent required of a possessor is the intent to repel such interference.[36] The "therefore" does not follow. There is nothing illogical about confining possessory remedies to people who intend to retain possession against all the world, whether or not it is sensible or consistent with Anglo-American law.

∼ WHAT HOLMES LACKED was a social theory to take the place of the kind of internal legal theory that he denigrated in the German theorists. We now have that theory; it is called economics.

Unless a valuable resource is subject to a right of exclusive use, control, and benefit, incentives to invest in the production of valuable goods will be suboptimal; for example, the owner of farmland will have

35. Holmes, note 13 above, at 213.
36. See id. at 219–220.

no assurance that he will be able to reap where has has sown.[37] Some resources, moreover, will be overused—for example, a pasture owned in common. None of the owners of the cattle pastured on it will consider the cost that their use imposes on each other by reducing the amount of forage. Efficiency requires property rights.[38]

Two polar systems of property rights can be imagined: ownership only in accordance with a system of paper titles, and ownership only by physical possession. Either would involve serious inefficiencies. A universal system of paper titles assumes that everything is already owned[39] and permits transfers only by formal conveyance (for example, the delivery of a deed), and so is helpless to deal with problems of acquisition of property that is unowned, whether because it was never owned or because it has been abandoned. Such a system would also leave undefined the status of nonowners who nevertheless have the exclusive use of property, such as tenants. And it would be helpless to deal with the inevitable mistakes to which a system of paper rights gives rise. The other polar regime, in which rights to the exclusive use of property are made to depend on physical control of the property, entails heavy investments in the maintenance of such control. It also makes no provision for rights to future as distinct from present use. An example is the appropriation system of water rights that is in force in the western states of the United States, under which one acquires a right to water by possessing, that is, using it (in irrigation, for example). This system encourages wasteful present use as a method of staking a claim to the future use of the water. The future use may be sufficiently valuable to the possessor to make the present wasteful expenditure worthwhile from his standpoint even though a system of paper rights might be more efficient from an overall social standpoint.

Thus an efficient legal regime of property rights is likely to be a mixed system, combining paper rights with possessory rights. We need to specify the efficient combination and compare it with the combina-

37. This is not a modern insight; it was well known to Hobbes and Blackstone, among many others.

38. Richard A. Posner, *Economic Analysis of Law* 36–37 (5th ed. 1998). On the economics of possession generally, see Richard A. Epstein, "Possession," in *The New Palgrave Dictionary of Economics and the Law*, vol. 3, p. 62 (Peter Newman ed. 1998); see also Dean Lueck, "First Possession," in id., vol. 2, p. 132.

39. An exception—the acquisition of title by a grant—is discussed below.

tion actually found in the legal system. We can begin with the question whether *unowned* property should be obtainable only by possession or also by grant or some other nonpossessory method. The general answer is, only by possession. Suppose a new, and to simplify analysis an uninhabited, continent were discovered. Would it be efficient to give the discoverer title to the entire continent before he had taken possession of it in the sense of occupying all or at least most of it? Probably not. Such an enormous reward would incite an excessive investment in exploration. The explorer who discovered the continent just one day before his rivals would obtain the continent's entire value. The prospect of obtaining a value so greatly in excess of that of his actual contribution to its creation would induce him, and likewise his rivals, to invest more than the social value of the investment in the quest.[40] An even more extreme case, one that was common in the early period of European exploration of other continents, was the effort by monarchs (including the pope) to create property rights in undiscovered lands by grant.

The efficient alternative to basing ownership of previously unowned property on either discovery or a grant is to base it on possession in the sense of physical occupation.[41] This reduces the *net* reward to being first, and so alleviates the problem of excessive investment, by forcing the would-be owner to incur costs of occupation. It also tends to allocate resources to those persons best able to use them productively, for they are the people most likely to be willing to incur the costs involved

40. Suppose that the prize (the exclusive right to exploit the newly discovered continent) is worth X, and that if there were only one potential discoverer he would spend $.1X$ to discover it and this would take him t years. But there are ten potential discoverers, and if they have an equal chance of being the first discoverer each will (assuming they are not risk averse) spend up to $.1X$ in the race to be first. The aggregate expenditure will be ten times what the single potential discoverer would spend. Suppose that as a result of the race, the continent would be discovered a year earlier; given the time value of money, this would increase the value of the discovery, say to $1.1X$, but the increase ($.1X$) would fall far short of the added cost ($.9X$). The race would thus be wasteful from a social standpoint. Lueck, note 38 above, points out, however, that there may be no race if one of the contestants has much lower costs than the others, so that it is apparent from the start that if there is a contest (and the contestants have equal access to the capital markets to finance the expense of the contest) he will win. In that event, the others will forbear to compete.

41. For an analogy to trademark law, see William M. Landes and Richard A. Posner, "Trademark Law: An Economic Perspective," 30 *Journal of Law and Economics* 265, 281–282 (1987). The economic principles of possession have many applications to intellectual property, but I shall not try to discuss them here.

in possession. A discoverer who could obtain title to the entire conti-nent just by declaration or filing would promptly turn around and sell off most or all of the land, because he would not be the most efficient developer of all of it. It is more efficient to give the people who are ac-tually going to possess the land the ownership right in the first place.

Consider the whale cases discussed by Holmes. If the right to the whale went to the first whaler to stick his harpoon into the whale even if the harpoon quickly fell out (or the line broke) without slowing down the whale, we might find the ocean blanketed with amateurs good at flinging harpoons but not good at actually killing whales. This would be an example of a socially wasteful race to be the first "discoverer" of valuable property. But if instead the law gives the property right in the whale to the whaler who kills it, this may discourage cooperative activ-ity that is essential to efficient whaling, as it is not to most hunting, where the rule that ownership can be obtained only by possession pre-vails. The "half a whale" solution that Holmes discusses can be under-stood as a response to the problem of discouraging cooperation. Al-though it is a step away from a pure system of possessory rights in the direction of a claims or prospect system,[42] it is remote from a system in which exclusive rights to whales (or to a newly discovered continent, to which a newly sighted whale is economically analogous) are created by granting those rights to the first person to discover the commercial value of whaling. It shows that an optimal regime of property rights is likely to combine possessory and nonpossessory rights.

The issue of possessory rights is further illustrated by Holmes's case of the safe with hidden banknotes in it. At common law the agent hold-ing the safe for its owner does not acquire possession of the notes; un-der Roman law, according to Savigny, he does. Considered from the standpoint of economics, finding lost property is a valuable service and should be encouraged. But as with the discovery of new continents, giving the finder the entire value of the property could lead to over-investment in exploration. A further problem, which has no counter-part in the case of continental discovery, is that giving the finder of lost property its entire value may make owners overinvest in safeguarding

42. For a much richer discussion of nineteenth-century whaling norms from an economic standpoint, see Robert C. Ellickson, *Order without Law: How Neighbors Settle Disputes* 196–206 (1991).

their property. Better than giving the finder ownership is giving him a reward, the domain of the law of restitution.[43] That is also better than dividing the found property between the original owner and the finder. Unless the property is readily divisible, a division will reduce its total value (not a problem with banknotes, however), and so the parties would have to expend resources on negotiating a transfer of one party's share to the other or both parties' shares to a third party, to preserve the property's integrity.

I have been assuming that the owner of the safe owned the banknotes. Suppose he didn't. Consider a clearer example: someone leaves his wallet, containing money, at a supermarket checkout counter. A customer picks up the wallet. The owner never claims it. Should the customer be entitled to retain possession of the wallet and money, or is the supermarket (the "locus in quo," as the cases say) entitled to it? The argument for the customer is that since it was he who found it, he deserves a reward; the supermarket did nothing. But if, knowing that he will be able to keep the wallet if the owner doesn't claim it, the customer walks off with it, it is less likely to be returned to the owner than if the wallet were left to be found by a supermarket employee. For when the owner of the wallet discovers its loss, he will check in the places that he has been that day, and the search will quickly lead him back to the supermarket.

It is on this basis, which owes nothing to careful parsing of "possession," that American law has traditionally distinguished between lost and mislaid items, "lost" meaning that the owner doesn't realize the property is missing. Not realizing that it is missing he is unlikely to search for it, and so the law awards lawful possession of lost property to the finder rather than, as in the case of mislaid property, to the owner

43. See Nadalin v. Automobile Recovery Bureau, Inc., 169 F.3d 1084 (7th Cir. 1999), and cases cited there; William M. Landes and Richard A. Posner, "Salvors, Finders, Good Samaritans, and Other Rescuers: An Economic Study of Law and Altruism," 7 *Journal of Legal Studies* 83 (1978); Saul Levmore, "Explaining Restitution," 71 *Virginia Law Review* 65 (1985). A case similar to the case of the safe, and also discussed by Holmes, is where "a stick of timber comes ashore on a man's land" (presumably without his knowing it). "He thereby acquires a 'right of possession' as against an actual finder who enters for the purpose of removing it." Holmes, note 13 above, at 223 (footnote omitted). The optimal solution may be to give the finder a reward while giving the property right to the landowner—assuming the stick of timber was unowned when it washed ashore.

of the place where it is found. The distinction is fragile and much criticized.[44] Why couldn't the finder of the mislaid item be given possession on condition that he leave his name and address with the supermarket so that the owner can contact him? But the point I want to stress is simply that the concept of possession does not drive the analysis when an economic view of the issue is taken. Whom to give possession to is determined by asking which allocation of possessory rights would be most efficient.

Another objection to allowing the customer-finder to keep either lost or mislaid property that is not claimed is that his reward may greatly exceed his cost, and we have seen that excessive rewards for finding tend to attract excessive resources into the activities that generate such rewards. True, it is only ex post that the customer-finder obtains this reward; that is, it is only if the owner did not claim his property. And this means that the finder's *expected* reward may have been small, since most people who lose valuable property make an effort to recover it. But since an employee of the supermarket would probably have found the wallet shortly after the customer did, the value of the customer's finding it may have been slight—in fact negative, for the owner will have more difficulty reclaiming it from a customer than from the supermarket even if the customer is required to leave his name and address with the supermarket.

Suppose the rule is, therefore, that the supermarket has lawful possession, but the customer-finder doesn't know or doesn't care what the law is and walks off with the wallet—and then he forgets it in the next supermarket he goes into. This time an employee of the supermarket finds it and the customer returns to the supermarket and claims it. Should he, the wrongful possessor, prevail over the subsequent lawful finder, the supermarket?[45] Presumably not; depriving him of possession is the only feasible sanction for his initial wrongful act, and the prospect of such deprivation may be the only feasible deterrent against wrongful takings.

The case of the safe casts light on whether physical control, either complete or in the attenuated form specified by Savigny (the power merely to reproduce that control), should be required for the mainte-

44. See, for example, R. H. Helmholz, "Equitable Division and the Law of Finders," 52 *Fordham Law Review* 313 (1983).

45. See Jesse Dukeminier and James E. Krier, *Property* 100–103 (4th ed. 1988).

nance as well as acquisition of possession. The answer given by economics is, in general, no. Such a requirement would lead to wasteful expenditures and also discourage specialization. Imagine that a tenant were deemed the owner of the leased premises because the landlord, by virtue of the lease, loses physical control over them; that is, he cannot barge into the premises during the term of the lease. Savigny gets around this problem by denying that the tenant is ever in possession, but we saw that that is an unsatisfactory solution. Far more sensible, though heretical in Savigny's system, is to recognize the joint possession of landlord and tenant and to parcel out the right to take legal action to protect their possessory interest between them in accordance with comparative advantage in particular circumstances. I mentioned the case where the tenant has not yet taken possession. To this can be added cases in which dispossession by an intruder takes place so late in the term that the tenant has little incentive to sue; cases in which the infringement is more harmful to the landlord than to the tenant (for example if the tenant is dispossessed by a dealer in illegal drugs, who proceeds to frighten away the other tenants); and cases in which the tenant simply lacks the resources to litigate against the infringer.

Yet Savigny is right to worry about joint possession, though not because it is inconsistent with the *definition* of possession, a purely formalistic point. Transaction costs are higher if the law, rather than placing the right to the use of property in one person, requires two or more people to agree with each other on how the property is to be used. The common law deals with this problem by allowing each joint possessor to insist on the partition of the jointly possessed property, so that the property becomes reconfigured as separate parcels each controlled by only one person. Of course this won't be permitted if the partition would greatly reduce the value of the property, as in Savigny's case of the statue's arm and head being separately owned. In such cases efficiency requires a presumption that the whole object is the thing possessed.

Savigny recognizes the problematic character of requiring exertion in order to maintain a possessory right, by requiring notice as a precondition to dispossessing a landowner. Suppose a tract of land was previously unowned, unclaimed, and unoccupied, and there is no paper title to it. The first possessor is therefore the owner. But what if he is not continuously present on the land? If someone else occupies the land, is *he* the possessor? Savigny's answer, which is no, is surely correct; a contrary answer would lead to wasteful expenditures by owners on fencing and patrolling land. It is one thing to condition acquisition of title to newly found property on possession, as I argued earlier; but once title is acquired by this route, it should be enough for the maintenance of that title to record it in a public registry of deeds in order to warn away accidental trespassers. That is a cheaper method of notice than elaborate signage and fencing, let alone the kind of present, pervasive use that might reasonably be required to obtain title to *terra incognita*. It is another example of why a system of purely possessory property right would be uneconomical.

Records are not infallible, however; nor do they ordinarily record abandonment. If a new occupier of land formally owned by another makes clear that he is claiming the land and the owner does nothing to contest the claim for years, the law shifts the ownership of the land to the new occupier, who is said to have acquired ownership by "adverse possession." The requirement of adverseness (implicit in my stipulating that the new occupier "is claiming" the land) is essential. Otherwise a tenant whose lease extended for the period of years required to obtain ownership by prescription (that is, by passage of time) would, at the end of that period, have become the owner of the leased property.

The tenant's possession is not "owner-like"; the adverse possessor's is. The root difference is in the possessor's intent, which can often be inferred from such "objective" indicia as the existence of a lease, the behavior of the owner (whether itself "owner-like"), and the behavior of the possessor, for example, whether he makes permanent improvements to the property, implying that he thinks of himself as the owner. Savigny was right, it turns out, to relate possessory rights to "ownerly" intentions. But he was wrong to suppose that such intentions should *always* be required to be present for a possessory right to arise.

The economic rationale of adverse possession, conceived as a method of shifting ownership without benefit of negotiation or a paper transfer, can be made perspicuous by asking when property should be deemed abandoned, that is, returned to the common pool of unowned resources and so made available for appropriation through seizure by someone else. The economist thinks this should happen when it is likely to promote the efficient use of valuable resources. As it is undesirable in general that property should remain in the common pool, the clearest case of abandonment is when a possessor deliberately "throws away" the property, in effect voluntarily returning it to the common pool. His act signifies that the property has no value in his hands. So by deeming the property abandoned and therefore available for reappropriation by someone else, the law encourages the reallocation of the property to a higher-valued use without burdening the system with negotiation costs. Similarly, the owner who does not react to the adverse possession of his property for years is indicating that he does not value the property significantly, which is the practical economic meaning of abandonment. A less clear case of abandonment, which I have already discussed, is where the owner loses the property and makes no effort to reclaim it, or gives up on reclaiming it; but that is an unlikely occurrence with land.

When an owner actually throws away his property, this indicates that he values it at zero dollars or less and so any finder who bothers to take the property is certain to be someone who values it more. Negotiation is not required in such a case in order to certify that the appropriation of the property by the finder is indeed a value-maximizing transaction, and so the costs of negotiation would be a deadweight social cost, a waste. But adverse possession is almost always of land, which is rarely thrown away, lost, or mislaid. When transaction costs are low, market transactions are a more efficient method of moving property to its socially most valuable uses than coerced transactions are. But transaction costs can be high even when one is dealing with parcels of land. The owner may be unknown. More commonly, the exact boundaries of his property are unknown, so that the adverse possessor doesn't know that he's encroaching or the owner that his property is being encroached upon. By the time the owner wakes up and asserts his rights, evidence may have faded and the adverse possessor may have relied on a reasonable belief that he is the true owner. Thinking the property his, he may have made an investment in it that will be worthless if he loses the property to the original owner, to whom the property may be worthless, as indicated by his having slept on his rights. When there is a gross disparity in the value that the only competitors for a good attach to it, transaction costs are likely to be high as each competitor vies for the largest possible share of that value.[46] Adverse possession is a

46. Suppose the land is worth $1 million to the adverse possessor (perhaps because he is aware of mineral deposits on it) and only $10,000 to the original owner. Then at any price be-

method of correcting paper titles in settings in which market-transaction costs are high;[47] it improves rather than challenges the system of property rights.

Savigny makes the interesting suggestion that an intention to abandon property can sometimes be inferred from negligence in the use of it.[48] It would be more straightforward to say that the neglectful possessor both implies by his conduct that the property is not worth much to him and creates the impression among potential finders that the property has indeed been abandoned and is therefore fair game. Deeming the property abandoned in these circumstances becomes a method of reducing transaction costs and increasing the likelihood that the property will be shifted to a more valuable use.

Economic analysis further implies that the right of adverse possession should be confined to cases in which the adverse possessor is acting in good faith—that is, he really believes the property is his. Otherwise the doctrine would encourage coercive property transfers in settings of low transaction costs. Confined to cases in which the true owner cannot easily be identified or found or seems clearly to have abandoned the property, the doctrine fulfills a traditional function of law conceived economically, that of mimicking the market in cases in which high transaction costs either prevent the market from bringing about an efficient allocation of resources or, as in the case of abandonment, would be a pure waste.

We can see by now the close relation between (as well as the interdependence of) possession and paper titles as methods of establishing property rights, and also the historical priority of the former. Possession, just like a deed of title recorded in a public registry, is, provided it is "open and notorious," as the cases on adverse possession say, a way of notifying the world of the existence of a claim.[49] It is likely to be the only feasible way in the earliest stages of society. The fence is prior to

---

tween $10,000 and $1 million both parties will be made better off by a sale. But each will be eager to engross as much of the difference as possible, and that may make it difficult for them to agree on a price without lengthy and costly bargaining.

47. Thomas W. Merrill, "Property Rules, Liability Rules, and Adverse Possession," 79 *Northwestern University Law Review* 1122 (1985).

48. *Von Savigny's Treatise on Possession*, note 20 above, at 270–271.

49. This function of possession is emphasized in Carol M. Rose, "Possession as the Origin of Property," 52 *University of Chicago Law Review* 73 (1985).

the paper title as a method of announcing a property right. Once understood as concerned with notice, a rule requiring an exercise of physical power to obtain or maintain a possessory right can be seen to involve a trade-off between the costs of particular physical acts that communicate a claim and the benefits of clear communication. The more elaborate the required acts, the more unmistakable the communication (the more they resemble a fence), which is good because the clear public definition of property rights lowers transaction costs and tends to optimize investment; but also the more costly this form of notice becomes. The costs of the most elaborate acts of notice by possession—acts of complete, continuous, and conspicuous occupation—will often outweigh the benefits. That is why a lesser degree of active possession will suffice to maintain a property right than would be necessary to acquire it.

Consider the colorful old case of *Haslem v. Lockwood*.[50] The plaintiff had raked horse manure dropped on the public streets into heaps that he intended to cart away the next day, that being the earliest he could procure the necessary transportation. The defendant beat him to the punch. The plaintiff sued for the return of the manure and won. This is the economically correct result. The original owners of the manure, who were the owners of the horses that had dropped it, had abandoned the manure; the plaintiff had found it. He took possession of it by raking it into heaps, and the heaps were adequate notice to third parties, such as the defendant, that the manure was (no longer) abandoned. To have required the plaintiff, in order to protect his property right, to go beyond the heaping of the manure—to fence it, or watch continuously over it, or arrange in advance to have a cart in place to remove the manure as soon as it was heaped—would have increased the cost of the "transaction" by which manure worthless to the original owner became a valuable commodity, without generating offsetting benefits.

When property is stolen, it is not deemed abandoned, and the purchaser from the thief, even if wholly and reasonably ignorant of the tainted source of his possession, has no right against the original owner. This rule can be defended as reducing the gain from and hence the likely incidence of theft. But there is more to a sound economic analysis, as is brought out by the much discussed issue of property rights in

50. 37 Conn. 500 (1871).

stolen art.[51] Many works of art were stolen during World War II, which ended more than half a century ago. It can be argued that if the original owner has done nothing to try to recover the work in all that time, his title should be cut off lest the current owner be reluctant to exhibit the work for fear of alerting his dormific predecessor; the work should be deemed abandoned. Were this the rule, original owners would have an incentive to take additional precautions to prevent the theft of their art. But creating such an incentive is not the unalloyed benefit that it may seem. The cost of these precautions, which might include refusing to allow the art to be exhibited widely, must be balanced against the cost of additional efforts by the purchaser to prevent the discovery of the art, as well as the additional search costs that an original owner will incur to discover his stolen art if he is entitled to get it back even from a bona fide purchaser from the thief. If the costs in concealment by the purchaser and search by the owner, under a system in which the original owner prevails, do not greatly exceed the costs in owner precaution under a system in which the bona fide purchaser prevails, the undesirability of making stolen goods more readily marketable is likely to tip the balance against allowing the purchaser to acquire title.

The problem is general, and harks back to the safes and wallets. If we make it too easy for finders to acquire title by possession of lost or mislaid goods, we incite owners to take additional precautions to prevent their goods from being lost or mislaid. These precautions involve real costs. We need rules that will economize on them. In the case of lost works of art, or other lost property of considerable value, the optimal solution may be to restore the work to the original owner but to entitle the finder to a reward large enough to encourage the search for lost art, but not so large as to make owners excessively cautious about risking the loss of their property.

Holmes thought it anomalous, we recall, that an employee should not be deemed to possess property that his employer had entrusted to him. But the rule makes economic sense. The entrustment (like that of the dinner plate to the tavern guest) is narrowly circumscribed, with little room left for the exercise of discretion by the custodian. So if the terms of the entrustment are deliberately violated, the inference of

51. See William M. Landes and Richard A. Posner, "The Economics of Legal Disputes over the Ownership of Works of Art and Other Collectibles," in *Essays in the Economics of the Arts* 177 (Victor A. Ginsburgh and Pierre-Michel Menger eds. 1996).

deliberate wrongdoing deserving severe punishment is easily drawn. There is no economic difference between the tavern guest who steals the plate and a person who enters the tavern and steals the plate without asking to be served and thus becoming a customer, or between the Brinks driver who makes off with his employer's cash-laden armored car and the stranger who put him up to the crime.

~ IN DESCRIBING legal thinking about possession as passing through three stages in the last two centuries—the first represented by the legal theory of Savigny, the second by the legal theory of Holmes, and the third by economic theory—I risk being misunderstood to be suggesting that Savigny missed the boat, that he was doubly in error in failing to use the functionalist approach of Holmes or the economic approach that has now operationalized it. That is not my intention. It is a mistake to suppose that every modern insight or approach was always available, so that the fact that it was not discovered or applied until recently is to be ascribed to the stupidity of our ancestors compared to ourselves. Different epochs have different needs. Savigny, remember, was aware of the importance of the "actual needs of daily life" in shaping law. But the actual need of daily life that he emphasized, appropriately for his time and place, was for clear and uniform legal rules. Germany in 1803 was divided into hundreds of independent states and its legal institutions were too weak and fragmented to bring clarity and uniformity to the law.[52] Especially in the western part of Germany (where Marburg, the site of the composition of Savigny's treatise on possession, is located), the French Revolution and its aftermath had unsettled, even disoriented, German thought. As we know from his later criticisms of codification, Savigny did not think Germany's legal culture ripe for the Benthamite project of starting from scratch with a clear and concise codification of functionally derived legal rules and principles. The alternative was to use the universities' intellectual resources to extract from Roman law—a highly sophisticated body of law—a set of clear principles to be the common law of Germany.

It is often said of particular issues in law that it is more important that the law be settled than that it be right. This is an aphoristic version

---

52. "The German-speaking lands were an extraordinary legal patchwork." Whitman, note 2 above, at 102.

of the argument for rules as distinct from standards. Rules abstract a few relevant facts from the welter of circumstances of each actual case and make the selected facts legally determinative. The consequence is an imperfect fit between rule and circumstances, resulting in some outcomes that are erroneous from the standpoint of the substantive principle undergirding the rule. This is a cost, but it must be traded off against the benefit of the rule in reducing the cost of litigation and in reducing legal uncertainty. Uncertainty is costly in itself and also may invite judicial corruption, whether financial or political, by making it difficult for outsiders to determine whether a judicial decision is in accordance with law. If it is especially urgent at a particular stage in a society's legal development to have clear legal rules, then the approach taken by Savigny to the law of possession may well be the best one to take—from an economic standpoint, as my discussion of the costs and benefits of rules versus standards has been intended to suggest.

Savigny provided a clear definition of possession and used it to deduce a host of specific rules. The structure is to some extent arbitrary but its clarity is an enormous plus. To devise such a structure may have been more important than trying to derive rules or standards from considerations of social policy. Not only because German law as Savigny found it was in urgent need of systematization,[53] but also because German disunity created a political need that Roman law could fulfill. That law provided a *lingua franca* that because of its ethnic and temporal remoteness was politically neutral compared to a system of law avowedly based on current social needs, needs that would differ across German states and inevitably be inflected politically. Consistently with Max Weber's belief that the law must attain "formal rationality" in order to provide the clear, definite, and politically neutral framework required for economic progress, Roman law may have contributed to the rise of commercial society in Europe[54]—a role for which Savigny cast it. The individualistic and (as I suggested earlier) "anti-feudal" bias of Roman law made a return to it, paradoxically, an important measure of modernization.

---

53. The jumble in which he found that law is typified by the work of the influential eighteenth-century jurist Moser. See Mack Walker, *Johann Jakob Moser and the Holy Roman Empire of the German Nation* 130–135 (1981).

54. See, for example, James Q. Whitman, "The Moral Menace of Roman Law and the Making of Commerce: Some Dutch Evidence," 105 *Yale Law Journal* 1841 (1996).

Savigny was also prescient in recognizing the importance of the universities as a force for intellectual unity in the face of Germany's political disunity. Drawing their students from all over Germany and focusing the research and teaching of their law faculties on the same body of legal principles, namely the Roman, universities became a substitute for a uniform judicial system.

Holmes found himself in a completely different situation from that of Savigny. The legal system of post–Civil War America was mature, sure-footed, and thoroughly professionalized. The nation was united after the trauma of the Civil War, and although it remained a federal system and the states retained a good deal of autonomy in matters of law, especially property law, there was a considerable homogeneity of approach. The American legal system (and one could rightly speak of *the* American legal system despite the laws of the different states) had the suppleness and enjoyed the public confidence to be able to adapt legal principles to current social needs without undue danger of sacrificing legitimacy or creating debilitating legal uncertainty. In that setting, the formalism of Savigny and his followers was felt as constraining rather than liberating.

But while Holmes was enthusiastic about throwing off the fetters of the past and making law serve current social needs, he was not able to specify those needs. *The Common Law* tends to treat them as inscrutable, arbitrary preferences, or even instincts. Holmes says at one point, characteristically, that "it is quite enough . . . for the law, that man, by an instinct which he shares with the domestic dog, . . . will not allow himself to be dispossessed, either by force or fraud, of what he holds, without trying to get it back again."[55] This tells us, perhaps, why there are possessory rights, but nothing about their contours. (Recall how he merely set out the three rules for obtaining possessory rights in whales, without indicating which was best, and how economics can differentiate among the rules.) The limning of those contours, the filling in of the picture, had to wait another century, when the tools of economics would attain the level of refinement required for dealing illuminatingly with the law of possession.

55. Holmes, note 13 above, at 213 (footnote omitted).

~ III
PSYCHOLOGY

~ 7

Emotion in Law

$\mathscr{T}$HERE ARE, as we glimpsed in Chapter 1, two basic conceptions of economics. One focuses on subject matter, and holds economics to be the study of markets; the other focuses on method, and holds economics to be the application of the rational-actor model to human behavior. Those who adhere to the second conception may seem to be on a collision course with psychology, the focus of which is on the nonrational and irrational components of human behavior. Psychologists argue with great plausibility that human behavior is *characteristically* nonrational, that the "rational man" of economics is rarely encountered in the real world, even in economic markets and certainly very rarely outside them. I examine this claim, in this part of the book (and to some extent in the next as well), as part of a broader interest in what psychology may have to offer to the understanding and improvement of law. A lot, I think—and much of it consistent with the rational model.

It is natural to begin such an inquiry with an analysis of emotion, the conventional antithesis of the rational faculty and clearly a matter with which the law must come to terms. Much of the behavior that law regulates is intensely emotional—think of the murder of an adulterous spouse, the kidnapping of a child by a parent denied custody, or the daubing of paint on a fur coat by an animal-rights activist. Or is shockingly devoid of emotion (the "cold-blooded" murder). Or arouses the emotions—often sympathy for the victim of a crime or a tort and indignation at the injurer, but sometimes sympathy for the injurer, as in killings by "battered wives"—of people who hear or read about the incident. The law itself is conventionally regarded as a bastion of "reason" conceived of as the antithesis of emotion. The law's function is understood to be to neutralize the emotionality that legal disputes arouse in the participants and lay observers. Yet anyone who has ever been involved in litigation as litigant, lawyer, judge, juror, or witness knows that this, the quintessential method of resolving legal disputes, is an intensely emotional process, rather like the violent methods of dispute resolution that it replaces.

The emotionality of acts that are regulated by the law, and the law's responses to that emotionality, raise a number of issues for the legal system. I address five in this chapter. First, how should the fact that a wrongful act is precipitated by an emotion affect the law's evaluation of the act? Should emotionality make the law come down harder or softer on the violator? I discuss this question with particular reference to "hate crime" laws,[1] and to provocation as a mitigating factor in criminal punishment. The second question is whether and how the law should use emotion. The third is what the emotional state of the law's administrators, whether judges, jurors, prosecutors, or police, should be. Should they be emotionless, like computers? If not, how precisely should emotion enter into their judgments? Fourth, what screens or filters should be used to ensure that the law's administrators are in the correct emotional state (whatever exactly that is) when carrying out their legal duties? Fifth, how can the law prevent the emotionality of the litigation process from frustrating efforts to settle cases before the process has run its full course?

We can get help in answering these questions from the cognitive theory of emotion, which originated with Aristotle and has been elaborated in recent years by philosophers and psychologists.[2] Challenging

---

1. "Hate crimes" should be distinguished from "hate speech," which I discussed in Chapter 2. Hates crimes are ordinary crimes, such as murder, that are motivated by hatred for the group (blacks or homosexuals, for example) to which the victim belongs.

2. See, for example, John Deigh, "Cognitivism in the Theory of Emotions," 104 *Ethics* 824 (1994); Jon Elster, *Alchemies of the Mind: Rationality and the Emotions* (1999), esp. pp. 283–331; Susan James, *Passion and Action: The Emotions in Seventeenth-Century Philosophy* 20–22 (1997); William E. Lyons, *Emotion* (1980); Martha C. Nussbaum, *Upheavals of Thought: A Theory of*

what despite Aristotle had become (not only in law) a thoroughly conventional antithesis between rationality and emotion, these modern theorists argue that emotion is a form of cognition. Not just in the obvious sense that emotional reactions are usually triggered by information, but also in the sense that an emotion expresses an evaluation of the information and so may operate as a substitute for reasoning in the usual sense. For example, when we react with anger to being informed of some outrage, the reaction expresses disapproval, an evaluation that we might have reached as the end point of a step-by-step reasoning process. The evaluative function of emotion implies that a failure to react to a particular situation with a particular emotion might demonstrate not a superior capacity to reason but instead a failure of understanding or, in the case of moralistic emotions such as compassion and indignation, a rejection of the society's moral code. Thus, particular emotional reactions in particular situations can often be praised as appropriate to the situation or criticized as inappropriate either because they are evoked by misinformation or because they are based on a perverse evaluation of the situation.

Another objection to dichotomizing reason and emotion is that it confusingly envisages a struggle between motivational and nonmotivational elements of personality. Reason is not (*pace* Kant) motivational; knowing what is the right thing to do must be conjoined with a desire to do the right thing for action to result. When we say that a person did not allow himself to give way to his emotions (for example, he resisted that piece of chocolate), we mean that an aversive emotion ("self-control"—the aversion to being weak-willed) was stronger than the attractive emotion.[3]

Nevertheless, it would be a mistake to think that the cognitive approach to emotion abolishes traditional concerns about emotionalism.

---

the Emotions (Cambridge University Press, forthcoming), esp. chs. 1 and 3; Keith Oatley, *Best Laid Schemes: The Psychology of Emotions* (1992); Ronald de Sousa, *The Rationality of Emotion* (1987); Robert C. Solomon, *The Passions* (1976); Michael Stocker with Elizabeth Hegeman, *Valuing Emotions* (1996); R. B. Zajonc, "Feeling and Thinking: Preferences Need No Inferences," 35 *American Psychologist* 151 (1980). There has been little effort to apply theories, cognitive or otherwise, of the emotions to law. But see the recent anthology *The Passions of Law* (Susan A. Bandes ed. 1999), where an earlier version of this chapter appears; and also "Symposium on Law, Psychology, and the Emotions," 74 *Chicago-Kent Law Review* 1423 (2000).

3. This is essentially Hobbes's view. See the helpful discussion of Hobbes and his critics in James, note 2 above, at 269–288.

The dichotomy of reason and emotion, misleading though it is, captures an important truth. We all have the experience of making mistakes because of pride, anger, or other emotions. An efficient method of cognition in some cases, emotion is an inefficient one in others. It short-circuits reason conceived of as a conscious, articulate process of deliberation, calculation, analysis, or reflection. Sometimes this is all to the good; emotion focuses attention, crystallizes evaluation, and prompts action in circumstances in which reflection would be interminable, unfocused, and indecisive.[4] But in situations in which making an intelligent decision requires careful, sequential analysis or reflection, emotion may, by supplanting that process, generate an inferior decision. Love notoriously can lead to bad judgments, and likewise fear and anger, the last inciting egocentric, polarized thinking that occludes relevant features of the situation that has engendered the anger.[5]

But it would be more precise to say that too much emotion or the wrong kind of emotion may generate the inferior decision. For as I shall argue in discussing emotion in judges, emotion is necessary to precipitate *any* decision that is not merely the conclusion of syllogistic or other purely formal reasoning—the kind of reasoning a computer can do better than a human being. Decision is a form of action, and there is no action without emotion.

Concretely, when we say that a person is "emotional" or that a person's judgment is distorted by "emotionalism" we mean that he has given undue salience to one feature of the situation and its associated emotional stimulus, neglecting other important features. So we might call a judge "emotional" who was so affected by the ghastly injuries of a tort plaintiff that he was blinded to the other legally relevant features of the case. We expect appellate judges to be less emotional in this sense than trial judges because remote from the emotionally most salient features of the case. They do not deal in person with the parties and witnesses but only with the lawyers and the trial transcript and other

4. Cf. Elster, note 2 above, at 291–293, discussing studies that show that persons rendered emotionally flat by brain damage have difficulty making decisions. Discussing the same studies, Arthur J. Robson, "The Biological Basis of Economic Behavior" 11–13 (forthcoming in *Journal of Economic Literature*), gives an explicit economic interpretation: emotion-driven choice operates as a rational, information-conserving, rule-of-thumb method of decision in the face of complexity.

5. Well described in Aaron T. Beck, *Prisoners of Hate: The Cognitive Basis of Anger, Hostility, and Violence*, pt. 1 (1999).

documents (with only the occasional photograph).[6] The design of the appellate process can thus be seen as a response to the danger of emotionalism viewed as the placing of too much weight on a salient feature of a complex situation. In everyday life we respond to this danger by various personal strategies such as trying to "control" our anger so that it will not cause hasty, ill-considered, quickly regretted actions.

The idea of emotion as a cognitive shortcut explains why jurors, like children, are more likely to make emotional judgments than judges. The less experienced a person is at reasoning his way through some problem, the more likely he is to "react emotionally," that is, to fall back on a more primitive mode of reaching a conclusion, the emotional. It is primitive in a quite literal sense. Emotions, like sex, are something we have in common with other animals, who having smaller cortexes than human beings rely more heavily than we do on emotions to guide their actions. The fact that emotions are discernible in the youngest infants is a further clue that we are dealing with an innate characteristic. Like other parts of our "animal," that is, our "natural," as distinct from our cultural, endowment, our suite of emotions probably was well adapted to the conditions of our ancestral environment, a term that evolutionary biologists use to describe the prehistoric period in which human beings evolved to essentially their present biological state. Our emotional repertoire may not be as well adapted to the conditions in which we live today. That is a reason for worrying that emotion may sometimes lead us astray, as by precipitating a decision that because of the complexity of the issue—a complexity that may not have been a common feature of the ancestral environment—would have been improved by careful, patient reasoning.

I do not want to leave the impression, as my description of emotion as a cognitive shortcut may have done, that every "correct" emotional reaction can be translated into an analytical judgment. Such a view would be excessively rationalistic. Many of our thoroughly approved emotional reactions are prior to any rational reconstruction, which in such cases is mere rationalization. Try giving a good "reason" for becoming upset at seeing an animal mistreated. I return to this point later.

6. See generally John C. Shepherd and Jordan B. Cherrick, "Advocacy and Emotion," 138 *Federal Rules Decisions* 619 (1991).

It should be apparent by now that the legal system could no more have a uniform policy toward emotion than it could have a uniform policy toward information or belief. The significance of the emotional component of behavior regulated by law is bound to depend, rather, on the purpose of the particular law. Take criminal law. If one assumes that its basic purpose is to limit dangerous activity, the question how it should treat emotion requires relating emotion to dangerousness; and obviously the relation varies not only across but within crimes. In the case of murder, the presence of strong emotion tends to mitigate the dangerousness of the criminal and the absence of strong emotion to aggravate it. The "cold-blooded killer" (psychopathic, affectless)—a murderer for hire, for example—is particularly dangerous. His propensity to kill is not confined to those rare situations in which a natural aversion to killing breaks down, as in the case of most crimes of passion, and his coolness will make it easier for him to maneuver to avoid being caught.

It might seem that the more "emotional" the crime, the more rather than less severe the punishment should be because a greater threat of punishment may be necessary to deter prospective criminals in those circumstances. But this is not correct. Not only do the greater ease of catching the emotional criminal and the lesser risk that he will repeat the crime (because it is situation specific and the situation is unlikely to recur) tend to offset the need to ratchet up the punishment to ensure deterrence and incapacitation, but in addition most crimes of passion involve an element of provocation by the victim, which may provide a reason for lighter punishment.[7] It is true that the lighter punishment will increase the likelihood of crimes against provokers by reducing the expected punishment cost of such crimes. But it will also reduce that likelihood by increasing the expected cost of provocation. The provoker will be more likely to be attacked if the expected punishment cost of the attacker is less, and knowing this people will be less likely to provoke. If the latter effect (reducing the crime rate by discouraging provocation) predominates, a reduction in the severity of punishment in cases of provocation should reduce the amount of crime.

Not all murders fit into either of the categories that I've been de-

---

7. See Alon Harel, "Efficiency and Fairness in Criminal Law: The Case for a Criminal Law Principle of Comparative Fault," 82 *California Law Review* 1181 (1994).

scribing—the "cold-blooded crime" and the "crime of passion." The "serial" killer, along with certain types of sex criminal (and many serial killers *are* sex criminals), are particularly dangerous because they are driven by powerful emotions to commit the same crime over and over again. Their emotion makes them more rather than less dangerous, so they are punished more heavily. In sum, the law recognizes that emotionality is a dimension of human behavior but its reaction to that fact is shaped by the purposes of particular laws applied to particular situations rather than by an overarching position on the goodness or badness of emotion.[8] Both the least and the most emotional criminals may be, as in the case of murder, the most dangerous and therefore the most deserving of harsh punishment. Granted, this conclusion assumes that the purpose of criminal law is to deter or otherwise prevent crime. Not everyone will accept that this is its purpose. But my general point holds regardless: the law cannot be expected to be flatly for or flatly against emotion or emotionality.

I am led to question whether there should be a separate category of "hate crimes" that are punished more harshly than the same offenses not motivated by hatred.[9] Like most emotions, hatred is morally neutral. Its moral valence depends on its object. Unless you are the kind of Christian rigorist who takes the Sermon on the Mount literally, as a guide to living in this world rather than (as it was intended) preparing for living in a next world believed to be imminent, you will not think it immoral to hate Hitler or Stalin. I would add—so far am I from being a moral rigorist—that I do not consider it immoral to hate criminals, philanderers, braggarts, or even beggars (nowadays, in the wealthy countries at least, mainly a species of con man), though I shall argue that it is wrong for officials, and in particular judges, when in the exercise of their office, to hate anyone. Crimes of passion are frequently motivated by hatred for the victim, and yet the emotionality of the act is properly regarded as a mitigating factor if it indicates that the act is

---

8. Hence I do not agree that the criminal law takes "an ambivalent stance toward emotions." Dan M. Kahan and Martha C. Nussbaum, "Two Conceptions of Emotion in Criminal Law," 96 *Columbia Law Review* 269, 325 (1996). That implies that the law ought to make up its mind whether it is for or against the emotions. The proper stance is a nuanced one, rather than either-or.

9. For an excellent discussion, see James B. Jacobs and Kimberly Potter, *Hate Crimes: Criminal Law and Identity Politics* (1998).

unlikely to be repeated because it was triggered by a confluence of circumstances that is unlikely to recur.

By the term "hate crimes" is meant something quite specific—that the object of the criminal's hatred is (1) a group rather than an individual, (2) the members of which are *not* outlaws, since if they were, it would not be a crime to prey on them. There may be merit to enhanced punishment in these circumstances even if the criminal law is concerned solely with dangerousness. First and least, the criminal whose target is a group rather than an individual may be more dangerous than the average criminal because he has more people in his sights, as it were. This point is dubious because it does not distinguish the hate criminal from the burglar, say, for whom every owner or occupant of residential or commercial premises is a potential victim. A better point is that if members of particular groups, such as southern blacks during the Jim Crow era, are less likely than other victims of crime to report a crime against them or to receive effective protection from police and other law enforcement authorities, the expected benefits to criminals (wholly apart from the emotional state of the criminal) of preying on members of the group will rise, warranting heavier punishment.[10] Third, heavier punishment is warranted if the psychological harm to the victim of such a crime is greater when the victim knows that the criminal is motivated in part or whole by hatred of the group to which the victim belongs, or if the crime imposes an emotional cost greater than a differently motivated but otherwise similar crime would impose on people who are fearful of becoming victims of crime, or if the perpetrator derives an added benefit from the crime in the form of enhanced status among his fellow bigots. Fourth, hatred differs from anger in often being "cold" rather than "hot."[11] The impulsiveness of a crime motivated by anger often makes it easier to apprehend the criminal, and so becomes a reason for a lighter punishment. The "cold" criminal, with his greater presence of mind, is likelier to take effective steps to avoid detection. Of course, anger often accompanies hatred (and vice versa), but not always.

The distinction between anger and hatred will help us to distinguish among three types of hate-crime perpetrators: cold-blooded bigots;

10. See Lu-in Wang, "The Transforming Power of 'Hate': Social Cognition Theory and the Harms of Bias-Related Crime," 71 *Southern California Law Review* 47, 57–58 (1997).

11. For a good discussion, see Elster, note 2 above, at 62–67

impulsive juveniles, who are in fact responsible for the majority of hate crimes;[12] and the deeply emotional hate criminal, symbolized by the "homophobe," who, pathologically anxious about his own sexual identity, kills a homosexual who propositions him. The last category of hate crime overlaps with the crime of passion and raises the question whether provocation should not result in a *lighter* punishment for many hate crimes. Homophobic murder is a crime of passion, and like other crimes of passion is situation-specific. But it also resembles the murder of prostitutes in not being confined to persons with whom the murderer has a direct relation, as he would with an adulterous spouse. In contrast, impulsive juveniles may be more deterrable than the homophobe because their emotions are less deeply engaged, or, conversely, they may be less deterrable because of the emotionality of youth.

Although hate crimes may on average be more dangerous than otherwise similar crimes not motivated by hatred for a group, the advocates of punishing them more heavily do not insist on linking greater punishment to greater dangerousness. The classic hate crime is the murder of prostitutes, as by Jack the Ripper and his many emulators. Punishing such murders more heavily than the average murder could thus be defended by reference to relative dangerousness. Yet it is not what advocates of enhanced punishment for "hate crimes" mean by the term. They mean crimes against members of groups for which they have a particular solicitude, such as blacks, Jews, and homosexuals.[13] "Hate crime laws . . . demonstrate the impact of identity politics on criminal law."[14] Defining hate crimes by reference to favored groups and thus severing the relation between group-hate crimes and dangerousness, these advocates inject politics into the criminal law, much as the Soviets did with their concept of "class enemies." If, for the sake of maintaining the political neutrality of criminal law, the proper criterion for grading criminal punishment is dangerousness, the presence and object of hatred are relevant only insofar as they bear on the criminal's dangerousness. A person who kills homosexuals because he hates homosexuals is more dangerous than a person who kills the man who has

12. Jacobs and Potter, note 9 above, at 89.

13. See, for example, Kahan and Nussbaum, note 8 above, at 269, 313–314, 350–355 (1996).

14. Jacobs and Potter, note 9 above, at 77.

cuckolded him, but not more dangerous than one who kills prostitutes because he hates prostitutes. As long as criminal sentencing takes full account of the bearing of the criminal's object on his dangerousness, the nonpolitical concerns that motivate advocacy of the "hate crime" classification are taken care of automatically and there is no need for the classification.

Not only is there no need; in such a case the use of the classification to alter the punishment is inconsistent with freedom of thought. If two crimes differ not at all in dangerousness but only in the fact that one is motivated by a belief that the judicial authorities reprobate—a belief, for example, that homosexuals are evil—then to punish that crime more heavily is to punish belief, not action. Compare two blackmailers of homosexuals. They differ only in that one does it purely for money and the other partially out of hatred of homosexuals.[15] Blackmail by the first blackmailer is not a hate crime; blackmail by the second is. To punish the second more heavily is to punish (to an extent measured by the increment of punishment of the second blackmailer over the first) an *opinion* about homosexuality. Opinions trigger emotions that may incite action. As the cognitive theory of emotion implies, when a criminal is punished more heavily because of the emotional state in which he committed the crime we may actually be punishing cognition, and therefore opinion or belief, rather than just "raw" emotion.

The Supreme Court has rejected this approach on the ground that hate crimes do more harm than other crimes because they are "more likely to provoke retaliatory crimes, inflict distinct emotional harms on their victims, and incite community unrest."[16] Yet the first point, about retaliation, implies that the weaker the group targeted is, the less likely it is to retaliate; hence under the Court's analysis the *less* harmful the crimes against it are.[17] The point about community unrest—assuming it's not just the first or second point in different words—may be valid, but probably only with respect to black on white and white on black crimes, which indeed have the potential to exacerbate our already serious racial tensions. The Court's point about "distinct emotional

15. I assume that their victim is unaware of their motive, as a manifestation of the second blackmailer's homophobia might increase the psychological harm to his victim, though this is far from certain, as we shall see shortly.

16. Wisconsin v. Mitchell, 508 U.S. 476, 487–88 (1993).

17. See Jacobs and Potter, note 9 above, at 88.

harms" may also have some validity,[18] but probably not[19] and in any event it is the sort of vague and coarse-grained justification for punishing opinions that the Supreme Court usually rejects. Is it really more distressing to be assaulted because you're a member of a group whom your assailant hates than because he hates you as an individual? If you're black, is it worse to learn that a white has tried to kill you because he hates blacks or that your son has tried to kill you to inherit your money? The answers will vary from case to case and this casts doubt on the adequacy of the hate crime categories to pick out the more serious crimes even apart from the arbitrariness of the categories and the lack of any urgent need for them. The question of relative harm can readily be handled either case by case or by a rule or standard based on a nonideological criterion such as the federal sentencing guideline that requires enhanced punishment of crimes against "vulnerable victims."[20]

And notice the paradox that enhanced punishment for hate crimes makes less sense when the crime is murder. For often the victim will not know the motivation of the murderer—indeed, often he will have no foreknowledge of the murder and hence incur no emotional distress (though other members of his group may). The hate crime statutes do not recognize this paradox.

The objection, in short, is not to varying the severity of punishment for crime according to the harm suffered by the victim or the deterrability of the criminal. It is to varying that severity in order to make a political or ideological statement or, what is often the same thing, to accommodate the pressures of politically influential groups. Ideology and interest-group politics have no proper place in a criminal justice system. In rejecting this precept the supporters of hate crime laws are playing with fire. It was not long ago that a political or ideological conception of the role of criminal law would have justified less, rather than more, legal protection for blacks, homosexuals, and other

18. As argued in Wang's article, note 10 above.
19. Jacobs and Potter, note 9 above, at 83–84.
20. See, for example, United States v. Lallemand, 989 F.2d 936 (7th Cir. 1993), upholding the enhancement where the victim of blackmail was a homosexual—but upholding it not because the defendant was motivated by hatred of homosexuals (it seems that his motivation was purely financial), but because the homosexual was deeply "closeted" and therefore highly unlikely to complain, which reduced the expected punishment cost to the blackmailer.

minorities. Proponents of hate crime laws may respond that in those bad old days the enforcement of the criminal law on behalf of these groups was often unenthusiastic. That is true. But there is a difference between failing to protect people adequately against private hostility and making that hostility a basis for increased legal punishment. The first practice is wrong; the second is wrong and sets a dangerous precedent.

All this is not to say that hatred and cognate emotions such as disgust and revulsion should have no place in criminal punishment. We must not confuse hatred of the victim by the criminal with hatred of (or disgust for) the criminal by society. The latter type of hatred is an ineliminable feature of criminal justice in at least three respects. First, disgust underlies the criminalizing of "immoral" conduct that cannot be shown to cause temporal harm to human beings, such as intercourse with or cruelty toward animals, desecration of corpses, and public nudity. Second, hatred informs the decision to impose capital punishment under the essentially standardless capital-sentencing regime created by the Supreme Court. And third, even when sentencing guidelines are used to curtail judicial discretion in sentencing and to do so in part by banishing many "emotional" factors, either the drafters of the guidelines or the judges in their diminished area of discretion are bound to consider emotional factors, such as remorse, that either increase or decrease the hatefulness of the criminal.

Disgust when sufficiently widespread is as solid a basis for legal regulation as tangible harm. To deny this—to contend that the only proper basis for criminal (or perhaps any) law is utilitarianism or some other moral theory—is to exaggerate the proper as well as the actual role of moral reasoning in the moral and criminal codes. Not when it lacks a "rational" basis, but when there is no consensus supporting it, does moral regulation become political or ideological in a disreputable sense. It is only the disintegration of the moral consensus concerning the evil of homosexuality that has made the laws against sodomy so questionable a feature of American criminal justice today.

In making this argument I am making a sympathetic bow toward the expressive theory of morality. A moral judgment is an expression of a strong attraction or repulsion to the behavior being evaluated. The cause of the emotional arousal need have nothing to do with any "reason" that might be offered by a moralist. Reasons can always be offered, but they have the air of rationalization. To offer an argument why parents should not be allowed to kill their infant children is to miss the point; it would be like arguing to someone who finds sex disgusting that there is no ground for his disgust. To place the entire criminal code on a "rational" basis would wreak havoc with our moral code.[21]

The Supreme Court in the name of the Constitution's cruel and unusual punishments clause forbids making capital punishment the automatic or even presumptive punishment for specific classes of act. The legislature can specify the classes of act that make a defendant "eligible" for the death penalty but the jury must be allowed to consider the eligible defendant's character in deciding whether to impose the penalty. The consequence is that the issue in capital sentencing hearings tends to be how hateful the defendant is. The defendant's lawyer tries to portray him as sick, deprived, or penitent, and the prosecutor tries to portray him as evil and remorseless. Since the moral category of evil, the medical category of crazy, and the social-psychological category of deprived all overlap and many murderers are found in the area of overlap, juries in capital cases are often left entirely to their own devices in deciding whether to decree death.

Judges and jurors want defendants to exhibit remorse,[22] that is, recognition of having done wrong and regret for the wrong and its consequences for the victims. But remorse is such an interior state of mind that the judicial system can never have much confidence that the defendant is remorseful rather than merely forensically resourceful. And the more he accepts responsibility for his act, thus demonstrating remorse, the more evil he makes the act and therefore the actor (himself) seem by depicting it as the product of his own depraved will rather than of evil companions, a deprived upbringing, an addiction, or a psychiatric illness.[23] In a capital case, with its elaborate sentencing hearings, the defendant will sometimes pursue a two-track strategy: he will take full responsibility for his crime in his own testimony while his "mitigation expert" presents evidence that the defendant is being too hard on

21. For a fuller defense of this way of understanding morality, see Richard A. Posner, *The Problematics of Moral and Legal Theory*, ch. 1 (1999); also Simon Blackburn, *Ruling Passions: A Theory of Practical Reasoning*, ch. 3 (1998).

22. See, for example, Todd E. Hogue and Jason Peebles, "The Influence of Remorse, Intent and Attitudes toward Sex Offenders on Judgments of a Rapist," 3 *Psychology, Crime and Law* 249 (1997).

23. This is a serious problem in administering the "acceptance of responsibility" punishment discount in the federal sentencing guidelines. See United States v. Beserra, 967 F.2d 254 (7th Cir. 1992).

himself, that really his crime was the product of circumstances rather than of a depraved will. Those who do not believe in free will as a metaphysical reality think that the only significance of the defendant's proclaiming his remorse is to show that he is not an open rebel against the legal system—something that would make him more dangerous both by example and as an indication that he is highly likely to commit further crimes when and if released from prison.

In discussing hate crimes I emphasized the case for basing criminal law on a policy of deterring or (normally through imprisonment) preventing the unjustified infliction of temporal harm rather than using the law to enforce current ideas of politically correct behavior or to randomize the imposition of capital punishment. But now we see that we can't push this view of the proper scope of the criminal law too far, given the lack of functional justifications for some of our deepest moral intuitions that we want to embody in law.

〜 RECENT INTEREST in the use of shaming penalties—mostly publicity of various sorts, such as requiring a convicted sex offender to display a poster in his front yard, or a bumper sticker on his car, that reads, "I am a convicted sex offender," or requiring vandals to clean sidewalks while wearing prison garb—brings into focus another question about the law's attitude toward emotion. This question is when if ever the law should try to induce an emotional state as a component of punishment. Shaming penalties recall a long history of public punishments designed to humiliate and degrade the convict and awe or frighten the spectators. This history had seemed to end, for the most part, with the rise of the prison in the nineteenth century, as a result of which criminal punishments are now normally administered if not quite in secret then at least out of the public eye.[24] But imprisonment has become so costly as to spark a renewed interest in alternative punishments, including shaming.[25] Since people can be made to experience

24. The story is told with great vividness in Michel Foucault, *Discipline and Punish: The Birth of the Prison* (1977).

25. See, for example, Dan M. Kahan, "What Do Alternative Sanctions Mean?" 63 *University of Chicago Law Review* 591 (1996); Kahan, "Social Meaning and the Economic Analysis of Crime," 27 *Journal of Legal Studies* 609 (1998); and for criticism, Toni M. Massaro, "The Meanings of Shame: Implications for Legal Reform," 3 *Psychology, Public Policy, and Law* 645 (1997); James Q. Whitman, "What Is Wrong with Inflicting Shame Sanctions?" 107 *Yale Law Journal* 1055 (1998).

"emotional distress" (the intentional infliction of which—except by the
state when it is punishing criminals!—is a tort), the shaming penalties
are a way of inflicting disutility on convicted criminals. Instead of depriving them of their liberty, the state subjects them to humiliation. It
may inflict the same disutility, and thus achieve the same deterrent effect, as imprisonment, but at lower cost.

The term "shaming penalties" is something of a misnomer. Often
they are designed to humiliate rather than to shame. A person is
shamed when he is discovered by his in-group, the people he respects
(often just his immediate family), to have engaged in conduct contrary
to the norms of the group. The exposure is the shame, and you don't
put a dunce cap on his head. The purpose of the dunce cap is to humiliate, to make a person an object of public ridicule and execration. However, when pressed, the modern advocate of shaming tends to retreat to
forms of publicity, such as the bumper sticker and the sign in your front
yard, as his preferred "shaming" penalties, and the more the penalty involves just exposure the more apt the term "shaming" is. Humiliation is
also involved, but not the deliberate "piling on" that is represented by
the dunce cap.

An alternative interpretation of exposure penalties to both shaming
and humiliation should be noted. The legal protection of privacy undermines regulation by social norms, because such regulation depends
on violations being detectable by ordinary citizens, the ostracizers
(norm enforcers). Stripping away privacy is thus a logical method of
seeking to enhance the effectiveness of norms in controlling behavior.
But shaming and humiliation are consequences of such stripping away
even when they are not intended.[26]

Despite the inexpensiveness of shaming, humiliation, or pure exposure penalties, there are a number of objections to them. One is that in
a society in which more than half the crime, or at least the detected
crime, is committed by blacks and Hispanics, yet the criminal justice
system is predominantly white and Anglo, a policy of imposing *humiliating* punishments on criminals is likely to exacerbate already serious
racial and ethnic tensions. Another concern is the paradoxical insensi-
tivity of the advocates of shaming penalties to the expressive, or signaling, function of punishment. An important signal that criminal punish-

---

26. Both shame and social norms are discussed at greater length in Chapter 9.

ment is intended to emit in our culture is official respect for the dignity of even the lowest of the low—namely, hateful criminals. That is why the lethal injection does not take the form of an injection of rat poison. In our society criminals are not, in Carl Schmitt's ominous phrase, "the enemy within," to be treated with all the consideration we accord to a foreign enemy. They are errant members of the community. To treat them as less, as children or animals, is to introduce into our public policy the kind of "we–they" thinking that history suggests[27] can lead to barbarous prison conditions, summary justice, and savage punishments. It's all right for private citizens to hate criminals; but the functionaries of the criminal justice system should not hate them, or at least express hatred for them.

Another objection to shaming penalties is that while the threat of imprisonment deters crime, imprisonment itself prevents crime so long as the offender remains in prison. This preventive effect is lost when public humiliation is substituted for all or part of a prison term. If there is no substitution—if the shaming penalty is tacked on at the end of the prison term, to increase the severity of the sentence—there is no cost savings, although there may be a gain in deterrence.

The preventive effect may not be lost entirely. The sign outside the sex offender's house serves not only to humiliate the offender but also to warn potential victims to keep away from him. But the preventive effect will be less than that of imprisonment unless the period in which the warning is required to be in effect is considerably longer than the term of imprisonment for which it is a substitute would be, for not all potential victims will learn of the warning or take effective precautions in response to it. This implies that the most effective shaming penalty is the one that is tacked on at the end of the normal prison sentence. But, to repeat, in that case there is no economizing on the cost of imprisonment except insofar as the publicity effect of the shaming penalty reduces recidivism by alerting potential victims or increases deterrence, that is, except insofar as by making criminal punishment more severe the shaming penalty reduces the amount of crime and so the aggregate cost of imprisoning criminals. And lengthening prison terms could have the same effect. For it is a mistake to suppose that making

27. But let's not forget the danger of relying too heavily on historical analogies. See Chapter 4.

prison terms longer must increase the prison population. To suppose that is to ignore the deterrent effect of the *threat* of imprisonment.

If, for example, a 1 percent increase in the length of prison sentences led to a 2 percent decrease in the incidence of crime, then, if nothing else changed, the prison population would decrease by roughly 1 percent. Suppose that at time t, before the increase in prison sentences, the number of criminals is 200, half (100) are caught and convicted, and the average prison term is 100 months, so that the aggregate prisoner-months for which the prison system must budget is 10,000. If at time $t + 1$, because of the deterrent effect of longer prison sentences, there are only 196 criminals (2 percent fewer), of which again half (98) are caught and convicted and each serves 101 months, the aggregate prison-months will fall from 10,000 to 9,898.

Another objection to shaming penalties is that if there is greater variance across persons in the disutility from humiliating punishments than in the disutility from loss of liberty, it will be more difficult to calibrate the humiliation punishment schedule. This is especially likely if more than one form of such punishment is employed.

∽ THE THIRD QUESTION that I said I would address in this chapter is the proper emotional state of the judicial officer, whether judge or juror. To what extent if any should his emotions be engaged by the case? A formalist, that is, one who thinks of legal analysis on the model of solving logical puzzles or mathematical problems, would probably answer, "Not at all." This would not be quite correct even on the formalist premise. Solving the most difficult logical and mathematical problems, the kind computers still can't solve, may require such emotions as wonder, delight, and pride; recall what I said earlier about the indispensability of emotion to decisionmaking. Nevertheless, a number of the strongest emotions, such as anger, disgust, indignation, and love, would be out of place. They would not only interfere with the problem-solving process rather than provide an efficient shortcut; they would also introduce substantive distortions in the law by depriving people of remedies to which they were entitled as a matter of law. Love for one of the litigants can prevent the judge from thinking straight about the issues, but it can also lead him, though he is clear-headed, to make an unjust ruling.

Cases that present difficult, in the sense not of analytically complex but of rationally indeterminate, questions of law obviously cannot be decided without bringing to bear moral feelings and political preferences. In these cases it might seem that a richer emotional palette would be appropriate, or at least inevitable. To a degree this is true, especially for someone who like me holds an essentially emotivist view of morality. But the danger of excessive emotionality in the decision of the difficult case must not be gainsaid. The more uncertain the decision-making task, the weaker will be the resistance that "objective" (in the sense of affectless) factors will offer to inappropriate emotion. Most people can add 2 + 2 correctly whatever their emotional state, but when the intellectual challenge is greater the danger that the response will be "swayed" by emotion is greater too. This is one reason for the rules designed to limit a judge's emotional involvement in a case, such as the rule that forbids him to sit in a case in which a relative is a party or a lawyer, or in which he has a financial interest.

Even in the easy cases, sound judicial decisionmaking is apt to require more emotions than just those that you need for performing any nonalgorithmic task. In particular it may require indignation and empathy. Indignation is the normal reaction to a violation of the moral code of one's society. More important, it is often the mode by which a violation is identified. As I suggested in discussing the emotional basis of morals offenses, it is often difficult to give a persuasive *rational* account of a moral rule, including a moral rule to which the law has annexed a sanction for violating. This is true whether the rule is against urinating or masturbating in public, against public nudity, against pederasty, against polygamy, against infanticide, for or against abortion, against involuntary euthanasia, against intercourse with beasts or human corpses, against mistreating animals, against gladiatorial combat, against adult nonprocreative incest, against prostitution and obscenity, against gambling, against self-slavery, against public executions, against mutilation as a form of criminal punishment, against selling or consuming some mind-altering substances (but not others), or against some forms of discrimination (but not others). We "know" that urinating in public is bad only because we have a revulsion against the idea of it. Many of our other moral convictions equally resist reflection or reexamination because they are embodied in tenacious, inarticulable emotions. And many of these nonrational convictions are embodied in the law and imposed on people who do not share them, or, more commonly, do not act in conformity with them because they derive utility from the conduct that the rule forbids.

I thus take the cognitive significance of emotion so seriously as to be unwilling to constitute reason the tribunal that reviews the emotions and decides which the law should encourage (tolerance, perhaps, but not disgust). The bedrock of many of our moral rules is emotion, not emotion-evaluating reason. Suppose that a legal rule intended, as many legal rules are, to attach sanctions to the violation of a moral rule that has no plausible social-functional justification were challenged before an emotionless judge. This judge would have difficulty rejecting the challenge because he would not have and could not be given rationally convincing reasons for the rule. The rule (say, against a mother's killing her infant) would strike him as arbitrary, whereas a person with a normal emotional endowment would reject the challenge out of hand because his emotions told him to do so. That is the correct response if you think as I do that it is not the proper business of judges to dismantle the moral code of their society or, what would come to much the same thing, to insist that it be rationalized convincingly.

The other emotion that is important for the judge to feel when he is faced with a case that cannot be decided by purely formalistic reasoning is empathy or fellow feeling. Empathy is one of the best examples of the cognitive character of emotion. The cognitive element in empathy is imagining the situation of another person; the affective element, which marks empathy as an emotion and not merely a dimension of rationality, is *feeling* the emotional state engendered in that person by his situation. My point is not that the judge should be partial to whichever party to the case tugs harder on his heartstrings. It is virtually the opposite. The importance of empathy in the performance of the judicial function is to bring home to the judge the interests of the absent parties, or in other words (the words of cognitive psychology, the subject of the next chapter) to combat the "availability heuristic." This is the tendency—we glimpsed it in the opening discussion of "emotionality"—to give too much weight to vivid immediate impressions, such as sight over narrative, and hence to pay too much attention to the feelings, the interests, and the humanity of the parties in the courtroom and too little to absent persons likely to be affected by the decision.

The availability heuristic is one of a long list of distortions in reasoning that have been identified by cognitive psychologists. Not all of them involve the emotions. The crooked appearance of a straight stick in water is an example of a perceptual distortion that owes nothing to emotion or emotionality. The availability heuristic crosses the line that separates the emotional from the "purely" cognitive; it is responsible for a number of tricks of memory that owe nothing to the emotionality of the events recalled or forgotten. But when triggered by the emotional charge of a particular feature of a situation, it is appropriately regarded as an example of a clash between emotion and reason. Its operation is illustrated by the debate over abortion. Before ultrasound images of early fetuses became common, the heuristic favored the proponents of abortion rights, because they could tell vivid stories and even show photographs of women killed by botched illegal abortions, whereas the abortion "victim," the fetus, was hidden from view. Ultrasound, by making the fetus visible, canceled the rhetorical advantage that the proponents of abortion rights had enjoyed by virtue of the availability heuristic.

The availability heuristic is conducive to short-sighted adjudication—whether excessive lenity for the murderer who makes an eloquent plea for mercy, his victim being unable to enter a counterplea by reason of being dead; or an excessive tilt in favor of the rights of tenants, oblivious of the effect on the rentals that other tenants will have to pay when landlords factor the court-engendered higher cost of rental housing into their other costs and pass a fraction, possibly a large fraction, of them onto tenants in the form of higher rentals; or a tax break for a struggling corporation, ignoring the fact that other firms will pay higher taxes as a result and will pass on a part of the additional cost to consumers. You don't need much in the way of empathy to be moved by a well-represented litigant pleading before you. The challenge to the empathetic imagination is to be moved by thinking or reading about the consequences of the litigation for absent—often completely unknown or even unborn—others who will be affected by your decision. The economic approach to law is empathetic because, although it does not wear its heart on its sleeve (rather, *because* it does not wear its heart on its sleeve), it brings into the decisional process the remote but cumulatively substantial interest of persons not before the court—such as future victims of murderers, future seekers of rental housing, future taxpayers, and future consumers. As Shakespeare has Angelo (in his role as judge) say in *Measure for Measure* in response to

Isabelle's plea that he show pity for her brother, "I show it most of all when I show justice; / For then I pity those I do not know, / Which a dismissed offense would after gall."[28]

There need be no tension between judicial detachment and judicial empathy. Detachment is not "cold" when it involves creating an emotional distance between the judge and the parties (and witnesses and others in his presence) in order to create space for an imaginative reconstruction of the feelings and interests of absent persons potentially affected by the judge's decision. The name that the legal system gives to this empathetic detachment is "judicial temperament." The judge who gets so emotionally involved in the immediacies of the case that he is blinded to the interests of the absent parties is said to lack judicial temperament; the most prominent recent example is the late Supreme Court Justice Harry Blackmun. We don't have an official name for the judge who displays the opposite form of emotionalism—a weird pride in maintaining a complete, inhuman indifference to the parties before him. But such judges are not admired.

So it would be misleading to say that good judges are less "emotional" than other people. It is just that they deploy a different suite of emotions in their work from what is appropriate both in personal life and in other vocational settings. Self-control is not only an emotion, but a strong emotion because it is a check on strong emotions.

∼ ANTICIPATING some of the discussion in Chapter 12, I now ask how the rules of evidence should be configured to help the judicial officer attain the proper emotional state sketched in the preceding section. The question can be focused by considering the issue of "victim impact" statements in death cases. The issue arose after the Supreme Court had held that defendants in such cases could present evidence designed to appeal to the jury's sense of mercy. Had the Court stopped there and not allowed similar evidence to be presented by the victim's family and friends—evidence designed to engender the same sympathy for the victim as the defendant was trying to engender for himself—the Court would have been distorting the process of empathetic consideration. The defendant, pitiably pleading for his life, would have been standing before the judge and jury in all his palpable humanity, while

---

28. *Measure for Measure*, Act II, scene 3, lines 127–129.

his victim, dead and gone, would have been invisible. Think of Antony in *Julius Caesar* exhibiting the body of Caesar at Caesar's funeral and bidding Caesar's wounds to plead for him. This is an early as well as fictional example of a victim impact statement, but it illustrates the point: the living occludes the dead and absent. The victim impact statement seeks to redress the balance; it is like my earlier example of the ultrasound picture of the fetus. Anyone genuinely concerned about the distorting effect on judgment of the availability heuristic, rather than merely concerned to reduce the number of executions, should approve the Court's decision to allow victim impact statements.[29]

It has been argued, however, that since the jury will have learned a lot about the victim during the guilt phase of the trial, evidence about the victim at the sentencing phase is redundant.[30] But that is also true about the murderer, whom defense counsel will have sought to present in a sympathetic light during the guilt phase. Moreover, much victim impact evidence concerns the effect of the victim's death on his survivors, and such evidence will not have figured in the guilt phase. And to the extent that the evidence *is* redundant, its emotional force—the focus of the objection—will be blunted.

Also unconvincing is the argument that the victim is more likely than the murderer to come from the same social class as the jurors and so the jury will require additional help in understanding the potentially mitigating circumstances of poverty or deprivation or discrimination that may have impelled the murderer to his crime. Taken to its extreme, the argument implies that when the murder victim is rich, and the jurors and murderer are of average income, victim impact evidence should be allowed but not mitigating evidence. More generally, it implies complicating the litigation process with considerations of class that are alien to American ideology. In any event, most murders are between members of the same social class, what used to be called the "lower" class. Most murder victims have the same background of deprivation as the murderers, so that the banning of victim-impact state-

29. Payne v. Tennessee, 501 U.S. 808 (1991).

30. These and other arguments against victim impact statements are summarized in Note, "Thou Shall Not Kill Any Nice People: The Problem of Victim Impact Statements in Capital Sentencing," 35 *American Criminal Law Review* 93 (1997). See also Susan Bandes, "Empathy, Narrative, and Victim Impact Statements," 63 *University of Chicago Law Review* 361 (1996); Martha C. Nussbaum, "Equity and Mercy," 22 *Philosophy and Public Affairs* 83 (1993).

ments would actually penalize the law-abiding poor. What is true is that allowing victim impact statements "discriminates" against murder victims who do not have loving relatives, and so it could be thought to cheapen the lives of the poor and friendless and to magnify the effect of social class on punishment. But this argues not for excluding victim impact statements but for appointing a friendless victim's representative to be Antony to the murderer's Julius Caesar and bid his dumb wounds to speak. To exclude victim impact statements may save a few murderers of the rich and popular but it will further cheapen the lives of the poor and marginal by reducing the likelihood that their murderers will be executed.

It is also not a good objection to the victim impact statement that it appeals to the jury's sense of vengeance rather than to the "nobler" emotion of mercy. Mercy is nobler than vengeance only in the sense of being less natural[31] and less practical. On both counts it is more appealing to our modern rigorists (many found in the academy), who, like the early Christians, seek to set themselves apart from the herd by living (nowadays they are much more likely simply to advocate—"think Left, live Right," as the saying goes) a life that is repugnant to most people and that if adhered to steadily by enough people would bring society grinding to a halt. Vengeance is problematic, but it is not irrational.[32] A vengeance culture, with the (to us) exaggerated and dangerous emphasis on honor that it encourages, is rational in times or places in which law is weak or nonexistent, even though its rationality depends on

31. Not *un*natural; it is closely related to altruism, and we know that some situations will generate altruistic impulses even toward strangers. The word "mercy" is often used, however, to denote the extreme of altruism that is associated with Christian ethical teachings.

32. See Robert L. Trivers, "The Evolution of Reciprocal Altruism," 46 *Quarterly Review of Biology* 35, 49 (1971); J. Hirshleifer, "Natural Economy versus Political Economy," 1 *Journal of Social and Biological Structures* 319, 332, 334 (1978); Richard A. Posner, *The Economics of Justice*, ch. 8 (1981) ("Retribution and Related Concepts of Punishment"); Posner, *Law and Literature*, ch. 2 (rev. and enlarged ed. 1998); Robert M. Axelrod, *The Evolution of Cooperation* (1984); Christopher Boehm, *Blood Revenge: The Enactment and Management of Conflict in Montenegro and Other Tribal Societies* (1984); Robert H. Frank, *Passions within Reason: The Strategic Role of the Emotions* 1–70 passim (1988); Stephen Wilson, *Feuding, Conflict and Banditry in Nineteenth-Century Corsica* (1988); William Ian Miller, *Bloodtaking and Peacemaking: Feud, Law, and Society in Saga Iceland* (1990); David J. Cohen, *Law, Violence, and Community in Classical Athens* (1995); Dov Cohen and Joe Vandello, "Meanings of Violence," 27 *Journal of Legal Studies* 567 (1998); Steffen Huck and Jörg Oechssler, "The Indirect Evolutionary Approach to Explaining Fair Allocations," 28 *Games and Economic Behavior* 13 (1999).

emotion to create the commitments necessary to make a decentralized system of purely informal enforcement work. The persistence of this system, albeit in much attenuated form, in the American South to this day[33] may seem puzzling. One might think that the South, because it has a substantially higher incidence of violence than the North, would be better off if the vestiges of the code of honor of the Old South[34] could be obliterated. Not necessarily; we would have to know what that level would be were there no code of honor. Maybe the demand for crime is so great relative to the resources of the criminal justice system in southern states that the code of honor continues to perform an essential deterrent function.

It is interesting to note that the code of honor is taken more seriously by southerners in close-knit families than in ones who are not in close-knit families.[35] This pattern makes good economic sense. The literature on revenge emphasizes the importance of the family in lending credibility to threats of retaliation. A murdered person who has no family has no one to revenge him, making the cost of not being part of a close-knit family very great in a vengeance culture. Presumably the southerners who break away from their families have alternative means of self-protection to the code of honor.

Apart from whatever conditions may explain the persistence of the code of honor in the South, some degree of vengeful emotion remains indispensable to the control and deterrence of criminal and other antisocial behavior. Without such emotion, relatively few crimes would be reported and deterrence would therefore often fail as a method of social control. Excess of mercy can be as socially destructive as excess of vengefulness. The turn-the-other-cheek morality of the Sermon on the Mount is not a practical formula for living. Mercy in sentencing means lighter sentencing; lighter sentencing leads to more crime; more crime means more victims of crime. So mercy for victims implies severity for criminals, and mercy for criminals implies multiplying the victims of crime. Mercy is on both sides of the balance but in one of the pans is also justice while in the other is—the availability heuristic, pushing for one-sided, short-sighted, sentimental penal practices.

33. See, for example, Cohen and Vandello, note 32 above.

34. On which see Jack K. Williams, *Dueling in the Old South: Vignettes of Social History* (1980).

35. See Cohen and Vandello, note 32 above, at 582.

I am not arguing that the law should open the door all the way to emotional appeals in litigation. An argument could be made for banning victim impact statements *and* pleas of mercy by defendants, in order both to minimize the operation of hatred in the sentencing process without distorting the balance between victim and murderer and to reduce the length and cost of criminal proceedings. And certainly there are emotional appeals that hurt rather than help the cognitive process, such as gruesome photographs of a murder victim that the prosecution wants to introduce into evidence not in order to establish victim impact but in order to establish guilt, the issue to which the photographs will often be irrelevant. Cognitive theorists of emotion, while right to complain about the excessive dichotomization of reason and emotion, should be the first to admit that emotion can get in the way of rational processes and engender avoidable mistakes.

In social evolution, law takes the place of vengeance as the principal method of deterring and redressing serious infringements of the norms of social cooperation. From this perspective lawsuits are merely a low-cost substitute for duels, feuds, brawls, and wars. The law channels, civilizes, and subdues, but does not eliminate, the anger and indignation that people feel when they believe that their rights have been infringed or that their interests are threatened by someone who accuses them of having infringed his rights. But in a legal system such as the American in which the number of legal disputes is very large in relation to the resources that the system is prepared to devote to their resolution, the bulk of those disputes must somehow be resolved before the litigation process has run its full course from complaint to judgment to exhaustion of all appellate remedies. Fortunately, there are strong incentives to settle a case at the earliest opportunity: litigation is much more costly than settlement and most people are risk averse and therefore prefer the certain equivalent to a chance. Even without risk aversion (but assuming risk neutrality rather than risk preferring, that is, a taste for gambling), virtually all cases would settle if the parties agreed on what judgment would be likely if the case did not settle. Suppose they agreed that the plaintiff had a 50 percent chance of winning $100,000 if the case went to judgment, and the cost of continuing to litigate was $10,000 to each party, and the cost of settling only $2,000 to each. Then the plaintiff would have an expected benefit of continuing the litigation of $42,000 ($100,000 x .5 − $10,000 + $2,000)[36] and the defendant an expected cost of $58,000 ($100,000 x .5 + $10,000 − $2,000), and so at any price between $42,000 and $58,000 both parties would be better off settling, and presumably they can negotiate to some point in that rather generous range.

The principal danger is that they will not arrive at identical estimates of how the case is likely to come out if it goes all the way to judgment. The specific danger is that each will exaggerate his own probability of winning, since it is that condition of "mutual optimism" that will compress or even eliminate the existence of an overlapping settlement range. The reactions of courts are not always easy to predict and, because of the value of surprise at trial, parties will often have strategic reasons to withhold information in their possession that might help their opponent to make a more accurate guess as to the likely outcome of continued litigation. Each may be reluctant, moreover, to be the first to suggest settlement, lest the suggestion signal weakness and cause the other party to stiffen his settlement terms. Both the convergence of the parties' estimates and, if there is convergence, negotiation to a mutually agreeable settlement point within an overlapping settlement range are less likely if the parties' minds are fogged by emotion, and specifically the kinds of emotion typically aroused by serious struggles. Anger begets righteousness, and a sense of righteousness is likely to increase confidence that the judiciary, as the repository of justice, will rule in one's favor; it may also make it difficult to perceive the merits of the opposing party's position. On both counts anger is likely to increase mutual optimism about the outcome of the litigation and thus reduce the probability of settlement.

A device by which the legal system with increasing frequency is trying to address the informational, strategic, and emotional issues that discourage settlement is the use of a mediator in settlement negotiations. A mediator is a neutral third party who, unlike an arbitrator (a private judge), has no decisional power. He might seem impotent, therefore, to bring about a settlement. Yet actually mediation addresses all three of the problems that I have identified. Since the mediator generally meets with the parties separately and his discussions with them are confidential, and so they are likely to be more candid with him than

36. Because the cost of settlement is saved if there is no settlement.

they would be with each other, he is in a position to form a more accurate impression of the actual strengths and weaknesses of the parties' respective positions than they are. And since he can make proposals for settlement, the parties need not know whether a proposal is emanating from them or from him (and therefore which party made the first proposal to settle, thus signaling weakness), and so they have a greater incentive to make a proposal to him for (covert) transmission to the other party than they would have to make a proposal directly to the other party. Finally and perhaps most important, the mediator is not the object of the parties' anger. His presence is a soothing one and encourages each party to make a realistic assessment of its chances if the litigation continues. And when he is negotiating with each party separately, and thus masking the anger of each from the other, they can negotiate a settlement without ever having to be in the same room with each other.

~ 8

Behavioral Law and Economics

$\mathcal{I}$N THE ARTICLE that provides the primary though not only text for the discussion in this chapter, Christine Jolls (economist and lawyer), Cass Sunstein (lawyer), and Richard Thaler (economist) endeavor to use the insights of behavioral economics—the application of psychology to economics—to improve economic analysis of law, which they believe to be handicapped by its commitment to the assumption that people are rational.[1] Since JST complain with some justice that economists and economically minded lawyers do not always make clear what they mean by "rationality," let me make clear at the outset what I mean by the word: choosing the best available means to the chooser's ends. For example, a rational person who wants to keep warm will compare the alternative means known to him of keeping

1. See Christine Jolls, Cass R. Sunstein, and Richard Thaler, "A Behavioral Approach to Law and Economics," 50 *Stanford Law Review* 1471 (1998) (hereinafter "JST"), reprinted in *Behavioral Law and Economics* 13 (Cass R. Sunstein ed. 2000); the other essays in that book; Jolls, Sunstein, and Thaler, "Theories and Tropes: A Reply to Posner and Kelman," 50 *Stanford Law Review* 1593 (1998); and Sunstein, "Behavioral Law and Economics: A Progress Report," 1 *American Law and Economics Review* 115 (1999); Jon D. Hanson and Douglas A. Kysar, "Taking Behavioralism Seriously: The Problem of Market Manipulation," 74 *New York University Law Review* 630 (1999); Russell B. Korobkin and Thomas S. Ulen, "Law and Behavioral Science: Removing the Rationality Assumption from Law and Economics," 88 *California Law Review* 1051 (2000). For an early discussion of the implications of behavioral economics for the economic analysis of law, see Thomas S. Ulen, "Cognitive Imperfections and the Economic Analysis of Law," 12 *Hamline Law Review* 385 (1989).

warm in terms of cost, comfort, and other dimensions of utility and disutility, and will choose from this array the means that achieves warmth with the greatest margin of benefit over cost, broadly defined. Rational choice need not be conscious choice or require a large cortex. Rats are at least as rational as human beings when rationality is defined as achieving one's ends (survival and reproduction, in the case of rats) at least cost. It is particularly important to emphasize that rationality does not entail either complete information or error-free reasoning from available information; information is costly (especially in time) to obtain, and processing information is costly in time and concentration, so a person is not necessarily being irrational if he sometimes acts on incomplete information or sometimes uses mental shortcuts, including the emotional short circuiting of reason that we examined in the preceding chapter, that may yield inaccurate results. These points may make it difficult, as we shall see, to distinguish between behavioral and nonbehavioral interpretations of economic or legal behavior.

Behavioral economics is not the only source of challenges to the rational model of human behavior, although it is the most sophisticated. The idea that the rational model is simply too "cold" is widespread and powerful, though we saw in Chapter 7 that "emotional" behavior can often be given a rational construal and though it is an elementary mistake to confuse a model with a description and condemn the first because it is not the second. I therefore want to begin at a slight distance from JST's article by examining very briefly two examples of seeming irrationality that owe nothing to the cognitive distortions emphasized by the behaviorists. One is the phenomenon so dramatically on display of late in the Balkans and parts of Africa and Asia of ethnic hatred, which may seem to defy any kind of rational explanation. In fact a signaling model (and signaling will play an important role later in this chapter) may furnish a clue to such an explanation. As Timur Kuran explains, the kind of "bandwagon effects" that caused a rapid escalation of ethnic violence in a previously peaceful Yugoslavia may have been rational every step of the way, even though the consequences were catastrophic for most of the people involved.[2] Tito died, and the benefits of ethnic solidarity rose because of uncertainty about the stability of the

2. Timur Kuran, "Ethnic Norms and Their Transformation through Reputational Cascades," 27 *Journal of Legal Studies* 623 (1998). See also Eric A. Posner, "Symbols, Signals, and Social Norms in Politics and the Law," 27 *Journal of Legal Studies* 765 (1998).

central government, while the costs of ethnic solidarity fell because it was no longer punished. Some Yugoslavs felt passionately about ethnic issues (and perhaps they had good reasons, though possibly of an entirely selfish kind), and they were now free to express their feelings. In these circumstances, the net cost, say to Serbians who were in fact indifferent to ethnic issues, of signaling loyalty to the group with which they have their most valuable interactions, a group containing the minority of Serbians who were passionate about these issues, fell. As more and more Serbians signaled their attachment to the Serbian cause, the pressure on the remaining Serbians to signal such attachment rose, since the fewer holdouts there were the more easily they would be identified and rejected as nonconformists. By such a process, as Kuran demonstrates, even a relatively slight jar to an equilibrium of no overt ethnic solidarity could rapidly give way to an equilibrium of lethal ethnic antagonisms.

My second example involves the contention by the philosopher Elizabeth Anderson that rational-choice economists are committed to assuming, with hopeless unrealism, that everyone is "a type-A personality," who "does not bow down to social convention, tradition, or even morality," who is instead "autonomous, self-reliant, consistent, coolly calculating."[3] This conception of rational-choice theory, which implies extruding from economics a host of distinguished economists, such as Gary Becker, who explicitly reject the type-A model in favor of a model of human choice that emphasizes altruism, limited information, habit, and emotion,[4] leads Anderson to argue that a person who accepts the authority of the Catholic Church is irrational because a type A won't take direction from anyone. She might as well say that it is irrational for her to accept the authority of high-energy physics, or for a piano student to accept the authority of his teacher.

Much of Anderson's article that I am criticizing is devoted to criticism of a book by Kristin Luker about women's decisions to abort.[5] Luker is not an economist, but she hypothesizes that a woman's deci-

3. Elizabeth Anderson, "Should Feminists Reject Rational Choice Theory"? (paper presented at the Conference on Social Norms, Social Meaning, and the Economic Analysis of Law, University of Chicago Law School, April 19–20, 1997).

4. I add that a type-A personality is not coolly rational, but indeed hotly emotional and even self-destructive. Yet even type As—or better, perhaps, workaholics—can usefully be modeled in economic terms: a type A is simply a person with an unusually high opportunity cost of leisure.

5. Kristin Luker, *Taking Chances: Abortion and the Decision Not to Contracept* (1975).

sion to abort is rational, and she tries to identify the benefits and costs that might—against the odds as it were—confirm the hypothesis. The book is not at first glance a promising candidate for a test of rational-choice theory, so that Anderson's choice of it as the test vehicle might be thought uncharitable toward the theory. Luker's sample consisted of women who had had abortions at an abortion clinic in California in the early 1970s, meaning that they were poor women who had come up losers at a time when legal abortion was new. And yet Luker's inquiry guided by the hypothesis of rationality is illuminating. It shows that although the decision to abort implies that the cost of pregnancy exceeds the benefits, that cost is merely an *expected* cost and may be outweighed by the benefits of unprotected sex. These benefits include avoiding violation of a religious norm against contraception, increasing the likelihood of marriage to one's sexual partner by concealing sexual experience, extracting a commitment from him,[6] and simply catering to his desire to avoid using a condom, which diminishes male sexual pleasure. The first benefit, avoiding a religious prohibition, Anderson deems irrational because Catholicism anathematizes abortion even more than contraception. This ignores the fact that pregnancy is a probabilistic rather than certain consequence of unprotected sex and that the choice of abortion is itself only a probability, not a certainty, when the decision to engage in unprotected sex is made. Anderson emphasizes the misconceptions that many women have about the probability of becoming pregnant as a result of particular sexual conduct, but to be poorly informed is not to be irrational.

Not everything in Luker's study is consistent with rational-choice theory. A degree of self-deception and confusion in the women in her sample is perceptible. But there is enough rationality to enable an economist to use the study to hypothesize a utility function for women facing a risk of abortion, a hypothesis that can be tested with data on changes in the cost and effectiveness of contraceptive methods, the risk of sexually transmitted disease, the availability of abortion, the level of welfare benefits for unmarried mothers, and women's job opportunities. If the predictions generated by the utility function survive con-

6. In Anderson's paraphrase of Luker, "If she gets pregnant, he will have to reveal how serious he is about her, and either agree to marry or break off the relationship. She either gains a husband, or the knowledge that he isn't worth further investment plus the freedom to seek a more marriage-worthy partner." Anderson, note 3 above.

frontation with the data, we have some basis for concluding that much behavior in the face of abortion risk is indeed rational.[7]

Let me turn back now to behavioral economics, and let me make clear at the outset of my discussion of it that I don't doubt that it's a source of valuable insights for law.[8] I used the availability heuristic in the preceding chapter and will use it again, along with other cognitive quirks that Jolls, Sunstein, and Thaler highlight, in the chapters on evidence. But JST overargue their case. Some of the points they make are new labels for old challenges to the economic model of behavior that owe nothing to behavioral economics in any distinctive sense, the sort of challenges I have been discussing up to this point. Others are best explained by reference to evolutionary considerations that play no role in behavioral economics. Others are only weakly supported.

Many of the insights that JST ascribe to behavioral economics are already a part of economic analysis of law, which without abandoning its commitment to the rational model of human behavior has abandoned the model of hyperrational, emotionless, unsocial, supremely egoistic, omniscient, utterly selfish, nonstrategic man (or woman), operating in conditions of costless information acquisition and processing, that JST in places appear to ascribe to it.[9] To take just one example for now, the availability heuristic is consistent with rationality once it is acknowledged that imaginative reconstruction requires more "effort" (that is, cost) than immediate perception. Recall the issue of "victim impact"

7. As argued in Tomas J. Philipson and Richard A. Posner, "Sexual Behaviour, Disease, and Fertility Risk," 1 *Risk Decision and Policy* 91 (1996).

8. For a useful survey of behavioral economics that differs from JST's in not highlighting legal applications, see Matthew Rabin, "Psychology and Economics," 36 *Journal of Economic Literature* 11 (1998). A more extended treatment by one of the leaders of the field is Richard H. Thaler, *Quasi Rational Economics* (1991). And for a brief critical discussion, see Jennifer Arlen, "The Future of Behavioral Economic Analysis of Law," 51 *Vanderbilt Law Review* 1765 (1998). Good discussions of the principles and findings of cognitive psychology that subtend behavioral economics can be found in Detlof von Winterfeldt and Ward Edwards, *Decision Analysis and Behavioral Research*, ch. 13 (1986); Albert J. Moore, "Trial by Schema: Cognitive Filters in the Courtroom," 37 *UCLA Law Review* 273 (1989); and especially Richard Nisbett and Lee Ross, *Human Inference: Strategies and Shortcomings of Social Judgment* (1980).

9. It is noteworthy that Professor Coase, whom JST properly regard as a principal founder of nonbehavioral law and economics (of which the Coase Theorem is indeed a cornerstone, as we saw in the Introduction), rejects the traditional economic model of man as a rational maximizer of his satisfactions. See Ronald H. Coase, *The Firm, the Market, and the Law: Essays on the Institutional Structure of Production* 4 (1988); Coase, "The New Institutional Economics," 140 *Journal of Institutional and Theoretical Economics* 229, 231 (1984).

statements discussed in the preceding chapter. The argument for allowing them into evidence in a capital case is precisely that without them the jurors or judge will have to exert extra effort to imagine the victim's suffering, in order to counterbalance the impact of the immediate perception of the suffering defendant, pleading for his life. The availability heuristic would be evidence of irrationality only if people never made adjustments for it. But we saw the legal system adjusting to it in deciding to admit victim impact statements into evidence, and we shall see further examples in Chapters 11 and 12.

Behavioral economics, JST explain, rejects the assumption that people are rational maximizers of their satisfactions in favor of assumptions of "bounded rationality," "bounded willpower," and "bounded self-interest." Let us examine these three assumptions.

Bounded rationality refers to the fact that people have cognitive quirks that prevent them from processing information rationally. These include, besides the availability heuristic, overoptimism, the sunk-cost fallacy, loss aversion, and framing effects. There is a good deal of evidence for the existence of these quirks. But because most of the evidence consists of experiments with students or of responses to surveys, it is unclear to what extent the quirks are due to serious, stubborn obstacles to rational action or merely to the operation of mental shortcuts in settings in which the optimal investment in thought is low because so little turns on thinking through the problem posed by the experiment or survey.

JST exaggerate the evidence by failing to distinguish between impediments to clear instrumental reasoning and preferences that enlightened observers may think silly. Consider the case of the person who will eat a lobster contentedly if he doesn't see it when it's alive but, if he's asked to pick it out of a lobster tank, will lose his appetite for it. JST would say that this person's mind had been fogged by the availability heuristic. An alternative interpretation is that he has different preferences for two different goods: one a lobster seen only after being cooked and the other a lobster seen before, in its living state, as well as after. These are different goods in the same way that a good that comes in pretty wrapping paper is different from one that comes in a brown paper bag. There is no basis for pronouncing a difference in preferences with regard to such pairs of goods irrational (although ethical criticism may be possible, as animal-rights advocates remind us) or for dismissing the difference as a product of "emotion." When people re-act with fright to a horror film, we might be tempted to say that they are being irrational, because the movie is make believe. But preferences cannot be divorced from emotion, or emotion from their stimuli, and so instrumental reasoning cannot be thought pervaded with irrational-ity merely because a frequent goal of such reasoning is a preference that we would not have if we were not emotional beings. The way to distinguish a real cognitive quirk from an emotion-driven preference is to ask whether if you point out to a person the "irrationality" of his ac-tion he either will change it or at least will admit that he's being irratio-nal. Obviously it would do nothing to a liking for horror movies to point out that they are make believe; the people who watch them know that already.

Moreover, the fact that human beings are not always rational, even that some are irrational most or all of the time, is not *in itself* a chal-lenge to rational-choice economics. Many people have an irrational fear of flying. It is an irrational fear rather than just an aversion that we may not share because the people who harbor it acknowledge that it is irrational. They know that the surface-transportation alternatives are more dangerous and they want above all to avoid being killed, yet they choose the more dangerous modes anyway. Their regret, embarrass-ment, and annoyance with themselves distinguish their case from that of the people who like horror movies. But their irrationality does not invalidate the economic analysis of transportation, although it may show why pecuniary and time costs, and accident rates, may not explain all the difference between the demand for air transportation and the demand for its substitutes. Most of the usual predictions that econo-mists make about behavior will go through: a fall in the price of air transportation will result in an increase in demand, as will a rise in the price of a substitute or a fall in the price of a complement. A preference can be taken as a given, and economic analysis proceed as usual, even if the preference is irrational.

Voting, one of JST's examples of irrational behavior, can be analyzed similarly. When viewed as an instrumental act, voting in a political election is irrational because it costs something (chiefly time) to vote yet there is no offsetting benefit to the individual voter because virtu-ally no such elections are decided by one vote. But treating the desire to vote as a given, like other expressive behavior (for example, applauding at a concert or other public performance), the economist can answer important questions about voting behavior. These questions include why the old vote more than the young, why retired people vote more than unemployed people (even though both groups might seem to have low costs of time), and why turnout is greater in a close election.[10] Turnout is greater in a close election not because one's vote is more likely to make a difference—even close elections are not decided by one vote—but because the costs of information are lower the more publicity an electoral contest generates, and close elections generate more publicity than one-sided ones.[11]

Bounded willpower is just a relabeling of weakness of will. Most of us have experienced the sensation of being torn between two selves—a "good" self that has our long-run welfare in mind and a "bad," short-sighted self—and of the "bad" self winning unless strenuous efforts are made to thwart it. Hyperbolic discounting is said to illustrate the operation of weakness of will, although it can equally well be understood in terms of information costs. A hyperbolic discounter increases his discount rate as the costs or benefits that he is discounting become more imminent. For example, if you asked me whether I would rather have $1,000 in the year 2011 or $800 in the year 2010, I would almost certainly say $1,000 in 2011. But if you asked me whether I would rather have $800 today or $1,000 a year from now, I might very well say $800 now. And this would mark me as a hyperbolic discounter. But the reason for the different reactions may simply be that I lack a clear conception of my consumption needs a decade hence; the reason may, in other words, be the imagination cost that I mentioned earlier. I cannot imagine what might make me pay in effect a huge interest rate to reallocate consumption from 2011 to 2010. The fact that knowledge and imagination are "bounded" just shows, what no rational-choice economist doubts, that information costs are positive.

Yet no one can doubt that there is such a thing as weakness of will, even if hyperbolic discounting is not a good example of it. Unlike the cognitive quirks ("bounded rationality"), however, it can be analyzed

10. See Richard A. Posner, *Aging and Old Age* 148–152 (1995).
11. An alternative explanation, stressing the incentive that political parties have to invest more in campaigns for elections that are likely to be close, is offered in Ron Schachar and Barry Nalebuff, "Follow the Leader: Theory and Evidence on Political Participation," 89 *American Economic Review* 525 (1999).

within the framework of rational-choice theory[12]—easily when we are torn between alternative courses of action because of uncertainty, less easily when there is no uncertainty, as in the case of refusing to keep chocolate in the house because of doubt about one's ability to overcome temptation. Explaining the second type of behavior in rational-choice terms may require abandoning a tacit assumption of most economic analysis—that the self is a unity—in favor of a conception of the person as a locus of different selves. All the selves are rational but they have—rationally—inconsistent preferences. Examples are a young self versus an old self, with the former unwilling to save money so that the latter can enjoy a high level of consumption; a pre-accident self unwilling to spend heavily on accident insurance versus a post-accident self that would have liked the pre-accident self to buy a lot of accident insurance; and in the case of the chocolate, a present-oriented self that lives for the moment and a future-oriented self.[13] (The last example is related to the first.) The assumption of a unitary self is not inherent in the concept of rationality used in economics; it is merely a convenient assumption in most situations that economists analyze.

As in this example, behavioral economists tend to give up on rational-choice economics too soon. Matthew Rabin writes that "a nominal wage increase of 5 percent in a period of 12 percent inflation offends people's sense of fairness less than a 7 percent decrease in a time of no inflation."[14] People know that not all wages will increase by the rate of inflation—inflation spells economic trouble; only with perfect indexing would real wages remain unaffected by it. So the failure of one's wage to rise by the rate of inflation need not imply that one's employer is critical of one's work. But a sharp wage cut out of the blue is often a signal of dissatisfaction with an employee's work, and so engenders anxiety or resentment.

JST remark that Gary Becker has demonstrated that random choice in a situation of scarcity will generate a downward-sloping demand curve,[15] from which they conclude that downward-sloping demand is

12. As acknowledged in Rabin, note 8 above, at 40.

13. See, for example, Thomas C. Schelling, "Self-Command in Practice, in Policy, and in a Theory of Rational Choice," 74 *American Economic Review Papers and Proceedings* 1 (May 1984); Richard A. Posner, "Are We One Self or Multiple Selves? Implications for Law and Public Policy," 3 *Legal Theory* 23 (1997).

14. Rabin, note 8 above, at 36.

15. Gary S. Becker, "Irrational Behavior and Economic Theory," 70 *Journal of Political Economy* 1 (1962), reprinted in Becker, *The Economic Approach to Human Behavior*, ch. 5 (1976).

not evidence in support of the rational model of behavior. Becker's argument is that consumers have limited budgets, and so on average, even if their purchasing decisions are made randomly, they will purchase less of a pricier good because a fixed amount of money will not buy as much of it. He did not suggest that most consumers *are* irrational, however, or that well-attested economic phenomena other than the downward-sloping market demand curve, such as the tendency of the prices of the same good to be equalized, could be explained without assuming rationality. Buyers do not in fact choose randomly. Rationality is the only reasonable explanation for their reactions to changes in relative prices.

The real significance of randomness in rational-choice economics is in further explaining why that economics can accommodate a good deal of irrational behavior without a fatal loss of predictive power. Most questions that economists ask concern aggregate rather than individual behavior, for example the effect on the quantity purchased of cigarettes of an increase in the cigarette excise tax, not the effect of the tax increase on Mr. Cigarette Smoker *A* or Ms. Cigarette Smoker *B*. Suppose the cigarette tax is increased by 2 percent and rational smokers respond by reducing their purchases of cigarettes by an average of 1 percent while the irrational ones respond randomly—some reduce their purchases by 50 percent, some actually increase their purchases, and so on. If the distribution of these random behaviors has the same mean as the rational smokers' reaction to the tax, the effect of the tax on the quantity demanded of cigarettes will be identical to what it would be if all cigarette consumers were rational. This is true no matter what fraction of cigarette consumers is irrational.

JST claim that economic analysts of self-destructive behavior, such as drug addiction and unsafe sex, use rationality as fancy dress for the tautological assertion that people choose what they prefer. Not so. The economic analysts to whom JST are referring assume that people do *not* want to become addicted or to contract AIDS. The analysts explore the conditions under which the costs of such behavior, steep as they are, are nevertheless outweighed by perceived benefits. They deduce from rational-choice theory, and then test empirically, nonintuitive hypotheses about these unconventional behaviors. An example is the hypothesis that the long-run price elasticity of addictive goods is high, rather than low as conventionally believed, because the rational addict expects his consumption of the addictive good to increase over time, and so an increase in the price of such a good (if the increase is expected to be long term) will have a greater long-term effect on his expenses than the same increase in the price of a nonaddictive good would have.[16] Another example is the hypothesis that the AIDS epidemic will cause an increase in the rate of unwanted pregnancies by inducing a rational substitution of condoms—which are good prophylactics against disease but mediocre contraceptives—for the pill, which is an excellent contraceptive but no prophylactic.[17]

Addiction, whether to crack cocaine or to unsafe sex, is weakness of will writ large; yet economists can model it in rational-choice terms. The existence of the irrationalities emphasized in behavioral economics need not derail rational-choice economics.

Bounded self-interest refers to the fact that people sometimes act out of motives (compendiously, for JST, "fairness") that do not seem explicable by self-interest even in the sense, which is now conventional in rational-choice economics, in which an altruistic act is self-interested. If an increase in A's utility will increase B's utility, this means that B is altruistic toward A and it may therefore be in B's self-interest to transfer resources to A. JST are not interested in altruism, positive or negative,[18] in the sense of interdependent utilities. They are interested in cases in which a person will do something for other people—or against other people—because he thinks it the fair thing to do.

JST's lumping fairness in with cognitive quirks and weakness of will suggests that behavioral economics is merely the negative of rational-choice economics—the residuum of social phenomena unexplained by it. JST don't connect their claim that "fairness," which they define in golden-rule terms—be kind to the kind, and unkind to the unkind—is important to some people some of the time to their claims that people have difficulty processing some types of information and subordinating short-run to long-run interests. Those are disabilities or insufficiencies; acting in accordance with notions of fairness is a strength. The cognitive quirks belong to cognitive psychology, weakness of will to the

16. See Gary S. Becker, Michael Grossman, and Kevin M. Murphy, "Rational Addiction and the Effect of Price on Consumption," 81 *American Economic Review Papers and Proceedings* 237 (May 1991), reprinted in Becker, *Accounting for Tastes* 77 (1986).

17. See Philipson and Posner, note 7 above.

18. Envy is an example of negative altruism—the situation in which a decrease in A's utility will increase B's utility.

psychology of neurosis and other abnormalities, and fairness to moral philosophy or moral psychology.

The picture that JST paint with their three "boundeds" drawn from different domains of psychological theory is of a person who has trouble thinking straight or taking care for the future but who at the same time is actuated by a concern with being fair to other people, including complete strangers. This may be a psychologically realistic picture of the average person,[19] and it responds to the familiar complaint that "economic man" is unrecognizable in real life. But it has methodological problems. In theory-making, descriptive accuracy is purchased at a sacrifice of predictive power. The rational-choice economist asks what "rational man" would do in a given situation.[20] Usually the answer is pretty clear and can be compared with actual behavior to see whether the prediction is confirmed. Sometimes it is not confirmed—and so we have behavioral economics. But it is profoundly unclear what "behavioral man" would do in any given situation. A compound of rational and nonrational capacities and impulses, he might do anything. There is neither a causal account of behavioral man nor a model of his decisional structure. These gaps give rise to many questions: Do cognitive quirks diminish as the costs of yielding to them rise? If so, why? Does weakness of will vary across people, and, again, if so why? Do JST believe that their own analysis is marred by cognitive quirks or weakness of will, or actuated by a sense of fairness, or of resentment at being treated unfairly?[21] If not, why not? And are the quirks curable? Is weakness of will curable?[22]

---

19. It is the implicit modern liberal conception of the average person—good, but inept, and for both reasons not very responsive to incentives, though perhaps rather plastic. The implicit conservative view of the average person, in contrast, is that he is competent but bad; hence conservatives place emphasis on incentives and constraints.

20. To repeat an earlier point, he need only be rational with respect to the particular choice confronting him. People who are morbidly fearful of flying are assumed to respond rationally to changes in ticket prices, even though it is difficult to give a rational account of their fears.

21. I give an example later of where JST appear to have succumbed to the hindsight fallacy, which is one of the cognitive quirks. Rabin, note 8 above, at 27 n. 21, claims that economists are subject to "same-evidence polarization," one of the cognitive quirks. Well, Rabin is an economist, as are Jolls and Thaler.

22. Not, can these problems be circumvented, as in my chocolate example, but can they be solved, so that people are no longer afflicted by cognitive deformities and lack of willpower. JST are curiously fatalistic about the quirks and the weakness. This may be because they have no theory of where these things come from. I return to this point at the end of the chapter.

These questions are made both urgent and mysterious by the under-theorization of behavioral economics. It is undertheorized because of its residual, and in consequence purely empirical, character. Behavioral economics is defined by its subject rather than by its method and its subject is merely the set of phenomena that rational-choice models (or at least the simplest of them) do not explain. It would not be surprising if many of these phenomena turned out to be unrelated to each other, just as the set of things that are not edible by man include stones, toad-stools, thunderclaps, and the Pythagorean theorem. Describing, speci-fying, and classifying the empirical failures of a theory is a valid and im-portant scholarly activity. But it is not an alternative theory.

Explanation and prediction must not be confused. It's easy to formu-late a theory that will explain, in the sense of subsume, all observations within its domain, however anomalous they are from another theoreti-cal standpoint. The trick is to relax whatever assumptions in the other theory made some of the observations anomalous. The rotation of the moons of Jupiter was anomalous in medieval cosmology because each planet (other than the earth, which was not considered a planet, but in-stead the center around which the planets revolved) was thought to be fastened to a crystalline sphere, which the moons would have collided with in their rotation. The anomaly could be dispelled by assuming that the sphere was permeable, or by assuming (as Cardinal Bellarmine did in his famous dispute with Galileo) that the telescopic observations that had disclosed the rotation of Jupiter's moons were a deceit by the devil. Whichever route was taken, the amended theory would not gen-erate any predictions about planetary satellites; all it would predict was that whatever would be, would be. Similarly, if rational-choice theory bumps up against some example of irrational behavior, the example can be accommodated by changing the theory to allow for irrational behav-ior, in other words, by substituting behavioralism for rationality. But there is no greater gain in predictive power than in the cosmology ex-ample; in both cases, in fact, there is a loss. If a theory is so vague or elastic that it cannot be falsified, neither it nor its predictions can be validated; everything that happens is by definition consistent with the theory. When people act rationally, the behavioralists do not treat this as contradicting the assumption of bounded willpower. When people resist temptations, thus demonstrating strength of will, this is not treated as contradicting the assumption of bounded willpower. And when they act selfishly, this is not thought to contradict the assumption of bounded self-interest. If people became more rational, this would be attributed to their having learned the lessons of behavioral economics, and so would operate to confirm rather than refute it. So the question arises, what if any observation would falsify the theory? If none, there is no theory but merely a set of challenges to the theory-builders, who in the relevant instances are rational-choice economists and evolutionary biologists.

"Fairness" is the vaguest word in the language but the clearest example of behavioral economics' lack of theoretical ambition. It can be made precise, however, and explained, and subsumed under a broad conception of rationality, with the aid of the evolutionary biology of positive and negative altruism. Evolutionary biology explains altruism as a trait that promotes inclusive fitness, defined as maximizing the number of copies of one's genes by maximizing the number of creatures carrying them weighted by the closeness of the relation.[23] The inclusive fitness of a social animal like man is greatly enhanced by his having a proclivity to help his relatives, and so it is plausible to suppose that this proclivity evolved as an adaptive mechanism.[24] In the prehistoric epoch in which our instinctual preferences were formed, people lived in tiny, isolated bands. Most members of one's community would have been either one's relatives or nonrelatives having very close affective ties to one (such as one's mate and his or her family) or at least very frequent—indeed virtually continuous—face-to-face dealings with one. In these circumstances it would not have been essential to have an innate capacity to discriminate between relatives and other intimates, on the one hand, and, on the other hand, those people—call them "strangers"—with whom one did not have repeated face-to-face interactions.[25]

23. So, other things being equal, having three nephews (each a 25 percent genetic copy of you) will contribute more to your inclusive fitness than having one child (a 50 percent genetic copy of you). The qualification ("other things being equal") is vital. If your three nephews were much less likely to survive to reproductive age than the one child, they would contribute less, at least on an expected basis, to your inclusive fitness than the child.

24. See, for example, Susan M. Essock-Vitale and Michael T. McGuire, "Predictions Derived from the Theories of Kin Selection and Reciprocation Assessed by Anthropological Data," 1 *Ethology and Sociobiology* 233 (1980).

25. Cf. Charles J. Morgan, "Natural Selection for Altruism in Structured Populations," 6 *Ethology and Sociobiology* 211 (1985); Morgan, "Eskimo Hunting Groups, Social Kinship, and the Possibility of Kin Selection in Humans," 1 *Ethology and Sociobiology* 83 (1979). This analysis is questioned, however, in Allan Gibbard, *Wise Choices, Apt Feelings: A Theory of Normative Judgment* 258 n. 2 (1990).

Conditions today are different. We interact a great deal with strangers. But our instincts are easily fooled when confronted with conditions to which human beings never had a chance to adapt biologically. That is why a pornographic movie can arouse a person sexually or a violent one frighten an audience, why people can love an adopted infant as much as they would their own biological child, why people are more frightened of spiders than of cars and of airplanes than of far more dangerous terrestrial forms of transportation, and why men do not clamor to be allowed to donate to sperm banks. Voting, giving to charities, and refraining from littering, in circumstances in which there is neither visible reward for these cooperative behaviors nor visible sanctions for defection, may illustrate an instinctual, and as it were biologically mistaken, generalization of cooperation from small-group interactions, in which altruism is rewarded (hence reciprocal) and failures to reciprocate punished, to large-group interactions in which the prospects of reward and punishment are so slight that cooperation ceases to be rational.[26]

Negative altruism is illustrated not only by envy (see Chapter 3) but also by the indignation we feel when someone infringes our rights. The extreme of indignation is the passion for revenge. This may seem the antithesis of rational thinking, because it flouts the economist's commandment to ignore sunk costs, to let bygones be bygones. Not that it is irrational to *threaten* retaliation in order to deter aggression; but if the threat fails to deter, carrying it out will often be irrational. No matter how much harm you do to the aggressor in return for what he has done to you, the harm that you have suffered will not be annulled. Whatever dangers or other burdens you assume in order to retaliate will merely increase the cost to you of the initial aggression. But if retaliation is futile for rational man, this will make the aggressor all the more likely to attack not the average man but—rational man. The aggressor will know that rational man treats bygones as bygones (or as economists say, ignore sunk costs) and is therefore less likely to retaliate than a less rational person. This calculation will lower the anticipated costs of committing aggression.

26. See Cristina Bicchieri, "Learning to Cooperate," in *The Dynamics of Norms* 17, 39 (Cristina Bicchieri, Richard Jeffrey, and Brian Skyrms eds. 1997); Oded Stark, *Altruism and Beyond: An Economic Analysis of Transfers and Exchanges within Families and Groups* 132 (1995). Generalization (less grandly, pattern recognition) seems an innate, and very valuable but of course fallible, capacity of the human animal.

What was needed for deterrence and hence survival in a human society before there were any formal legal or political institutions, and thus before it was possible to make a legally enforceable commitment to retaliate against an aggressor, was an *instinctual* commitment to retaliate. People who were endowed with an instinct to retaliate would have tended to be more successful in the struggle for survival than others. Sometimes retaliation ends in disaster; but inability to make a credible threat to retaliate renders a person virtually defenseless in a prelegal, prepolitical society. The desire to take revenge for real or imagined injuries—without calculating the net benefits of revenge at the time it is taken, because such calculation would, as I have suggested, reduce the credibility of the threat to retaliate and so would invite aggression that would in turn reduce a person's inclusive fitness—may therefore have become a part of the human genetic makeup.

I have contrasted rational man with vengeful man, but the contrast is superficial. The real contrast is between ex post and ex ante rationality. Having an unshakable commitment to retaliate may be ex ante rational by lowering the risk of being a victim of aggression, even though, if the risk materializes, acting on the commitment will then (that is, ex post) become irrational. Put differently, a certain emotionality may be a component of rationality, which I defined at the outset as suiting means to ends rather than as a particular form of ratiocination.

We can see in this example how bringing evolutionary biology into the picture—an alternative strategy to that pursued by JST—enables the concept of rationality to be enlarged to cover phenomena (not only fairness but at least one of the cognitive quirks, the sunk-costs fallacy) that JST classify as irrational. One more step, however, is necessary to give a complete account of the concept of fairness as used by JST. We must consider why a person may become indignant not only when his own rights are infringed but also when another person's rights are infringed. The key is altruism (so positive altruism lies at the base of negative altruism). This is easy to understand in the case in which the person whose rights have been infringed is a relative or close friend. But it is operative even when he is a stranger. For in that case the phenomenon of "fooling the instincts" is in play and the attenuated but nonetheless positive altruistic feelings that we have even for complete strangers engenders a corresponding indignation if the stranger's rights are infringed.

This analysis may explain what has long puzzled moral philosophers—why we are more indignant at the driver who runs down a child carelessly than at the more careless driver who through sheer luck misses the child.[27] The altruistic instinct is triggered in the first case but not the second. We are hurt in the first case by the loss of the child even though it is not our own child. There is no loss in the second case.

JST's principal example of how fairness can trump rationality is drawn from the "ultimatum game," which is played as follows. *A* is given an amount of money. He can offer as little or as much of it as he pleases to *B*. If *B* accepts the offer, *A* gets to keep the rest; if *B* refuses, neither gets anything. One might suppose, therefore, that however large the stakes, *A* would offer only a penny, since he would expect *B* to accept the offer rather than go away empty-handed. Yet in fact the *A*'s in the ultimatum game invariably offer the *B*'s a substantial fraction of the stakes. The explanation that JST give for this result is that the proposer (*A*) and the respondent (*B*) share a concept of fairness. But this is just a labeling of the result of the game; the process that generates it remains mysterious in their analysis.

We can make progress by viewing the game through the lens of negative altruism. To gain anything from playing the game, the proposer has to make an offer generous enough to induce the respondent to accept. As this necessity exists whether or not the proposer has any sense of fairness, there is nothing even remotely irrational—hence nothing that requires a concept of fairness to explain—about his offering more than a penny. So we can forget about the proposer and concentrate on the respondent, and ask, Why won't he take the penny? For the same reason that I would not kiss JST's collective feet for $1,000. The offer of the penny would signal to the respondent the proposer's belief that the respondent holds a low supposal of his own worth, that he is grateful for scraps, that he accepts being ill-used, that he has no pride, no sense of honor.[28] This weak-spirited creature is just the type who in a prepolitical, vengeance-based policy would have been stamped on by

27. See, for example, Bernard Williams, "Moral Luck," in his book *Moral Luck: Philosophical Papers 1973–1980* 20 (1981); also Williams, "Moral Luck: A Postscript," in his book *Making Sense of Humanity, and Other Philosophical Papers 1982–1993* 241 (1995).

28. Consistent with this suggestion, an experimental study found that "proposers [in the ultimatum game] do not want to be fair, but rather want to appear fair, in order to prevent the responder from rejecting the offer." Werner Güth and Eric van Damme, "Information, Strategic Behavior, and Fairness in Ultimatum Bargaining: An Experimental Study," 42 *Journal of Mathematical Psychology* 227, 242 (1998).

his aggressive neighbors and, thus deprived of resources, have left few offspring. The neighbors would have trampled on his rights because they would have known that he had no sense of *having* any rights and was in any event too diffident to act in defense of them. It is from the aggressive neighbors that most of us moderns are descended, and we reveal our prideful genetic heritage in a wide variety of settings, one of which is the ultimatum game. The game itself shows that this heritage continues to be rational in a range of instances—it is what enables the respondents in the ultimatum game, and their counterparts in analogous real-world situations, to avoid complete defeat. The vengeful spirit was the basis of the nuclear deterrent that contributed, perhaps vitally, to avoiding a world war for half a century. As I emphasized in Chapter 7, it is also the basis of most reporting of crime in those situations, which are common, in which neither the victim of the crime nor any other potential reporter or witness of it anticipates a selfish gain from reporting.[29]

I mentioned signaling, but not to suggest that the respondent in the ultimatum game is seeking a reputation for toughness because he expects to be playing the game again with the same proposer. That would be an easy case for rational-choice analysis. The difficult case is where there is no prospect of repeat play—indeed, no observation at all of the player's moves. In that case, the response of turning down an insultingly low offer is in a narrow sense emotional rather than rational, but in a broader sense rational because the emotion that generates it is part of a cognitive-emotional complex that enables the making of commitments that are rational ex ante.

The acid test of the rationality of the players in the ultimatum game would be if the offer, though a minute percentage of the stakes, was large in absolute terms.[30] Suppose the stakes were $1 million, and the offer was $10,000. Although the offer would be meager in relative

29. One would like to see a series of ultimatum-game experiments in which the proposers make the same offers to respondents who differ both among themselves and from the proposers in age, sex, income, and education, viewed as proxies for or sources of differences in status, self-esteem, or other plausible correlates of the sense of pride that causes respondents in the game to reject chintzy offers. We might learn how closely the ultimatum game corresponds to status struggles among chimpanzees and other monkeys who resemble our protohuman ancestors.

30. L. G. Telser, "The Ultimatum Game and the Law of Demand," 105 *Economic Journal* 1519 (1995).

terms (only 1 percent of the stakes), one would be surprised if many respondents refused it. The demand of a rational person for the "goods" of pride, self-esteem, and vengeance is not perfectly inelastic, and so as the price of these goods rises from $10 (say) to $10,000, we can expect the amount demanded to decline and thus more offers to be accepted.

Another focus of behavioral economics, loosely related to fairness in representing a kind of primitive sense of entitlement, is the "endowment effect." This is the tendency to value what one has just by virtue of having it, even if it was acquired recently. When students in an experiment are given coffee mugs that they are free to sell to other students, few sales take place, because the "owners" of the mugs mysteriously charge a higher selling price than the other students are willing to pay. But this is not really so mysterious, quite apart from the point made in Chapter 6 that the only "rights" in prehistoric society were possessory rights, and so people who didn't cling to what they had would have been at a disadvantage. Maybe the outcome of the coffee-mug experiment is a vestige of a rational adaptation to a vanished situation.

In any bargaining situation, the potential seller (a student who had been given a mug) is likely at first to demand a higher price than the potential buyer is willing to offer. Bargaining proceeds until the demand and offer cross or the parties give up. When the good in question has a very low value, abandonment of the bargaining process before its completion is common. That is why in real-life rather than experimental settings, low-value items are usually sold at a fixed, take-it-or-leave-it price rather than being subject to bargaining.

The more common case in which the endowment effect is observed is where the good that one is asked to part with has been in one's possession for a long time; and here the reluctance to part with it can be understood in straightforward rational-choice terms.[31] Any rational person who owns a good, except the marginal owner, values it above the market price—otherwise he would sell it. This implies that owners of the good as a class value it more than nonowners do.

An alternative explanation draws on the idea of rational adaptive

31. The analysis that follows is drawn from Richard A. Posner, *Economic Analysis of Law* 20, 95–96 (5th ed. 1998).

preference. We rationally adapt to what we have, and would incur new costs to adapt to something new. A person who is blinded in an accident must incur costs to adapt to being blinded. But a blind person who through a doctor's negligence fails to regain his sight has already adapted to being blind, so his loss of (prospective) sight imposes a smaller cost than the sighted person's loss of sight.

It may be objected that to speak of adaptive preferences, as of multiple selves, violates the rational-choice economist's normal assumption of stable preferences. But obviously people's preferences change. All the assumption can signify is that ordinarily it is facile and uninteresting to explain a change in behavior (for example, a fall in demand for some good as a result of an increase in its relative price) by saying that peoples' preferences changed. That's like "explaining" irrational behavior by saying that people aren't always rational—a true statement, but not a helpful one. Rejecting the facile invocation of preference changes doesn't place beyond the bounds of economics the explanation why certain undoubted preference changes do occur.[32]

Surveys of attitudes toward national parks and other recreational public lands reveal dramatic endowment effects. Asked how much money they would demand to sell their rights to use such lands, people give much higher figures than when they are asked what they would offer to buy the rights. This disparity need not be thought irrational. It may reflect the remoteness of such a hypothetical transaction from our experience with markets (Sen's point that I noted in Chapter 3). Or it may simply reflect the absence of close substitutes for access to national parks.[33] Absence of a close substitute implies that a good could not be replaced easily if it were lost. So the owner demands a high price to part with it. But if he doesn't own it, he may be unwilling to pay much for it because he doesn't know what he is missing; by hypothesis, nothing he owns is much like it.

These examples may offer greater insight into normal human behavior than classroom experiments do. In a modern economy the sale of goods and services (other than labor) is to a considerable extent

---

32. On the economics of preference formation, see generally Gary S. Becker, *Accounting for Tastes* (1996).

33. See Daniel S. Levy and David Friedman, "The Revenge of the Redwoods? Reconsidering Property Rights and the Economic Allocation of Natural Resources," 61 *University of Chicago Law Review* 493 (1994).

professionalized. Most individuals, including virtually all university students—the principal experimental subjects of behavioral economics, which relies much more heavily than standard economics on experiments—are buyers but not sellers, and moreover are buyers from stores and other institutions rather than, with rare exceptions, individuals. When we have something to sell we usually sell through middlemen, such as real estate brokers, rather than directly to the ultimate consumer. Experimental situations in which the subjects are asked to trade with each other are artificial, just like surveys asking us to value national parks in pecuniary terms, and so we cannot have much confidence that the results generalize to real markets.

Here is another example of the importance of the difference between hypothetical and real situations. When married people are asked the probability that they will divorce, they give very low numbers, usually around 5 percent; yet the current divorce rate is 50 percent or higher. Does this show that people are irrationally optimistic? Not necessarily. People do not behave as if they *really* believed their probability of divorcing was low. The rise in pre- and postnuptial agreements, the high age at first marriage, the fact that women increasingly hedge against the risk of divorce by establishing themselves in the market before they marry, the low birth rate, the increased incidence of premarital cohabitation (a kind of "trial" marriage), and the low marriage rate are all responses (in part anyway) to "gut feeling" recognition that the risk of divorce is in fact very high. Social scientists who used the divorce estimates obtained by the behavioralists either to predict the divorce rate or to dismiss marriage as an irrational institution would understand modern marriage less well than social scientists who model prospective spouses as rational actors.

If the endowment effect makes sense from a rational-choice perspective in a variety of real-world settings, the results of the coffee-mug experiment may illustrate nothing more mysterious than the operation of habit—which is not irrational. Habitual behavior occurs when cost and benefit are time-dependent and cost is negatively related to time and benefit positively related to it.[34] Not only is it cheaper to brush one's

34. Gary S. Becker, "Habits, Addictions, and Traditions," 45 *Kyklos* 327, 336 (1992), reprinted in Becker, note 32 above, at 118; Marcel Boyer, "Rational Demand and Expenditures Pattern under Habit Formation," 31 *Journal of Economic Theory* 27 (1983). The obverse case—cost positively, benefit negatively, related to time—is that of boredom.

teeth after brushing has become habitual, but to stop brushing (maybe in response to convincing evidence that it was actually bad for one's teeth) would make one uncomfortable. Breaking a habit, like breaking an addiction (an extreme example of habit), causes withdrawal symptoms, though in the case of a mere habit they usually are slight and fleeting. Habit formation is one way in which "learning by doing" works; tasks are performed more quickly and with less effort when they become habitual. If acting in accordance with the endowment effect is rationally habitual because of the real-world examples given earlier (such as rational adaptive preference), this may explain the outcome of the coffee-mug experiment even though that outcome is irrational if habit is ignored.

There is an even deeper problem with the experiment. Earlier I pointed to signaling as a possible explanation for the results of the ultimatum game, but dropped the suggestion on the assumption that play was anonymous. Even if that assumption is correct, the conclusion that signaling cannot possibly explain the outcome of the game need not follow. For if the type of behavior that is the subject of the experiments is characteristically observed by other people rather than being anonymous, the experimental behavior may be similar as a matter of habit or inertia. A more interesting point is that the assumption of anonymity may not be correct. Most behavioralists' descriptions of their experiments do not mention what if any efforts were made to protect the experimental subjects' anonymity. Yet if a player's behavior is observed by the teacher and by the other students, the experiment will be an occasion for the subjects to signal the possession of traits, for example generosity in the ultimatum game and wealth in the coffee-mug experiment (the recipient of the mug signals by his refusal to sell it that he doesn't need money), that may enhance his reputation with the teacher or the other students. The incentive to engage in such signaling will distort the results of the experiment.[35]

According to the coffee-mug experimenters,[36] transactions cost were neglible yet nevertheless there was an endowment effect: students given the mugs at the outset of the experiment demanded a price

35. The discussion that follows draws from Gertrud M. Fremling and Richard A. Posner, "Market Signaling of Personal Characteristics" (unpublished, November 2000).

36. Daniel Kahneman, Jack L. Knetsch, and Richard Thaler, "Experimental Tests of the Endowment Effect and the Coase Theorem," 98 *Journal of Political Economy* 1325 (1990).

roughly twice as high as the others were willing to pay, so there was very little trading even though the initial distribution was random rather than based on how much the students valued the mugs. In contrast there was no reluctance of the same students to trade tokens redeemable in cash. This could just be a case of reluctance to sell a consumer good in response to a small increase in price because willingness to sell would signal an elastic demand and hence that the person is not affluent.

Loewenstein and Issacharoff added the following twist in their version of the coffee-mug experiment: whether one received the mug depended on how one scored on a short test administered at the beginning of their experiment.[37] When it was the low scorers who received the mugs, they did not value them any more highly than the high scorers who did not receive them. But when it was the high scorers who received the mugs they valued them much more highly than the low-scoring nonreceivers did. The signaling interpretation of these results is that when received by low scorers the mugs were in the nature of booby prizes, and this lowered their value because possession of them conveyed a negative signal; it marked the possessor as a low scorer. The low scorers would have been eager to part with this symbol of their poor performance on the test.

In a well-known paper, Richard Thaler (the "T" of "JST") presents several cases that he says falsify the predictions of rational-choice economics, yet all can be seen to involve signaling. The first case is that of Mr. R, who "bought a case of good wine in the late '50's for about $5 a bottle. A few years later his wine merchant offered to buy the wine back for $100 a bottle. He refused, although he has never paid more than $35 for a bottle of wine."[38] Thaler thinks that R's reaction is due to the endowment effect (p. 44), but a more plausible explanation is that R wants others to view him as being well-to-do and having high opportunity costs of time. A professional wine trader would be proud to make a large profit by selling the wine at a high price. But R is a consumer, who by refusing the high offer of $100 signals that he can afford to consume

37. George Loewenstein and Samuel Issacharoff, "Source Dependence in the Valuation of Objects," 7 *Journal of Behavioral Decision Making* 157 (1994).

38. Richard Thaler, "Toward a Positive Theory of Consumer Choice," 1 *Journal of Economic Behavior and Organization* 39, 43 (1980). Further page references to this article appear in the text of this chapter.

the wine even though it (opportunity) costs him that much to do so. He also signals that he is too busy to be bothered by such a trivial matter as returning a bottle of wine to the dealer in order to get $100, while his unwillingness to pay more than $35 a bottle signals not poverty but a disdain for hedonistic consumption. By signaling affluence, busyness, and frugality, he makes himself a more attractive potential transacting partner, whether in markets or in personal interactions.

Thaler's second example, again offered to show the operation of the endowment effect, is that of Mr. *H*, who "mows his own lawn. His neighbor's son would mow it for $8. He [Mr. *H*] wouldn't mow his neighbor's same-sized lawn for $20" (p. 43). Indeed, very few people would consider asking a neighbor or colleague to mow their lawn or clean their house for money. But the reason may be that the request would signal a belief that the neighbor or colleague is so necessitous, or perhaps so lacking in pride or self-esteem—or so greedy—that he is willing to perform low-status work. In other words, the offer conveys a negative signal about the offeree. It is insulting and will be resented, and so will not be made unless the offeror wants to insult the offeree.

Context is all-important here. Many teenagers do mow lawns for money and so it would not be rude to inquire whether a neighborhood teen would do yardwork. Few teenagers, even those possessing considerable status within their cohort, are able to find part-time, high-paying, prestigious jobs, and even if his parents are wealthy the teenager may be expected to work so as to learn to shoulder responsibilities or earn pocket money to buy things his parents refuse to buy for him. As it is already assumed by everyone that the teenager is not a high-class worker, a proposal that he do yardwork is not a challenge to his status and therefore is not offensive and likewise, of course, if the proposal is to a person known to make his living as a yardworker. Also different is asking your neighbor or colleague to do something for you as a "favor," for here the signal is that he is altruistic, not that he is poor, desperate, or lacking in a sense of self-worth.

Thaler gives a third example of what he considers irrational behavior:

Two survey questions: (a) Assume you have been exposed to a disease which if contracted leads to a quick and painless death within a week. The probability that you have the disease is 0.001. What is the maximum you would be willing to pay for a cure? (b) Suppose volunteers were needed for research on the above disease. All that would be required is that you expose yourself to a 0.001 chance of contracting the disease. What is the minimum payment you would require to volunteer for this program? (You would not be allowed to purchase the cure.) (pp. 43–44)

The typical response to (a) is only $200 but to (b) is $10,000, and Thaler again ascribes the difference to the endowment effect. With students as experimental subjects, there may well be a liquidity effect that would explain the difference; but a more interesting interpretation is that being deliberately exposed to a disease (b) is degrading. It resembles experiments on laboratory animals, prisoners of war, and inmates of prisons and insane asylums—all "persons" of low status. There is no comparable connotation to refusing to purchase an expensive cure. So while the probability of death is the same in (a) and (b), the latter involves an additional cost, that of emitting a negative signal about one's status.

Thaler gives an example of how regret can induce irrational reactions. "Mr. *A* is waiting in line at a movie theater. When he gets to the ticket window he is told that as the 100,000th customer of the theater he has just won $100. Mr. *B* is waiting in line at a different theater. The man in front of him wins $1,000 for being the 1,000,000th customer of the theater. Mr. *B* wins $150. Would you rather be Mr. *A* or Mr. *B?*" (p. 52). Some people, according to Thaler, choose to be Mr. *A* and Thaler's explanation is that "the knowledge that he just missed winning causes regret to Mr. *B*" (id.). Signaling again provides an alternative explanation. Mr. *A* is a winner; Mr. *B* is a loser who received a large booby prize. Although no accomplishments are involved in this particular example, being a winner draws attention to oneself and may create a reputation for being lucky. An even clearer example is a competition of ability or skill. The fastest runner receives more status from being Number One than from being faster by some particular number of seconds than the second-best runner. Rank order, because it conveys the *essential* information so efficiently (which is why many prospective employers would prefer to know a candidate's class rank than his grade-point average), can have a value in itself that a small sum of money cannot equal.

Signaling is *to* someone and therefore in experimental settings, where the reaction of the professor and the other students to any signals conveyed by the subject's response could be important, the *degree* of anonymity may affect the outcome. Most of the experiments are "anonymous" only in the sense that the answers that the experimental subjects give to the questions they are asked are not publicly announced. Most take place in a single class period and are discussed by the students and professor afterward, and in those discussions the veil must often slip. Since the items traded or not traded in these experiments are usually worth only a few dollars but the opinions of the professor and fellow students are likely to matter greatly to each student, it is plausible that the students would demonstrate some degree of self-consciousness in their answers and hence that the answers would be likely to contain a signaling component. The prospect of future classroom discussions or informal chats between students after the experiment can affect the students' responses even if the responses were completely anonymous when made. For example, if somebody claimed to have answered a question in a certain way but classroom discussion revealed that all the answers given fell in a different range, the lie would be unmasked.

In an experiment on the endowment effect using lottery tickets rather than coffee mugs,[39] the experimenters found to their surprise that the tickets generally traded for much higher prices than the expected payoff. But a follow-up survey revealed that the students had been anxious to participate in the lottery because the "social pleasure of participating in the lottery with the group outweighed the value of the prize."[40] If social influence has such a large effect on the value of the stakes, it is possible that signaling, a form of social interaction, may explain some or much of the seemingly irrational behavior of the experimental subjects. A student in one experiment asked "Is this 'Candid Camera'?" and a student involved in a study that was much like the one with coffee mugs but that involved pens instead said "I feel silly waiting around to exchange one pen for another for just a shekel [a small unit of Israeli currency], but it seems to be the 'correct' thing to do."[41] It is

39. Jack L. Knetsch and J. A. Sinden, "Willingness to Pay and Compensation Demanded: Experimental Evidence of an Unexpected Disparity in Measures of Value," 99 *Quarterly Journal of Economics* 507 (1984).

40. Id. at 513 n. 8.

41. Maya Bar-Hillel and Efrat Neter, "Why Are People Reluctant to Exchange Lottery Tickets?" 70 *Journal of Personality and Social Psychology* 17, 23–24 (1996).

"silly" to sit around for a long time to make a small transaction because it signals low opportunity costs of time.

The ultimatum game, as we saw, tests for the influence of altruism and concepts of fairness on the behavior of the experimental subjects and likewise the "dictator" game, in which the players are told to divide a sum with another person, as in "If you get $10, how would you split it with another subject in a different classroom?" A high fraction of the "dictators" give nontrivial fractions of the stakes and in the ultimatum games the fractions are even higher. Behavioralists ascribe the difference to the offeror's concern that the offeree will reject a highly unfavorable split because he will consider it "unfair" or "insulting." There is an alternative explanation. An individual who gives something *voluntarily*, as in the dictator game, signals that he is an altruist or at least that he cares whether others *think* he is an altruist.[42] A small offer in the ultimatum game not only signifies a lack of altruism (or lack of caring about being thought an altruist) but also is an offensive challenge to the offeree's status (my earlier example of being unwilling to kiss JST's six feet for $1,000). Knowing that acceptance of the penny offer will convey a negative signal about the offeree, the offeror will fear rejection and will therefore have an incentive, quite apart from his own signaling motives, to make a much more generous offer. By refusing the ungenerous offer the offeree is also signaling his affluence. The price of signaling pride, self-esteem, or related personal characteristics by such a refusal is forgoing the money offered by the offeror.

The degree of anonymity affects the outcome of the dictator game.[43] The more anonymous the game, the smaller the "dictator's" gift. This result supports the signaling hypothesis, as does the accidental finding in the same study that in an experiment in which a high degree of anonymity was supposed to be guaranteed by requiring each "dictator" to place his gift in a sealed envelope, many students did not do so and their choice was not random. "There was a pronounced tendency for

42. Another possibility is habitual behavior. The dictator game resembles tipping, see Bradley Ruffle, "More Is Better, But Fair Is Fair: Tipping in Dictator and Ultimatum Games," 23 *Games and Economic Behavior* 247, 258 (1998), a social norm "enforced" by the dirty looks that a waiter will give a person who fails without cause to leave a tip within the customary range.

43. Elisabeth Hoffman, Kevin McCabe, and Vernon L. Smith, "Social Distance and Other-Regarding Behavior in Dictator Games," 86 *American Economic Review* 653 (1996).

those leaving no money to seal their envelope, and for those leaving positive amounts of money to not seal their envelopes."[44] In like vein it has been found that "if fairness is a social norm guiding distribution behavior, it needs monitoring, i.e., it can prevail only in environments where behavior is observable."[45] Another study found that anonymity increases the willingness of offerees in the ultimatum game to accept the offering player's "ultimatum."[46]

All this is not to deny that altruism, and not just a desire to be thought an altruist, is at work in the dictator and ultimatum games. Especially when the players in the ultimatum or dictator game are students in the same class, acquainted with each other and to some extent, at least, friends, or when the prospective offerees are traditional objects of charity,[47] we would expect a degree of altruistic behavior even if none of the players had, as posited by the behavioralists, a concept of "fairness." But we also expect the tendency to engage in such behavior to be amplified by the benefits for one's reputation of appearing to be generous and trustworthy.[48]

It has been claimed that "the outcomes of ultimatum, dictatorship and many other bargaining games have more to do with manners than [with] altruism" because by turning down small offers the respondents in the ultimatum game show that they are not altruistic toward the offeror.[49] It is correct that altruism is not the complete explanation for

---

44. Id. at 656.

45. Güth and van Damme, note 28 above, at 243.

46. Gary E. Bolton and Rami Zwick, "Anonymity versus Punishment in Ultimatum Bargaining," 10 *Games and Economic Behavior* 95 (1995). See also Iris Bohnet and Bruno S. Frey, "Social Distance and Other-Regarding Behavior in Dictator Games: Comment," 89 *American Economic Review* 335 (1999); Bohnet and Frey, "The Sound of Silence in Prisoner's Dilemma and Dictator Games," 38 *Journal of Economic Behavior and Organization* 43 (1999); Catherine C. Eckel and Philip J. Grossman, "Are Women Less Selfish than Men? Evidence from Dictator Experiments," 108 *Economic Journal* 726 (1998); Duncan K. H. Fong and Gary E. Bolton, "Analyzing Ultimatum Bargaining: A Bayesian Approach to the Comparison of Two Potency Curves under Shape Constraints," 15 *Journal of Business and Economic Statistics* 335 (1997).

47. See Catherine C. Eckel and Philip J. Grossman, "Altruism in Anonymous Dictator Games," 16 *Games and Economic Behavior* 181 (1996).

48. For evidence of this, which further supports a signaling interpretation of the results of the behavioral experiments, see Kevin A. McCabe, Stephen J. Rassenti, and Vernon L. Smith, "Reciprocity, Trust, and Payoff Privacy in Extensive Form Bargaining," 24 *Games and Economic Behavior* 10 (1998).

49. Colin Camerer and Richard H. Thaler, "Anomalies: Ultimatums, Dictators and Manners," *Journal of Economic Perspectives*, Spring 1995, pp. 209, 216.

these outcomes—only saints are altruistic toward people who insult or otherwise mistreat them. It is thus no surprise that respondents in the ultimatum game do *not* turn down stingy offers when they know that the offer is made by a computer,[50] since there is neither a revenge motive nor a signaling motive for rejecting such an offer. Notice also that the "revenger" who turns down the small offer in order to keep offerors "honest" is a kind of altruist; his self-sacrificing behavior contributes to the maintenance of an efficient social order. All this has nothing to do with "manners," a term that connotes an unthinking reflex based on early training or "culture" and remote from considerations of self-interest.

Another reason for caution in interpreting the empirical findings of behavioral economics is selection effects, which suggest that the experimental and real-world environments will differ systematically. The experimental subjects are chosen more or less randomly; but people are not randomly sorted to jobs and other activities.[51] People who cannot calculate probabilities will either avoid gambling, if they know their cognitive weakness, or, if they do not, will soon be wiped out and thus be forced to discontinue gambling. People who are unusually "fair" will avoid (or, again, be forced out of) roughhouse activities—including highly competitive businesses, trial lawyering, and the academic rat race. Hyperbolic discounters will avoid the financial-services industry. These selection effects will not work perfectly, but they will drive a wedge between experimental and real-world consequences of irrationality. It would thus be interesting to compare the subsequent career paths, and earnings, of students who score high in rationality in experiments conducted by behavioral economists with those who score low.

I have been emphasizing experimental results, but they do not exhaust the empirical evidence marshaled by the behavioralists against nonbehavioral economics. For example, JST point to the phenomenon of criminals' discounting of future punishments, argue that such discounting is hyperbolic, and conclude that the rational-choice approach to crime and punishment is refuted. I explained earlier why I don't consider hyperbolic discounting necessarily inconsistent with rationality, but even if it is, JST's analysis is unconvincing.

A peculiarity of criminal punishment, when it takes the form of im-

---

50. Id. at 215.

51. With the partial exception of jury service—which is a reason to repose greater confidence in the results of mock-jury studies, as I point out in Chapter 12.

prisonment, which is the standard form it does take in this country, is that a reduction in its probability cannot easily be offset by an increase in its severity. The only way to increase severity is to add prison time at the end of the criminal's sentence. If the sentence is already long, any increments of length will have little weight in the criminal's calculations, simply because of ordinary, not hyperbolic, discounting. For example, lengthening a prison sentence from 20 to 25 years will increase its disutility (in "present value" terms, that is, as reckoned by the defendant when he is deciding whether to commit a criminal act that would expose him to such a punishment) by much less than 25 percent; at a discount rate of 10 percent, the increase will be only about 6 percent.

But I am willing to grant that many criminals are hyperbolic discounters rather than merely ordinary discounters. Indeed I think it likely. For we must consider the selection effects of a criminal punishment system. If it is designed to deter, then criminals—which is to say, the part of the population that is *not* deterred—will not be a random draw from the population. We can expect the undeterrable to have peculiar traits, including, in a system in which punishment takes the form of imprisonment, an abnormal indifference to future consequences. Most criminals are not very intelligent and this may make it hard for them to imagine future pains. This does not show that a criminal justice system should be designed on the assumption that the population of *potential* criminals, the people we think we can deter from becoming actual criminals, is dominated by hyperbolic discounters.

What is true is that any *personal* discount rate[52] higher than necessary to adjust for the risk of death is suspect from the narrowest rational-choice standpoint, as it implies an arbitrary preference for present over future consumption. But this present orientation can be profitably analyzed in terms of rational choice, as I suggested earlier, either through the concept of multiple selves (the present self is in control of a person's present actions, and disavalues the welfare of the person's future selves) or because of information costs that make it difficult to imagine our state of mind in the future.[53]

52. A term I use to distinguish *interest* rates, which are a function not only of time preferences, default risk, and administrative costs but also of the supply of capital, from nonmonetary discount rates. Interest rates might be high not because people had a strong preference for present over future consumption but because capital was scarce for unrelated reasons.

53. See Becker, note 32 above, at 11–12; Becker and Casey B. Mulligan, "On the Endogenous Determination of Time Preference," 112 *Quarterly Journal of Economics* 729 (1997).

Selection effects also explain some at least of the phenomenon of overoptimism (the "winner's curse"). People are more likely to want to enter an activity if they think they will do well in it. But the competition among such people will reduce the likelihood of success, so that viewed ex post their original expectations will seem inflated.

JST's most interesting, and from the standpoint of law and public policy potentially most important, example of a departure from rationality is that of mandated childbirth health insurance, a reassuringly concrete real-world phenomenon, moreover. The fact that wages in the study they cite[54] fell when it was imposed by the full cost of the coverage implies that the workers valued the coverage at its full cost[55] even though, before it was imposed, they did not value it that highly. For if they had, the employer would have provided it voluntarily. The implication that JST draw is that the coverage changed the women's preferences; something they didn't like before they had it they did like once they got it, just as in the case of the coffee mugs.

Yet their interpretation of the study is at best suggestive. For there is again a selection problem—or rather two such problems. Women planning to have children will be attracted to employments in which childbirth insurance is available,[56] thus competing down wages. And given the insurance, women will be more likely to have children, and this will make them less productive and lower their wages. The author of the study speculates that the insurance may have resulted in an excessive number of cesarean sections[57]—indicating a thoroughly rational reaction by the women and the medical profession to the availability of a new funding source for obstetrical procedures.

Not the study itself, which does not mention behavioral economics, but JST's analysis of it, arbitrarily combines the premises of behavioral economics with those of rational-choice economics. JST assume that employees are governed in their employment behavior by the endow-

54. Jonathan Gruber, "The Incidence of Mandated Maternity Benefits," 84 *American Economic Review* 622 (1994).

55. If they didn't, the employer would be forced to "swallow" some of the additional cost of the program.

56. It is unclear from Gruber's article what exceptions if any the state laws that were his principal subject made in coverage. But even if all employed people were fully covered, the laws would tend to attract women of childbearing age and intentions from the home into paid employment.

57. Gruber, note 54 above, at 640.

ment effect, but also that if before the law made childbirth insurance coverage mandatory employees had valued it at or above its cost, employers would have offered it without any prodding by government. The fact that they did not is taken by JST to imply that the employees did not value it at more than its cost. But this is to assume that before the law was passed employers and employees alike were perfectly rational. It is true that before the law was passed the endowment effect was not in play. But the endowment effect is only one of a number of irrationalities that JST believe pervade labor markets. They do not explain why none of them was operating before the imposition of mandatory childbirth insurance.

To show that parties to lawsuits do not recontract after the plaintiff has succeeded in obtaining an injunction, which is offered as proof that the Coase Theorem is false,[58] they rely on a study by Ward Farnsworth[59] that has a sample size (twenty) too small to be statistically significant. And if the courts in his study "got it right"—that is, granted injunctions only in cases in which the plaintiff had more to gain from the injunction than the defendant had to lose from it—there would be be no occasion for a corrective transaction by the parties to the lawsuit. Yet JST generalize from Farnsworth's study that once people have received a court judgment they will be unwilling to negotiate with the opposing party. In fact it is not unusual for parties to settle a case after judgment in the trial court, rather than take their chances with an appeal.[60] JST may have meant to confine their observation to cases in which a judgment has become final after exhaustion of appellate remedies. If so, it greatly weakens the inference they wish to draw from Farnsworth's study, that the endowment effect prevents advantageous postjudgment transfers. If a case that has become final through exhaus-

58. I don't think JST actually mean that the theorem is false; they are speaking loosely. The theorem is a tautology. They must mean that if the theorem is recast as the hypothesis that the assignment of property rights is irrelevant if transaction costs are lower than the benefits of reassigning the rights, the hypothesis is false.

59. Ward Farnsworth, "Do Parties to Nuisance Cases Bargain after Judgment? A Glimpse inside the Cathedral," 66 *University of Chicago Law Review* 373 (1999), reprinted in *Behavioral Law and Economics*, note 1 above, at 302.

60. About a quarter of all cases filed in federal courts of appeals are disposed of, before full briefing, without judicial action. Computed from Richard A. Posner, *The Federal Courts: Challenge and Reform* 72 (1996) (table 3.6). An unknown, but not trivial, percentage of these are settled, along with a very small percentage of cases briefed and argued but not yet decided.

tion of appellate remedies could have been settled, because the remedy sought by the plaintiff would cost the defendant more than it would benefit the plaintiff, the case would have been settled earlier—at the latest after the judgment in the trial court and before the appeal. And this point suggests that Farnsworth's findings vindicate rather than challenge rationality. Had the parties waited until all appeal rights had been exhausted before working out the value-maximizing resolution of their dispute—if final judgments turned out to be the preliminary to negotiations that undid them—it would mean that the parties had irrationally failed to economize on their expenses of litigation.

In support of a radical proposal for curtailing tort liability by requiring plaintiffs to bear a heightened burden of proving negligence, JST rely on impressionistic evidence that juries are too favorable to plaintiffs. They ascribe this favoritism to hindsight bias, gliding over the possibility that it might be actuated by considerations of "fairness," perhaps distributive in nature—the sense that defendants or their insurers have "deep pockets" to pay for the plaintiff's injuries. Appeals to fairness are ubiquitous in tort cases.[61] But my main criticism is of basing so radical a proposal on such limited evidence. We shall see in Chapter 11 that there is evidence that juries in tort cases favor defendants rather than plaintiffs.

In support of an argument that the availability heuristic has given rise to "legislation by anecdote," JST offer their own anecdote, about how the highly publicized rash of illnesses of people living near Love Canal gave rise to the Superfund law: "The behavioral account of Superfund is that the availability of 'Love Canal' as a symbol for the problem of abandoned hazardous waste dumps greatly intensified public concern, to the point where a legislative response became nearly inevitable, no matter what the actual facts might be."[62] It is unclear what this narrative, plausible though it is, owes to behavioral economics or to any other organized body of thought.

JST cite a study which hypothesized that each side in teacher collective-bargaining negotiations, in seeking to bolster its negotiating position with data on teachers' wages in comparable communities, would "adopt self-serving judgments about which communities are 'compara-

61. See, for example, James A. Henderson, "Judicial Reliance on Public Policy: An Empirical Analysis of Products Liability Decisions," 59 *George Washington Law Review* 1570 (1991).
62. Jolls, Sunstein, and Thaler, note 1 above, at 1521.

ble,' and impasses may result from such judgments."[63] This is no more surprising than that each side in a lawsuit will make self-serving judgments about which cases provide the closest analogies to the case at hand or which facts are most probative. JST contend that the strategic incentive to make self-serving judgments was eliminated in the collective-bargaining study by the fact that the only audience for the responses in the study was the study's authors. This is naive. Negotiators are unlikely to drop their (rational) biases when talking to professors, especially since they may lack confidence that their disclosures will remain confidential. JST are correct that there is such a thing as role bias, that it is common among lawyers and negotiators, and that it may be a factor in why not all cases settle, though most do. But the study adds nothing to the intuition.

To demonstrate the power of behavioral economics to explain laws that stump the conventional economist, JST merge usury laws, which have nothing to do with shortages; the avoidance of price gouging, which is not a legal imposition but a presumably compensated buffer of the risks faced by customers; and laws against ticket scalping, which are in force in fewer than half the states and which coexist mysteriously with laws permitting ticket brokers to buy in bulk from the theater and resell at "scalpers" prices.

The lack of relation between usury laws and the other two types of law is shown by the fact that there is no "reference point" interest rate and therefore no benchmark for triggering the sense of indignation that is the relevant component of JST's concept of fairness. Lenders do not typically refuse to lend to risky borrowers at above-market rates, whatever exactly "market" means in this context. Banks quote a prime rate, but not necessarily the same rate, to their best customers and charge everyone else—that is, the riskier borrowers—more. (All a "prime rate" means is the bank's best interest rate.) Mortgage lenders charge varying numbers of points. Bonds, a form of loan, are rated for risk, and the lower-rated bonds pay higher interest rates without anyone crying "usury!" Credit card interest is much higher than bank-loan interest. Long-term interest rates usually differ from short-term rates. Interest rates on secured loans are lower than those on unsecured loans. Interest rates fluctuate with inflation, and of course with the de-

63. Id. at 1502.

mand for and the supply of capital. Even in consumer credit transactions, the focus of modern usury laws, there is no uniformity in interest
rates, as many of my examples show. And can these laws have *any* effect
today, when one considers that credit card and installment credit interest rates often approach 20 percent yet are lawful?

What may have misled JST is that if a borrower has a *really* high risk
of default, there may be no interest rate that will make the loan worthwhile to either lender or borrower. This is especially likely because the
higher the interest rate, the greater the risk of default, since an interest
rate is a fixed rather than a variable cost of the borrower. That is why
the riskiest loans and resulting astronomical interest rates are the domain of the loan shark, who, facing an unusually high risk of default,
employs the threat of force in lieu of the milder remedies that are all
that are available to the legal lender.

JST suggest that the same concept of fairness that explains usury
laws, price-gouging laws, and ticket-scalping laws explains laws forbidding prostitution and refusing to enforce surrogate-motherhood contracts, laws forbidding the sale of body parts and political votes, and
laws refusing to enforce the contracting around of laws against race and
sex. This is a heterogeneous collection of laws, and to refer them to
"pervasive judgments about fairness"[64] is not to explain them. JST
should explain what all these laws have in common, give some form and
content to their idea of "fairness," and consider the possibility of competing explanations for the laws, such as that they serve politically powerful special interests or are a product of misunderstandings unrelated
to any of the three "boundeds." (Voters have little incentive to become
well informed about policies, especially since they vote for representatives rather than for the policies themselves.) For example, limits on
adoption prices are supported by nonprofit adoption agencies, which
are concerned about competition from profit-making adoption agencies, and by public ignorance of the consequences of price ceilings.

I have been focusing on the significance of behavioral economics for
positive analysis, but I wish to consider briefly its possible normative
implications. On the one hand, the picture of the human being that
JST draw is one of unstable preferences and (what turns out to be related) infinite manipulability. If you give a worker childbirth coverage,

64. Id. at 1516.

she'll like it (endowment effect); but if you don't give it to her, she'll dislike it (more precisely, won't want to pay for it in lower wages). If you force her to take an HIV test, she'll thank you afterwards, even though she fought kicking and screaming against having to take it. If you describe the threat of breast cancer to a woman in one way, she'll want a mammogram, but if you describe it in another although logically equivalent way, she won't. It seems then that the politically insulated corps of experts that JST favor would be charged with determining the populace's authentic preferences, which sounds totalitarian. On the other hand, nothing in JST's analysis exempts "experts" from the cognitive quirks, from weakness of will, or from concerns with fairness. The expert, too, is behavioral man. Behavioral man behaves in unpredictable ways. Dare we vest responsibility for curing irrationality in the irrational? Have we then a standoff?

One might have thought that behavioral economics had at least one clear normative implication: that efforts should be made through education and perhaps psychiatry to cure the cognitive quirks and weakness of will that prevent people from acting rationally with no offsetting gains. Even if, as I believe, the sunk-costs fallacy has biological roots, it should not be impossible to educate people out of it. Behavior therapy has enabled many people to overcome their fear of flying, which I suspect has more tenacious biological roots. JST treat the irrationalities that form the subject matter of behavioral economics as unalterable constituents of human personality. All their suggestions for legal reform are of devices for getting around, rather than dispelling, our irrational tendencies.

~ 9

Social Norms,
with a Note on Religion

$\mathscr{A}$ SOCIAL NORM ("norm" for short) is a rule that is neither promulgated by an official source, such as a court or a legislature,
nor enforced by threat of legal sanctions, yet is regularly complied with
(otherwise it wouldn't be a rule).[1] The rules of etiquette, including
norms of proper dress and table manners; the rules of grammar; standard business practices; and customary law in prepolitical societies and
private associations are all examples of norms. Norms might seem to
belong more to sociology than to psychology; but my focus will be on
the enforcement of norms, and the keys here are psychology, including
the psychology of emotion,[2] and economics.

A full understanding of law requires careful consideration of norms.
The behavior of judges, for example, is primarily norm- rather than
law-driven. And law is older than political society, which means that it
originates as a set of norms—and in the case of public international law
it remains largely a set of legally unenforceable norms because of the
absence of world government. Even in societies that have strong governments, norms are both a source of law and, often, a cheap and effective substitute for law (but sometimes they are an antagonist to law).
There are norms against stealing and lying, but also laws against these

1. I do not require, however, that it be internalized as a preference, as in the definition of
norm used in Gary S. Becker, *Accounting for Tastes*, ch. 11 (1996).

2. See Jon Elster, *Strong Feelings: Emotion, Addiction, and Human Behavior* 98–102 (1999).

behaviors. The two kinds of rule differ in the mode of creation, the definition of the offense, the procedure for administering punishment, and the punishments themselves. Laws are promulgated by public institutions, such as legislatures, regulatory agencies, and courts, on the basis of well-defined deliberative procedures, and are enforced by the police power of the state, which ultimately means by threat of violence. Norms are not necessarily promulgated. If they are, it is not by the state; otherwise they would be laws. Often a norm will result from (and crystallize) the gradual emergence of a consensus. Norms are enforced by internalized values, by refusals to interact with the offender, by disapproval of his actions, and sometimes by private violence.

Norms are a seductively attractive method of social control because of the presumptive legitimacy in our culture of private ordering and because a rule may be desirable yet its formulation and promulgation too costly a project relative to the benefits for the state, with its crowded agenda and cumbersome procedures, to undertake. A rule against poor table manners, for example, is hardly suitable for embodiment in law. But norms also have a number of drawbacks relative to laws. A norm is even more of a public good than a law, since no one person or political party can claim credit for creating a norm. And the cost of inflicting penalties for violating a norm cannot be financed by mandatory taxation and so must be shouldered voluntarily by those who enforce it. Because of these attributes of norms, it may seem obvious that they would be underproduced and underenforced from a social standpoint. But that is not necessarily so. Norms, like laws, can be bad, in which case the obstacles to their creation and enforcement may actually promote social welfare. A related but subtler point is that because norms, once created, are difficult to uncreate, the stock of norms may be large even though the flow is small.

The focus of the scholarly literature on norms has been on their importance and their efficiency or inefficiency.[3] In this chapter I focus in-

3. Illustrative recent contributions are Lisa Bernstein, "Opting Out of the Legal System: Extralegal Contractual Relations in the Diamond Industry," 21 *Journal of Legal Studies* 115 (1992); Avner Greif, Paul Milgrom, and Barry R. Weingast, "Coordination, Commitment, and Enforcement: The Case of the Merchant Guild," 102 *Journal of Political Economy* 745 (1994); Robert D. Cooter, "Decentralized Law for a Complex Economy: The Structural Approach to Adjudicating the New Law Merchant," 144 *University of Pennsylvania Law Review* 1643 (1996); and the articles collected in *Reputation: Studies in the Voluntary Elicitation of Good Conduct* (Daniel B. Klein ed. 1997).

stead on how norms operate and so on the variety of sanctions that enforce norms, the degree of underenforcement associated with each type of sanction, and the varying difficulty of creating norms enforced by each type of sanction.[4]

Sometimes the sanction is built into the violation, as when a person who drives on the wrong side of the road risks crashing into another car and injuring himself as well as others, though the sanction may not be adequate—even in the case of driving on the wrong side of the road—because the violator may consider the cost of the violation only to himself and not to other people as well. The most effectively self-enforcing norms are those that are constitutive of advantageous transactions. If you don't speak the language, you can't make yourself understood. If you don't play chess by the rules, you're not playing it at all, so if you *enjoy* playing chess, you won't cheat unless the net expected gain is very great.

This point may explain the efficacy of the norms governing judicial behavior. I am speaking not of those norms that are backed by law, such as the rule against taking bribes, but of those subtler, informal norms that adjure the judge to suppress his personal or partisan sympathies, to disregard public blame or praise, to control his emotions, and to follow precedent rather than his own values—in short, to adhere to the traditional "rule of law" virtues. Compliance with these norms is far from uniform, because there are incentives to deviate and the costs of deviation are small. But the question is why there is *any* compliance. The answer lies in recognizing on the one hand that the private costs of compliance are low because the law-backed rules of judicial behavior (not only must the judge not take bribes, but he must not sit in cases in which he or his relatives might derive a pecuniary benefit from his decision) make it difficult for the judge to profit from partiality, and on the other hand that the private benefits of compliance are substantial. They are substantial because the "rule of law" norms are the constitutive rules of the practice of judging; if you don't obey them, you're not playing the judicial "game." Law school and the judiciary teach the game to new lawyers, and judicial selection procedures select for persons who *want* to play the judicial game rather than some other game,

4. The discussion that follows draws on Richard A. Posner and Eric B. Rasmusen, "Creating and Enforcing Norms, with Special Reference to Sanctions," 19 *International Review of Law and Economics* 369 (1999). See also Eric A. Posner, *Law and Social Norms* (2000).

such as partisan politics. This is true even when judicial appointments are elective rather than appointive or when appointments are based on patronage or ideology rather than merit. Self-selection is present in the decision to seek judicial office whether by election or appointment.

The violator of a norm may feel bad about his violation because of education and upbringing, quite apart from any loss of benefits or any external consequences. Most people would feel at least a twinge of guilt about stealing even if they believed they were certain not to be caught. Shame is a distinct sanction for the violation of a norm from guilt. The violator may feel that his action has lowered himself either in his own eyes (a "multiple self" situation—see Chapter 8—in which the individual is both the actor and the observer of his actions) or in the eyes of other people. One can feel shame even if there is no element of wrongdoing, no breach of a moral code. One can be ashamed of doing something stupid that harms nobody simply because behaving stupidly is failing to live up to one's self-image. One can also be shamed—though the better word would be "humiliated" (see Chapter 7)—for engaging in conduct that violates a moral code that is not one's own, so that there is no question of feeling guilt. The people who were paraded through the streets in dunce caps during China's "Cultural Revolution" felt humiliated even if they disapproved of the regime and therefore felt no guilt at violating its norms.

Guilt in particular might be thought a type of automatic or self-enforcing sanction, since the violator perceives the violation as a cost to himself, much like the risk of being injured if he drives on the wrong side of the road. But it differs in requiring an investment to create it. People must choose a level of effort to exert in instilling the potential for feeling guilt into other people (sometimes even themselves), as well as the amount of guilt to try to instill. The sense of guilt may be innate, but it is sharpened and focused by formal schooling, by purposive moral influence by parents and relatives, and, possibly most important, by the *examples* offered by both adults and peers.

Parents have both a selfish and an altruistic interest in instilling a sense of guilt in their children. (So they may instill too much guilt, from the standpoint of the child's long-run self-interest, for offenses such as rudeness, or ingratitude, to one's elders.) A child who has a sense of guilt is more likely to conform to norms; and other people's knowledge of this will help him later in life by making him a more reliable transacting partner. But rational parents will not want to create guilt feelings so strong as to block even an efficient breach of the norm. It is often advantageous to violate a norm, especially if others are adhering to it. Rational parents will also endeavor to maintain marginal deterrence of norm violating: they won't try to make a child feel as guilty about not brushing his teeth as about shoplifting.

Consider the following example of parents' decision whether to instill guilt about theft in their daughter. When she is grown an employer will decide whether to hire her, and if she is hired she will decide whether to steal from the employer. Assume that the value of the job (salary) to the daughter is 40, the benefit to the employer from her work is 50, the value of both the gain to her and the loss to the employer from theft is 30, and the theft cannot be detected. The daughter's net pecuniary gain from being hired and committing theft is then 70 (40 + 30), and the employer's payoff from hiring the daughter is −20 (50 − 40 − 30). Assume that the daughter will suffer guilt pangs that subtract G from her utility if she steals, provided that her parents had instilled a sense of guilt in her. Assume further that the parents and the daughter have the same interests and that the employer can determine (perhaps from the daughter's school record, references, and personal deportment) whether she indeed has a sense of guilt.

If G is less than 30, the parents will have no incentive to instill a sense of guilt, since whether they do so or not their daughter will steal if hired because the payoff to her from stealing, $70 - G$, exceeds 40, the value of the job (without theft) to her. Knowing all this, the employer will not hire her, as his net expected gain would be negative. But if G exceeds 30, the parents will instill a sense of guilt in their daughter; she will refrain from stealing if hired; and so the employer will hire her, because her payoff from honest working, 40, will exceed her gain from dishonest working, yielding the employer a net benefit from hiring of 10 (50 − 40).

Implicit in the example is the important point that the private and social costs of a norm violation may diverge. The violator may gain more than he loses, and knowing this parents may instill a lesser sense of guilt and lower threshold of shame than society as a whole might desire. This suggests that the controlling forces in society will be reluctant to delegate all moral instruction to parents, especially if the society relies heavily on norms rather than laws to constrain behavior. And the divergence between the private and social costs of violating norms suggests that parents may have a greater incentive to instill shame in their children than to instill guilt. The optimal strategy from the child's selfish—which may be the parents' altruistic—viewpoint is to violate norms but not get caught. To the extent that it is an external sanction and thus depends on information, shame may provide the right (from a private, not a social, standpoint) incentive for optimal cheating by punishing the violator only when the violation is detected.

In the case where G is more than 30, the parents, by having reduced the payoff to their daughter from stealing on the job, have benefited her because of the reaction of the third party, the employer, to their action. And notice that while she could not have obtained the job unless she had the potential to feel guilty, she will not suffer any actual pangs of guilt, because she is honest. To say that "she is honest"—that is, to remark a disposition that has become unconscious—is to suggest that the norm of honesty has become a habit that the daughter will feel uncomfortable breaking even after reaching adulthood and even in the face of a contrary tug of "self-interest."[5] I pointed out in the preceding chapter that in habits as in addictions, cost, which may be purely psychological, is negatively related to time, and benefit is positively related to it. Once a practice becomes habitual, the benefit-cost ratio of compliance becomes strongly positive, so that an interruption is felt as a real cost even when the actual harm from the interruption is trivial.

The internalization of norms through habituation may seem highly efficient because it reduces the cost of compliance. But of course the norms may be bad ones. Even if norms tend to be efficient within the group in which they are felt as binding, they may be dysfunctional for society as a whole, an example being a norm against informing against a coconspirator.

Internalization of norms has another dark side, though this conclusion depends on controversial ethical assumptions. It reduces human freedom when freedom is viewed functionally in terms of scope of choice rather than formalistically as freedom from legal constraints. When norms are enforced by external sanctions, the individual balances the benefits of violation against the costs. When norms are inter-

5. See Assar Lindbeck, "Welfare State Disincentives with Endogenous Habits and Norms," 97 *Scandinavian Journal of Economics* 477, 479 (1995).

nalized, he does not make a choice—it has been made for him, by his parents, teachers, or peers.[6] If we value choice either instrumentally or ethically, we may think it desirable to reduce the domain in which people comply unthinkingly with norms—the domain of the "unthinkable," of *unquestioning* obedience. In the nightmare world of George Orwell's *Nineteen Eighty-Four*, there is no formal law; the rulers have succeeded in exacting unquestioning obedience from virtually the entire population by instilling social norms through brainwashing.

Thus, contrary to the "conservative" belief that the trend toward more regulation by law and less by social norms signifies a loss of freedom, an increased reliance on law to control antisocial behavior may signify an increase in considered, consciously reasoned human choice. But the qualification in "may" is important. To pose the issue as unthinking obedience versus consciously reasoned human choice is too stark. The temptation to disobey may be checked by a pang of conscience that imposes a cost on disobedience without entirely destroying, as a law might do, the power of choice.

Even when divorced from guilt, shame can, like guilt, operate as a sanction though other people take no action against the violator. If a professor's arrest for patronizing a prostitute is publicized, he feels ashamed before his colleagues even though none of them mentions the arrest to him, or perhaps *because* none of them mentions it—their silence, an embarrassed reaction to the shameful act, is evidence that the act was indeed shameful and cannot just be laughed off.

Although shame does not depend for its efficacy on revealing information about the violator's character, that is often an element: the man who is caught driving while drunk is revealing that he probably drinks heavily on a regular basis, and his consciousness of people's reaction to the revelation may be what mainly engenders the feeling of shame in him. Self-revelation can be a factor too: someone titillated by his first sight of sexually deviant pornography may be ashamed to discover inclinations within himself that he never suspected he had.

Shame is often a by-product of the imposition of a bilateral or multilateral sanction. When people criticize a norm violator, they are trying to impose a multilateral sanction; but the *disutility* of the criticisms to

6. Unless one deliberately sets out to make a practice, such as brushing one's teeth after every meal, habitual in order to reduce the cost of the practice.

the violator, and thus the efficacy of the sanction, may be due entirely to shame. If the violator shrugs off the criticisms as a product of ignorance, malice, or envy, and in addition anticipates no bad consequences for him from the communication of the criticisms to other people, the criticisms will fail as a sanction.

What the sanctions I have discussed thus far have in common is that enforcement is costless—and when the norm violator's action conveys (often unwittingly) valuable information about himself the cost of enforcement may actually be negative. A student wears casual clothing to a job interview, unintentionally signaling that he doesn't care a great deal whether he gets the job or not. So he doesn't get it, and the would-be employer is better off. The student's "breach" of the dress code for job applicants is "punished" by his not getting the job.[7] The punishment is light because by hypothesis the student doesn't care very much about getting the job. But the cost of punishment to the punisher (the employer) is actually negative, because by shunning the violator the punisher avoids an unwanted association. And likewise if a man beats a woman and is punished by not being able to find any other woman willing to associate with him; here the cost of punishment to the violator is heavy, but the cost of enforcement is low (or even negative) because the violator has shown by his actions that associating with him has little or no (and often negative) value. Ostracism can be cheap to the ostracizers.

The personal or commercial characteristics revealed by the violation of a norm may be only distantly related to the violation yet still convey valuable information. Consider the following example: Nature chooses 90 percent of workers to be "steady," with productivity $p = x$, and 10 percent to be "wild," with productivity $p = x - y$. A worker decides whether to marry or not. Marriage adds utility of m for a steady worker and $-z$ for a wild one. The employer, observing whether the worker is married but not whether he is wild, offers him a wage of wm or wu depending on whether he is married or not. The employer has no intrin-

---

7. See Eric A. Posner, "Symbols, Signals, and Social Norms in Politics and the Law," 27 *Journal of Legal Studies* 765 (1998); Eric Rasmusen, "Stigma and Self-Fulfilling Expectations of Criminality," 39 *Journal of Law and Economics* 519 (1996); Rajiv Sethi and E. Somanathan, "The Evolution of Social Norms in Common Property Resource Use," 86 *American Economic Review* 766 (1996); Niloufer Qasim Mahdi, "Pukhtunwali: Ostracism and Honor among the Pathan Hill Tribes," 7 *Ethology and Sociobiology* 295 (1986).

sic reason to care whether the worker is married. Wild workers are less productive, but whether they are married has no effect on their productivity. The only significance of marriage for the employer is that it signals steadiness. The payoffs received are pw for the employer if he succeeds in hiring the worker, wu for a married employed worker, w for an unmarried employed worker, u for a married unemployed worker, and 0 for an employer who does not hire a worker and for an unmarried worker who is not hired. If z exceeds y the employer will pay wages of $wu = x - y$ and $wm = x$, the steady worker will get married, and the wild worker will stay single.

There is no danger that unmarried workers will marry in order to fool the employer into paying them a higher wage, because by definition these are the workers for whom the wage premium is less than the disutility to them (stemming from their "wildness") of marriage. Their reluctance might be overcome by a subsidy for marriage, but if so the subsidy would reduce the productivity of labor by depriving employers of useful information about the marginal product of their workers. The same is true, however, of taxing marriage; the marriage signal would be destroyed if marriage were taxed out of existence. And likewise if government forbade employers to use an applicant's marital status in making a hiring decision. These points illustrate the danger in government's fiddling with norms.

Informational sanctions for the violation of norms may seem to lack proportionality. A trivial violation of a norm, if the violation signals the offender's probable unreliability as a friend or business acquaintance, may precipitate ostracism that will impose a cost on the violator that exceeds the social cost of his breach. But this need not be excessive punishment. It corrects an asymmetry of information and by doing so confers a social benefit that is distinct from its deterrent effect.

Let me distinguish now between two types of costly sanctions for norm violations, the bilateral and the multilateral. Sometimes the violator of a norm exposes himself to costly punishment by just one other person, whose identity is specified by the norm. The jealous husband who shoots his wife's seducer, or who merely divorces his wife (whom he loves) after discovering her adultery, incurs substantial costs to punish the violation of a norm. Creating adequate incentives for administering punishment costly to the punisher may require second-order norms, such as norms of vengeance that supplement bilateral costly sanctions with multilateral ones by ostracizing anyone who is unwilling to carry out his duty of avenging an injury.[8] In this example, punishment is facilitated by reducing its net cost, which is the difference between the cost of punishing and the cost of not punishing. The cost of punishment can also be reduced by releasing the punisher from the ordinary sanctions, formal or informal, for the punishing behavior. Ordinarily a person who insults someone in public is severely criticized, but if the insult is intended as punishment for the other person's norm violation, the insult is likely to be excused.

Mention of vengeance is a reminder of the importance of the emotions as enforcers of norms[9]—a point that is also vital to understanding the *emergence* of law. The honor code of the Old South, which I mentioned in Chapter 7, was a relic of a revenge-based system of law—more precisely, of prelaw. Before there were governments, what we now call law was a system of social norms that were obeyed partly out of fear of ostracism and partly out of fear of revenge. The impulse to lash out in "blind rage" against an aggressor, regardless of the balance of costs and benefits as they appear when the victim must decide whether to retaliate, is the instinctive response to the infringement of one's "rights" conceived of as the fundamental conditions for surviving and reproducing.

Finally, the violator of a norm may be punished by the costly actions of several or many other people. For example, a divorced man may find that he is no longer invited to dinner in the community, even though he is "the life of the party."[10] Multilateral punishments require more information than bilateral ones. The free-rider problem is exacerbated because more people are involved, but ameliorated because each punisher's cost of punishment can be less for the same total deterrent.

8. Jon Elster, *The Cement of Society* 127 (1989).

9. See also Jack Hirshleifer, "On the Emotions as Guarantors of Threats and Promises, in *The Latest and the Best* 307 (John Dupre ed. 1987); Robert H. Frank, *Passions within Reason: The Strategic Role of the Emotions* (1988).

10. The categories of guilt and shame correspond to "first party" sanctions in Robert Ellickson's terminology, bilateral costly sanctions to his "second party," and multilateral costly sanctions to his "third party." Robert C. Ellickson, *Order without Law: How Neighbors Settle Disputes* 130–131 (1991). He does not include the automatic and the informational sanctions in his taxonomy because they are not methods of enforcing norms as he defines "norm." Other definitional issues are addressed in Richard H. McAdams, "The Origin, Development, and Regulation of Norms," 96 *Michigan Law Review* 338 (1997).

Consider the Amish practice of shunning offenders against church rules. Like other Mennonites, the Amish have norms both against violence and against going to court. Excommunication, with resulting ostracism, is therefore the maximum punishment.[11] But it is effective because the Amish constitute an isolated subculture *from which exit is costly*. The qualification is essential. Ostracism is an effective sanction only if there are net benefits from remaining within the group. Creating those benefits can be exceedingly costly, however. The Amish do not permit their children to be educated beyond elementary school. This makes it difficult for Amish to function in the larger culture and thus raises the cost of exit, but at the price of limiting their potential income.

The thickness of the membrane that separates the member of an isolated subculture from the larger culture that surrounds it depends on the larger culture's tolerance of difference as well as on how different the subculture is. The more tolerant the larger culture, the easier it will be for the member of the subculture to escape into the alien surround without heavy cost. A culture of intolerance can foster good behavior by strengthening normative regulation by groups within the society. A group can *thrive* in consequence of being discriminated against; its members, however, may be either better or worse off than if they could readily assimilate to the larger society.[12]

Even if there is a high degree of cultural nonconformity by a group and intolerance of nonconformity by the larger society, ostracism will not be a feasible sanction unless there are net benefits to being an ostracizer. Because ostracizers are unpaid norm enforcers, there is a potential free-rider problem; each will have an incentive to hang back from undertaking costly action, hoping that others will step forward. Emotion plays a role in overcoming this tendency and so, as noted earlier, does self-interest in a more conventional sense; we saw that the cost of ostracism to the ostracizers will sometimes be negative. This is one reason that norms are more likely to be effective the smaller the group that is subject to them. Repetitive transactions, which are more

11. See John Howard Yoder, "Caesar and the Meidung," 23 *Mennonite Quarterly Review* 76 (1949). For a theoretical discussion of costly ostracism in a repeated game, see David Hirshleifer and Eric Rasmusen, "Cooperation in a Repeated Prisoner's Dilemma with Ostracism," 12 *Journal of Economic Behavior and Organization* 87 (1989).

12. See Eric A. Posner, "The Regulation of Groups: The Influence of Legal and Nonlegal Sanctions on Collective Action," 63 *University of Chicago Law Review* 133 (1996).

frequent among members of a small group than among members of a large one,[13] both reduce the cost of ostracism to the ostracizers—all they have to do is cease transacting with the violator, and this may be privately as well as socially advantageous—and make it easier to identify norm breakers.

A notable feature of American society is religious pluralism, and we should consider how this relates to the efficacy of governance by social norms in view of the historical importance of religion as both a source and enforcer of such norms. On the one hand, religious pluralism facilitates norm shopping, both because a person can find a sect that does not constrain his activities and because he can find one that constrains them in a way that he finds desirable. Belonging to a church that punishes deviance can be as useful to one's long-term welfare (in quite materialistic terms) as having parents who instill guilt. On the other hand, pluralism can promote the enforcement of norms by facilitating the emergence of many *small* sects, since, as we have seen, regulation by norms is more effective in a small group than in a large one. But it is the community's own norms that are enforced, not those of the larger society; and there may be a divergence between the two sets of norms.

The conditions that conduce to effective enforcement of norms—small membership and a high cost of being ostracized—are most likely to be satisfied in isolated, primitive communities. This may explain how something like law could emerge, as a system of social norms, before there was any centralized authority to enforce it. A contributing factor is that regulation by informal norms is more feasible if the society is static, as primitive societies tend to be. Large norm changes are difficult to arrange without a centralized authority because of their high cost and the temptation to free ride that the high cost creates. Evolution, being a process of slight, incremental, and often, therefore, cheap change, can overcome this obstacle to the creation of norms, but it is slow. So if a society is changing rapidly, regulation by norms is unlikely to satisfy the society's regulatory needs.

◇ CONSIDER NOW the creation, destruction, and alteration of norms. A norm is a "public good" in the strong sense that its cost does not rise if more people use the norm and that people who do not contribute to its enforcement cannot be denied its benefits. Any good with

13. As emphasized in Ellickson, note 10 above, at 177–180.

such characteristics is for obvious reasons in danger of being underproduced, and so norms are likely to be underproduced. But by the same token, once a norm is created, it is hard to change. Creating a norm requires promulgation of the norm and the creation of sanctions for its violation. Eliminating a norm requires promulgation, too, and also the destruction of the expectations and tastes that support the sanctions for its violation—a process of taste-changing that may be as costly as their creation in the first place. *Changing* a norm, which requires elements of both destruction and creation, can be the most difficult trick of all.

Not always, to be sure. If "goodbye" became an inefficient form of farewell, individuals could shift to "take care" without cost. Anyone who changed would be able to convey the same meaning as before and would not be thought worse of by other people. Many writers have switched from using "he" as the indefinite nonneuter pronoun to "he or she" or "she." The writer's meaning is still apparent, as in the case of shifting from "goodbye" to "take care," but in the he/she case the violation of the grammatical norm distracts the reader and slows down communication, leading some writers to employ elaborate periphrasis to avoid having to use a pronoun. The rapidity with which the norm has nevertheless changed is a result of the importance to many people of signaling a belief in feminist goals. The norm has not changed all the way, however, because some writers wish to signal their rejection of what they take to be an extremist feminist ideology or simply attach more weight to writing well than to being seen as politically correct.

In both these examples, altering an existing norm is feasible because it can be done gradually and hence without centralized direction. But try reversing traffic signals so that red meant "go" and green meant "stop," or changing the rules of the road from driving on the right to driving on the left. Such a norm change would have to be adopted by everyone at once, unlike minor language changes, in order to avoid enormous transition costs. The habitual character of compliance with these norms would add to the cost of change.

Trying to switch from one language to another, as opposed to changing usage within a single language, would present a similar problem on a vaster scale.[14] National languages do change, but ordinarily it is

14. See Richard Adelstein, "Language Orders," 7 *Constitutional Political Economy* 221 (1996).

through an intermediate stage of bilingualism. More common has been reform in writing, as in the simplification of Chinese characters in the twentieth century,[15] the replacement of the Gothic alphabet by the Roman in Germany after the Second World War,[16] and the increasing substitution in Korean writing of the highly phonetic Korean "alphabetic syllabary" for Chinese characters.[17] But in the Chinese and Korean cases the change was effected by government, just as in the case of Sweden's overnight change from driving on the left to driving on the right.[18]

The problem of transitions that I have been discussing is our old friend (from Chapter 4) path dependence, and it can help explain why it is often desirable that norms should change slowly even when the change is in the direction of a clearly superior norm. Because the superior norm may take time to phase in, there might be a rent in the fabric of social control if the older, inferior norm were to disappear before the transition was complete. The gradual decline of vengeance as an extralegal normative system for deterring and punishing crime paralleled the increasing efficacy of law's methods of crime prevention. Had the vengeance norm collapsed suddenly, anarchy would have resulted because the legal methods of crime control (involving police, judges, lawyers, and so on) were not yet well developed.

The overdeveloped sense of honor in white males of the Old South, the similar "macho" values of poor young black males in our cities today, and the surprisingly resilient "coolness" of cigarette smoking are all examples of norms that apparently are dysfunctional under current conditions but that nevertheless persist. They illustrate the earlier point that the destruction as well as the creation of norms is a public good, so that it is possible for the flow of norms to be too small but the

---

15. See, for example, Insup Taylor and M. Martin Taylor, *Writing and Literacy in Chinese, Korean and Japanese*, ch. 8 (1995); *Language Reform in China: Documents and Commentary* (Peter J. Seybolt and Gregory Kuei-ke Chiang eds. 1979).

16. Kenneth Katzner, *The Languages of the World* 71 (new ed. 1995).

17. See Taylor and Taylor, note 15 above, pt. 2. The Korean alphabet, introduced by the government early in the fifteenth century, shows that the reform of writing is not a recent invention. Failed attempts to change languages abound. Consider Ireland's attempt to expand the use of Gaelic, or Canada's attempt to spread the use of French. There have been notable successes, but most have been the result of conquest; an exception is the revival of Hebrew (the use of which had shrunk largely to ritual occasions) as the national language of Israel.

18. See "Sweden Tells Traffic to Keep to the Right," *Business Week*, Sept. 2, 1967, p. 26.

stock of norms too large. Norms enforced by guilt and shame are particularly difficult to create or to change because they are heavily influenced by social conditioning mediated through the family, an institution highly resistant to governmental efforts to change its beliefs and
practices.

When frequent change is itself a norm, as in the case of women's
fashions, the impression of frequent and easy norm change can mislead. The surprise would be if the "change norm" itself changed suddenly—if one year women's fashions were identical to the previous
year's. And Timur Kuran has shown how norms that appear to be very
strong can suddenly evaporate, enforced as they are only by people's
beliefs that other people will continue to enforce them.[19]

Understanding how norms change can help us understand how they
are created. When incremental change is feasible, even complex norms
can evolve from meager beginnings, given enough time. Comparing
the scene depicted on Achilles' shield in book 20 of the *Iliad* with modern norms of judicial behavior, one gets a glimpse of how those norms
could, over a period of more than 2,500 years, have evolved from rudi-
mentary procedures. The shield depicts informal, voluntary arbitration
before a lay tribunal. This is remote from modern litigation (though
not so remote from modern arbitration), yet it is easy to trace a step-
by-step evolution from ancient to modern practices of dispute resolution.

We have now to consider the place of norms in an overall system of
social control, and hence the role of law in relation to norms. I make
five points. The first concerns the law's role as a supplemental enforcer
of norms. Norms are a more effective method of social control than
law when individual violations are too trivial, or the difficulty of proving guilt too great, to justify the expense of trials, police, and prisons.
But often the sanctions for violating norms are too weak to deter
enough people from committing offenses, while the creation of norms
proceeds too slowly to provide all the rules necessary for the governance of society—so laws have their place too. Apart from creating new
norms in the form of law, government can prescribe supplemental punishments for the violation of existing social norms if the informal sanction for violation is inadequate. It does this for theft, for example.

19. Timur Kuran, *Private Truths, Public Lies: The Social Consequences of Preference Falsification*
(1997).

Legal sanctions for the violation of norms are particularly important when many people in a society are impervious to informal sanctions. They may lack guilt and shame, may not mind ostracism (because they have no valuable transactional opportunities regardless of their norm compliance), and have no reputation to lose; but they still are vulnerable to the law's tangible sanctions.

Second, law has a role both in regulating and protecting the private sanctions for the violation of norms. The legal process is designed to minimize the likelihood of erroneously imposing formal legal sanctions. Elaborate protections of the innocent are not necessary with regard to most of the conduct that norms rather than laws regulate because the sanctions for violation are not severe. But when violations are punished by especially severe extralegal sanctions, a public hearing to correct the erroneous imposition of the sanction may be warranted. This is the economic rationale for the provision of legal remedies against defamation, which is an informational sanction for the violation of norms; it operates by destroying reputation, thus discouraging people from dealing with the defamed person. But because defamation is an important sanction for violating norms, the law must not punish it uncritically or too severely, and in particular must not punish *truthful* defamation; that would strike at the heart of the system of informational sanctions for the violation of social norms. Notice that if the penalty for slander (oral defamation, as opposed to written, which is governed by libel law) is too high, people will be afraid to gossip for fear they don't have the story exactly right. Gossip is an important facilitator of sanctions for violating norms.[20]

To take a more extreme, and, in fact, archaic example, if bilateral sanctions such as shotgun marriages are to work, the law may have to relax its monopoly on force. It has been argued that the change in the 1960s in the norms governing births out of wedlock was due to the rise of birth control and abortion, which reduced the benefits of shotgun marriages.[21]

20. See Sally Engle Merry, "Rethinking Gossip and Scandal," in *Toward a General Theory of Social Control*, vol. 1, p. 271 (Donald Black ed. 1984).

21. George A. Akerlof, Janet L. Yellen, and Michael L. Katz, "An Analysis of Out-of-Wedlock Childbearing in the United States," 111 *Quarterly Journal of Economics* 277 (1996). Most such marriages, of course, were not literally enforced by the threat of violence; nor do I suggest that permitting such threats would be warranted by the social costs of out-of-wedlock births, substantial though those costs are.

Third, government can supply incentives for administering private sanctions for violating a norm. Consider the enforcement of contracts that provide for arbitration of disputes arising under them. A contract is a set of norms constructed by the parties to the contract. If the law enforces arbitration awards (as it does), it gives legal backing to the private formation and enforcement of norms. Contracts create norms tailored to highly specific and even idiosyncratic activities that a centralized legal authority would lack sufficient information to regulate. (By the same token, the law refuses to enforce contracts that are against public policy—that is, that create bad norms.) The legal enforcement of contracts reinforces (complements) rather than creates norms that would not otherwise exist or be obeyed because many contracts are adhered to, despite a lack of feasible means of legal enforcement, by considerations of reciprocity.

Fourth, government can foster the creation of norms. In the case of coordination norms, government can promulgate the new norm, as in the examples I gave earlier. When guilt and shame are the sanctions, government can help to instill these in children and adults alike. But because moral and intellectual education can work at cross-purposes, an increase in the resources devoted to education is not a dependable means of promoting governance by norms. By emphasizing the acquisition of knowledge and intellectual skills, a typical modern education encourages the student to think for himself. In the process it equips him with intellectual tools for circumventing moral norms, such as rationalization, casuistic reasoning, discovering latent inconsistencies between moral norms, pluralism, moral skepticism (values are not objective, are matters of opinion), and even nihilism.[22] Ignorance of alternatives is a powerful constraint on free choice. Exposing students to alternative norms encourages norm shopping, which may result in students' opting out of irksome moral constraints as adults. The well-documented moral differences between cities and rural areas[23] illustrate

22. See Richard A. Posner, *The Problematics of Moral and Legal Theory* 70–75 (1999); Matthew Rabin, "Moral Preferences, Moral Constraints, and Self-Serving Biases" (Wkg. Paper No. 95–241, Dept. of Econ., Univ. of Cal. at Berkeley, Aug. 1995).

23. See, for example, Edward L. Glaeser and Bruce Sacerdote, "Why Is There More Crime in Cities?" 107 *Journal of Political Economy* S225 (1999); Robert J. Sampson, "The Effects of Urbanization and Neighborhood Characteristics on Criminal Victimization," in *Metropolitan Crime Patterns*, ch. 1 (Robert M. Figlio, Simon Hakim, and George F. Rengert eds. 1986).

the importance of norm shopping as a phenomenon, though another factor is that ostracism is less effective in a setting in which most interactions are with strangers.

"Liberal" education, in short, is "freeing" education and one of those freedoms is from norms. Whether education is *effective* in this or any other respect is, of course, the despair of teachers at all levels. Nevertheless, what appears to be a long-term movement away from regulation by norms and toward regulation by law may reflect an inverse relation between a society's level of education and the efficacy of normative regulation.

Education can undermine social governance by norms in another way. In general, within limits apparently not yet reached, the more highly educated a nation's population is, the wealthier the nation is. The cost of being ostracized, as a sanction for violating a norm, is negatively related to a society's income level. In a wealthy society, the individual is less dependent on the good will of his particular community— either because he's wealthy himself, or has a social safety net under him, or is highly mobile because he has portable vocational and social skills. These considerations make normative regulation what economists call an inferior good, that is, one the demand for which falls with increases in income. And another: privacy is a superior good, and so there is more of it in a wealthy society; and privacy reduces the efficacy of norms by depriving neighbors, acquaintances, gossips, and scandal sheets of the information needed for shame, informational, and multilateral sanctions.[24] The more the law protects privacy, the more it increases the demand for law as a substitute for regulation by norms. I am led to doubt the realism of supposing, as some communitarians and social conservatives do, that American society may be ripe for a moral revolution that will restore governance by norms to the high place it once occupied.

Finally, government has a role to play in combating bad norms. It can target the bad-norm entrepreneurs, as in the successful campaigns to reduce street crime in New York City and elsewhere. By removing from the streets aggressive panhandlers, vandals, drunks, junkies, prostitutes, gang members, loiterers, and other visibly antisocial persons,

---

24. Yuval Tal, *Privacy and Social Norms: Social Control by Reputational Costs* (unpublished diss., University of Chicago Law School, 1997).

the police remove exemplars of deviant behavior who if allowed to flourish unmolested might establish norms for the more timid members of the community to adopt.[25] The law can also reduce the benefits of compliance with bad norms by creating effective legal remedies for deliberate injuries; those remedies will reduce the benefit of a vengeance norm based on personal honor. Or it can increase the cost of complying with the norm, most simply by affixing a legal penalty such as by making dueling a crime. Since, however, the heart of an honor-based vengeance system is a readiness to act without regard to the balance of costs and benefits, increasing the costs of compliance with a bad norm is not so simple as it may seem.[26] Once a legal penalty is affixed, compliance with the norm may signal the dueler's honor even more effectively. But honor implies indifference only to *certain* costs, in much the same way that indigence may make one indifferent to uncollectable fines but not to imprisonment. The proper "currency" in which to punish dueling is to make it dishonorable, as by disqualifying the dueler from the public offices that a man of honor is duty-bound to fill.[27]

Lawyers think that the law is a shaper (not just an enforcer) of norms, much like education. The evidence for this conjecture is weak, as I noted in reference to constitutional law in the Introduction. Against it can be cited evidence that subgroups will often go their own way, adhering to norms that serve their special needs but violate the applicable legal norms, which may have been created without consideration of those needs.[28] The divergence may come about through sheer (rational) ignorance of the law—an ignorance that is especially likely to be found precisely where the law is nonintuitive, and hence more costly to understand, because it is inconsistent with the norms of a person's immediate community. Law can undermine good norms as well as bad ones by reducing a group member's incentive to comply with the group norms, since he can look outside the group—to the law—for protection.[29]

25. See Dan M. Kahan, "Social Influence, Social Meaning, and Deterrence," 83 *Virginia Law Review* 349 (1997).

26. I am treating the dueling norm, I think realistically, as secondary to the honor code—that is, as an enforcement norm rather than a substantive norm.

27. Lawrence Lessig, "The Regulation of Social Meaning," 62 *University of Chicago Law Review* 943, 971–972 (1995).

28. A major theme of Ellickson, note 10 above.

29. See Posner, note 12 above.

⟨⁓⟩ No DISCUSSION of social norms, or for that matter of the role of emotion in the regulation of human behavior, can be complete without an examination of the role of religion. Adam Smith taught that religious sects must be small in order to overcome free-rider problems among their members and thus shape their moral behavior effectively; his discussion was thus very much in the spirit of the modern economic analysis of social norms. David Hume emphasized that an established religion is likely to dampen religious fervor by reducing competition among religions—another nice economic point. The present state of religious belief in Western Europe supports Hume's conjecture.[30] The nations of Western Europe have established churches, but except in Ireland the level of religiosity of the population is very low relative to the United States,[31] which forbids established churches.

Smith's and Hume's analyses differ not only in the value they ascribe to religion but also in their implications for public policy toward religion. Smith believed that religion was on balance useful in shaping moral values, while Hume believed that on balance it was destructive because it fomented war, civil strife, superstition, and persecution. The destructive potential of religion is illustrated in this country today by religiously inspired attacks on abortion doctors and clinics and efforts to discourage the teaching of the theory of evolution, and in some other countries by protracted, large-scale sectarian violence. There is need to trade off the norm-related benefits emphasized by Smith of fostering small sects, implying the absence of an established church, with the costs emphasized by Hume of religious strife and oppression, consequences of religion that he thought argued for an established church, implying a reduction in the number of sects. In the limit, an established church might have a complete religious monopoly, and Smith's aim would be completely defeated and Hume's completely achieved.

The modern economic literature on religion[32] emphasizes two activ-

30. For empirical evidence, see Laurence R. Iannaconne, "The Consequences of Religious Market Structure: Adam Smith and the Economics of Religion," 3 *Rationality and Society* 156, 169 (1991).

31. See, for example, *Gallup Report No. 236*, May 1985, pp. 50, 53.

32. See, for example, Laurence R. Iannoccone, "Household Production, Human Capital, and the Economics of Religion," in *The New Economics of Human Behavior* 172 (Mariano Tommasi and Kathryn Ierulli eds. 1995); Iannoccone, "Progress in the Economics of Religion," 150 *Journal of Institutional and Theoretical Economics* 737 (1994); Iannoccone, "Sacrifice

ities of religious groups, both related to norms though the first more centrally. The first is their effort to increase the costs of defection, or exit, by inculcating their members with deviant characteristics of behavior or appearance, a kind of branding; I mentioned the Amish earlier. But one of the best examples is secular. It is the decision of the Zionists, who were religious unbelievers, to make Hebrew rather than German or English the official language of what was then Palestine. One effect was to make it more difficult for future generations of Jews in Palestine to emigrate.

It is an open question whether under the conditions prevailing in a modern society religion contributes a great deal to the enforcement of social norms. The example of the Amish is pretty isolated. This is not an accident; assuming that the values and manners of the larger society are optimal in some sense—for why else *are* they the values and manners of the larger society?—the price that a group pays for cultivating deviant values or manners is very high for its members.

Consider the parallel example of orthodox Jews. Wielding an effective threat of ostracism, they have been able to achieve a commanding position in the international trade in diamonds without recourse to the law to enforce the norms of the trade.[33] But they are only a small fraction of the Jewish population. Although Jews as a whole have very high levels of income and education, most Jews are nonobservant or marginally observant. The astonishing Jewish economic and professional success in the United States has gone hand in hand with Jewish assimilation, as measured for example by the current 50 percent intermarriage rate. One is not surprised to find, therefore, that the Jewish income advantage is inverse to orthodoxy: orthodox Jews have lower incomes on average than conservative Jews, and conservative Jews lower incomes on average than reform Jews.[34] For the Jews, at least, and perhaps gen-

and Stigma: Reducing Free-Riding in Cults, Communes, and Other Collectives," 100 *Journal of Political Economy* 271 (1992); Edward L. Glaeser and Spencer Glendon, "The Demand for Religion" (unpublished, Harvard University Department of Economics, Oct. 23, 1997); Glaeser and Glendon, "Incentives, Predestination and Free Will," 36 *Economic Inquiry* 429 (1998).

33. See Bernstein, note 3 above.

34. Esther I. Wilder and William H. Walters, "Ethnic and Religious Components of the Jewish Income Advantage, 1969 and 1989," 68 *Sociological Inquiry* 426 (1998). See also Esther I. Wilder, "Socioeconomic Attainment and Expressions of Jewish Identification, 1970 and 1990," 35 *Journal for the Scientific Study of Religion* 109, 123 (1996); Barry A. Kosmin and Seymour P. Lachman, *One Nation under God: Religion in Contemporary American Society* 266 (1993).

erally in the conditions prevailing in modern society, the increase in the efficacy of normative regulation that is brought about by cultivating distinctive dispositions and practices is more than offset by the loss of transactional opportunities that such dispositions and practices cause. This point has general application to efforts to substitute regulation by social norms for regulation by law.

The second religious activity emphasized in the modern literature is the effort to shape the values and preferences of the members of a religious group by various forms of indoctrination that to the unsympathetic are simply methods of brainwashing. The secular analogue here is totalitarianism, and it is evident that the fascists and the communists borrowed a number of techniques from the Catholic Church in their ultimately unsuccessful (or only partially successful) effort at mass brainwashing.[35]

Of considerable interest as well is the competition between government and religion in the inculcation of norms. By insisting in the name of the Constitution that public schools be entirely secular, the courts increase the demand for the services of (private) religious institutions and by doing so strengthen religion.[36] What social conservatives denounce as the antireligious character of the Supreme Court's religion decisions may actually be one of the reasons that Americans are more religious than most of the populations of other modern nations.

But the existing economic literature on religion, preoccupied as it is with religion's role in relation precisely to the subject of this chapter, leaves out much that one would like from a theory of religion. A fascination with norms should not be allowed to occlude the other functions of religion. A notable omission from the economic literature is any analysis of the *content* of religious doctrines. For purposes of discouraging defection by raising its costs, the rationality of religious doctrine or ritual may be irrelevant. But explaining those doctrines and rituals, rather than treating them as arbitrary, should also be a concern of a theory of religion and it may not be entirely beyond the scope of economics to contribute to such an explanation. Religious practices that

35. I develop this theme in my article "Orwell versus Huxley: Economics, Technology, Privacy, and Satire," 24 *Philosophy and Literature* 1 (2000).

36. Richard A. Posner, "The Law and Economics Movement," 77 *American Economic Review Papers & Proceedings* 1, 11 (May 1987). See also Michael W. McConnell and Richard A. Posner, "An Economic Approach to Issues of Religious Freedom," 56 *University of Chicago Law Review* 1 (1989).

we are liable to dismiss out of hand as products of mere superstition may on closer examination reveal economizing properties. Take what we deride as female "genital mutilation" (what used to be called, less pejoratively but misleadingly, "female circumcision," but is more precisely and neutrally described as clitoridectomy and infibulation). The main practitioners are African Moslems, who are polygynous (Islam permits polygyny), and a possible function is reducing female sexual pleasure in order to reduce the temptations to female adultery in a polygynous society.[37] The temptations are great because a man's wives live in separate households among which he circulates with limited sexual contact with, and limited surveillance of, each wife.

Functionalism is a perilous mode of explanation, I know; it is usually easy—too easy—to imagine a function for any social practice, however weird, but difficult to establish the causal relation between its functionality and its adoption and persistence. But there is enough plausibility to the suggested explanation of female genital mutilation to warrant further inquiry before deciding that the practice is irrational, rather than merely distasteful to us.

I go further and claim that religion cannot be understood *primarily* as a system for inculcating values any more than economics can be understood primarily as a system for inculcating values, although one function of graduate education in economics is to inculcate certain professional values, such as honesty in the use of data and properly crediting the contributions of other scholars. Religion is a system parallel to and indeed competitive with—in ancient and primitive cultures continuous with or even indistinguishable from—science for understanding and controlling one's social and physical environment. It offers answers to important questions, such as how the world came to be, how human life originated, and what happens to us when we die, and it offers techniques, such as prayer, divination, and sacrifice, for controlling nature, prevailing in war, and so on.

The religion of the ancient Greeks was naturalistic, pragmatic, and protoscientific. The gods were plausible personifications of the various natural forces and human dispositions; and efforts to propitiate the gods, mainly through sacrifice, were plausible although mistaken attempts to control the natural environment—the same aim that modern

37. See Richard A. Posner, *Sex and Reason* 256–257 (1992).

science and technology pursue with greater success. The competition among religions, and between religion and its secular alternatives, such as Marxism and science, has always been, in part anyway, a competition among theories. One reason for the success of Protestantism, especially Calvinist Protestantism, may be that the doctrine of grace is closer to scientific ways of thinking about human behavior than Catholic doctrine is. The idea that God determines *before we are born* who shall be saved and who damned is a deterministic theory of behavior, just like the scientific outlook on behavior. (In other words, read grace for genes.) And recall that the success of Christianity was apparently due in part to the example of the martyrs, whose calmness in the face of death signaled a sincere belief in the tenets of their religion. Later, both Christianity and Islam were able to win many converts by arguing that their military conquests showed that God was on their side. In short, religions frequently succeed through rational appeals.

Mention of martyrs and conquests brings to the fore the epistemological difficulties faced by religion. The most compelling version of the scientific method involves propounding hypotheses that can be falsified by reference to data (whether generated by experiments or otherwise) whose interpretation is independent of the particular values or perspective of the scientists who observe the data. In some cases, such as the theory of evolution, the central hypothesis of the theory cannot be tested on data; the evolution of man and other primates from a common ancestor cannot be observed. But often and in that instance the hypothesis can be tested indirectly but still reliably, whether by laboratory experiments in breeding fruit flies or other animals (or plants) that reproduce very rapidly, or by the study of geographically isolated animal populations, or the fossil record, or by DNA comparisons between related animal populations, or by computer simulations. No single approach to explaining the unobservable phenomenon may be decisive but the consilience of a large number of different approaches, combined with the absence of a plausible alternative hypothesis, may justify accepting the explanation, though always just tentatively.

Religious theories are generally not tested in a similar way, although there are exceptions: when a religion predicts that the world will end on a certain day, and the day comes and goes without incident, the falsification of the prediction is taken by most people to establish the falsity of the cult's creed. Most religions have shied away from making falsifiable predictions, instead making predictions that are either impossible to test, such as predictions concerning the afterlife, or that are very difficult to test, such as predictions concerning the efficacy of prayer, since it is understood that many things may prevent a prayer from bringing about the desired effect other than that there is no god listening to it. Religions commonly appeal to testimony, for example the testimony of the alleged witnesses to Christ's miracles, or seek to enhance the credibility of the claims by signaling, as in the examples in a previous paragraph.[38] (The drawbacks of testimony as a basis for justified belief are discussed in the next chapter.)

Many religions have striven to create a monopoly of belief, since religious diversity may create skepticism. For example, Pascal's famous wager (even if the probability that God exists is very slight, since the gain—eternal life—from believing in Him if He does exist is infinite, the expected gain from "betting" that he does exist must be positive) is infeasible if there is competition between religions. No longer is it a safe bet, since if you bet on the "wrong" God (one that does not in fact exist), you may be punished by the true God.[39] The vitality of religion in America, despite Americans' religious pluralism, may appear to refute the suggestion that pluralism stimulates skepticism; but as we are about to see, much American religious belief may be merely notional.

The theory of evolution eliminated the strongest *scientific* argument for religion, the argument that anything as complicated as the human organism must reflect conscious design, implying an awesomely powerful Designer—what else *could* explain it? Darwin answered this rhetorical question, and ever since only a minority of educated people have looked to religion as a source of scientific truths, an alternative to scientific theory.

Science and religion historically have competed as technologies (methods of controlling the environment) and not just as theories about the structure of the world. Religion traditionally had a large component of magic, while science is the source of most of our modern "magic." Since scientific magic turns out to be more effective than reli-

38. Rodney Stark, *The Rise of Christianity: A Sociologist Reconsiders History* 173 (1996). Stark's book emphasizes devices by which religions enhance the credibility of their claims. See especially id., ch. 8.

39. It's still a good bet if agnosticism is punished as severely as the "wrong" belief; but it may not be.

gious, religion has tended to withdraw from direct competition, instead becoming increasingly metaphysical and psychological, catering to our dislike of uncertainty by offering answers to questions that science cannot yet answer and to our fear of death by offering the promise of an afterlife.[40] A parallel development occurred with philosophy, another quondam competitor of science; it has largely ceded the task of explaining the natural world to science.[41] There is an analogy to the rise of abstraction in art when photography displaced art's function in portraiture and other realistic depiction. Competition from a new technology induced artists to seek new markets. In the same way, the rise of scientific technology displaced religion away from magic and toward metaphysics and psychology, as well as toward the social functions emphasized in the economic literature.

Because intellectually more sophisticated people are quicker to discover the intellectual inadequacies of existing religion, new religions draw their votaries disproportionately from the ranks of such people, rather than, as one might have supposed, from the credulous.[42] This implies a lively competitive process in the religious "market," and rapid adaptation to the advances of its scientific and technological competitors.

At a time when religion was the principal source of scientific knowledge and practical technology (control of weather, and so forth), it was not necessary to offer such psychological balm as a happy afterlife; Greek religion famously did not. As religion retreated on the scientific front, its social and psychological functions came to the fore. Here too it faced, and is facing, the competition of science, not only psychiatry and pharmacology but also life-extending and pain-reducing medical advances that reduce the demand for spiritual comforts.

As religion, at least in the prosperous, technologically progressive

40. See Ignacio Palacios-Huerta and Jesús J. Santos, "An Essay on the Competitive Formation of Preferences" (unpublished, Amos Tuck School of Dartmouth College and University of Chicago Graduate School of Business, Nov. 26, 1995).

41. The analogy would be closer, however, if one were considering the shift from religion to science as a system for explaining natural phenomena; few people, even among believing Christians, think any more that the story in Genesis of the expulsion of Adam and Eve from the Garden of Eden is a plausible explanation of why snakes lack limbs or how female human beings came into existence. Yet for centuries the Genesis story was the most widely believed explanation of these phenomena.

42. Stark, note 38 above, ch. 2.

nations, increasingly cedes theory and magic to science and substitutes therapeutic and social functions, its grip on behavior loosens. Its power to awe and to threaten diminishes. This recession (what Nietzsche called "the death of God") is concealed from Americans by the fact that a significant fraction of the American population, perhaps a tenth, still believes in biblical inerrancy and so rejects a good deal of modern science. But the behavioral significance of this belief is open to question. It is necessary to distinguish between two types of belief, the notional and the action-impelling. The distinction corresponds to that between cheap talk and credible commitment ("putting your money where your mouth is") in the theory of strategic behavior (game theory). Recall that one consequence of religious pluralism may be to enable people to find a religious niche in which their preferred behavior is unconstrained, even applauded. If you choose the length of your tether from among a large array of alternatives, you are likely to end up with a very long one. Although there is nevertheless a robust negative correlation between religiosity and criminality in the United States,[43] what drives this result is church membership and activities—the social dimension of religion—rather than beliefs (for example in hell).[44] This supports Adam Smith's thesis that the significance of religion for behavior is in facilitating governance by social norms, although his further suggestion that the effect is inverse to the size of the group has not been supported.[45] It is noteworthy that there is great religious enthusiasm, particularly Muslim, in U.S. prisons, yet it seems not to affect the rate of recidivism. It might, conceivably, increase it, since the relevant social

43. See Lee Ellis and James Peterson, "Crime and Religion: An International Comparison among Thirteen Industrial Nations," 20 *Personality and Individual Differences* 761 (1996); T. David Evans et al., "Religion and Crime Reexamined: The Impact of Religion, Secular Controls, and Social Ecology on Adult Criminality," 33 *Criminology* 195 (1995); Jody Lipford, Robert E. McCormick, and Robert D. Tollison, "Preaching Matters," 21 *Journal of Economic Behavior and Organization* 235, 244 (1993); Brooks B. Hull and Frederick Bold, "Preaching Matters: Replication and Extension," 27 *Journal of Economic Behavior and Organization* 143 (1995); William Sims Bainbridge, "The Religious Ecology of Deviance," 54 *American Sociological Review* 288 (1989); Rodney Stark, Lori Kent, and Daniel P. Doyle, "Religion and Delinquency: The Ecology of a 'Lost' Relationship," 19 *Journal of Research in Crime and Delinquency* 4 (1982); Lee Ellis, "Religiosity and Criminality: Evidence and Explanations of Complex Relationships," 28 *Sociological Perspectives* 501 (1985).

44. See Ellis and Peterson, note 43 above, at 765–766; Evans et al., note 43 above, at 210.

45. See Hull and Bold, note 43 above.

group is criminal and its norms presumably are those congenial to criminality.

The magnitude of the effect identified by Smith, however, at least under modern conditions, may be doubted. And today, as always, religion is a common source of violence, which was Hume's concern. Like nationalism, religion reduces the expected costs of violence. If you think you're really just a cell in a larger organism called Turkey or Poland or Germany, so that your death means no more than the death of one cell in a human body does, or if you think your soul is immortal and your body will be resurrected, then you will think it less costly to be killed in pursuit or defense of some ethnic or religious goal. It is one thing for a religion to inculcate beliefs that increase the utility of the votary, such as a belief in eternal life, and quite another to induce people to act ethically, implying subordination of self-interest to other values. There is, as I have been emphasizing, a tension between the beneficent effects of religion in encouraging governance by social norms, effects that Adam Smith stressed and that depend on the social rather than epistemological dimension of religion, and the destructive effects of religion—effects based on its truth claims and thus on its epistemological dimension—that worried Hume.

~ *IV*

EPISTEMOLOGY

～ *10*

Testimony

$O_{\text{NE OF THE MOST}}$ important things that a legal system does is to resolve factual disputes. Most legal disputes turn on disagreements, real or feigned, over what happened in the incident that gave rise to the dispute, rather than over what the governing rule should be. Even when the facts are not disputed, there is often disagreement over whether they "add up" to a violation of some legal duty; and such disagreements—disagreements over whether for example the defendant's admitted conduct amounted to negligence—can, as we shall see in the next chapter, usually be decomposed into purely factual disputes.

Much of the dissatisfaction with the American legal system stems from a belief that the system is not very good at resolving factual disputes. This skepticism has a distinguished philosophical lineage.[1] Many philosophers have doubted the truth value of "testimony," a term they use in a broad sense that includes but is not limited to the kind of evidence that is admissible at a trial. Testimony in the broad sense is any statement, oral or documentary, that is used to try to persuade a person of some fact. My birth certificate is "testimony" to my age, parentage, name, and place of birth. It happens to be imperfect testimony, as testimony so often is, because on the birth certificate my name is given as "Allen Richard Posner," but I have always gone by the name "Richard

---

1. See C. A. J. Coady, *Testimony: A Philosophical Study* (1992).

A. [for Allen] Posner." As this example brings out, skepticism about testimony is closely related to skepticism about historical knowledge, since both refer to past events that cannot be directly observed.

A factual determination made on the basis of testimony, as by judge or jury in a trial, is perforce based not on the tribunal's own firsthand knowledge but on what other people have said or written. As a source of knowledge, therefore—if it can ever be a source of knowledge—testimony differs from perception, memory (a kind of second-order perception), and inference (logical or inductive reasoning from knowledge acquired by perception or memory). Even when testimony is not secondhand—is not, that is, what the law calls "hearsay evidence," discussed in Chapter 12—the factual determination based on it is. The factfinder (judge or jury) cannot get behind the secondhand evidence and verify it by reference to what really happened, because there is no access to what really happened other than through the witnesses. Sometimes, after the trial, the truth of what happened becomes established beyond doubt. But this is rare, and so in the usual case the findings made on the basis of a trial cannot be proved correct; verdicts rest on testimony all the way down, so to speak. Skeptics about testimony are bound, therefore, to be skeptics about the factual accuracy of verdicts.

Like any belief founded on testimony, a finding of fact made by a judge or jury resembles the formation of a belief purely on the basis of the authority of some assumed expert concerning a matter that one is incapable of investigating oneself or perhaps even of understanding. And deferring to the authority of experts is in fact one of the traditional examples of basing belief on testimony rather than on perception, memory, or inference.[2] Since most of our beliefs are based on the testimony of authorities, philosophers' doubts that beliefs based on testimony can be accorded the status of knowledge are likely to strike a practical person as little more than a terminological quibble. Indeed, for reasons that Wittgenstein demonstrated, these doubts probably aren't even good philosophy.[3] Because of the limitations of time and intellect, we perforce base most of our beliefs on testimony, such as the

2. See, for example, Douglas N. Walton, *Appeal to Expert Opinion: Arguments from Authority* (1997), applying this point to the testimony of expert witnesses, a topic I take up in Chapter 12.

3. Ludwig Wittgenstein, *On Certainty* (1969), esp. ¶¶144, 240, 282, 288, 604.

testimony of scientists concerning cosmological and microscopic phenomena. Most of these beliefs are as reliable as those we form on the basis of perception, memory, or inference, and many are more reliable. This is true even though we judge the reliability of testimony largely on the basis of other testimony (I believe that my birth certificate has the date of my birth right in part because of what I have heard about governmental recording of vital statistics and in part because of what my parents told me my date of birth was), and even though we can be fooled by testimony. Much of it is indeed false, but we also make many mistakes in perception, misremember, and use faulty inferential procedures or err in their application.

Even Hume, who was famously skeptical about testimony (specifically the testimony of alleged witnesses to the resurrection of Christ),[4] thought it *generally* reliable. But he thought it possible to repose confidence in testimony only after verifying firsthand the witness's credibility; and this is rarely possible. Most judgments of credibility rest on testimony that we cannot, or at least do not, verify. "That babies are born of women in a certain way is known to all of us and it is a fact of observation but very many of us have not observed even one birth for ourselves"[5] and few of us have interrogated the observers or otherwise sought to verify their credibility. Testimony is, as the birth example demonstrates, a fundamental rather than a derivative source of knowledge, entitled to epistemological parity with perception, memory, and inference.[6]

Still, because judgment on the basis of testimony is undoubtedly highly fallible,[7] though not uniquely so, a large space is opened for

4. David Hume, *An Enquiry concerning Human Understanding* §10, pt. 1 (1748).

5. Coady, note 1 above, at 81.

6. This is the theme of Coady's important book. For the clearest statement of his argument, see id. at 143–151. See also Wittgenstein, note 3 above; Alvin I. Goldman, *Knowledge in a Social World*, ch. 4 (1999).

7. This is one of the themes of Orwell's great novel *Nineteen Eighty-Four*. By rewriting the documents—the testimony—on which knowledge of the past is based, the Party controls the past. "The mutability of the past is the central tenet of Ingsoc. Past events, it is argued, have no objective existence, but survive only in written records and in human memories. The past is whatever the records and the memories agree upon. And since the Party is in full control of the minds of its members [as well as of all records], it follows that the past is whatever the Party chooses to make it" (p. 176 of 1961 New American Library paperback ed.). Notice the conflation of testimony and memory here. Needless to say, Orwell himself was not a postmodernist; it is a striking implication of his novel that totalitarians are postmodernists.

questioning the accuracy of legal judgments and for seeking improvements in the legal factfinding procedures themselves. I try in the next chapter to create, with the aid of economic theory, a framework for evaluating legal factfinding, the domain of the law of evidence. I point out that the law does not and should not strive for perfect accuracy in the determination of facts. So some skepticism about the reliability of legal testimony is certainly warranted. But there can be too much, the excess reflecting a heroic conception, Platonic in origin, of the power and duty of the individual (though in Plato only the exceptional individual) to ground his beliefs in his individual reason rather than deferring to the testimony of others. Skepticism about testimony can easily misfire, leading to an unwarranted loss of confidence in the accuracy of the legal system, as we can see with a case, originally obscure, that has achieved a certain celebrity as a result of deeply misguided journalistic attention.

In 1990 a federal jury convicted Sheila McGough, a criminal defense lawyer in Alexandria, Virginia, of fraud, perjury, witness intimidation, and related crimes, and she was sentenced to three years in prison. Her conviction and sentence were affirmed and a subsequent motion for a new trial on the basis of newly discovered evidence was denied and that denial was also affirmed. After being released from prison she wrote the well-known journalist Janet Malcolm that she had been framed because her pertinacious efforts to defend her clients had irritated federal prosecutors and judges. Malcolm investigated the matter and concluded that McGough had indeed been unjustly convicted. "It seems scarcely possible that in this country someone could go to prison for merely being irritating, but as far as I can make out, this is indeed what happened to Sheila McGough,"[8] though Malcolm does not believe that the judges and prosecutors involved in the proceedings against McGough had "framed" her in the sense of deliberately fabricating a case against a person whom they believed to be innocent.

Malcolm's book straddles two genres, both nourished by the tradition of skepticism about testimony. The first is that of revisionist legal history, in which a historian or investigative journalist tries to show that a trial, whether of a Dreyfus, or a Sacco and Vanzetti, or an Alger

---

8. Janet Malcolm, *The Crime of Sheila McGough* 6 (1999). Subsequent page references to her book appear in the text of this chapter.

Hiss, produced a miscarriage of justice. The second, illustrated by such works as Melville's *Billy Budd* and Camus's *The Stranger*, uses a real or, as in those two examples, a fictional legal proceeding to raise deep questions about the law's capacity to find truth and do justice. Janet Malcolm wants to show that the legal system failed to do justice in Sheila McGough's case but she also wants to suggest that it cannot do justice in any case, because of its epistemological and ethical inadequacies.

Revisionists usually pick a well-known case, and so there is a public record that can be consulted to evaluate their claims. Malcolm picked an obscure case, and while there is a public record in the technical sense—a trial transcript, briefs, and other documents that are available for public inspection in a government archive—it is not published and it is not readily available to people outside the federal judiciary. (The opinions of the trial and appellate judges in her cases are also unpublished.) Most of her readers will therefore find it impossible to evaluate her claims, and so they will remain blissfully unaware that her use of the record was selective and misleading. I'll summarize the evidence presented at McGough's trial and then discuss how Malcolm tries to exonerate her "exquisite heroine" (p. 161), as she calls McGough, from legal and moral responsibility.

In 1986 McGough was retained by a con artist named Bob Bailes (actually this was only one of the names he used) to defend him against a federal prosecution for bank fraud and for using false social security identification numbers to deceive. McGough knew about the multiple names, knew too that Bailes had a long criminal record, even knew that he was being investigated by the FBI for selling fraudulent insurance charters. Knowing these things she should have been on her guard—should have known the kind of person she was dealing with. Bailes implausibly represented to potential investors that the insurance charters, which he had forged, authorized the purchaser to engage in the insurance business anywhere in the United States without complying with pesky state-law restrictions. Eventually he was convicted of this fraud, too, and was sentenced to 25 years in prison, having by this time accumulated an extremely long criminal record. He has since died.

While McGough was preparing Bailes's defense in the bank fraud case, he used her law office to conduct his insurance scam. Responding to an ad for the charters that he had placed in the *Wall Street Jour-*

nal, two men named Manfredi and Boccagna, represented by a lawyer named Morris, began negotiating with Bailes to buy two of the charters. Bailes demanded a deposit of $75,000, which Morris and his clients insisted be placed in McGough's attorney trust account and be refunded to them if the deal fell through. All three testified that McGough repeatedly assured them that the deposit would remain in her trust account until the deal closed. As soon as the deposit was made, however, she checked out all but $5,000 of it to Bailes, who told her to keep the rest for herself, which she did. Shortly afterward she received a letter from Morris requesting confirmation that the money for the deposit would remain in her trust account. She neither answered the letter nor did anything to restore the $75,000 to the account.

The money had been put up by an investment banker named Mac-Donald (Morris's clients had been in effect brokers for the deal). As he began looking into the charters that he had agreed to buy, he became suspicious. His lawyer, Blazzard, asked McGough whether the $75,000 was still in her trust account, and she told him that it was, though she had disbursed it to Bailes and herself almost two weeks before. She told MacDonald that some of the insurance companies authorized by the charters were up and running; none was.

MacDonald soon realized that he had been had. He demanded that McGough return his $75,000, and when she refused he sued her for the money. In the deposition that she gave in that suit, she denied having represented Bailes in connection with the sale of the insurance charters. This was a lie, made under oath, and material to MacDonald's suit.

On the eve of trial in *MacDonald v. McGough*, McGough's lawyer submitted to the court two documents, entitled "Superseding Contracts," purportedly signed by Manfredi (one of Morris's clients, remember). The documents purported to be contracts between Bailes and Manfredi that superseded the original contracts for the sale by Bailes of the insurance charters to Boccagna and Manfredi. Unlike the original contracts, the "Superseding Contracts" made the $75,000 deposit that the purchasers had put up nonrefundable, and so cut the ground out from under MacDonald's suit. But Manfredi's signature on the "Superseding Contracts" had been forged, almost certainly by Bailes, from whom McGough had obtained the documents for use in the trial. She tried unsuccessfully to get Manfredi's forged signature notarized by a friend of Bailes named Cain. The day after he refused to do so, she threw in the towel and settled MacDonald's suit for the full $75,000 that he had sought. The natural inference is that she flinched at the prospect of going to trial on the basis of forgeries.

Back in 1986, during the negotiations with Morris's clients, another prospective purchaser of the phony charters had appeared. This man, Johnson, met with Bailes and McGough in McGough's office. Bailes demanded a nonrefundable deposit of $25,000. Johnson insisted that it be refundable and that it be retained in McGough's trust account until the deal closed. Bailes and McGough agreed to these conditions and the money was duly wired to her account—and she immediately checked it out to Bailes, all but $7,200, which she kept. Johnson later wired another $12,500 to her account, and this amount too Bailes and McGough divvied up between themselves. The deal with Johnson, unlike that with MacDonald, actually closed, with McGough signing for Bailes because he was in prison. They had agreed to give Johnson documents showing that the charter he had bought was indeed usable in all fifty states. No documents were forthcoming and when Johnson complained to McGough she said the reason for the delay was that Bailes was "on the road"; actually he was in prison.

A third transaction involved partners named Irwin and Sali. McGough denied she had ever received the $25,000 deposit that they made, yet it was proved that Irwin had wired it to her trust account and she had promptly disbursed it to Bailes. When Sali (Irwin having died) demanded the deposit back, she threatened to sue him and to have him arrested.

She was deeply involved in the insurance scam and must at some point have realized that she was a participant in a fraud. But that was just the beginning. Bailes devised another fantastic scheme, this one for getting himself released from prison into the custody of McGough. The implementation of the scheme began with her filing petitions for bankruptcy on behalf of assetless corporations owned by Bailes. Then she filed on behalf of other shell corporations owned by Bailes claims against the bankrupts, at the same time pleading for the release of Bailes into her custody on the ground that if he were out of prison he could take the necessary steps to see that the creditors of the bankrupt corporations were repaid. Nonexistent debtors sought relief from nonexistent debts owed to nonexistent creditors. McGough not only prepared numerous pleadings and motions in these fraudulent proceedings; she also procured and paid lawyers to represent the sham creditors.

By this time, a grand jury was investigating McGough. Shortly after she learned the identity of three witnesses that the government was planning to call before the grand jury, Bailes decided to bring a $50 million lawsuit against each of them. McGough took the complaint in the suit to the federal court for filing, but refused to pay the filing fee. As a result the complaint was not accepted for filing, although the defendants were served with a copy.

There was other evidence of fraud, witness intimidation, and related crimes as well by McGough. She did not take the stand in her defense.

The case that I have outlined struck the trial judge, the jury, and the appellate judges as open and shut. The only puzzle was McGough's motivation. It does not appear to have been financial. The deposit moneys that she appropriated from her trust account were slight in relation to the time that she spent representing Bailes. During most of that time she received no compensation from him at all and yet she abandoned all her other clients to devote full time to his affairs. It is possible that she was romantically involved with him—she was a never-married woman in her forties during the period in which she represented him—but it is more likely that she was simply "taken in" by him. By all accounts he was charming and plausible—a true con *artist*. She believed in him and would stop at nothing to advance his interests and rescue him from the clutches of the law.

Let us see how Malcolm tries to refute the case against McGough. One of her methods is to quibble over evidentiary details. Almost every legal case is replete with loose ends, discrepancies, inconsistencies, questionable witnesses, bits of evidence that don't fit or that contradict other bits. A defense lawyer will often try to use such impurities to plant doubts in the mind of jurors, who may have an idealized conception of how guilt is proved. Manfredi testified that he had been present when lawyer Morris read to McGough over the phone the letter Morris was sending her directing her to hold his clients' $75,000 deposit in her trust account. But the telephone company's records show that the call lasted only a minute. That may have been too short a time for him to have read the letter out loud, although it is less than a page long. Morris had had several conversations with McGough during the same period of time, and, testifying four years later, Manfredi may have mixed them up. There is no question that the deposits—not only the deposit that Morris's clients made on behalf of MacDonald but also the Johnson and Irwin-Sali deposits—were made to McGough's trust account. The only purpose could have been to make sure they weren't disbursed before the deals closed, so that if they didn't close, the depositors would be assured of getting their money back. McGough's claim that each deal "was a no-free-look-deal and that she was not an escrow agent" (p. 72), though convincing to Malcolm, is actually incredible. Had that been the nature of the deal, the deposit would have been made to Bailes's bank account—and he did have one, contrary to what McGough told Malcolm. Put differently, McGough had no reason of her own to want the deposit money placed in her trust account. It must have been the depositors' idea, and the purpose could only have been to keep the money out of Bailes's hands until the deal closed.

McGough's "no-free-look" claim was further undermined by her failure to reply to Morris's letter, which was explicit that it was indeed a "free-look" deal and that McGough was to keep the money in her trust account until the deal closed. If this understanding had been incorrect, McGough would presumably have told Morris lest she be accused of misappropriating the money that had been deposited in her trust account.

Testimony doesn't come labeled "true" or "false." It must be evaluated with reference to the motive and competence of the witness relative to any witnesses who may be giving contrary testimony, the internal consistency of his testimony and its consistency with the other testimony in the case, the common-sense plausibility of his testimony, and so forth. This process of sifting, weighing, and comparing testimony will often dispel or defuse the doubts about the reliability of testimony to which the philosophical tradition has drawn attention. In McGough's case it allows us with considerable confidence to attribute Manfredi's testimonial error to imperfect memory, to credit the essence of his testimony, and to dismiss McGough's denial as a lie.

Malcolm makes much of the fact that Morris was disbarred and later sent to jail, although these events occurred after McGough's trial and were unrelated to it, and that Manfredi and Boccagna were disreputable characters (and likewise Zinke, another participant in the brokering of the sale of the charters)—probably con artists themselves. But neither MacDonald nor his lawyer, Blazzard, have been accused of wrongdoing. And the fact that a prosecution witness has a criminal record, while it should raise a warning flag, does not invalidate his testimony. Criminal defense lawyers criticize, with good reason as we shall see in Chapter 12, the use of a defendant's criminal record to undermine his credibility; and what is sauce for the goose is sauce for the gander. The shadiness of Morris's clients is not inconsistent with their having wanted their deposit to be retained in a lawyer's trust account until the deal with Bailes closed. Shady characters may well be more rather than less suspicious than the average person of the people they do business with and so may be particularly eager to have the protection against the shadiness of others that a trust account affords—though in the end Boccagna and Manfredi managed to avoid putting up any money; it all came from MacDonald.

Regarding McGough's effort to get those forged "Superseding Contracts" that she dropped into MacDonald's suit against her notarized, Malcolm argues that since "copies of the contracts were already part of the court record of the case [McGough's lawyer having already filed them], it was out of the question" that McGough would have asked Cain to notarize the signature on them (p. 67). Not at all; a notarized signature would have tended to rebut the inference of forgery that the jury would have been invited to draw had the case gone to trial. And while it is true that Cain himself was shady and that McGough's lawyer in the MacDonald case gave testimony at her criminal trial that contradicted some of Cain's testimony, the lawyer admitted that he had not been present at the meeting in Cain's hotel room at which, according to Cain's testimony, McGough asked Cain to notarize the document. A friend of Bailes, Cain had no motive to give false testimony against Bailes's accomplice.

Malcolm claims that Johnson's lawyer lied when he testified that McGough had said that Bailes was "on the road" when Johnson closed the deal for the charter. The lawyer was indeed mistaken. The statement had been made later, when Johnson became impatient for the documentation that he needed in order to launch the insurance company in all fifty states. But the confusion of dates is irrelevant to the fraudulent character of the statement. It is another example of the loose ends found in all legal cases. It also calls into question the strand in the philosophical tradition that treats memory as a more authentic basis of knowledge than testimony.

Malcolm's most naive defense of McGough consists simply of crediting her denials. Yet those denials were not made under oath—remember that McGough did not testify at trial, where false testimony would have exposed her to a sentencing enhancement for perjury[9] (as distinct from the perjury that she committed earlier, at her deposition in MacDonald's suit against her). They were made to Malcolm, years after the trial. Naively crediting these unsworn, implausible denials, Malcolm is oblivious to the possibility of being conned by a con artist's lawyer. She may believe that you can tell whether a person is telling the truth by the sincerity of the person's manner. This belief, which research has exposed as fallacious,[10] is the very premise of successful con artistry, for which McGough as Bailes's accomplice may have had a gift. Because the demeanor of a witness can be so misleading, I do not feel at a disadvantage in assessing McGough's truthfulness by reason of not having "venture[d] beyond the trial transcript" and thus not having interviewed her and the other witnesses in her case, as Malcolm did in preparing her book.[11]

She has a condescending attitude toward McGough, who reminds her of "a corporate wife from Scarsdale, in town for a matinee" (p. 11). It doesn't occur to her that McGough could con *her.* And so in crediting McGough's avowal of naiveté about Bailes's business dealings, Malcolm fails to register the significance of McGough's boast to her that in her career as an executive of a foundation before she went to law school in her late thirties she had "had the responsibility of negotiating contracts for" her employer (p. 160). Malcolm also fails to note the incongruity of McGough's admitting to her that Bailes had forged a document yet claiming that the government had framed him. Malcolm exhibits almost comical credulity when, catching McGough—whose "devotion to truth," Malcolm says, "was an inspiring given" (p. 130)— in a lie, she remarks: "Her confession to me that she had misled Quarles was only further evidence of her honesty. She could have

---

9. See U.S. Sentencing Guidelines §3C1.1 and Application Note 4.

10. Judges and juries are all too often fooled by good liars. Michael J. Saks, "Enhancing and Restraining Accuracy in Adjudication," 51 *Law and Contemporary Problems,* Autumn 1988, pp. 243, 263–264. Should journalists be thought less credulous? Notice that if Malcolm did not believe McGough, she probably would not have a book. It was in her professional and pecuniary interest (at least short term) to be credulous.

11. Letter to the Editor from Janet Malcolm, *New Republic,* May 31, 1999, p. 4.

fudged or equivocated, but she had chosen to tell the shameful truth about herself" (id.). To confess to lying is proof of telling the truth? Come again?

Anyway she *did* fudge. Quarles, who had answered the *Wall Street Journal* advertisement but wisely decided against purchasing any of the insurance charters, had testified that in response to his "point-blank [question] whether anything had happened to Bob Bailes within the past two weeks" (p. 129), McGough had not disclosed that Bailes had been convicted of bank fraud. McGough admitted to Malcolm that she had misled Quarles by telling him "that nothing was final, that things were on appeal" (id.). But that was not Quarles's testimony, and he was a defense witness. He testified that she hadn't told him about the conviction, that he had learned about it for the first time years later. If she had told him that "things were on appeal," he would surely have followed up by asking what "things" were on appeal. McGough's version of their conversation is incredible.

The ethically most dubious, but rhetorically most effective, means by which Malcolm tries to make her reader doubt McGough's guilt is to ignore much of the damaging evidence presented at McGough's trial. Given the inaccessibility of the trial record to most of Malcolm's readership, this tactic of suppression echoes the fraud of which she seeks to exonerate her "exquisite heroine." Malcolm does not mention McGough's appropriation of Johnson's $25,000 deposit. She does not mention McGough's dealings with Irwin and Sali at all, which included not only the appropriation of another $25,000 deposit but also the threat to have Sali arrested. She does not mention the multimillion dollar lawsuits against the grand jury witnesses. It is not to be believed that Bailes alone had conceived these suits—that McGough was merely his messenger girl in bringing the papers to the courthouse. The defendants named in these suits—the people the suits were intended to harass and thus dissuade from testifying before the grand jury—were witnesses against her, not against him.

Malcolm does mention the accusation that McGough participated in the sham bankruptcies of Bailes's shell corporations. But by not commenting on whether the accusation was true or false, she makes it seem unrelated to McGough's prosecution and indeed implies that its only significance was to set the stage for a further accusation, which she denies on the basis of a letter McGough wrote her, that McGough had misled a federal judge with respect to Bailes's custody. McGough did mislead the judge, by concealing from him that a previous judge had refused to release Bailes. But that lie was less culpable than the countless acts of fraud that she committed with respect to the fraudulent bankruptcies. And Malcolm misses the most important point in McGough's letter, the statement that she had sought Bailes's release "so he could work with attorneys on a Chapter 11 [bankruptcy] case" (p. 117). That case was a sham, one of the sham bankruptcies that McGough filed for Bailes. She *had* to know this, and so she was lying to Malcolm, who should have realized it.

Malcolm does not mention the unimpeached testimony of lawyer Blazzard concerning his conversations with McGough; his name does not appear in the book. She does not mention that the "almost preternatural[ly] honest" McGough (as Malcolm characterizes her, p. 6) committed perjury in her deposition in the case brought against her by MacDonald when she claimed not to have represented Bailes in connection with the insurance charters. That perjury was one of the fourteen felonies of which McGough was convicted.

All the evidence that Malcolm ignores supports the charges against McGough, and taken all in all leaves no doubt that they were true— something that few readers of Malcolm's book who have not looked at the actual record of McGough's trial will realize.

Malcolm seeks to undermine confidence in McGough's guilt in other ways, such as by changing the subject. She invites the reader to consider the possibility of malevolent motives on the part of federal prosecutors and federal judges angered by McGough's efforts on behalf of her clients before she met Bailes. This possibility is reduced to the vanishing point by the fact that McGough did not practice law in the federal system before she became involved with Bailes; his prosecution for bank fraud was her first federal case.

Malcolm invites the reader to consider the even more alarming possibility that the American legal system is incapable of making truthful determinations of guilt and innocence; and it is here particularly that one catches a distorted and amplified echo of the philosophical tradition of mistrusting testimony. She says that "in a sense, everyone who is brought to trial, criminal or civil, is framed" because "the deck is stacked against the accused" (p. 14), and that "the prosecutor prosecuting an innocent person or the defense lawyer defending a guilty client actually have an easier task than their opposite numbers" (p. 26). The basis for this nutty claim is that because "truth is messy, incoherent, aimless, boring, absurd," it can prevail at trial only if it is "laboriously transformed into a kind of travesty of itself" (id.). So McGough was convicted *because* she is incapable of lying ("almost preternatural[ly] honest"); her habit of compulsive truth-telling condemned her to being disbelieved.

"Law stories," Malcolm explains, "are empty stories. They take the reader to a world entirely constructed of tendentious argument, and utterly devoid of the truth of the real world, where things are allowed to fall as they may" (pp. 78–79). What is this "real world" of which Malcolm is speaking? Can she be serious in suggesting that law is *nothing* but tendentious argument, that it is *utterly* devoid of truth? In so suggesting, she undermines her own claim to have established McGough's innocence. If the legal process is incapable of discovering the truth, how likely is it that journalism is capable of discovering it? If legal testimony is utterly untrustworthy, how likely is informal testimony to a reporter to be trustworthy?

In a pitch to readers convinced of McGough's guilt, Malcolm seeks to enlist sympathy for her heroine by depreciating the gravity of Bailes's crimes. She does this in two ways—by romanticizing con artists and by ridiculing their victims. Con artists are called "con artists," she explains, "precisely in recognition of the qualities they share with regular artists," such as "love of freedom" (p. 8). This could be said of most criminals; they are irked by the restraints that the law tries to place on their freedom of action. What is true of con artists—what is, indeed, their stock in trade—is that they are charming. This enables them to tap into the vein of admiration in American culture (as in the earlier English culture that produced such works as *Moll Flanders* and *The Beggar's Opera*) for romantic outlawry.[12] Malcolm writes in a long tradition of depreciating, to the point of admiring, the con man.[13]

12. On which see Martha Grace Duncan, *Romantic Outlaws, Beloved Prisons: The Unconscious Meanings of Crime and Punishment*, pt. 2 (1996).

13. "A confidence man prospers only because of the fundamental dishonesty of his victim . . . Confidence men are hardly criminals in the usual sense of the word, for they prosper through a superb knowledge of human nature; they are set apart from those who employ the machine-gun, the blackjack, or the acetylene torch. Their methods differ more in degree than in kind from those employed by more legitimate forms of business." David W. Maurer, *The Big Con: The Story of the Confidence Man and the Confidence Game* 16 (1940).

Part of con artists' appeal lies in the fact that they often prey on greedy, credulous, and sometimes crooked people—at best "born suckers" and at worst fellow con artists, a possible description of Morris and his clients. But Bailes was not *just* a con artist; the bank fraud for which he was prosecuted in the case in which McGough first represented him was a straightforward case of obtaining a bank loan by making false statements (backed by forged documents) concerning the borrower's assets. It is false that his criminal career consisted solely of "the various petty chicaneries he committed in order to eat and to pay for gas" (p. 42). In the course of a long criminal career he not only stole many hundreds of thousands, probably millions, of dollars (the insurance scam alone got him at least $250,000) but also imposed large costs on the legal system and public-records offices with his incessant filings of forged and otherwise phony documents and of frivolous claims, lawsuits, and bankruptcy petitions. The burdens that criminals like Bailes impose on the legal and administrative systems are not trivial. Malcolm ridicules them by saying that "the mess Bailes created in the registrar's office was not the crime he was indicted for. But it was the crime he was convicted of" (p. 42). She dismisses the registrar's complaint of having to spend more than 100 hours "trying to sort out the mess that Mr. Bailes had caused" as "one among the many moans and whimpers that echo through the chronicles of Bailes's passage through the courts" (id.). What she should have said is that Bailes's victims included not only the people and institutions that he defrauded but also the taxpayers who bear the costs of the legal and administrative services that he abused.

Not all victims of con artists deserve to be defrauded, moreover. Many are simply financially unsophisticated. Their ruination by con artists is not pretty. One would have to be an extreme Social Darwinist to believe that con artistry should be condoned as a method of winnowing the commercial and consumer flocks of their weaker members. Whether any of Bailes's victims over the course of his long career fit that description is unclear. But Malcolm errs in suggesting that *all* of them were his "spiritual colleagues" (p. 9). The banks that Bailes defrauded were not. And MacDonald appears to have been an innocent victim. Malcolm has her doubts about this but her principal criticism of him is that he was "a patsy without a patsy's philosophical bent," who rather than "sadly stumble away in the direction of his next disaster," which Malcolm thinks is how a con artist's victim should react when he discovers he's been had (a nice Darwinian touch, that), tried to get his money back and to get McGough prosecuted into the bargain, being "a harsh and punitive man" (p. 16). In criticizing MacDonald, Malcolm is blaming the victim with a vengeance: not only for being victimized in the first place, but for trying to get the victimizer punished. There is an echo of Nietzsche, who thought it a sign of weakness for the victim of an injury to seek redress for it rather than shrug it off.[14]

Malcolm's remark that Bailes had been convicted for gumming up the bureaucracy's recordkeeping, rather than for the actual crime with which he was charged, puts one in mind of the intimation in *The Stranger* that Meursault, charged with murder, really was convicted because he had not cried at his mother's funeral. That is, he was convicted because he was a nonconformist in a stifling bourgeois milieu. Malcolm thinks that Bailes was punished severely for bank fraud because when he was arrested he was living in his car, which was filled with dirty clothes and dirty dishes. "Dirty clothing and dirty dishes are no federal crime; but federal judges no less than juries form their impressions and act on them" (p. 41). Another Camusian touch is Malcolm's claim that the jury deliberated for only six hours before convicting McGough because it was the day before Thanksgiving and the jury "evidently need[ed] the afternoon hours for shopping" (p. 6). There is no ground for this slur on the jury's conscientiousness.

A further embarrassment to Malcolm's account is that her compulsive truth teller, this martyr to truth, exercised her constitutional right not to testify at her trial.[15] Malcolm accepts McGough's explanation that she was afraid that if she testified she would be bound to say things that would harm Bailes. Had McGough testified, Malcolm believes, she would have been acquitted. Her decision to sacrifice herself for her client raises McGough, in Malcolm's eyes, to heroic stature. McGough's "refusal to label [Bailes] a con man and write him off" stands for "something rather magnificent . . . a bracing idealism" (p. 43).

Everyone who is charged with a crime is entitled to the loyalty of his lawyer, but within limits. The lawyer is not to commit crimes on his cli-

14. See, for example, Friedrich Nietzsche, *Thus Spoke Zarathustra: A Book for All and None*, pt. 2, p. 95 (Walter Kaufmann trans. 1966).

15. In the next chapter I question the justification for this right, but justified or not it is not a truth-protective feature of the legal process.

ent's behalf. No legal system could tolerate such behavior. Breaking the law to spring one's client may be *morally* justified if the legal system is fundamentally unjust, or perhaps even if, within the framework of a basically just system, the defendant is indeed being "framed" and there is no lawful way to rescue him. But Bailes was just a crook, as Malcolm in her soberer moments acknowledges—and indeed reminds McGough. The idea that he would have been acquitted of bank fraud or his other crimes, or not charged at all, had he not caused extra work for government clerks is a fantasy. McGough was not fulfilling "a lawyer's obligations to his client . . . to the letter" (p. 44). Those obligations do not include perjury, bankruptcy fraud, breach of fiduciary obligation, suborning perjury, and the other crimes that she committed.

Malcolm's book disserves the public by making light of crimes that involve "merely" fraudulent activity, rather than violence or drug dealing, and by undermining confidence in the criminal justice system. Bailes, the career criminal, almost a one-man crime wave, is recast by Malcolm as a lovable nonconformist, a modern-day Huck Finn. The system of criminal justice is redescribed as an engine of oppression. By the end of the book Bailes is Robin Hood and McGough is Joan of Arc.

～ 11

The Principles of Evidence
and the Critique of
Adversarial Procedure

$\mathcal{T}$HE LAW OF EVIDENCE is the body of rules that determines what, and how, information may be provided to a legal tribunal
asked to resolve a factual dispute. The importance of the accurate resolution of such disputes to an economically efficient system of law has
been discussed at length,[1] although the economic literature dealing
with the rules themselves is scanty in relation to the scope and importance of evidence law.[2] I hope to show in this and the following chapter
that economics, with the help of an empirical literature on trials and
evidence that is largely psychological in orientation, as well as with
help from Bayes's theorem, other aspects of decision theory, and the
principles of statistical inference, can illuminate a wide range of issues
bearing on the accuracy and legitimacy of the law's methods for resolving factual disputes.

1. See, for example, Richard A. Posner, "An Economic Approach to Legal Procedure and
Judicial Administration," 2 *Journal of Legal Studies* 399 (1973); Louis Kaplow, "Accuracy in
Adjudication," in *The New Palgrave Dictionary of Economics and the Law*, vol. 1, p. 1 (Peter
Newman ed. 1998); Kaplow, "The Value of Accuracy in Adjudication: An Economic Analy-
sis," 23 *Journal of Legal Studies* 307 (1994).

2. I cite much of it in this chapter and the next. For a useful bibliography, see Jeffrey S.
Parker and Bruce H. Kobayashi, "Evidence" (forthcoming in *Bibliography of Law and Economics*). A larger literature deals with the economics of pretrial discovery and procedure generally
and somewhat overlaps the issues discussed in this chapter. See Richard A. Posner, *Economic
Analysis of Law*, ch. 21 (5th ed. 1998), and references cited there.

Many professors of the law of evidence, and even a few judges,[3] would, if asked, say that *of course* the American system of finding facts at trial is inefficient, ludicrously so, and redeemed if at all by the noneconomic values that the system protects. But that assessment is founded on incomplete analysis and on misleading anecdotage[4] that is itself an artifact of a worthwhile feature of the American system—the high degree of public scrutiny that it invites and enables. Neither cheap nor highly accurate, our adversarial system is radically imperfect from the Utopian standpoint so often, though mistakenly, used to evaluate social institutions. It may not be inferior to the alternatives, including the Continental inquisitorial system much touted in some quarters of the American legal academy.

Evidence can be approached from the direction of economics by any number of paths. The simplest would be to take up the various rules piecemeal and examine their economizing properties. Another would be to deduce the optimal system of dispute resolution from economic theory and compare it with the actual systems in use in this and other countries. A third would begin with the epistemological and psychological literatures dealing with rational inquiry.[5] A fourth would build from what is now an extensive empirical literature on the actual operation of the various methods (especially the jury, the focus of this literature) for determining facts at trial.[6] A fifth would inquire how the

3. A classic statement is Marvin E. Frankel, "The Search for Truth: An Umpireal View," 123 *University of Pennsylvania Law Review* 1031 (1975).

4. As pointed out in Marc Galanter, "An Oil Strike in Hell: Contemporary Legends about the Civil Justice System," 40 *Arizona Law Review* 717 (1998), and in two notable recent studies of jury awards: Deborah Jones Merritt and Kathryn Ann Barry, "Is the Tort System in Crisis? New Empirical Evidence," 60 *Ohio State Law Journal* 315 (1999); Neil Vidmar, Felicia Gross, and Mary Rose, "Jury Awards for Medical Malpractice and Post-Verdict Adjustments of Those Awards," 48 *DePaul Law Review* 265 (1998).

5. A good recent treatise on rational decisionmaking is David A. Schum, *The Evidential Foundations of Probabilistic Reasoning* (1994). With specific reference to the pros and cons of a Bayesian approach to the law of evidence, see *Probability and Inference in the Law of Evidence: The Uses and Limits of Bayesianism* (Peter Tillers and Eric D. Green eds. 1988). I discussed some of the epistemological issues involved in the use of the legal process to make factual determinations in my book *The Problems of Jurisprudence* 203–219 (1990), but I no longer agree with everything I said there, particularly my criticisms of the jury system.

6. This literature is well illustrated by Roselle L. Wissler, Alan J. Hart, and Michael J. Saks, "Decisionmaking about General Damages: A Comparison of Jurors, Judges, and Lawyers," 98 *Michigan Law Review* 751 (1999); Michael J. Saks, "What Do Jury Experiments Tell Us about How Juries (Should) Make Decisions?" 6 *Southern California Interdisciplinary Law*

private sector resolves disputes, since private dispute resolvers have stronger incentives than public ones to maximize the net benefits of the dispute-resolution process. A sixth approach would be to examine all the possible goals of the law of evidence and try to establish the weight that economic goals should be given.

The easiest approach to begin with is the second, which involves asking how, if we were writing on a clean slate and trying to design a system for the resolution of factual disputes in litigation that would be economically efficient in the broadest sense, we would frame our inquiry. I propose two equivalent ways. The first is to model factfinding as a problem in search, analogous to searching for a consumer durable,[7] with the correct answer to the question of, say, did X shoot Y corresponding to the utility-maximizing choice between two brands of dishwasher.[8] The process of obtaining, sifting, marshaling, presenting, and (for the trier of fact) weighing evidence confers benefits and imposes costs. (Social and private benefits and costs must be distinguished, but that is for later.) Benefits are a positive function of the probability (p) that if the evidence is considered by the trier of fact the case will be decided correctly, and of the stakes (S) in the case. Assume for simplicity that the benefits are simply the product of the two terms, hence pS, where p is a positive function of the amount of evidence (x); then the full expression for the benefits of the search is $p(x)S$. With enough evidence p might equal 1, meaning that a trial would be certain to produce the correct outcome. The costs of the trial (c) are also a positive function of the amount of evidence.

On these assumptions, the net benefits ($B(x)$) of the search for evidence in a case are given by

(1) $$B(x) = p(x)S - c(x)$$

Journal 1 (1997); Richard Lempert, "Civil Juries and Complex Cases: Taking Stock after Twelve Years," in *Verdict: Assessing the Civil Jury System* 181 (Robert E. Litan ed. 1993); and Donald Wittman, "Lay Juries versus Professional Arbitrators and the Arbitrator Selection Hypothesis" (University of California at Santa Cruz, Economics Department, unpublished, July 11, 2000).

7. See, for example, Sridhar Moorthy, Brian T. Ratchford, and Debabrata Talukdar, "Consumer Information Search Revisited: Theory and Empirical Analysis," 23 *Journal of Consumer Research* 263 (1997); Asher Wolinsky, "Competition in a Market for Informed Experts' Services," 24 *RAND Journal of Economics* 380 (1993).

8. A dichotomous choice is assumed in both the legal and consumer examples for the sake of simplicity; nothing of analytical relevance turns on the assumption.

The optimum amount of search—the amount that maximizes net benefits—is then the amount that satisfies

(2) $p_x S = c_x$

where the subscripts denote derivatives. In words, the search should be carried to the point at which marginal cost and marginal benefit are equated. The amount of evidence at the optimum point will be greater the higher the stakes in the case, the lower the cost of obtaining evidence, and the greater the effect of evidence in increasing the likelihood of an accurate outcome.

For this optimum to exist, it is enough if $p(x)$ is increasing at a decreasing rate ($p_{xx} < 0$) and that c_x is nondecreasing ($c_{xx} \geq 0$).[9] These conditions are plausible. The first implies that as more and more evidence is obtained, the effect of additional evidence on the outcome of the case will decrease, especially if the searcher begins the search with the most probative evidence—the rational procedure unless that evidence is particularly costly to obtain.

To refine the analysis a bit, suppose that there are n possible sources of evidence, the sources are independent of each other (that is, discovering valuable evidence in one does not help the searcher find valuable evidence in any other), and each source has a known probability (p) of yielding valuable evidence, a known value (V) of that evidence should it turn out to be obtainable from the source, and a cost (c) of exploring the source to discover whether it will yield the evidence. Then for each source there will be an expected net gain from searching of $pV - c$. If we are searching among the sources for the best one (for example, the best expert witness for our case, or the best character witness, or, in

9. The second condition implies that there are no economies of scale in searching for evidence. A simple version of Equation (1) that satisfies both conditions is

(1a) $B(x) = (x/(x + 1))S - cx$

where p takes the specific value of $x/(x + 1)$ and $c(x)$ the specific value of cx (constant costs). The optimum amount of evidence (x^*) is then

(2b) $x^* = (S/c)^{1/2} - 1$

and is greater the higher the ratio of the stakes in the case to the unit cost of the evidence. But notice that it increases at a diminishing rate as that ratio rises.

The condition that c_x be nondecreasing is not strictly necessary. It is enough if it decreases less rapidly than the benefits of the search decrease, so that $p_{xx}S < c_{xx}$.

general, one witness or document where there are alternative possibilities), rather than seeking to cumulate evidence, it can be shown that we should continue the search until we find a source that yields evidence having a value greater than $(pV - c)/p$ for all the unsearched sources.[10] Since $(pV - c)/p$ is, equivalently, $V - c/p$, and $V > c/p$ for all $c > 0$, this means stopping at the first success if each success has the same evidentiary value. In the event of failure, we should next explore the source having the highest p (assuming constant V and c), lowest c, or highest V.

If the searcher cannot determine in advance which evidence is most likely to be fruitful, his search procedure will resemble random sampling, and as the size of a sample grows, the value of additional sampling in conducing to a more accurate result will rise at a falling rate. (Roughly speaking, accuracy increases by the square root of the sample size.) So again there will be declining marginal utility of search. Indeed, as we shall see, beyond some point that marginal utility may turn negative. At the same time, the cost of additional searching is unlikely to fall as the search widens and in fact may well begin to rise as the initial leads run out. The reasons for hedging ("unlikely") are twofold: a heavy initial investment in gathering evidence may generate leads that for a time enable the searcher to obtain additional evidence at low cost; and when aggregated over all cases the cost of searching for evidence may fall with increases in the amount of evidence obtained because more accurate factfinding increases the deterrence of wrongful conduct, which in turn reduces the number of cases and hence the aggregate costs of the legal process.

To see how accuracy in factfinding relates to deterrence, notice first that the expected cost of punishment (EC) is actually the difference between the expected cost of punishment if one commits a crime ($EC_g = p_g S$, where p_g is the probability of punishment if the accused is guilty and S is the sentence) and the expected cost of punishment if one does not commit a crime ($EC_i = p_i S$, where p_i is the probability of punishment if the accused is guilty, and S is as before). Hence $EC = p_g S - p_i S$; equivalently, $EC = (p_g - p_i)S$, making it transparent that if punishment is imposed randomly, so that the probability of punishment is the same regardless of guilt (that is, if $p_g = p_i$), the expected punishment cost for committing the crime will be zero. The more accurate the process of determining guilt is, the less random punishment will be, and so the

10. See Martin L. Weitzman, "Optimal Search for the Best Alternative," 47 *Econometrica* 641, 646–648 (1979).

greater will be the law's deterrent effect.[11] To put this point differently, greater accuracy in the determination of guilt increases the returns to being innocent.

The point is not limited to criminal law. It applies to all areas of law in which the deterrence of unlawful behavior is an objective. It shows what a good investment expenditures on evidence can be. But there is a danger of exaggeration if one fails to distinguish between punishment that is truly random and punishment that merely has a random component. Suppose that a person with a criminal record is quite likely to be convicted of any subsequent crime that he is charged with even if he did not commit that crime. This will reduce the effect of the criminal law in deterring him from committing subsequent crimes. But at the same time it will increase deterrence against his committing the first crime by increasing his (long-term) expected punishment, and it will also cause people with a criminal record to steer clear of activities in which they might be arrested and falsely charged. So inaccuracy can increase as well as reduce deterrence,[12] though my guess is that the latter effect will predominate in most cases, even that of convicting second and other subsequent offenders of crimes they have not committed. If law enforcers concentrate their limited resources on such offenders because they are easier to convict regardless of guilt, the expected punishment of first offenders will decline because the authorities will devote fewer resources to prosecuting them.

Deterrence plays a starring role in the economic analysis of evidence because it links the concern with accuracy that is so central to the evidentiary process with the economist's conception of law as a system for creating incentives for efficient conduct. Since the accurate determination of facts at trial is important to the efficacy of law in imparting efficient incentives, accuracy in adjudication is an economic as well as a moral and political value.

An alternative way of modeling the search for evidence, one that derives from familiar economic models of procedure and of negligence,[13] is as a process of cost minimization. Let p now be the probability of an

11. Posner, note 1 above, at 412.

12. For other examples of how inaccuracy in adjudication can actually enhance social welfare, see Michael L. Davis, "The Value of Truth and Optimal Standards of Proof in Legal Disputes," 10 *Journal of Law, Economics, and Organization* 343 (1994).

13. See Posner, note 1 above, at 401 (procedure); William M. Landes and Richard A. Posner, *The Economic Structure of Tort Law* 58–60 (1987) (negligence).

erroneous rather than of a correct outcome, and pS the cost of the error (the probability of error weighted by the stakes). Suppose that $p = 0.1$, implying that, on average, one of ten cases will be decided incorrectly. If the average stakes in these cases are \$100,000, then the expected cost of error is \$10,000. The specific assumption that pS equals the social costs of error is arbitrary. But it is a reasonable guess that the social cost of an erroneous outcome will generally rise with the dollar equivalent of the stakes in the case. I will both defend and qualify this assumption shortly.

The social goal of the evidentiary process is to minimize the sum of the cost of error and the cost of error avoidance, that is, to minimize

$$(3) \qquad C(x) = p(x)S + c(x)$$

Formally this is done by differentiating $C(x)$ with respect to x and setting the result equal to zero, yielding

$$(4) \qquad -p_xS = c_x$$

That is, the search for evidence should be carried to the point at which the last bit of evidence obtained yields a reduction in error costs equal to the cost of obtaining the evidence. For this optimum to exist, it is enough if increases in x have a diminishing effect in reducing pS and if, as before, c_x is nondecreasing.

"Costs," so emphasized in this model, may seem too narrow a concept to serve as a criterion for choosing among alternative rules of evidence. But this depends on how "costs" are defined. The costs of the search for evidence, in a proper economic analysis, should not be limited to time and other direct costs. They should include as well the indirect costs that result from the incentive effects of the search process. Consider the rule that limits the use of evidence that after the accident giving rise to the plaintiff's suit the defendant repaired the condition that caused the accident; the worry is that allowing such evidence would discourage repairs and so increase the risk of future accidents, and therefore expected accident costs.

Many law professors prefer to take account of the indirect costs and benefits of rules of evidence by invoking multiple goals of the law of evidence[14] rather than just that of accuracy in factfinding. The econo-

---

14. See, for example, Michael L. Seigel, "A Pragmatic Critique of Modern Evidence Scholarship," 88 *Northwestern University Law Review* 995 (1994), and references cited there, including influential articles by Laurence Tribe and Charles Nesson.

mist will agree that accuracy (p in Equations (1) through (4)) is not the only goal. Indeed, it is better described not as a goal at all but rather as one of the factors that determine the net benefits of a search for evidence. Other goals discussed in the evidence literature, such as providing catharsis to quarreling parties, resolving disputes in a manner acceptable to the community, safeguarding interests in personal liberty, and protecting other values (as in the subsequent-repair example), are likewise best regarded not as distinct goals but rather as factors influencing one element or another in the basic models. Not only can noneconomic concerns thus be accommodated within a framework of economic analysis; the basic insight of economic analysis of evidence law—that the law is engaged in making trade-offs between the accuracy and cost of trials—is a familiar and even orthodox theme in noneconomic writing about evidence law.[15] The economic approach serves more to refine and extend than to challenge the intuitions of the legal professional.

I can be a little more precise about how additional evidence nudges a factual inquiry toward an accurate conclusion. In the most intuitive version of Bayes' theorem, the posterior odds (the odds after a new piece of evidence, x, is considered) that some hypothesis (say that X shot Y) is correct are obtained by multiplying the prior odds by the ratio of (1) the probability that the evidence would have been observed if the hypothesis were true to (2) the probability that the evidence would have been observed even if the hypothesis were not true. Thus

$$(5) \qquad \Omega(H|x) = L \ x \ \Omega(H)$$

where Ω is odds,[16] H is hypothesis, and L (called the "likelihood ratio") is $p(x|H)/p(x|{}^{\sim}H)$. Suppose that the new piece of evidence is testimony by bystander Z that he saw X shoot Y. Suppose further that the prior odds ($\Omega(H)$) are 1 to 2 that X shot Y, while the probability that Z would testify that he saw X shoot Y if X did shoot Y is 0.8, and the probability

---

15. See, for example, Jon O. Newman, "Rethinking Fairness: Perspectives on the Litigation Process," 94 *Yale Law Journal* 1643, 1647–1650 (1985).

16. $\Omega(H|x) = p(H|x)/p({}^{\sim}H|x)$, and $\Omega(H) = p(H)/p({}^{\sim}H)$. The tilde (${}^{\sim}$) means "not." So if, in the example in the text, the probability, given X shot Y, that Z would testify that he saw the shooting is 0.4, and the probability that, given X did not shoot Y, Z would nevertheless testify that he saw him do it is 0.1, then the odds that X shot Y are 4 to 1 (or, equivalently, 4). If (before Z's testimony) the probability that X shot Y was 0.1 and the probability that he did not 0.2, the odds that X shot Y (the prior odds) would be 1 to 2 (or 0.5).

that he would testify that he saw X shoot Y if X did not shoot Y is 0.1, so that the likelihood ratio is 8. The posterior odds that X shot Y will therefore be 4 to 1.

Several qualifications should be noted. One is that the stakes in a case are an imperfect measure of the social benefits of gathering additional evidence. Imagine a dispute over liability under a statute that was repealed after the dispute arose but that still, not having been repealed retroactively, governs the dispute. If a lot of money is involved, the optimum *private* investment in evidence gathering may be very large because victory will confer or conserve substantial economic rents. Yet the social benefits from a correct decision might be nil. (Or might not: the expectation that any dispute arising under the statute would be resolved by accurate methods, come what may, might have induced efficient behavior when the statute was in force, and honoring that expectation may be necessary to induce efficient behavior under statutes currently in force.) The general point is that parties may underinvest in the search for evidence in some cases because accuracy in adjudication confers benefits on nonparties by increasing the deterrent efficacy of the law, while overinvesting in other cases for rent-seeking reasons. But generally the larger the stakes the more important it is from a social as well as a private standpoint that the case be decided correctly. Inaccuracy that reduces deterrence and hence compliance with law will impose greater social costs the bigger the case. It is more important to deter billion-dollar than million-dollar oil spills resulting from negligence.

A second qualification is that altering posterior odds may not have much if any social value even if the likelihood ratio of the new evidence is high, as in our shooting example, where it was 8. The value will depend on the prior odds and on the decision rule. Suppose that the prior odds (as a consequence of the previously presented evidence) that X shot Y are not 1 to 2 but 1 to 10, and that for X to be held liable for the shooting the trier of fact must find that the odds that he did it are at least 1.01 to 1 (the preponderance standard). Then the new evidence, since it would not lift the posterior odds above the threshold (multiplying the prior odds by a likelihood ratio of 8 yields posterior odds of only 1 to 1.25), would have no value. This would also be the case if, with the prior odds unchanged at 1 to 2, the trier of fact must reckon the odds to be at least 9 to 1 (one possible interpretation of the proof beyond a reasonable doubt standard) in order to find against *X*; for the posterior odds are only 4 to 1.

A final qualification is that investments in evidence may yield benefits that go beyond altering the outcome of particular cases. Take the simple case in which the outcome of a trial depends solely on the ratio of the investments of each side. *A*, say, will beat *B* if *A* spends twice as much as *B*; otherwise *B* will win. Then a proportional reduction in each side's expenditures will not alter the outcome. But it may well reduce the amount of information generated for the consideration of the tribunal, and by doing so may increase the variance of the actual as distinct from the expected outcome and also increase the likelihood of an appeal by reducing confidence in the accuracy of the outcome of the trial.

⟋ I WANT TO EVALUATE the criticisms that one hears with increasing frequency of our adversarial system of adjudication. The benefits and costs of searching for evidence, and so the optimal kind and amount of such search, vary with the type of searcher and it is the difference in who searches for evidence that mainly distinguishes the adversarial system, which prevails in most of the English-speaking world, from the inquisitorial system, which prevails in most other countries, notably those of the European continent and Japan.

Begin with the case in which the only searcher is a professional judge. That is a caricature of the inquisitorial system. Although lawyers play a smaller role in developing evidence in an inquisitorial system than they do in an adversarial one, it is not trivial; it also varies from country to country. But as I want to make the contrast between the systems as stark as possible, I shall treat tendencies as if they were their extremes[17] and therefore not only ignore the role of the lawyer as an

17. The *very* simplest example of factual inquiry would be that of a parent investigating a dispute between two of his or her children. Bentham seems to have considered this the appropriate model for the system of legal evidence, though not a model to be followed slavishly. See Jeremy Bentham, *Rationale of Judicial Evidence*, vol. 1, pp. 6–8 (J. S. Mill ed. 1827). See generally Laird C. Kirkpatrick, "Scholarly and Institutional Challenges to the Law of Evidence: From Bentham to the ADR Movement," 25 *Loyola of Los Angeles Law Review* 837 (1992). For descriptions of the differences between adversarial and inquisitorial handling of evidence problems, see Mirjan R. Damaška, *Evidence Law Adrift* (1997); John H. Langbein, "The German Advantage in Civil Procedure," 52 *University of Chicago Law Review* 823 (1985); David Luban, *Lawyers and Justice: An Ethical Study* 93–103 (1988).

evidence searcher in this inquisitorial system but also treat trial by jury as the sole form of trial in the adversarial system.

It might appear that the searcher-judge would be an extremely efficient searcher, because of selection, training, and experience.[18] But maybe not. Because it is difficult to evaluate legal factfinding and thus to criticize a judge for having made erroneous findings or praise him for good ones, the judge's incentive to exert himself to do a good job will be limited. If he is highly paid, moreover, the cost of search may be substantial. And the amount of search conducted will depend on the number of judges and auxiliary judicial personnel, a number that may be determined without much regard to the socially optimal amount of search. In addition, the public may lack confidence in the judge's search and in the conclusions he draws from it because the process of judicial inquiry in an inquisitorial system, like grand jury proceedings in the United States, is carried on mainly behind closed doors. There is also a danger that the judge will render the "popular" result in a case, irrespective of justice.

In the adversarial process exemplified by the modern American civil jury trial,[19] the search for evidence is conducted separately by the lawyers for the opposing sides and presented to a nonexpert, ad hoc, multiheaded tribunal for decision. Because trial lawyers are compensated directly or indirectly on the basis of success at trial, their incentive to develop evidence favorable to their client and to find the flaws in the opponent's evidence is very great and if it is a case involving large monetary stakes their resources for obtaining and contesting evidence will be ample. If size of stakes is a proxy for the social costs of an inaccurate decision, there will be at least a rough alignment between the amount of search that is actually conducted and the amount that is socially optimal.

The amount of search is driven not by the stakes alone but also by the likely effect of the marginal bit of evidence on the outcome. Recall

18. It is often remarked as though the point were obvious that the inquisitorial approach is "more efficient" than the adversarial approach. E.g., Craig M. Bradley, "The Convergence of the Continental and the Common Law Model of Criminal Procedure," 7 *Criminal Law Forum* 471 (1997).

19. Few civil cases are actually tried; the vast majority are settled. But the terms of settlement are shaped by expectations concerning the length, the cost, and, above all, the outcome if the case were tried.

from Equation (2) that the marginal benefit of a piece of evidence is given by $p_x S$, where p_x is the impact of the evidence on the probability that the trial will reach the right result (whether from a social or, as here, where we are considering the incentives of lawyers rather than judges, a private standpoint). This implies that, other things being equal, more evidence will be obtained the closer the case is.[20] For the closer the case is, the greater an effect on the outcome additional evidence is likely to have and so the more likely such evidence is to be furnished to the trier of fact. If the case is one-sided, additional evidence, even though highly probative considered by itself, may have no effect on the outcome.

The incentive to present more evidence the closer the case has a tendency to promote efficiency, but no stronger statement is possible. It is easy to imagine cases in which the additional evidence induced by the closeness of the case has no social product. Suppose that party A can increase the probability of a favorable outcome by 1 percent by adducing one more bit of evidence at a cost of x. And suppose that his opponent, B, can nullify that 1 percent shift in A's favor by adding another bit of evidence, evidence favorable to B, also at a cost of x. If each party puts in his additional evidence, a cost of $2x$ will be incurred without any change in the expected outcome. The example, however, is somewhat unrealistic. If A can anticipate B's response, he will have no incentive to put in the additional evidence. A and B will jointly benefit from agreeing to keep the evidence out and an agreement by the parties to limit evidence will normally be enforced. If lawyers were perfect agents of their clients, such stipulations would be more common than they are.

The competitive character of the search process, and the presentation of the results to a body of amateur judges (the jurors) that does not itself participate in the gathering of the evidence, make it difficult to situate the adversarial system on a continuum with the inquisitorial. The model for the latter is a police investigation, but for the former it is the debate. The debater's tools are the tools of rhetoric, the set of techniques for inducing belief in matters involving irremediable uncertainty that often is due to the audience's lack of sophistication but more fundamentally to the oft-remarked fallibility of "testimony" in

---

20. See also Avery Katz, "Judicial Decisionmaking and Litigation Expenditure," 8 *International Review of Law and Economics* 127 (1988).

the general sense discussed in Chapter 10. As emphasized by theorists of rhetoric beginning with Aristotle—who was more forgiving of inexact reasoning than Plato—an important dimension of effective rhetoric (called the "ethical appeal") is making the speaker, as well as the speech, credible. The economics of consumer search again provides a helpful analogy.[21] Some consumer goods are what are called in economics "credence goods." A good is a credence good if the consumer cannot readily determine its quality by inspection or even use, so that he has to take its quality "on faith."

The importance of credibility in a rhetorical system of justice, and the incentives of lawyers to enhance the credibility of their witnesses without regard for the truth, explain the emphasis that adversary systems place on cross-examination and rebuttal, and the corresponding suspicion of hearsay evidence, which, defined functionally, is simply testimony that is not subject to cross-examination. The witness can be cross-examined, but not the out-of-court declarant whose "testimony" the witness is repeating.

The significance of cross-examination is often misunderstood, and its social value consequently underappreciated, because of failure to consider the deterrent effect of the right to cross-examine. Because cross-examination *can* destroy a witness's credibility, it rarely does so in practice, and so is mistakenly denigrated. The witness whose credibility would be destroyed by cross-examination will not be called at all or will try to pull the sting of the cross-examiner by acknowledging on direct examination the facts that a cross-examiner could be expected to harp on.

The adversary system makes it difficult for litigants to signal the strength of their case. Just as poker players must bluff occasionally to avoid revealing the strength of their hand and thus losing the strategic advantage of secrecy, so a lawyer who has a weak case must pretend to have a strong one in order to avoid tipping his hand. One might expect some lawyers to specialize in strong cases, so that the fact that the lawyer had been retained would signal that the case was strong, and thus induce a favorable settlement. This would be a cheap and reliable method of signaling, but it does not appear to be widespread.

The adversary system may seem less efficient than the inquisitorial merely because it involves two or more searchers—the lawyers for the

21. For a fuller discussion, see Richard A. Posner, *Overcoming Law*, ch. 24 (1995).

opposing parties—rather than one (the judge). There is duplication, hence added cost. And because the searchers are not disinterested, the system needs procedures for preventing concealment and distortion of evidence. When permitted, as they are in the American legal system, lawyers assist their witnesses to make the witness's story credible; lawyers understand the importance to effective rhetoric of the ethical appeal. But such assistance is not altogether a bad thing. It can remind the witness of true facts that he may have forgotten, help him to articulate his recollections in an intelligible form, and show him how to testify in compliance with the rules of evidence.

Because the private benefits of searching for evidence may exceed or fall short of the social benefits, privatizing the search (as in the adversarial system) may result in too much or too little evidence from a social standpoint, as we have seen, whereas in principle—a tremendous qualification, obviously—the inquisitorial judge can continue his search for evidence until he reaches the point at which marginal cost and marginal benefit intersect and can stop right there. But the judge in the adversary system can at least limit the amount of search that the lawyers do, not only by curtailing pretrial discovery, setting an early trial date, and limiting the length of the trial (all measures that judges in our system are authorized to employ), but also by excluding evidence at trial under the authority of Rule 403 of the Federal Rules of Evidence. As we shall see in the next chapter, that rule authorizes exclusion when the probative value of the tendered evidence is clearly outweighed by, among other things, its effect in prolonging or confusing the trial. It is true that by the time a Rule 403 motion is made, the evidence will be gathered. But parties are unlikely to gather evidence if they expect the judge to exclude it at trial. The function of the rules of evidence in limiting the external costs generated by an adversary system is one reason why such rules are less important in an inquisitorial system.[22]

The rules cannot force the parties to search more than the case is

<hr>

22. See Gordon Tullock, *Trials on Trial: The Pure Theory of Legal Procedure* 151–157 (1980); Franklin Steir, "What Can the American Adversary System Learn from an Inquisitorial System of Justice?" 76 *Judicature* 109 (1992); Konstantinos D. Kerameus, "A Civilian Lawyer Looks at Common Law Procedure," 47 *Louisiana Law Review* 497, 500 (1987). An alternative approach would be a regulatory ("Pigouvian") tax on evidence; but there would have to be a subsidy for those cases in which the parties underinvest in evidence from a social standpoint. The implementation of such a tax-subsidy scheme would, unfortunately, require far more information than the government could feasibly obtain.

worth to them merely because the additional search would confer a social benefit. But they can nudge them a little in this direction, as we shall see when we get to the rules governing the burden of producing evidence to the court.

Because the jury is an ad hoc tribunal, a significant amount of time is spent at the outset of trial in the selection of its members. And because it is inexperienced a professional judge is needed to guide it, and the pace of the trial is retarded by the need to educate the jurors in the rudiments of their job. Civil jury trials in federal court are on average more than twice as long as civil bench (that is, judge) trials.[23] And this means that there is no saving of judge time by employing a jury; rather the contrary, though with some offset because the judge does not have to actually decide the case or write an opinion. The rules of evidence, it is frequently argued, would be largely unnecessary if there were no jury trials; they are mainly designed to protect laymen from making cognitive errors as a result of inexperience. And so the formulation and application of those rules are another cost of trial by jury.

Trial by jury also magnifies differences in ability between opposing counsel; for fear of interfering with the jury's decisionmaking, the judge cannot easily redress the balance by questioning the witnesses himself or suggesting lines of argument, as he could in a bench trial. This is not entirely a bad thing. It has the consequence that trial by jury penalizes bad lawyers more than nonjury trials do, and so may produce in Darwinian fashion a higher quality of lawyer than bench trials in which the judge may seek to compensate for the inadequacies of the weaker lawyer. Yet "quality" in this context includes the unscrupulous mastery of deceitful rhetorical tricks, illustrating the point that Darwinian processes are not necessarily normative.

Finally, and seemingly most tellingly, it may seem obvious that the jurors' inexperience and naiveté will reduce the likelihood of an outcome that corresponds to the true facts of the case. Not only do the jurors have higher information costs than professional judges do; they may be more subject to cognitive illusions and emotionalism than a professional judge who has "seen it all before." But this is only part of the picture. The competitive character of the adversary process gives the searchers (the lawyers) greater incentives to search hard than

23. Richard A. Posner, *The Federal Courts: Challenge and Reform* 193 n. 1 (1996).

under a system in which the judge is the principal or only searcher.[24] Competition always involves duplication of effort, yet more often than not yields more than offsetting benefits, and it may do so in a trial. To put this differently, the adversarial system relies on the market to a much greater extent than the inquisitorial system does, and the market is a more efficient producer of most goods than the government is.

Professor Langbein, a distinguished defender of the inquisitorial approach, recognizes that the adversarial approach has the advantage that it "aligns responsibility with incentive" and "is an undoubted safeguard against official sloth." But he offers a "straightforward" answer to this concern: "The judicial career must be designed in a fashion that creates incentives for diligence and excellence."[25] This is easier said than done, and may in fact be infeasible in America's political culture.[26] Some evidence of this is the widespread dissatisfaction with American administrative agencies, which employ methods and procedures (expert judges, no jurors, relaxed rules of evidence, and more control by the tribunal over evidence gathering) that resemble those of inquisitorial systems.

We must not rest on a dogmatic preference for market allocation of resources, but must consider concretely how competition might conduce to optimal evidence gathering. It might do this not only by inducing greater efforts by each side to find evidence than a judge in an inquisitorial system would exert, but also by inducing greater efforts to find the flaws in the other side's evidence.[27] Not greater efforts across the board—rather, greater efforts the larger the stakes and the closer the case, hence greater in those cases where a more thorough and careful canvass, marshaling, and evaluation of evidence is likely to confer greater social benefits. In general, moreover, the party having the objectively stronger case will be able to obtain evidence favorable to it at lower cost than the opposing party can obtain evidence favorable to it-

24. See Mathias Dewatripont and Jean Tirole, "Advocates," 107 *Journal of Political Economy* 1 (1999).

25. Langbein, note 17 above, at 848.

26. As argued in John C. Reitz, "Why We Probably Cannot Adopt the German Advantage in Civil Procedure," 75 *Iowa Law Review* 987 (1990).

27. The latter point is emphasized in Giuliana Palumbo, "Optimal 'Excessive' Litigation in Adversarial Systems" (Wkg. Paper No. 98–01, ECARE, Université Libre de Bruxelles, June 1998).

self.[28] So the competitive system of gathering evidence will tend to favor the party who would win in an error-free world.[29]

The adversarial system also facilitates the drawing of reliable inferences from evidentiary gaps.[30] If one party ought to be able to obtain evidence favorable to itself at low cost, its failure to present such evidence will allow the trier of fact to infer that there is no such evidence and the party should therefore lose. Silence becomes a signal.

Although the average juror may be less bright, and will certainly be less experienced in adjudication, than the average judge, "two heads are better than one"—and six, eight, or twelve inexperienced heads may be better than the one experienced head when they pool their recollections and deliberate to an outcome. The judge does not merely preside, moreover; he can take the case away from the jury by granting a new trial or, if the evidence is completely one sided, a directed verdict or judgment notwithstanding the verdict, if the jury seems to him to have screwed up. The twelve heads are really thirteen. And depending on the type of case, the jurors may be more like the witnesses and parties, in terms of social background, occupation, education, life experience, race, mores, and outlook, than the judge is. That may make it easier for them to understand, and to determine the credibility of, the witnesses than it is for the judge to do so. This is likeliest to be true in personal-injury tort cases and in criminal cases, but together these two categories account for most jury trials.[31]

And if judges as well as jurors are prone to make cognitive errors of

28. Ideally, the cost of producing favorable evidence should be infinite to the party who deserves to lose. If it were, the fact that parties have incentives to lie under a regime of competitive evidence gathering would not lead to erroneous results. See Chris William Sanchirico, "Games, Information, and Evidence Production: with Application to English Legal History," 2 *American Law and Economics Review* 342 (2000).

29. Luke M. Froeb and Bruce H. Kobayashi, "Naive, Biased, Yet Bayesian: Can Juries Interpret Selectively Produced Evidence?" 12 *Journal of Law, Economics, and Organization* 257 (1996). See also Paul Milgrom and John Roberts, "Relying on the Information of Interested Parties," 17 *Rand Journal of Economics* 18 (1986).

30. See Hyun Song Shin, "Adversarial and Inquisitorial Procedures in Arbitration," 29 *RAND Journal of Economics* 378, 404 (1998).

31. In the most recent year for which statistics are available (1996 for state cases, 1997 for federal), 74 percent of all jury trials in the United States were either personal-injury tort cases or criminal cases. Computed from Brian J. Ostrom and Neal B. Kauder, *Examining the Work of State Courts, 1996: A National Perspective from the Court Statistics Project* 25, 28 (1997); *Judicial Business of the United States Courts: 1997 Report of the Director of the Administrative Office of the United States Courts* 152–154, 359–361 (1997) (tables C–4, T–1). The state figure on

the sort discussed in Chapter 8, or to be overcome by emotion (see Chapter 7), then trial by jury may be more accurate than trial by judge, in which there is no gatekeeper protecting the trier of fact from confusing or excessively prejudicial evidence. The point is less that we need rules of evidence because we have juries than that we have no mechanism for enforcing rules of evidence against judges. There would have to be a screening judge to keep inadmissible evidence from the trial judge but the latter would be humiliated by being deemed unable to keep inadmissible evidence of which he was aware from influencing his decision. Yet probably he *would* be unable to keep from being influenced by such evidence. Indeed, it isn't even certain that judges are less prone to cognitive illusions than jurors (though I'll note later some evidence that they are). The literature on these illusions provides some basis for thinking that market settings tend to dispel or at least reduce them,[32] but none for thinking that government processes have similar effects.[33]

Gatekeeping is one way of combating cognitive illusions; another is the adversary process itself. If the lawyer for one party uses "framing" to influence a witness's testimony, the other lawyer can on cross-examination reframe the question to offset the effect of his opponent's framing. This is another respect in which the adversarial system (with jury) may be better at dealing with cognitive illusions than the inquisitorial system.

Jurors have, moreover, a certain freshness that many judges lack. The judge may be case-hardened and therefore less likely to attend to the particulars of a new case. Suppose that by virtue of having presided in many similar cases the judge reckons at the outset of a new case that the odds that the defendant is guilty are 100 to 1. He will have little incentive to pay close attention to the evidence presented at trial, because evidence of the defendant's guilt will not alter the judge's judgment,

---

which this estimate is based is only an approximation, however, as there is no comprehensive "personal injury" category, which I have therefore approximated by the sum of "auto [torts]" and "medical malpractice."

32. See, for example, Vernon L. Smith, "Rational Choice: The Contrast between Economics and Psychology," 99 *Journal of Political Economy* 877, 884–888 (1991); Colin Camerer, "Individual Decision Making," in *The Handbook of Experimental Economics* 587, 674–675 (John H. Kagel and Alvin E. Roth eds. 1995).

33. See Christine Jolls, Cass R. Sunstein, and Richard Thaler, "A Behavioral Approach to Law and Economics," 50 *Stanford Law Review* 1471, 1543–1545 (1998).

while evidence of the defendant's innocence, unless extremely powerful, will not push the judge's posterior odds into the range in which he
would acquit the defendant. For example, if in a case in which the
judge's prior odds are 100 to 1 in favor of guilt the evidence creates a
likelihood ratio of 8 to 1 that the defendant is not guilty, the judge's
posterior odds on guilt will still be 12.5 to 1.

All this is perfectly rational. But when the pattern becomes understood, litigants will no longer have an incentive to produce much evidence. (To see this, think of the extreme case in which the judge has
made up his mind irrevocably about the correct outcome of the case
before any evidence is presented.) Eventually the accuracy of the litigation process will be severely compromised, as the judge's priors,
formed on the basis of trials in which the parties did put in a lot of evidence, become less and less accurate. The problem will be aggravated
by confirmation bias, the tendency to interpret evidence in the way
most consistent with one's priors.[34] The fact that the life-tenured judge
on a fixed salary pays no penalty for succumbing to this bias undermines his resistance to it. The dangers stemming from strong priors
are less acute in trial by jury.

A related point is that judges by virtue of their experience may take
shortcuts to decision, while jurors, being new to the process, may think
more carefully about the evidence. The judge's snap decision may be as
good as the jurors' more deliberate one—but it may not be better.

With its adversary character, and the need to present the evidence all
at once (a jury can't be kept together indefinitely, whereas a judge can
try a case in stages over an indefinite period of time and delay issuing
his decision until long after the trial has ended),[35] the American jury
trial is more easily monitored by the public than an inquisitorial process modeled on a police investigation. This is important in a culture
that distrusts officials—and so is the delegation of a large part of the
judicial function to nonofficials, the jurors, and the lawyers (though

34. See Matthew Rabin, "Psychology and Economics," 36 *Journal of Economic Literature* 11,
26–28 (1998), and references cited there.

35. Damaška, note 17 above, ch. 3, emphasizes the compression of the adversarial compared to the inquisitorial trial and attributes it to the jury. In the United States as in Europe,
judge trials tend to last longer from beginning to end (although the amount of actual trial
time is less) because, not having to keep a jury together, the judge can interrupt the trial to attend to other business.

when representing the government in court they usually are government employees). With so much of the judicial function privatized, the number of professional judges required to staff the courts is much smaller than in inquisitorial judiciaries,[36] and this pattern caters to public mistrust of officialdom.

Another way of understanding the pattern is that a decision to have a small number of judges drives up the cost of their search, so that the search function devolves on others, the lawyers and jurors, who might be considered excessively high-cost searchers (relative to benefits) if judges were plentiful and judge search therefore cheap. The fact that Americans mistrust officials more than do people in most other countries that are otherwise similar to the United States may therefore be the fundamental reason for our retention of the adversary system. England may seem a counterexample. It too has retained the adversary system, yet the English population is famously (if diminishingly) respectful of officials. Functionally, however, the English legal system is closer to the legal systems of the Continent than to that of the United States.[37]

American mistrust of officials has resulted, moreover, in most of our judges' being elected rather than appointed and in keeping judicial salaries well below the opportunity costs of the ablest lawyers, on both grounds raising doubts about judicial quality[38] and thus producing a vicious cycle—vicious if you don't like juries, that is. Because American judges are mistrusted, American judges really are less trustworthy than judges in a culture of greater respect for officials. This in turn narrows the competence gap between judges and jurors, and so reduces the error costs of jury trials relative to bench trials. The gap is further nar-

---

36. For example, the ratio of lawyers to judges is 54.59 to 1 in the United States compared to 6.07 to 1 in France, 6.86 to 1 in Germany, and 2.86 to 1 in Switzerland. Richard A. Posner, *Law and Legal Theory in England and America* 28 (1996) (table 1.1).

37. Id. at 20–36.

38. Though drawing an adverse inference from the salary differential is complicated by two factors. First, if judicial salaries were higher, the result might be a greater incentive on the part of politicians to treat judgeships as patronage plums; the judgeship would be worth more to the politician's friend or backer and so more to the politician. Second, judicial like military salaries are depressed by monopsony. There is only one employer of federal judges in the United States, just as there is only one employer of military personnel. So if you want to be a federal judge, or a soldier, you cannot rely on competition among prospective employers to give you a salary comparable to what you would enjoy in an alternative employment.

rowed by the fact that, when judges are elected, repeat litigants, such as insurance companies, and specialized trial lawyers, such as the tort plaintiffs' bar, have strong incentives to channel campaign contributions to judges who favor their interests. The incentives are blunted, and the bad effect on justice reduced, if decisional responsibility is shared with jurors. A jury system counteracts judicial bias and reduces the incentive to bribe judges.[39] It counteracts political bias as well, a potentially important factor especially in a system of elected judges. The judge who sits without a jury cannot "blame" the result on others; he can diffuse responsibility if he sits with a jury. And jurors unlike judges do not have career incentives to render verdicts that are popular with whoever controls judicial careers.

Doubts about the competence of jurors are influenced by the assumption that jurors constitute a random sample of the lay population, but that assumption is false. In both the federal and state court systems, the names of potential jurors are taken mainly from voter registration lists or lists of actual voters, so that people whose sense of civic responsibility is insufficient to motivate them to register to vote are in effect disqualified from serving on a jury. (States, however, often supplement voter lists with other sources of names, such as lists of licensed drivers and of taxpayers, which may not select for civic responsibility.) The people whose names are chosen are sent summonses to jury duty but the most irresponsible recipients ignore them and there is rarely any follow-up. Then when the cooperators are questioned by the judge as part of the process of selecting the jury for the particular case, the potential jurors who do not want to serve make up excuses and are usually let off. Then challenges for cause hive off the jurors who are likely to be partial to one side or another and peremptory challenges enable the lawyers to act on inarticulable hunch to eliminate some of the prospective jurors who remain. The prospects who make it through this gauntlet are not a random sample of the inhabitants of the federal judicial district but generally are above average in competence, civic-mindedness, and sense of responsibility, except that peremptory challenges are sometimes used to exclude the ablest prospective jurors—the ones most likely to see through the case presented by the lawyer making the challenge. Contrary to legend, retired people are underrepresented

39. Dewatripont and Tirole, note 24 above, at 30.

rather than overrepresented on juries.[40] So, however, are the busiest people, and some of them would make first-class jurors.

Even assuming that jurors are on balance as competent to resolve factual disputes as (American) judges, we might worry that they have no incentive to exert themselves. They are less likely than judges to be criticized publicly for reaching the "wrong" result (though this, as we saw, can be a good thing as well as a bad); they have no career stakes in doing their job as jurors well; and their financial incentive to conduct a careful search of evidence is nil. Yet almost all judges who sit with juries are struck by their conscientiousness, whether or not the judge agrees with the jury's verdict. Part of the explanation is the screening for conscientiousness that I have mentioned. More important is what might be called the theatrics of trial by jury. American judicial systems strive, apparently with some success, to create an atmosphere in which the jurors, caught up in the drama of decisionmaking, do their best to render a sound verdict. This is no more (or less) surprising from the standpoint of rational choice than the fact that an audience can be frightened by a scary movie even though everyone knows that it's make believe.

Well-publicized instances of crazy jury trials—interminable, uncivil, lawless, resulting in outlandish verdicts and other egregious miscarriages of justice, or all these things at once—have convinced some observers that the American system is grossly inefficient.[41] But there are pitfalls in relying on anecdote to shape public policy in a nation as vast and as blanketed by the media as the United States. The very fact that the American jury trial facilitates public evaluation—that the mistakes of the system are harder to bury—guarantees that the system will look less efficient than one that operates behind a veil.

For the sake of clarity I have been contrasting polar systems for gathering and evaluating evidence in litigation—an inquisitorial system without any participation by lawyers in the evidentiary process and an adversarial system of jury trials. Actual systems are mixed—lawyers do play an evidentiary role in the Continental legal systems and only a small fraction of American cases are decided by juries—and their best features could be combined. The jury could in principle be abolished

---

40. Richard A. Posner, *Aging and Old Age* 152 (1995).

41. This position is argued from an economic standpoint in Gordon Tullock, "Defending the Napoleonic Code over the Common Law," 2 *Research in Law and Policy Studies* 2 (1988), and in Tullock, note 22 above, ch. 6.

without jettisoning the adversary system. England has largely abolished the civil jury, but England's system is, in other respects as well, far from adversary in the American sense. More cases could be channeled into arbitration, which mostly uses lay judges but ones who, unlike jurors, have expertise. A number of suggested and some already implemented reforms of the adversary system and corresponding reforms of the inquisitorial system[42] offer promise of enhancing efficiency. Here are some designed to make trial by jury more accurate:[43]

1. Restoring the size of the civil jury to the traditional twelve (from six or eight, its size in the federal system at present), in order to obtain greater diversity of experience, which is important because determining probabilities with regard to the sorts of uncertainty involved in a trial draws heavily on the adjudicator's common sense, which is shaped in turn by people's experiences; to exploit the Condorcet jury theorem on the superiority of collective to individual judgment;[44] and to reduce variance in outcomes by drawing on a larger, though still small, sample of the community.[45]

42. See, for example, Palumbo, note 27 above, at 2, 19–20. On the growing convergence between the Continental (inquisitorial) and Anglo-American (adversarial) systems, see, for example, *Criminal Justice in Europe: A Comparative Study* (Phil Fennell et al. eds. 1995); John D. Jackson, "Playing the Culture Card in Resisting Cross-Jurisdictional Transplants: A Comment on 'Legal Processes and National Culture,'" 5 *Cardozo Journal of International and Comparative Law* 51 (1997); Kerameus, note 22 above.

43. Many of these are discussed in Saks, note 6 above, and Lempert, note 6 above, at 220–231, and are summarized in American Bar Association, Section of Litigation, "Civil Trial Practice Standards" (Feb. 1998). See also Michael Honig, "Jury Trial Innovations," *New York Law Journal*, Nov 9, 1998, p. 3.

44. See, for example, Bernard Grofman and Guillermo Owen, "Condorcet Models, Avenues for Future Research," in *Information Pooling and Group Decision Making* 93, 94 (Bernard Grofman and Guillermo Owen eds. 1986). The theorem requires that each juror make an independent judgment, that each have a probability greater than 0.5 that his judgment is correct, and—critically—that the jury arrives at its outcome by majority vote. Suppose that each member of a twelve-person jury has a 0.6 probability of being correct. Then the jury will reach the incorrect result only if seven members are wrong, and the probability of this is 0.47, which is less than 1 percent. Under a rule of unanimity, the probability of error would be 40 percent. But given that juries deliberate, there is no doubt that an articulate majority is often able to win over dissenters and obtain a unanimous verdict.

45. For evidence that larger juries increase accuracy and reduce variance, see Saks, note 6 above, at 14–15, 42–43; Michael J. Saks and Mollie Weighner Marti, "A Meta-Analysis of the Effects of Jury Size," 21 *Law and Human Behavior* 451 (1997). Some cases are so huge that a single jury, even with twelve members, is too small to ensure accuracy commensurate with the stakes. This is a problem in mass-tort class actions, when claims with aggregate stakes of liter-

2. Imposing educational qualifications on jurors in highly complex litigation.

3. Encouraging jurors to take a more active role in the search process by permitting them to take notes; to ask questions of the lawyers, witnesses, and judge; to read daily transcript; and, more doubtfully, to call witnesses.

4. Instructing jurors on the law before and during as well as at the close of trial.

5. Explaining to jurors the basic rules of evidence so that they do not draw inappropriate negative inferences from the withholding of evidence from them. Jurors' ignorance of the rules of evidence can lead them to entertain ungrounded suspicions of the honesty of lawyers and witnesses and to draw erroneous "missing evidence" inferences.[46]

6. Avoiding legal jargon in instructions—a problem so general that some empirical studies have found "that instructed jurors have no better grasp of the law than uninstructed jurors"![47]

7. Changing the rules of evidence so as to combat some of the cognitive quirks that beset decision makers.

8. Shortening trials as much as possible so that jurors do not experience information overload.

Accuracy is only one of two factors to be considered in an economic analysis of evidence; cost is the other. But most of the suggested reforms are virtually costless and some, like compressing the trial, might actually reduce costs. The most costly-seeming reform would be to increase the size of the jury. The larger the jury, the higher the opportunity costs of taking jurors from their ordinary pursuits. More jurors

---

ally billions of dollars may be combined for trial before a single jury. The solution is to have a sample of the cases tried before separate juries. See Michael J. Saks and Peter David Blanck, "Justice Improved: The Unrecognized Benefits of Aggregation and Sampling in the Trial of Mass Torts," 44 *Stanford Law Review* 815, 841–851 (1992); In re Rhone-Poulenc Rorer, Inc., 51 F.3d 1293 (7th Cir. 1995).

46. For analysis and examples, see Bruce A. Green, "'The Whole Truth?': How Rules of Evidence Make Lawyers Deceitful," 25 *Loyola of Los Angeles Law Review* 699 (1992).

47. Saks, note 6 above, at 35; see also Reid Hastie, David Schkade, and John Payne, "A Study of Juror and Jury Judgments in Civil Cases: Deciding Liability for Punitive Damages," 22 *Law and Human Behavior* 287, 304 (1998). It may, however, fall into the category of problems that are hopeless but not serious. The instructions are determined before the lawyers' closing arguments to the jury, and the lawyers are not permitted to argue to the jury legal positions inconsistent with the instructions. In effect, then, the lawyers instruct the jury, but they do so consistently with the law as laid down by the judge.

would be needed and trials would be longer because jury selection and
jury deliberations would both be more protracted. There would also be
more hung juries, and hence more retrials. But the added costs might
well be offset by the fact that more accurate factfinding (which having a
larger jury, within limits, promotes) should produce better deterrence,
resulting, as noted earlier, in less wrongful conduct and so in fewer trials. Also, the settlement rate is higher the more predictable the outcome of the trial is.

I don't want to go overboard in praise of the large jury. Arbitration,
which as a privately created and financed method of adjudication provides a valuable though not infallible benchmark for evaluating the efficiency of public systems of adjudication, rarely involves more than
three arbitrators and usually there is only one. The implication is that
the costs of a larger panel would exceed the benefits that I have just
been stressing. But the implications are blurred by the fact that cases
selected for arbitration differ systematically from those adjudicated in
courts. Almost all are contract cases in which the parties agreed in the
contract itself to arbitrate disputes arising out of it, and perhaps in most
of them the parties did not anticipate disputes likely to involve stakes
large enough to warrant more than a brief and informal process of resolution. Although many multimillion dollar contracts provide for arbitration and rarely if ever do they provide for arbitration by a panel of
more than three arbitrators, most contract cases, even when the stakes
are huge, are decided on the basis of the language of the contract.
Messy factual disputes of the sort that a large panel of factfinders might
be better able to resolve are avoided. The benefits of additional arbitrators may therefore be slight even in large cases.

Another variable in the design of trial by jury is the voting rule. Unanimity is the traditional rule, but some states have relaxed it. It is difficult to say whether this is a good idea, apart from the effect on the
number of cases that hang, which may however be slight if the unanimity requirement gives way to a lesser supermajority requirement (for
example, conviction or acquittal by a 10–2 vote).[48] On the one hand,
deliberation is likely to be more perfunctory if unanimity is not re-

48. See Alvin K. Klevorick and Michael Rothschild, "A Model of the Jury Decision Process," 8 *Journal of Legal Studies* 141, 155 (1979); Edward P. Schwartz and Warren F. Schwartz,
"Decisionmaking by Juries under Unanimity and Supermajority Voting Rules," 80 *Georgetown Law Journal* 775, 787 (1992).

quired. On the other hand, unprincipled compromises, which may be necessary to secure unanimity, are also less likely.

Opponents of the jury system can point to two types of genuine empirical evidence to support their opposition. First, experimental evidence (limited, however, to a single study) indicates that judges are less subject to hindsight bias than jurors.[49] Second, the conviction rate is lower in bench trials than in jury trials. The significance of this lies in the fact that in most states the decision in a criminal case as to whether the trial shall be to a judge or to a jury is entirely the defendant's. If juries are less accurate guilt determiners than judges, innocent defendants will choose to be tried by judges rather than run the risk of jury mistake, while guilty defendants will choose to be tried by juries, hoping *for* a mistake; and so the acquittal rate will be higher in bench trials—and it is.[50]

Kevin Clermont and Theodore Eisenberg present some parallel evidence for civil cases: in products liability and medical malpractice cases, bench trials strongly favor plaintiffs and jury trials strongly favor defendants.[51] The plaintiff's choice of a bench trial, if he has a strong case, is explicable on the same ground as the criminal defendant's choice of bench trial if *he* has a strong case. The puzzle is why the civil defendant doesn't choose a jury trial if he has a weak case and thus needs a mistake by the trier of fact in order to prevail. The authors think that defendants' lawyers have bought into popular misconceptions that juries are inveterately pro-plaintiff. An alternative possibility is related to the assumed greater accuracy of judges. To say that juries are less accurate than judges is to say that there is greater variance in outcome in jury than in nonjury cases. A defendant who has too weak a case to have any realistic hope of escaping being held liable to the plaintiff may be harmed by this variance. Suppose that the range of possible damages awards by a judge is $10,000–$100,000 (for a mean of $55,000), but for a jury in the same case is $0–$110,000 (same mean). Then a defendant who has no chance of persuading the jury to award zero damages has

49. See W. Kip Viscusi, "How Do Judges Think about Risk?" 1 *American Law and Economics Review* 26 (1999).

50. Gerald D. Gay et al., "Noisy Juries and the Choice of Trial Mode in a Sequential Signalling Game: Theory and Evidence," 20 *RAND Journal of Economics* 196 (1989).

51. Kevin M. Clermont and Theodore Eisenberg, "Trial by Jury or Judge: Transcending Empiricism," 77 *Cornell Law Review* 1124, 1162–1166 (1992).

more to lose from being tried by a jury than by a judge. It is because in a civil case the jury determines the size of the sanction, but in a criminal case the judge does, that jury inaccuracy is likely to work to the disadvantage of the guilty defendant in the civil case and to his advantage (as noted in the preceding paragraph) in the criminal case.

A defendant who has a weak case will, however, tend to prefer a jury trial when the jury is asked to make a binary decision (such as guilty or innocent, liable or not liable), because in such a case variance can only work to his benefit by reducing the expected punishment. Suppose all judges are average, and the average judge will convict this defendant. The average jury will also convict him, but one in ten juries will acquit him. Then he is better off choosing a jury trial.

What I am calling "jury inaccuracy" need not reflect a difference in competence. It could reflect simply a difference in variance resulting from the fact that there are many more jurors than there are judges and they are more diverse because they lack the uniformity of outlook and experience that judges tend to have by virtue of common training and vocation. Yet jurors doubtless are somewhat more lawless than judges because they do not internalize the values of law-following to the same extent as most judges. That is why we have rules that forbid revealing to the jury that the defendant in a tort case has liability insurance. But this point is somewhat to one side of the question of factfinding competence; more studies are needed before it can be concluded with any confidence that the American jury is a less accurate factfinder than the American, or even the European, judge. If it is less accurate, however, it is probably less efficient, at least in civil cases. The direct cost of jury trials plainly exceeds that of bench trials. Only if a great deal of value is assigned to John Stuart Mill's "education in citizenship" rationale for the jury, or to some other political value of jury trial, are the added costs likely to be offset by greater benefits—except in criminal cases. Distrust of officials is too great in America for people to be willing to entrust their liberty solely to professional judges.

A final concern about the jury, and one that also casts doubt on proposals to restore the size of the jury to the original twelve members, arises from the psychological literature on group polarization. This literature finds, contrary to widespread intuitions concerning juries and other committees, that groups tend to reach more extreme results than the average member of the group; that is, group deliberations tend to be polarizing.[52] A number of explanations have been offered; none commands full agreement. What is disturbing is that none of the explanations (a common one is that people taking extreme positions argue with greater conviction, and this sways the moderates) suggests that the polarized outcomes are more rational than those that would be reached by the average member of the group deciding on his own, without deliberation. The implication is that twelve heads may, after all, not be better than one—and may in fact be worse if, for example, a greater variance in jury verdicts is considered undesirable whether because of risk aversion or other factors.

∽ I WANT TO MOVE now to other issues in the law of evidence besides the relative merits of the adversarial and inquisitive systems, starting with burden of proof. Burden of proof has two aspects. The first is important only in an adversary system, where the tribunal does not participate in the search for evidence. This is the burden (duty) of submitting evidence to the tribunal, as distinct from the burden of persuading the tribunal that one ought to win the case. The two burdens are intertwined; for one thing, the burden of persuasion generally determines who has the burden of production. The plaintiff's burden in an ordinary civil case is to show that his position is more likely than not correct. In other words, if at the end of the trial the jury either thinks the defendant should win or doesn't know which side should win—the evidence seems in equipoise—the plaintiff loses. This makes a plaintiff who puts in no evidence very likely to lose; so it makes sense, as a way of economizing on the time of the tribunal (as well as of reducing nuisance litigation), to require the plaintiff, as a precondition to getting to trial, to submit evidence that if believed would be likely to carry the day with the jury, before the defendant is required to submit any evidence.[53] This assumes that the cost to the plaintiff of obtaining this evidence is

---

52. See, for example, David G. Myers and Helmut Lamm, "The Group Polarization Phenomenon," 83 *Psychological Bulletin* 602 (1976); Markus Brauer, Charles M. Judd, and Melissa D. Ginter, "The Effects of Repeated Expressions on Attitude Polarization during Group Discussions," 68 *Journal of Personality and Social Psychology* 1014 (1995); David Schklade, Cass R. Sunstein, and Daniel Kahnemann, "Deliberating about Dollars: The Severity Shift," 100 *Columbia Law Review* 1134 (2000); cf. Rabin, note 34 above, at 26–28, on confirmation bias—which Rabin also calls "same-evidence polarization."

53. See Bruce L. Hay, "Allocating the Burden of Proof," 72 *Indiana Law Journal* 651 (1997).

not disproportionately greater than the cost to the defendant of obtaining contrary evidence (if there is any). But the assumption is reasonable; modern pretrial procedures for discovering evidence in the possession of the opposing party make the costs of searching for evidence pretty symmetrical.

The burden of persuasion rests on the plaintiff for the main claim but on the defendant for affirmative defenses, such as consent, statute of limitations, laches, accord and satisfaction, incapacity, preemption, and res judicata, and the burdens of production are allocated accordingly. It would be particularly inefficient to require the plaintiff to anticipate and produce evidence contravening the indefinite number of defenses that a defendant might plead in a given case. Such a requirement would also force the plaintiff to do the defendant's legal research for him. The plaintiff would have to identify and counter defenses that the defendant might not have been aware of as well as some that the defendant might have good tactical or evidentiary reasons not to plead or that he might decide not to plead simply because he had one clearly dispositive defense and so didn't have to waste his time with others. For example, if the statute of limitations is a plausible defense in only 5 percent of cases, making the plaintiff plead and prove that his suit was timely would impose costs with no corresponding benefits in 95 percent of cases. This suggests that the nineteenth-century rule that the plaintiff in a negligence case had to prove his freedom from contributory negligence as well as the defendant's negligence would have been sound from an economic standpoint only if either (1) contributory negligence was a likely defense in the vast majority of such cases, or (2) because pretrial discovery was very limited, it would have been much more costly for the defendant than for the plaintiff to determine whether the plaintiff had been negligent.

The economic rationale of rules governing the burden of production is further illustrated by the *McDonnell Douglas* rule.[54] Applied mainly in employment discrimination cases, the rule permits the plaintiff, say in a case of racial discrimination in hiring, to establish his prima facie case, and thus withstand a motion for summary judgment by the defendant, with evidence merely that he was qualified for the job but was passed

54. See McDonnell Douglas Corp. v. Green, 411 U.S. 792 (1973); see also Furnco Construction Corp. v. Waters, 438 U.S. 567 (1978).

over in favor of someone of another race. But the rule does more: satisfying the just-described burden of production creates a presumption of discrimination, meaning that if the defendant puts in no evidence the plaintiff is entitled to summary judgment. The probability that he lost the job opportunity *because* he was discriminated against might not seem very high if the only evidence is as described. But this suggestion disregards the evidentiary significance of missing evidence. If the defendant, who after all made the decision to give the job to someone other than the plaintiff, maintains complete silence about the reason for his action, an inference arises that the reason was indeed discrimination. Were the reason otherwise he should have been able without great difficulty to produce some evidence of that.

If the defendant breaks his silence and gives a noninvidious reason for his action, and the plaintiff is unable to present evidence casting doubt on that reason, then the plaintiff loses, again without a trial. If, however, the plaintiff is able to create doubt about the genuineness of the reason given by the defendant, then the case goes to the jury and the *McDonnell Douglas* rule falls out. A jury that disbelieves the reason given by the defendant can infer that the plaintiff was indeed discriminated against, but it need not do so;[55] it may conclude that the defendant is embarrassed by the reason, though it was not discriminatory, that motivated its action and so is concealing it.

The *McDonnell Douglas* rule is sometimes thought to be motivated by a desire of "liberal" judges to make it easier for the plaintiff to prevail in a discrimination case. My analysis suggests that the rule is justifiable in neutral terms of minimizing cost, specifically of minimizing the cost of trial in cases in which the parties can be induced to show their hand before trial. It is true that the significance to be drawn from the defendant's silence before trial, the silence that dictates judgment to the plaintiff able to make the very slight prima facie case required, is an artifact of the *McDonnell Douglas* rule itself. In the absence of a production-forcing presumption, the natural inference from the defendant's refusal to volunteer an explanation for his action would be that the defendant wasn't going to do the plaintiff's work for him; let the plaintiff use pretrial discovery to find out what may have been behind

---

55. See the comprehensive discussion of this issue in Fisher v. Vassar College, 114 F.3d 1332 (2d Cir. 1997) (en banc).

the defendant's action of which the plaintiff is complaining. Still, given that it is easier for the defendant to explain and produce evidence concerning its decisionmaking process, the presumption can be justified as reallocating production burdens in accordance with a neutral criterion of comparative cost advantage.

Let me turn to the burden of persuasion. In the typical civil trial there is no basis for supposing that type I errors (false positives, such as convicting an innocent person) on average impose higher costs than type II errors (false negatives, such as an erroneous acquittal). So it is enough to justify a verdict for the plaintiff that the probability that his claim is meritorious exceeds, however slightly, the probability that it is not. But because the cost to an innocent defendant of criminal punishment may well exceed the social benefit of one more conviction of a guilty person in maintaining deterrence and preventing the person from committing crimes for a period of time—namely, while he is imprisoned pursuant to his conviction—type I errors are more serious than type II errors in criminal cases and therefore are weighted more heavily in the former by the imposition of a heavy burden of persuasion on the prosecution.[56]

Trading off type I and type II errors is a pervasive feature of evidence law. Consider disputes over whether a given police lineup is unduly "suggestive." If the other persons in the lineup resemble the defendant very closely, the chance of a type I error (mistakenly identifying the defendant as the criminal) is minimized, because the defendant does not "stand out." But the chance of a type II error (mistakenly failing to identify the defendant as the criminal) is increased, because it is easier to confuse the defendant with the other persons in the lineup.

Another way to understand the difference between the criminal and civil burdens is by reference to the inherent advantages of the prosecution in a criminal case, compared to a private plaintiff, in an adversary system of justice, that is, a system of competitive evidence search. The government has enormous prosecutorial resources.[57] It can allocate

56. Posner, note 1 above, at 408–415.

57. In cities with a population of a million or more, the average budget of the local prosecutor's office exceeds $25 million. Carol J. DeFrances and Greg W. Steadman, "Prosecutors in State Courts, 1996" 1 (U.S. Dept. of Justice, Bureau of Justice Statistics, NCJ 170092, July 1998). Annual appropriations for the offices of the U.S. Attorneys, which prosecute most federal criminal cases, aggregate some $1 billion. *Budget of the United States Government, Fiscal Year 1999, Appendix* 594 (1998).

these across cases as it pleases, extracting guilty pleas by the threat to concentrate its resources against any defendant who refuses to plead and using the resources thus conserved to wallop the occasional defendant who does invoke his right to a trial. This is like the case in which unequal access to capital markets makes predatory pricing a rational strategy.[58] The analogy is closest when, as is the commonest case, the defendant cannot afford to hire counsel but is dependent on court-appointed counsel, who except in capital cases are kept on a short financial tether. Even the rare defendant who can afford to hire counsel will normally be unable to match the resources that the government can credibly threaten to pour into a case. The burden of proving guilt beyond a reasonable doubt is a partial offset (like the provision of counsel to indigent defendants) to the inequality of the parties' resources for gathering and presenting evidence. In an inquisitorial system, where the search is conducted by a presumably disinterested judge, the need for a heavier burden of proof in a criminal than in a civil system is attenuated.

A complicating factor is that prosecutors in either system may be disinterested too, since, unlike private lawyers, their incomes are not tied directly to success in litigation. But economic theory, as well as common sense and observation, suggests that the desire to win, weighted by the stakes in the case (roughly, the sentence if the defendant is convicted), is the most important argument in the prosecutorial utility function and thus that prosecutors have incentives similar to those of private lawyers. Being a prosecutor is rarely a terminal job; it is a stepping stone. Future employers will evaluate a prosecutor by his success in litigation, which will be seen as a function of his win rate weighted by the opposition that he had to overcome in order to win; the opposition will usually be greater the graver the offense charged.

When asked to express proof beyond a reasonable doubt as a probability of guilt, judges generally pick a number between 0.75 to 0.95 (depending on the judge); jury quantifications are similar.[59] These may seem shockingly low figures, implying that as many as a quarter of the people convicted of crime are innocent. Not so. The higher the crime

58. See, for example, Douglas G. Baird, Robert H. Gertner, and Randal C. Picker, *Game Theory and the Law* 183–184 (1994).

59. See National Research Council, *The Evolving Role of Statistical Assessments as Evidence in the Courts* 201–204 (Stephen E. Fienberg ed. 1989); Joseph L. Gastwirth, *Statistical Reasoning in Law and Public*, vol. 2: *Tort Law, Evidence, and Health* 700–702 (1988).

rate in relation to prosecutorial resources, the more thoroughly prosecutors will screen cases for easy ones to win, and these will tend to be drawn from the tail of the distribution of suspects that contains the suspects who are most likely to be guilty in fact. The heavy burden of persuasion and the other procedural advantages of criminal defendants increase the incentive of prosecutors to go after the guiltiest by making it difficult to convict a defendant, notwithstanding the disparity in resources between the prosecuting authorities and all but the wealthiest defendants, unless the case is one sided against him. If because of prosecutorial screening only 1 percent of the persons prosecuted are innocent, then even if *all* defendants are convicted, only 1 percent of convicted persons will be innocent. And that is an exaggeration. Not all persons who are prosecuted are convicted, and normally it is much easier (*pace* Janet Malcolm) for an innocent than for a guilty defendant to create enough doubt of guilt in the trier of fact to induce an acquittal.

Tight screening implies not only that guilty people are not prosecuted but also that most people who are prosecuted and *acquitted* are actually guilty. In the previous example, if a 10 percent acquittal rate is assumed, then 99 percent of the defendants who are acquitted would actually have been guilty if the probability of acquittal was random with respect to innocence and 90 percent if all innocent defendants were acquitted.[60] This implies that when crime rates rise faster than prosecutorial resources, entailing an even finer mesh in the screening of cases to pursue, courts or legislatures would have to reduce the procedural advantages of defendants if society were to maintain the same balance between the probabilities of convicting the innocent and of acquitting the guilty. This point suggests a possible nonideological basis for the Supreme Court's swing against the rights of criminal defendants in the 1970s and 1980s. Had those rights been preserved intact, the rise in crime rates in that era (which greatly exceeded the increase in the number of prosecutions)[61] would have had the paradoxical effect of making it easier for guilty defendants to avoid punishment. That in turn would

---

60. Of 10,000 defendants, then, 100 (1 percent) are assumed to be innocent. If 1,000 of the defendants are acquitted (10 percent) and the probability of acquittal is the same regardless of innocence, then in that group of 1,000 1 percent will be innocent and therefore 99 percent guilty. If all 100 innocents are acquitted, then 900 of the acquitted defendants must be guilty (90 percent). "Juries are not particularly good at evaluating eyewitness testimony . . . If they return few erroneous convictions it is because they are given few opportunities to judge innocent defendants." Samuel R. Gross, "Loss of Innocence: Eyewitness Identification and Proof of Guilt," 16 *Journal of Legal Studies* 395, 432 (1987).

have reduced the expected cost of punishment, and so driven crime rates even higher, unless there were an offsetting increase in the severity of punishment for those (fewer) criminals who were caught and convicted.

The assumption in the preceding paragraph of crime rates rising faster than prosecutorial resources suggests an alternative response to rising crime rates to curtailing defendants' procedural rights: increasing prosecutorial budgets. Courts could exert pressure on legislatures to do this by holding the line on procedure and invalidating (as cruel and unusual) steep legislative increases in the severity of criminal punishments. Legislatures would be forced to choose between increasing prosecutorial budgets and higher crime rates that would place additional pressure on the courts to relax procedural safeguards. As I noted in the Introduction, the courts chose not to play this game of chicken with federal and state legislators.

Although the burden of persuasion is much lower in a civil case and most plaintiffs do not operate with a resource constraint (thanks to contingent fees), there is no reason to suppose that a higher fraction of civil than of criminal cases are decided incorrectly. Burden of persuasion has less to do with the number of errors than with the distribution of errors between sides. More undeserving plaintiffs than undeserving prosecutors win, but fewer undeserving civil defendants than undeserving criminal defendants win. What makes it likely that most cases, civil or criminal, are resolved correctly is simply that it is usually cheaper to obtain persuasive evidence on the side of truth. But a selection effect makes the overall accuracy of the system difficult to observe. The procedural system as a whole is more accurate than the trial component of it, but it is the latter that is visible. One-sided cases are more likely to be settled before trial, usually with little publicity, than toss-ups are,[62] and so the latter are overrepresented on the trial docket, which is highly visible. Hence a criminal justice system that disfavors plea bar-

61. Between 1960 and 1996, the "crime index" compiled by the FBI and reported in the FBI's annual *Uniform Crime Reports* grew almost sevenfold. During the same period federal criminal prosecutions grew by a third (see annual reports of the Director of the Administrative Office of the U.S. Courts). For state criminal prosecutions, there are data only from 1977. Between then and 1994, the number of prosecutions actually declined slightly (as estimated by the Court Statistics Project of the National Center for State Courts), a period during which the crime index was growing by a third.

62. See George L. Priest and Benjamin Klein, "The Selection of Disputes for Litigation," 13 *Journal of Legal Studies* 1 (1984).

gaining (like the German) is bound to appear more accurate than our system. The more that plea bargaining is discouraged, the more one-sided cases there will be in the trial mix.

It is now generally accepted that since all evidence is probabilistic—there are no metaphysical certainties—evidence should not be excluded merely because its accuracy can be expressed in explicitly probabilistic terms, as in the case of fingerprint and DNA evidence.[63] But courts are reluctant to take the next step and hold that, given the modest burden of persuasion in civil cases, the explicit probability that the plaintiff's essential evidence is true need only exceed 50 percent, however slightly. Suppose that the plaintiff is hit by a bus, and it is known that 51 percent of the buses on the road where the plaintiff was hit are owned by Bus Company *A* and 49 percent by Company *B*. The plaintiff sues *A* and asks for judgment on the basis of this statistic alone; he tenders no other evidence. If the defendant also puts in no evidence, should a jury be allowed to award judgment for the plaintiff?[64] The law's answer is "no,"[65] and has so much intuitive appeal as to make the example Exhibit A in the case against using Bayes' theorem, or mathematical probability generally (or perhaps any theory of probability), to guide or interpret legal factfinding. We can think of the civil burden of persuasion as requiring posterior odds of a shade over 1 in favor of the plaintiff (say 1.048, which is 51/49), because a tie goes to the defendant. If the prior odds are assumed to be 1 to 1, on the theory that the jury begins hearing the evidence—in our hypothetical case it is the evidence, which is the only evidence they do hear, concerning the percentage of buses of each company on the route in question—without

63. See, for example, United States v. Hannigan, 27 F.3d 890, 893 n. 3 (3d Cir. 1994).

64. For the most thorough discussion of this famous chestnut of modern evidence scholarship, see Gary L. Wells, "Naked Statistical Evidence of Liability: Is Subjective Probability Enough?" 62 *Journal of Personality and Social Psychology* 739 (1992).

65. See Richard W. Wright, "Causation, Responsibility, Risk, Probability, Naked Statistics, and Proof: Pruning the Bramble Bush by Clarifying the Concepts," 73 *Iowa Law Review* 1001, 1050–1051 (1988), and cases cited. The hypothetical case in the text is a variant of Smith v. Rapid Transit, Inc., 58 N.E.2d 754 (Mass. 1945), where the court held that it "was not enough" "that mathematically the chances somewhat favor the proposition that a bus of the defendant caused the accident." Id. at 755. Kaminsky v. Hertz Corp., 288 N.W.2d 426 (Mich. App. 1979), is sometimes cited as being contrary to *Smith*, but this is not an accurate reading. Quite apart from the fact that the corresponding percentages were 90 percent and 10 percent, there was nonstatistical, as well as statistical, evidence pointing to the defendant's ownership of the truck that had caused the accident.

any notion of who has the better case, then the posterior odds are equal to the likelihood ratio. This is 1.048, and since it exceeds 1 the plaintiff should win—which almost no legal professional believes.

The cause of this disbelief, however, is not or at least should not be doubts about mathematical probability, but rather the tacit assumption that the statistic concerning the ownership of the buses is the only evidence that the plaintiff can obtain.[66] It is the implausibility of this assumption that powers the intuition that the plaintiff should lose. If the statistic is the plaintiff's only evidence, the inference to be drawn is not that there is a 51 percent probability that it was a bus owned by A that hit the plaintiff but that the plaintiff either investigated and discovered that it was actually a bus owned by B (and let us say that B is judgment-proof and so not worth suing), or that he has simply not bothered to conduct an investigation. If the first alternative is true, he should of course lose; and since it may be true, the probability that the plaintiff was hit by a bus owned by A is less than 51 percent.

He should lose even if the second alternative is true (that he didn't bother to investigate). The court should not be required to expend any of its scarce resources of time and effort on a case until the plaintiff has conducted a sufficient search to indicate that an expenditure of public resources is reasonably likely to yield a significant social benefit. That is implicit in the decision discussed earlier to place the burden of producing evidence on the plaintiff rather than on the defendant. Suppose it would cost the court system $10,000 to try even a barebones case. This expenditure would be worthless from the standpoint of deterring accidents should it turn out that the bus was owned by B. It makes sense for the court to require some advance investigation by the plaintiff in order to increase the probability that a commitment of judicial resources would be worthwhile. And likewise if there is an external benefit to getting right which bus company is responsible for the plaintiff's injury; for the law can increase the probability of getting it right by compelling the plaintiff to do a more thorough investigation than it might be in his strictly private interest to do.

If, however, the ratio of buses owned by A to those owned by B on

66. Another problem, which however I shall ignore (though it is relevant in showing the artificiality of the example), is that the plaintiff must prove more than the ownership of the bus to obtain a judgment—notably, he must prove that the accident was due to the bus company's negligence.

the route in question is much higher than 51/49, then the case against allowing "naked" statistical evidence to carry the plaintiff's burden of production is weakened. The law recognizes this not only in the obvious cases of fingerprint and DNA evidence but also in its adoption of such presumptions as that a properly addressed, stamped, and mailed letter will reach the addressee, a purely statistical presumption because it is applied without regard to the particulars of the case (beyond those required to satisfy the conditions of the presumption) and yet can determine the outcome.[67] Even in the 51/49 case, if there is other evidence against A there is an argument for admitting the statistical evidence because the additional evidence, even if weak, will (and rightly, under Bayes' theorem) affect the factfinder's posterior odds.[68]

Suppose both parties do conduct a thorough investigation yet are unable to come up with any additional evidence bearing on the ownership of the bus. There is no longer a basis for suspicion that the plaintiff really believes that a bus owned by Company B hit him or for punishing him for not having investigated more. But there are still reasons for dismissal. The costs of trying these cases are likely to exceed the social benefits. If 1,000 such cases are tried, we can expect 510 correct decisions (that is, 510 decisions in which the defendant was in fact the injurer) and 490 incorrect ones, while dismissing all of the cases can be expected to yield 490 correct decisions and 510 erroneous ones. The social benefits of the twenty additional correct decisions that trying the 1,000 cases would produce—benefits in more perfect deterrence of negligent accidents—would probably fall short of the social cost of 1,000 trials. Worse, the social benefits may be negative. If the law is that Company A's market share is enough for liability and no other evidence is available, then Company B's incentive to take care will plummet because it will know that A will be liable for any accidents that B causes.[69] B will have succeeded in externalizing its accident costs.

Another issue concerning statistical evidence is whether the result of

67. See Richard D. Friedman, "Generalized Inferences, Individual Merits, and Jury Discretion," 66 *Boston University Law Review* 509, 515 (1986).

68. See Steven C. Salop, "Evaluating Uncertain Evidence with Sir Thomas Bayes: A Note for Teachers," *Journal of Economic Perspectives*, Summer 1987, p. 155.

69. See Eric B. Rasmusen, "Predictable and Unpredictable Error in Tort Awards: The Effect of Plaintiff Self-Selection and Signaling," 15 *International Review of Law and Economics* 323 (1995).

a statistical investigation should be given any weight in a trial unless the result is statistically significant at the 5 percent level,[70] meaning that the probability that the investigation would have yielded this result even if the hypothesis that it was trying to test was false is no greater than 5 percent. The 5 percent test is a convention that academic researchers employ (as I did in Chapter 3 and do so again in Chapter 13), though not one to which the research community adheres rigidly. Social scientists often report results that are significant only at the 10 percent level, while if the results are significant at the 2 percent or 1 percent level the researcher will point out that these results are more robust than those that are significant only at the 5 percent level; they are "highly significant" rather than just "significant." So there is no magic to the 5 percent criterion; and to exclude *from a trial* statistical evidence that failed to reach the 5 percent significance level would imply that eyewitness testimony, too, should be inadmissible unless the probability that the testimony would have been given even if the event testified to had not occurred was less than 5 percent.

A low significance level may, it is true, reflect an unsound method of statistical estimation, an incorrect specification of the hypothesis being tested, or the omission of relevant variables that if included would have caused the hypothesis to be rejected. When any of these factors is present, the same kind of suspicion will arise as in the bus case. But if the study has been conducted responsibly and has withstood a hammering from the opponent's expert, yet the significance level does not reach the conventional 5 percent level, it would not be a good reason for excluding the evidence that a social scientist would be violating the norms of his discipline by reporting results that do not attain the con-

70. This is a common interpretation of Hazelwood School District v. United States, 433 U.S. 299, 311 n. 17 (1977), and Castaneda v. Partida, 430 U.S. 482, 496 n. 17 (1977), as noted without endorsement in Thomas R. Ireland et al., *Expert Economic Testimony: Reference Guides for Judges and Attorneys* 237 (1998). See also Alpo Petfoods Inc. v. Ralston Purina Co., 913 F.2d 958, 962 n. 4 (D.C. Cir. 1990); Ottaviani v. State University of New York, 875 F.2d 365, 372 (2d Cir. 1989); Ford v. Seabold, 841 F.2d 677, 684 (6th Cir. 1988). But the interpretation is incorrect, as noted in Orley Ashenfelter and Ronald Oaxaca, "The Economics of Discrimination: Economists Enter the Courtroom," 77 *American Economic Review Papers and Proceedings* 321, 323 (May 1987). For criticism of using significance levels as criteria of admissibility, see Richard Lempert, "Statistics in the Courtroom: Building on Rubinfeld," 85 *Columbia Law Review* 1098, 1099–1103 (1985). And see generally David L. Faigman et al., *Modern Scientific Evidence: The Law and Science of Expert Testimony*, vol. 1, pp. 118–121 (1997).

ventional significance. Anyway, he would not be violating them; the 5
percent convention is not that rigidly adhered to. More important, the
convention is rooted in considerations that have no direct relevance to
litigation, such as the need to ration pages in scientific journals.[71] And
fears that jurors are dazzled by evidence that involves explicit probability estimates, and so give such evidence more weight than a good
Bayesian would do, appear to be unfounded; jurors appear to give such
evidence *less* weight that they should.[72]

But we must not overlook the *cost* of weak statistical evidence. The
less robust the results of a statistical study offered as evidence, the more
time will have to be spent at trial exploring the design of the study.
Given the difficulty that judges and jurors have in understanding and
weighing statistical evidence, there is an argument (akin to that for the
hearsay rule) for excluding statistical evidence that the relevant profession, for whatever reason, considers weak.

Another feature of the mathematical theory of probability that has
drawn fire is the product rule: the probability that two (or more) independent events is true is the product of the probabilities that each of
them is true. For example, the probability of coming up with heads on
three consecutive fair tosses is .125 ($.5 \times .5 \times .5$). This leads to the paradox that the standard burden of proof instructions to a jury in a civil
case, at least if taken literally, will often imply that the jury should find
in favor of the plaintiff even if the probability that his claim is valid is
much less than 0.5.[73] For the jury will be instructed to rule for the

71. A similar point is made in an emerging economics literature on clinical trials and other
social experiments: benefits from adherence to statistical conventions (randomization, sample
size, significance, and so on) must be traded off against costs. See, for example, Tomas
Philipson, "The Evaluation of New Health Care Technology: The Labor Economics of Statistics," 76 *Journal of Econometrics* 375 (1997).

72. See Brian C. Smith et al., "Jurors' Use of Probabilistic Evidence," 20 *Law and Human
Behavior* 49 (1996). Wells, note 64 above, attributes this to a cognitive quirk and suggests that
it might be offset by a redescription of statistical evidence. See id. at 748–750. With reference
to a paternity suit in which blood tests showed a 99.8 percent probability that the defendant
was indeed the father, Wells states that "one suspects that the plaintiff would have won the
suit if the expert had reframed his testimony to say that 'based on a blood test that is 99.8%
accurate, I conclude that the defendant is the father' rather than 'based on a blood test, there
is a 99.8% probability that the defendant is the father.'" Id. at 749.

73. See Ronald J. Allen, "A Reconceptualization of Civil Trials," 66 *Boston University Law
Review* 401 (1986), and Allen, "The Nature of Juridical Proof," 13 *Cardozo Law Review* 373,
409–420 (1991).

plaintiff if it is satisfied that he has proved each of the elements of his claim by a preponderance of the evidence even if the elements are independent, that is, their probabilities are uncorrelated. It's as if the jury were being told that as soon as it finds one element proved by a preponderance of the evidence, it should assume that that element has been proved to a certainty. In other words, the jurors are being told to be bad mathematicians! In the simple case in which the plaintiff, to prove his case (C), must prove just two elements (A and B), and the burden of persuasion is proof by a preponderance of the evidence, and the elements are both independent and equiprobable, so that $p(C) = p(A) \times p(B)$ and $p(A) = p(B)$, then for the plaintiff actually to carry his burden of persuasion ($p(C) > 0.5$) the jury would have to find $p(A) = p(B) > 0.707$, that is, that the probability of each element exceeds 0.707, not, as it will be instructed, 0.5. If the arbitrary assumption of equiprobability is dropped, then the jury would have to find an even higher probability of one or the other element. For example, if it found $p(A)$ to be 0.6, it would have to find $p(B) \geq 0.834$ in order to conclude that the plaintiff had carried his burden of persuasion.

But perhaps the real function of the instruction is different: to indicate to the jury that a chain of inferences cannot be stronger than its weakest link. Even if the plaintiff has proved the defendant's negligence to a certainty, if the probability that the defendant's negligence caused the injury of which the plaintiff is complaining is 0.5 or less the plaintiff should still lose, since causation is an essential element of the negligence tort. As in this example, moreover, the number of elements of a plaintiff's claim is, except for purely formal requirements, rarely more than two, and the two are rarely independent.

Most important, the realistic benchmark for evaluating the plaintiff's case is not the null hypothesis but the defendant's case. Suppose the plaintiff's case has two elements—that a person hit him and that the person was the defendant's employee, elements which are independent of each other—and the jury reckons the probability of the first element at 0.6 and of the second at 0.7, for a joint probability of 0.42. This still leaves the question: What *did* happen? Did the plaintiff fabricate his claim? Was he injured, but by someone else? If the injurer was not the defendant's employee, what was his status? Mulling over these questions the jury may rationally conclude that the plaintiff's story, even though it has doubtful features, is more plausible than the alternative story told by the defendant (maybe the defendant has told *no* story), and therefore that the plaintiff should win. This was the core of Hume's argument against miracles. No doubt it was unlikely that the laws of nature could explain the phenomena attested as miraculous. But it was even less likely that those laws had been suspended in these cases; to put it differently, it was more likely that the witnesses of the alleged miracles were lying or mistaken.[74] As we might put it, the naturalists had proved their case by a preponderance of the evidence.

In Hume's case there were only two possibilities: either the alleged miracles were miracles, or they were not. In a legal case, the plaintiff might tell one story (the story that if true shows that he should win the case), the defendant might tell another, less probable story, and yet there might also be additional possible stories. If the plaintiff's story had a probability of 0.42 of being true, the defendant's story a probability of 0.30 of being true, and the probability that another story or stories is true was 0.28, then the plaintiff should lose because he has failed to prove that his story is more likely than not true.

The essential point, however, is that nothing in probability theory forbids working backward from a joint probability to individual probabilities. After considering all the alternatives, the jury might be quite confident that it was an employee of the defendant who hit the plaintiff. Suppose the jury reckoned that joint probability at 0.7. If one pointed out to the members of the jury that they couldn't have come to this conclusion consistently with reckoning the individual probabilities at 0.7 and 0.6, they would quickly be led to recalculate those probabilities. They would say something like, "Until we considered the case as a whole we didn't realize how *much* more likely than not it was that the plaintiff was indeed hit and that the person who hit him was indeed the defendant's employee."

This discussion bears also on the criticism that Bayes' theorem does not take account of the fact that the weight and completeness of the ev-

---

74. The relevance of Hume's distrust of testimony (see Chapter 10) is that if testimony were always trustworthy, his argument would fail. But it doesn't require philosophical doubts, quite probably misplaced for the reasons explained by Coady's book which I cited in that chapter at note 1, about the validity of testimony to realize that witnesses frequently are mistaken. William Kruskal, "Miracles and Statistics: The Casual Assumption of Independence," 83 *Journal of the American Statistical Association* 929 (1988), thus emphasizes the importance to a proper evaluation of Hume's thesis of whether the testimony of the various witnesses to miracles was independent, in which event the credibility of the testimony would be enhanced.

idence bearing on a hypothesis, and not just the odds that we might give on its correctness if we are betting folk, are important to people's judgments.[75] In fact, weak evidence and missing evidence do affect the odds that a person would be willing to give that some hypothesis was correct. In the bus case, for example, it would be reckless to give odds of 51 to 49 that the plaintiff was hit by a bus owned by Company A were there were no evidence other than the statistic. For the failure of the plaintiff to come up with any other evidence would give rise to an inference that it was actually B's bus that struck the plaintiff, that the plaintiff knows this, and that he has sued A only because B is judgment-proof. Nor does one have to be a gambler to think in terms of odds. A nongambler facing a decision whether to undergo an operation will be interested in the odds of the operation's being successful. Or maybe this example shows that we're all gamblers in a sense.

The significance of Bayes' theorem for the law of evidence is mainly as a reminder that estimating probability is a useful and rational way of dealing with uncertainty, that one should update one's estimates as new information flows in, and that the impact of new information on one's ultimate conclusion depends on one's priors, that is, on the probability that one estimated before beginning to consider evidence. The last point suggests a possible way of thinking about "bias" as a ground for excusing a prospective juror or recusing a judge. Ideally we want the trier of fact to work from prior odds of 1 to 1 that the plaintiff or prosecutor[76] has a meritorious case. A substantial departure from this position, in either direction, marks the trier of fact as biased, with the bad effects that I discussed earlier in reference to the judge who has strong priors in a system in which judges rather than juries are the decision makers. Although the clearest case of bias is where the judge or jury not only has a prior belief about the proper outcome of the case but holds the belief unshakably—that is, refuses to update it on the basis of evidence—it is not a complete response to a charge of bias that

75. See, for example, L. Jonathan Cohen, "The Role of Evidential Weight in Criminal Proof," in *Probability and Inference in the Law of Evidence: The Uses and Limits of Bayesianism*, note 5 above, at 113.

76. I do not think the "presumption of innocence" requires that the judge or jury in a criminal case weight the prior odds in favor of the defendant. The significance of the presumption is in requiring the prosecutor to bear a heavy burden of persuasion, that is, in setting the posterior odds high.

the judge or juror has an "open mind" in the sense of being willing to adjust his probability estimate in the light of the evidence presented at the trial. Any rational person will do that. (What I just called the "clearest case" of bias is thus a case of irrational bias.) The judge's prior odds, if he is a Bayesian, will still have an influence on his posterior odds and hence (at least in a close case—an important qualification for reasons explained earlier) on his decision.

This discussion implies that inquisitorial systems will be less concerned with bias than adversarial ones. If the judge dominates the search for evidence, the problem that his strong (albeit accurate) priors would discourage search by the lawyers and so eventually make his priors less accurate by reducing the flow of relevant information to him is less serious, because the role of the lawyers in the search process is smaller.

We should distinguish between prior beliefs about the proper outcome of the case and those prior beliefs that judges and jurors inevitably and rightly bring to the factfinding process—priors that constitute "common sense," such as the belief that witnesses are likely to shade evidence to make themselves look good. The ideal factfinder is not a *tabula rasa;* he simply reserves judgment on whether the plaintiff or defendant in this particular case should win. But even if impartiality thus means only lacking a prior belief (that is, prior to hearing evidence in the case) about the outcome of the case, it still has a downside: ignorance and inexperience. The problem is especially serious in the case of trial by jury. The strength of the jury system, constituting at least a partial offset to jurors' lack of expertise in adjudication, is its pooling of persons of diverse experience and perspective. When lawyers for both sides are free (as they are) to use peremptory challenges to exclude jurors who seem predisposed in favor of the opposing party, the epistemic diversity of the jury is impaired.[77] Deliberation might be fostered if the system, instead of striving to have jurors whose prior odds are 1 to 1, created balanced panels each composed of jurors having equal but opposite odds in favor of (and against) the plaintiff. But this seems infeasible. Alternatives include reducing the number of peremptory challenges and increasing the size of the jury.

77. Edward P. Schwartz and Warren F. Schwartz, "The Challenge of Peremptory Challenges," 12 *Journal of Law, Economics, and Organization* 325 (1996).

I have limited my discussion thus far to questions of fact, questions, that is, of a "who did what to whom, when, where" character. It is clear that a judge, whether the trial judge or an appellate judge, has a comparative advantage over a jury when it comes to deciding questions of law. But the line between a question of fact and a question of law is not always clear. Negligence is a legal concept; but is the question whether the defendant was negligent a legal or a factual question? The answer usually given is that it is both or neither and is perhaps best described as a "mixed" question of law and fact or a question about the application of a legal concept to a set of facts. I believe, on the contrary, that it is a pure question of fact, and so the law is right to leave it to the jury subject to the same deferential review as other factual determinations that juries make. This is most easily seen when the concept of negligence is expressed in the terms of the Hand formula (see Chapter 1). That is, the defendant is negligent if $B < PL$, which is to say if the burden (cost) of avoiding the accident was less than the cost of the accident (L for loss) discounted (multiplied) by the probability that the accident would occur unless the burden of avoidance was shouldered. Each determination required to apply the formula is factual rather than legal in character: estimating B, P, and L, multiplying P and L, and determining whether PL is larger than B. No legal knowledge is required to make any of these determinations (as would be the case if the jury were asked to decide what negligence is), which when made answer the question whether the defendant was negligent. I believe, but will not try to demonstrate here, that most other questions (called by lawyers "mixed questions of fact and law" or "ultimate questions of fact") concerning the correct application to the facts of the case of a legal standard, such as possession, voluntariness, and good faith, could similarly be decomposed into pure questions of fact.

~ 12

The Rules of Evidence

$\mathcal{T}$HE FEDERAL RULES OF EVIDENCE, enacted by Congress in 1975 and amended from time to time since (most recently in 1998), together with the Notes of the Advisory Committee on the Rules of Evidence, constitute a compendious as well as authoritative guide to the modern law of evidence. I shall use these rules as the skeleton of my further discussion of evidence law, skipping however a number of the less important or less problematic provisions. Besides these omissions, it is important to note that the formal rules of evidence codify only a fraction of the law of evidence. Some of the most important rules of evidence, being limited to particular fields of substantive law, are classified as parts of those fields rather than as parts of the law of evidence. Examples from tort law are the doctrine of res ipsa loquitur, the awarding of damages for loss of a chance (eliding intractable issues of proof), and (to the same end) rules allocating liability among negligent defendants when the causal contribution of each cannot be determined. Examples from contract law are the parol evidence and "four corners" rules and the statute of frauds, all designed to reduce the number of intractable credibility issues in trials for breach of contract. Likewise affecting the evidentiary process are the laws punishing perjury, which are classified with criminal law rather than evidence law, and statutes of limitations, which reduce the likelihood that questions concerning events in the distant past will have to be answered at trial. Of particular importance in criminal trials today, the federal sentencing guidelines direct the sentencing judge, in cases in which the defendant testifies, to impose additional punishment (for obstruction of justice) if the judge determines that the defendant perjured himself.

The evidentiary rules embedded in tort and contract law, the imposition of criminal sanctions for perjury and obstruction of justice, and statutes of limitations show, incidentally, that the law is not entirely naive about the ability of judges and juries to resolve credibility issues. In most cases, as the law recognizes, there are no completely reliable methods of determining whether a witness is testifying truthfully. As I pointed out in Chapter 10, a witness may be a good actor, in the sense of a person able to create the appearance of honesty, or a good liar, in the sense of a person able to weave a plausible and internally consistent fiction, or both.

I begin with Rule 103(a), which provides among other things that a ruling admitting or excluding evidence cannot be made the basis of a motion for a new trial or of reversal on appeal "unless a substantial right of the party [against whom the ruling went] is affected." In other words, harmless errors will be overlooked. The harmless error doctrine is not limited to evidentiary rulings, but, partly because such rulings are so frequent in a trial, they are the most frequent candidates for harmless error treatment. More important, judgments of harmlessness depend on assumptions about the understanding of the trier of fact.

Harmless error plays a particularly important role in criminal appeals, and they are the focus of my discussion. Because most criminal defendants do not pay for their lawyer, they will appeal their conviction or sentence even if the probability of reversal is slight; although the expected benefits of appealing may be slight, the expected costs are zero. Minor errors therefore figure prominently in criminal appeals and this makes clear the need for a doctrine of harmless error to head off remands that would be all costs and no benefits. But despite the common-sense (and economic) appeal of the harmless error principle, it may often confer an undeserved, or at least unintended, advantage on prosecutors.[1] The rule is biased in their favor because the appellate court, not having witnessed the trial (and, especially, not having ob-

---

1. As a practical matter, only prosecutors benefit from the rule in criminal cases, so rare are appeals by prosecutors.

served the jury), lacks good information for assessing the likelihood that the errors affected the outcome. The appellate court perforce assesses the likely effect of the errors on the *average* jury, whereas the prosecutor may know that the particular jury before which he is prosecuting the defendant has an above-average propensity to acquit so that he may have to manipulate the jury's emotions if he is to secure a conviction. And so an error may look harmless to the appellate court yet have been harmful. Moreover, it takes a highly disciplined judge to vote to reverse a conviction when he thinks the defendant guilty even if he acknowledges to himself that the defendant might have been acquitted but for an error at trial and so is entitled by law to a new trial.

The foregoing analysis can be formalized as follows. Let p be the probability of conviction; a the probability of affirmance given conviction (the prosecutor is assumed to be unable to appeal, and the defendant is assumed to appeal in every case in which there is a conviction), so that $1 - a$ is the probability of reversal; b the benefit to the prosecutor or prosecution-minded judge of a conviction; c the cost of a trial to the prosecutor (for simplicity, assume that the cost to him of defending an appeal by the defendant is zero—it will in fact usually be quite low relative to the cost of trial); x the set of tactics that involve violating procedural and evidentiary rules that favor the defense;[2] and y the other inputs into getting a conviction. Increases in x and y increase p, the probability of conviction; increases in x also decrease a, the probability that a conviction will be affirmed; increases in y also increase c.

If the prosecutor employs x, there are three possible consequences: conviction followed by affirmance; conviction followed by reversal followed by a retrial at which, we can assume, the variables are as they would have been in the first trial if $x = 0$; and acquittal, which generates no gain to the prosecutor and leaves him with a net loss measured by c. The prosecutor's net expected gain (G) when he employs x is therefore the sum of his gain if there is an affirmed conviction $(p(x,y)b - c(x,y))$, his gain if there is a reversed conviction followed by a retrial $(p(x,y)(p(y)b - c(y)))$ which may end in acquittal or conviction, and his (negative) gain if there is acquittal $(0 - c(x,y))$, with the first gain being

2. Perhaps the most common such tactic is inviting (without actually asking—that would be reversible error) the jury to infer the defendant's guilt from his failure to take the stand. This "abuse," however, is an artifact of the existence of the privilege against being forced to incriminate oneself—a privilege that, as we shall see, is not easy to justify on economic or other grounds.

discounted by the probability of affirmance (a) and the second by the probability of reversal $(1 - a)$. Thus,

(1) $\qquad G = a(x)p(x,y)b - c(x,y) + p(x,y)(1 - a(x))(p(y)b - c(y))$
$\qquad\qquad - c(x,y)$

(The reason that p and c are not shown as functions of x in the reversal-retrial state of the world is that by assumption $x = 0$ in that state.)

The effect of x (abusive tactics) on G is complex. It raises G by increasing the probability of a conviction but lowers it by increasing the probability of a reversal of the conviction and by increasing the prosecutor's costs. The possibility that the net effect is to increase G thus cannot be excluded and is increased if we consider the substitutability of x for y (of violating procedural or evidentiary rules for other inputs into obtaining a conviction). For then the effect of using abusive tactics, while it includes as before reducing the probability of a conviction that will stick and thus increasing the likelihood of having to incur the cost of a second trial ($c(y)$), is also to reduce the cost of the first trial. This is an additional reason to believe that if the effect of abusive tactics in reducing the probability that the defendant's conviction will be affirmed is low because of the harmless error rule, the rule encourages deliberate error by the prosecution. This is especially likely if the substitution effect of x on y is large, that is, if abusive tactics are a cheap and effective substitute for legitimate forensic tactics.

Even if the doctrine of harmless error thus invites prosecutors to commit deliberate errors, this might be efficient if prosecutors only committed such errors when faced with a jury *irrationally* prone to acquit. That might indeed be the consequence of the doctrine if appellate courts were omniscient. For then they could forgive prosecutorial errors if but only if the defendant was in fact guilty. If, however, the appellate court cannot tell whether the defendant is guilty—if all it knows is whether an average jury would have convicted the defendant had it not been for the errors—then the prosecutor may have an incentive to use deliberate errors to convict the innocent. How great an incentive, one does not know; it depends on the weight of purely careerist ambitions in prosecutorial utility functions. To be on the safe side, one might wish to modify the doctrine of harmless error to exclude from its operation *deliberate* errors committed or induced by prosecutors and make these cause for automatic reversal.

Federal Rule of Evidence 105 directs the judge to instruct the jury to limit its consideration of evidence admissible for one purpose (or against one party) but not for another. The assumption is that although the jury heard the inadmissible evidence, it is capable of disregarding it if instructed to do so. The assumption is not always indulged. For example, if the admissibility of a confession is in issue, the issue must be heard outside of the jury's hearing (Rule 104(c)), since if the confession were to be ruled inadmissible the jurors could not be expected to put it out of their minds in deciding whether the defendant was guilty. But in general, limiting instructions are deemed efficacious, not only in the circumstances with which Rule 105 deals but also when used to "cure" the erroneous or inadvertent admission of inadmissible evidence: the judge tells the jury to disregard it.

Empirical evidence as well as common sense suggests that courts greatly exaggerate the efficacy of limiting instructions.[3] A limiting instruction is very likely to be completely ineffectual unless the judge is able to explain why, as with certain types of hearsay, the evidence isn't probative. If it is probative (or emotionally compelling),[4] though inadmissible, the limiting instruction seems more likely to rivet the jurors' attention to the evidence than to get them to disregard it even if the judge explains the basis for the instruction.[5] For this reason, lawyers will often not request a limiting instruction though entitled to it. And notice how in a criminal trial the deemed but doubtful efficacy of limiting instructions cooperates with the doctrine of harmless error in encouraging prosecutors to resort to abusive tactics if they fear that acquittal is likely otherwise. For the likeliest response to an improper question or comment is neither a mistrial nor a reversal, but an impotent limiting instruction.

There is, it is true, a difference between belief and acceptance. Belief is involuntary, so telling someone not to believe something without

3. See Michael J. Saks, "What Do Jury Experiments Tell Us about How Juries (Should) Make Decisions?" 6 *Southern California Interdisciplinary Law Journal* 1, 26 (1997), and studies cited there.

4. The standard example is a gruesome photograph of a murder victim. On the capacity of such photographs to prejudice the jury's consideration of the logically distinct issue of guilt, see Kevin S. Douglas, David R. Lyons, and James R. P. Ogloff, "The Impact of Graphic Photographic Evidence on Mock Jurors' Decisions in a Murder Trial: Probative or Prejudicial?" 21 *Law and Human Behavior* 485 (1997).

5. For evidence, see Kerri L. Pickel, "Inducing Jurors to Disregard Inadmissible Evidence: A Legal Explanation Does Not Help," 19 *Law and Human Behavior* 407, 422–423 (1995).

giving him a reason to think that it is not credible is ineffective to alter the person's beliefs; that is the basis of skepticism about limiting instructions. But antiskeptics might point out that one can refuse to act on a belief. You might believe the defendant guilty yet accept that he should be acquitted because you don't believe it with the requisite degree of certitude.[6] In other words, burden of persuasion is properly regarded as involving acceptance rather than belief. The prior odds, the posterior odds, the likelihood ratios created by particular pieces of evidence are all matters of belief; but what posterior odds shall give the victory to plaintiff or defendant is a matter of acceptance. And this is a distinction that jurors should be able to understand.

The problem with using this insight to rehabilitate the limiting instruction is that when a jury is deliberating, it is very difficult for it to disregard the inadmissible evidence that it heard and was told to ignore, even if it wants to do so, and base judgment only on the admissible evidence. If jurors were explicit Bayesians, and calculated likelihood ratios for each bit of evidence, then they could disregard the evidence that they had heard but been told to ignore. They don't proceed in this fashion, but instead intuitively, and they cannot be expected to determine the posterior odds on the basis of less than all the evidence they heard, the essential point being that the posterior odds are founded on belief rather than on acceptance.

When the ineffectuality of limiting instructions is pointed out, judges tend to respond that the jury system *presupposes* that jurors obey the instructions given them by the judge.[7] By this the judges seem to mean that the jury system would have to be abandoned if the presupposition were acknowledged to be incorrect. That is untrue. The jury sys-

6. See L. Jonathan Cohen, *An Essay on Belief and Acceptance* 117–125 (1992).

7. "Our theory of trial relies upon the ability of a jury to follow instructions." Opper v. United States, 348 U.S. 84, 95 (1954). A "crucial assumption underlying our constitutional system of trial by jury [is] that jurors carefully follow instructions." Francis v. Franklin, 471 U.S. 307, 324 n. 9 (1985). "A central assumption of our jurisprudence is that juries follow the instructions they receive." United States v. Castillo, 140 F.3d 874, 884 (10th Cir. 1998). Not all judges fool themselves. Learned Hand, for example, called the limiting instruction "the recommendation to the jury of a mental gymnastic which is beyond, not only their powers, but anybody's else." Nash v. United States, 54 F.2d 1006, 1007 (2d Cir. 1932). Occasionally courts concede the ineffectuality of a limiting instruction. See, for example, Bruton v. United States, 391 U.S. 123 (1968) (reversing conviction where jury was permitted to consider a codefendant's confession that implicated the defendant).

tem presupposes *some* degree of compliance by jurors with the rules laid down by the judge to guide them, but not 100 percent. Perfect compliance with rules is rarely attained in any department of life, and is particularly unlikely in the case of an ad hoc body that has only weak incentives to comply, since jurors are neither penalized for bad performance nor rewarded for good. It is not even clear that jurors pay much attention to the instructions on the law, as opposed to instructions to disregard particular evidence, and yet as we saw earlier such lack of attention need not fatally undermine the rationality of the jury system.

The Federal Rules of Evidence define relevance as "having any tendency to make the existence of any fact that is of consequence to the determination of the action more probable or less probable than it would be without the evidence" (Rule 401). The rules make relevant evidence admissible and irrelevant evidence inadmissible (Rule 402), but relevant evidence may be excluded "if its probative value is substantially outweighed by the danger of unfair prejudice, confusion of the issues, or misleading the jury, or by considerations of undue delay, waste of time, or needless presentation of cumulative evidence" (Rule 403). These rules make economic sense. In Bayesian terms, evidence is relevant if its likelihood ratio is different from 1 and irrelevant if it is 1.[8] Irrelevant evidence so defined has zero social benefits, though it may confer a private benefit by confusing or prejudicing the jury.

The Advisory Committee Notes to Rule 401 point out that evidence can be relevant even though it bears on an undisputed fact, because it may help to make the fact clear—and thus assist in establishing correct likelihood ratios. If a relevant fact is unclear, though undisputed, the jury may not give it the proper weight in its calculations. A related point, borrowed from signaling theory, is that a certain amount of redundancy may increase rather than reduce the intelligibility of a communication.[9]

Rule 403, in requiring an explicit comparison of benefit and cost, is central to an economic analysis of the law of evidence in much the same way that the Hand formula is central to the economic analysis of the law of torts. It sets forth a cost-benefit formula for deciding the most common question in the law of evidence, which is whether to admit or

---

8. See Richard O. Lempert, "Modeling Relevance," 75 *Michigan Law Review* 1021 (1977).
9. David A. Schum, *The Evidential Foundations of Probabilistic Reasoning* 443 (1994).

exclude evidence. It bears the same relation to Equation (4) in Chapter 11 ($-p_x S = c_x$), the economic formula for the optimal amount of evidence, as the Hand formula does to the economic formula for the optimal amount of care ($-p_x L = c_x$).[10] The cost-benefit formula implicit in Rule 403 can also be used to evaluate particular rules of evidence,[11] just as the Hand formula is used in economic analysis of law as a standard for evaluating specific rules of tort law. Rule 403 does, it is true, place a thumb on the scale ("*substantially* outweighed"), but this may be necessary to prevent the judge from taking over the factfinding task from the jury by excluding most of the evidence that favors the side the judge thinks should lose.

Rule 403 is not as carefully drafted as it could be. It runs together three distinct grounds for excluding relevant evidence: (1) emotionality (one source of "unfair prejudice" and of "misleading the jury"), (2) cognitive overload ("confusion" and other forms of "misleading the jury"), and (3) "waste of time" (which seems synonymous with "undue delay" and "needless presentation of cumulative evidence"). At a first pass, the first two grounds relate to the cognitive limitations of the trier of fact, and so go to the benefits of the evidence in determining truth, while the third goes to cost, the right-hand side of Equations (1) through (4) in Chapter 11. But this is not precise. To begin with, two distinct types of cognitive limitation should be distinguished. The first, often called "bounded rationality" and encountered in Chapter 8, arises from the fact that people do not have zero costs of absorbing and analyzing information, and so encounter problems of overload. This type of cognitive limitation is entirely consistent with rationality, which does not presuppose zero costs of acquiring and processing information. The second type of cognitive limitation, however, is the domain of the cog-

---

10. I have relabeled D as L and A as c, in William M. Landes and Richard A. Posner, *The Economic Structure of Tort Law* 60 (1987) (eq. 3.9), to highlight the isomorphism of the formula for the optimal amount of care with Equation (4). The cost-benefit interpretation of Rule 403 is mentioned in Louis Kaplow, Note, "The Theoretical Foundation of the Hearsay Rules," 93 *Harvard Law Review* 1786, 1789 (1980). See also Thomas Gibbons and Allan C. Hutchinson, "The Practice and Theory of Evidence Law—A Note," 2 *International Review of Law and Economics* 119 (1982).

11. This was essentially Bentham's approach. He thought that there should be no rules of evidence, but that in particular cases the judge should be allowed to exclude particular items of evidence on grounds of "vexation, expense, and delay." Jeremy Bentham, *Rationale of Judicial Evidence*, vol. 1, p. 1 (J. S. Mill ed. 1827).

nitive illusions and emotional distractions, the domain of irrational thinking, also discussed in Chapter 8. Ground (1) (what I've called emotionality) corresponds to this second type of cognitive limitation and ground (2) (cognitive overload) to the first. Keeping evidence from the jury is an alternative to what might be time-consuming and ineffectual efforts at enlarging and debiasing the jury's cognitive capacities.

Another way to think about this function of Rule 403 and of the rules of evidence generally is as a corrective to the jury's lack of incentive to overcome its cognitive limitations by "thinking hard" about the issues that it is asked to resolve. Jurors have no monetary incentives to do a careful job; by screening from them evidentiary materials that would make their job even more difficult and thus require them to exert greater mental efforts without any compensation, the rules of evidence reduce the jurors' costs and so increase their product.

Ground (2) also interacts with (3) (waste of time): repetition and protraction can make it harder for the trier of fact to make a correct judgment, as well as increasing the direct costs of the trial. As more and more evidence is introduced, additional evidence even if relevant is likely both to be wasteful in the sense of yielding diminishing benefits in greater accuracy with no corresponding diminution in cost and confusing in the sense of actually reducing accuracy. This point suggests that the optimal length of a jury trial may in most cases be quite short; the benefits of additional evidence are likely to decline at an accelerating rate while the costs are constant—or even rise—as the litigants cast further and further afield.

We can explore this point by modifying Equation (1) in Chapter 11 to allow the amount of evidence (x) to have both a positive and a negative effect on the probability of a true result, as in

$$(2) \qquad B(x) = p(b_1 x - b_2 x^2)S - c(x)$$

where b_1 measures the effect of a unit of x in increasing the accuracy of the trial and b_2 its effect in decreasing that accuracy by confusing or overloading the jury. The latter effect is assumed to increase at an increasing rate with increases in the amount of evidence (hence the squaring of x). Depending on the values of b_1 and b_2, adding evidence may, beyond some point, actually reduce the accuracy of the trial and thus reduce efficiency even if the additional evidence is costless. Alternatively, confusion and overload could be thought of as indirect costs of evidence that increase with the amount of evidence, in which event the last term in Equation (1) in Chapter 11 ($c(x)$) might be approximated by $c_d x + c_i x^2$, where c_d is the direct costs of the evidence and c_i the indirect costs.

Evidence that is cumulative must be distinguished from evidence necessary to complete a mosaic of proof. A costly bit of "additional" evidence might be justified because it linked up with other evidence to establish the truth convincingly.

Notice how by excluding irrelevant, and also relevant but on balance unhelpful, evidence, Rules 402 and 403 counteract the incentive of the parties in some cases to overinvest in evidence from a social standpoint. We should expect these rules to be invoked most often in big-money cases, for it is in such cases that the risk of overinvestment is greatest.

The subsequent rules in Article IV of the Federal Rules of Evidence particularize the general standard of Rule 403 with reference to recurrent issues. Rule 404 excludes (with various exceptions)[12] evidence of a person's character when used to show that he probably acted "in character" on the occasion involved in the litigation. The principal consequence is to exclude evidence that a criminal defendant has a criminal record unless, as we shall see, he testifies. Such evidence is relevant, because a person who has committed a crime in the past has by doing so indicated a below-average propensity to comply with the criminal laws. But it is only weakly probative, especially since repeat offenders are punished more heavily than first-time offenders in part precisely to offset any greater propensity to commit crimes that their previous offenses or offenses have revealed. If recidivists are punished heavily enough, the propensity to commit a second or subsequent offense may be reduced to the same level as the propensity to commit a first offense.

The principal concern with this class of evidence, however, is not lack of probative value. It is the danger that a jury will give such evidence too much weight, or, what is more likely, that it will convict on less evidence, believing that it doesn't much matter if the defendant is innocent of the particular crime for which he is being tried, since he is a member of the criminal class and probably has committed other crimes for which he has not been punished.

---

12. Most of the rules contain exceptions; this qualification should be borne in mind throughout, as I do not repeat it.

The Rule 404 exclusion is somewhat porous, though. For one thing, evidence of prior crimes may be used to prove facts other than propensity, such as motive, absence of mistake, or *modus operandi* (see Rule 404(b)). If, for example, a defendant is being tried for the murder of a witness who had been responsible for the defendant's earlier conviction, that conviction would be admissible to prove the defendant's motive for committing the present crime. There is also a blanket exception when the defendant is charged with rape or child sexual molestation and the prior crimes involved similar acts.[13] The exception may have an economic rationale—most clearly in the molestation case—that is closely related to the motive exception in Rule 404(b). Most people do not have a taste for sexually molesting children. As between two possible molesters, then, only one of whom has a history of such molestation, the history establishes a motive that enables the two suspects to be distinguished; and prior-crimes evidence is admissible to prove motive. Unlike a molester, a thief, unless he is a kleptomaniac, does not have a taste for theft. Theft is merely instrumental to his desire for money, and there are many substitute instruments. The fact that a defendant accused of theft committed a prior theft doesn't show that he "likes" theft and so does not furnish a motive for his committing the current theft with which he's charged.

It has been argued that a rational juror, aware of the inadmissibility of prior-crimes evidence, and so knowing that he won't find out whether the defendant is a habitual or first-time offender, will assume that that there is some probability greater than zero but less than 1 that the defendant is indeed a habitual offender, and so will underestimate the guilt of the habitual offender and overestimate that of the first-time offender.[14] The assumption that jurors behave in such a way is exceedingly unrealistic, and the authors present no evidence that it is nevertheless correct. Their better point is that if prior-crimes evidence were freely admissible, and jurors were highly prone to convict habitual offenders whether or not the evidence showed guilt, deterrence would be undermined. The expected cost of punishment of habitual offenders would fall because that cost is a function not of the probability of punishment per se, but, as I noted earlier, of the difference between

13. Fed. R. Evid. 413, 414; cf. Fed. R. Evid. 415.

14. See Joel Schrag and Suzanne Scotchmer, "Crime and Prejudice: The Use of Character Evidence in Criminal Trials," 10 *Journal of Law, Economics, and Organization* 319 (1994).

the probability of punishment given guilt and the probability of punishment given innocence. (A partial offset, however, is that there would be an additional disincentive to *becoming* a habitual offender.) The expected cost of punishment of first-time offenders would fall also. Prosecutors would find it so much easier to convict habitual offenders whether or not guilty that their incentives to prosecute first-time offenders would be impaired, assuming that prosecutors operate with a budget constraint and, as suggested in Chapter 11, want to maximize convictions weighted by length of sentence, subject to that constraint.

The most important exception to the exclusion of character evidence, found in Rule 609, concerns the use of such evidence in cross-examination. If a defendant has been convicted within the previous ten years of a crime involving fraud or other deceit, the prosecutor (or plaintiff—the rule applies to civil cases as well as criminal ones and to all witnesses, not just the parties) has a right to use that conviction on cross-examination to "impeach" (challenge the credibility of) the defendant's testimony. Any other felony conviction within the ten-year period can be used for this purpose as well if the judge concludes that its probative value outweighs its prejudicial effect.

The rationale of the rule is that a person who has flouted the criminal law in the past is unlikely to take seriously his oath to testify truthfully. This may be; but it is doubtful that he is *more* unlikely to take his oath seriously than a first-time offender who thinks he can lie his way to an acquittal.[15] That is, there is no basis for supposing recidivists more likely than first-time offenders to lie; both are criminals, and the incentive of a criminal to lie seems unrelated to whether he has committed one crime or more than one. What is probably true, though only loosely related (through the heavier punishment of recidivists) to whether the defendant is a recidivist, is that a defendant is more likely to lie the heavier the punishment he faces if he's convicted. If so, then the relevant datum is the punishment he faces, not whether he is a recidivist as such. On balance, there is probably no benefit in enhanced accuracy to allowing prior-crimes evidence to be used in cross-examination. But there is a cost—the same cost as allowing prior-crimes evidence to be used to prove a criminal propensity. Despite the limiting instruction to which the defendant is entitled, the jury cannot be ex-

---

15. If the defendant is innocent, presumably he will give truthful testimony.

pected to confine its consideration of prior-crimes evidence to the issue of the defendant's credibility. By reducing the probability that a habitual offender who testifies will be acquitted, and so by deterring habitual offenders from testifying—and with much the same effect, since the jury is apt to infer guilt from the defendant's failing to testify (and this, once again, regardless of any limiting instructions)—the rule undermines the deterrence of habitual offenders.

Rule 407 excludes evidence that the defendant took remedial measures after the accident or other incident that is the basis of the plaintiff's suit. I mentioned the rule in the preceding chapter and suggested that its purpose is to encourage such measures. I recur to it here in order to consider another possibility, that the rule is designed to combat hindsight bias—what in prospect may have been highly unlikely may in retrospect appear to have been inevitable.

To the extent that that is the rule's purpose, I suspect that the rule is unnecessary. Hindsight bias is the cognitive illusion of which we are all aware, as is indicated by the currency of such expressions as "the wisdom of hindsight." What is more, the concept of a "freak accident" is familiar, and it encapsulates the idea that accidents can be *very* low probability events. One might expect the defendant's lawyer to be able to explain to a jury that while of course the accident did happen, the probability that it would have happened was slight.[16] Furthermore, hindsight bias is often rational, for example when the occurrence of an accident shows that a hypothetical possibility was a real one; and thus it is often not an illusion at all.[17]

Granted there is experimental evidence that juries are subject to the irrational form of hindsight bias.[18] But the evidence is limited and also

16. For experimental evidence that hindsight bias can be reduced or even eliminated by emphasizing the role of chance in human affairs and hence the probabilistic character of many events, see David Wasserman, Richard O. Lempert, and Reid Hastie, "Hindsight and Causality," 17 *Personality and Social Psychology Bulletin* 30 (1991).

17. See Mark Kelman, "Behavioral Economics as Part of a Rhetorical Duet: A Response to Jolls, Sunstein, and Thaler," 50 *Stanford Law Review* 1577, 1583–1584 (1998); Mark Kelman, David E. Fallas, and Hilary Folger, "Decomposing Hindsight Bias," 16 *Journal of Risk and Uncertainty* 251 (1998).

18. See Susan J. LaBine and Gary LaBine, "Determinations of Negligence and the Hindsight Bias," 20 *Law and Human Behavior* 501 (1996); Kim A. Kamin and Jeffrey J. Rachlinski, "Ex Post ≠ Ex Ante: Determining Liability in Hindsight," 19 *Law and Human Behavior* 89 (1995). In contrast, in an experimental study using state court judges as the experimental subjects, W. Kip Viscusi, "How Do Judges Think about Risk?" 1 *American Law and Economics Review* 26 (1999), found much less hindsight bias than the previous studies had found.

weak—though not because it is based on experiments using mock juries. Even though the behavior of mock juries cannot automatically be extrapolated to real ones, an experiment designed to test a difference (such as between an ex ante and an ex post determination of care) need not be invalidated by the discrepancy between experimental and real-world conditions.[19] To reject the studies of hindsight because the experimental subjects were not real jurors one would need a reason to think that if mock jurors exhibit hindsight bias, real ones do not; and it is by no means obvious what that reason would be. The problems with the studies are particular rather than general. In neither the LaBine and LaBine nor the Kamin and Rachlinski study were the juries instructed on burden of proof; in neither did they deliberate; and in both they may have favored liability in the ex post situation not because of hindsight bias but because of their substantive views on liability (many jurors probably believe that people who cause accidents should pay for them regardless of fault).[20] There is experimental evidence that deliberation increases the accuracy of jury verdicts.[21] And the fact that an instruction that warned the jury about hindsight bias had no effect in the Kamin and Rachlinski study (no such instruction was given in the LaBine and LaBine study) supports the conjecture that what looks like hindsight bias is really just a difference in substantive standards. Of course this point cannot be of much comfort to supporters of the jury, since it implies that the jury is disobeying the law; and such disobedience will generate legally unsound outcomes as surely as cognitive illusions will.

Concerning the broader issue whether cognitive illusions seriously undermine the accuracy of the factfinding process in trials and if so what ought to be done, given that judges may be subject to them to the same or almost the same extent as jurors, I point out that if the direction of the resulting bias is known it can be offset by revising other features of the legal process. Suppose, for example, that juries have a pro-

19. Saks, note 3 above, at 8.

20. See LaBine and LaBine, note 18 above, at 512; Kamin and Rachlinski, note 18 above, at 100–101; Kelman, note 17 above, at 1584. Hence Rule 411 excludes evidence that the defendant had liability insurance.

21. See, for example, Reid Hastie, David Schkade, and John Payne, "A Study of Juror and Jury Judgments in Civil Cases: Deciding Liability for Punitive Damages," 22 *Law and Human Behavior* 287, 305–306 (1998); Gail S. Goodman et al., "Face-to-Face Confrontation: Effects of Closed-Circuit Technology on Children's Eyewitness Testimony and Jurors' Decisions," 22 *Law and Human Behavior* 165, 200 (1998).

pensity to acquit guilty defendants but judges do not have a propensity
either to acquit guilty defendants or to convict innocent ones. Then, as
we saw earlier, the innocent defendants will tend to waive their right to
a jury; and so we need to worry only or mainly about the guilty ones.
We can discourage them from exercising their right to trial by jury by
increasing the reward for "acceptance of responsibility," which under
the federal sentencing guidelines is essentially a sentencing discount
for pleading guilty and thus waiving all trial rights. Jacking up the reward for pleading guilty need not be done by reducing the sentences of
those who plead guilty and thus undermining deterrence. It can equally
well be done by increasing the sentences of those who do not plead
guilty.

Hearsay or secondhand evidence is evidence of what someone who is
not a witness said, offered to establish the truth of what the out-of-
court declarant said. One might have thought that a rule governing the
admissibility of hearsay evidence would be a footnote to Rule 403, but
instead, because of the rule's complexity, it gets its own article of the
Federal Rules of Evidence (Article VIII). More radically, one might
wonder why there needs to be a hearsay rule at all. The only reason to
have rules excluding evidence that does not impose indirect costs (evidence such as that of subsequent repairs) is that the inexperienced trier
of fact, the jury, will give too much weight to the evidence even if given
a limiting instruction or other guidance by the judge. But much of the
"evidence" on which people act in their personal lives and their careers
is hearsay, so one might expect them to be experienced in sifting and
weighing hearsay evidence. As I noted in Chapter 10, from the standpoint of the judge or jury *all* evidence in a case is secondhand.

Even so, the hearsay rule can probably be justified by the "waste of
time" factor in Rule 403, or more precisely the costs of the trial process. Because the jury, unlike the judiciary in an inquisitorial system,
does not engage in an active search for evidence, it cannot terminate
the evidentiary process at the point at which the benefits of a further
search would exceed the costs. The hearsay rule helps to do this for the
jury by excluding an indefinite mass of generally dubious evidence.[22]
The many exceptions to the rule allow into evidence those forms of

22. For a contrary view, argued from a broadly economic perspective, see Kaplow, note 10
above, at 1794–1803.

hearsay that have probative value equivalent to that of firsthand evidence, a good example being a statement against the witness's pecuniary or penal interest—a kind of statement that one is unlikely to make unless it is true. The hearsay rule can also be understood as working in tandem with Rules 402 and 403 to counteract the incentives operating in some cases to overinvest in evidence. Still, it might be better to discard the categorical rule against hearsay—a rule that has so many exceptions as to be a veritable Swiss cheese—in favor of the flexible standard of Rule 403. Then particular items of hearsay evidence would be excluded not because they were hearsay but because, in the circumstances, their probative value was insufficient to justify the time and cognitive effort required to admit and evaluate them.[23]

Rule 501 of the rules of evidence deals with "privilege," that is, the right of a party to exclude evidence on grounds normally unrelated to the interest in accuracy. The rule does not enumerate the privileges recognized in federal litigation but provides merely that the existence of privilege shall be governed by federal or, where appropriate, state common law, except as superseded by statutes or the Constitution. I shall examine the more important privileges, beginning with the marital privileges, of which there are two. The *testimonial* privilege applies to all communications, whether made before or during the marriage, the public disclosure of which might undermine the marriage; but only the spouse asked to testify can invoke this privilege. The *marital-communications* privilege, the one I'll focus on, can be invoked by either spouse but is limited to communications made during the marriage. Its rationale is similar to that of the rule on subsequent remedial measures: collateral costs. A confession to one's spouse that one had committed a crime would be highly probative evidence of guilt, but is excluded out of fear of weakening the marriage by making spouses distrustful of each other. That the fear is justified is doubtful. The privilege might actually induce some people to marry who wouldn't otherwise, and marriages induced by a desire for evidentiary advantage are unlikely to be stable. More important, by lowering the cost of crime for married people, the privilege encourages (though no doubt only very slightly) such people to commit crimes; and the commission of a crime by a spouse is a

23. Essentially the position advocated in Richard D. Friedman, "Truth and Its Rivals in the Law of Hearsay and Confrontation," 49 *Hastings Law Journal* 545, 550–560 (1998).

highly destabilizing event for a marriage. A stronger argument could be made for the privilege if it were limited to civil cases.

Even if the benefits of marital privilege are slight, the costs in valuable evidence forgone may also be slight and so on balance there may be little gain from abolition. If the privilege were abolished and this were widely known, spouses would be much less likely to make damaging admissions to each other; and so abolition would not create a cornucopia of valuable evidence. This is in contrast to Rule 407. Allowing evidence of subsequent repairs to be introduced at a trial would reduce the incentive to make such repairs but would not come close to eliminating it, because of the benefits of the repairs in averting future liability. Indeed, those benefits may be so great as to justify abolishing the rule. But my point is only that abolishing the rule would generate some evidence. The benefits of admitting wrongful conduct to one's spouse are smaller than the benefits of taking measures to avoid otherwise quite likely future liability, and so abolishing marital privilege might cause such admissions to quite dry up.

The most important privilege is the lawyer-client privilege: the lawyer cannot be forced to divulge statements made to him by his client in the course of their professional relationship. I want to focus on the application of this privilege to statements made in the course or contemplation of litigation, rather than to statements made in the course of seeking legal advice with respect to contemplated acts.[24] As in the case of a confession to one's spouse, a confession to one's lawyer would be highly probative evidence of guilt. The rationale for its exclusion is that the adversary process would not work well if parties could not speak to their lawyers in complete confidence. To evaluate this rationale, we must consider, as with the subsequent-repairs rule and the marital privileges, what the consequences of abrogating the lawyer-client privilege would be. One consequence would be to make clients much more guarded about what they told their lawyers. As a result, not much valuable evidence would be obtained by making lawyers subject to being called as witnesses against their clients. So once again the benefits of abolishing the privilege, unless "chilling" lawyer-client conversations were considered a public good, would be slight. Another consequence

24. The different considerations applicable to the two types of statement are emphasized in Louis Kaplow and Steven Shavell, "Legal Advice about Information to Present in Litigation: Its Effects and Social Desirability," 102 *Harvard Law Review* 565 (1989).

of abolishing the lawyer-client privilege would be that potential litigants would invest more in learning at least the rudiments of law so that they could speak to their lawyers with minimum risk of making damaging admissions. Abrogating the privilege might thus increase enrollment at law schools!

Third, lawyers, fearful of extracting damaging admissions from their clients, might fail to elicit from them information that the client was unaware would demonstrate that his case had merit.[25] Fourth, and probably most important, abrogation would encumber the trial process and confuse juries. The same person might be appearing both as the advocate for a party and as a witness against that party—that, or the party would have to change lawyers as soon as he discovered that he had made a damaging admission to his current lawyer. He might have to change lawyers more than once, since he would be telling his story to each new lawyer in turn.

The case for an evidentiary privilege is greatly weakened if the people entitled to invoke it either don't know about it or would not be affected by its abrogation.[26] In the limiting case, where abolition of a privilege would have no deterrent effect on the creation of evidence, abolition would be all benefits and no costs. The lawyer-client privilege is well known, but consider the psychotherapist-patient privilege. Apparently most people are unaware that such a privilege exists[27]—and how many people of the few who are aware of it, and who were minded to consult a psychotherapist despite the continuing stigma that mental illness carries in our society, would be deterred by fear that the psychotherapist might someday be called as a witness against him?[28]

The point I've been emphasizing that abrogating rules of privilege might yield only a meager evidentiary harvest is applicable as well to the much-criticized rule excluding evidence obtained by an illegal search or seizure. Such evidence generally is highly probative, and

25. This point is emphasized in Ronald J. Allen et al., "A Positive Theory of the Attorney-Client Privilege and the Work Product Doctrine," 19 *Journal of Legal Studies* 359 (1990).

26. See American Bar Association, Section of Litigation, "Civil Trial Practice Standards" 100–102 (Feb. 1998).

27. Daniel W. Shuman and Myron S. Weiner, "The Privilege Study: An Empirical Examination of the Psychotherapist-Patient Privilege," 60 *North Carolina Law Review* 893, 925 (1982).

28. Some; the dispute giving rise to litigation might cause psychological distress that would prompt one to consult a psychotherapist, provided it would not hurt one's litigation chances.

sometimes essential, and its exclusion has seemed a disproportionate sanction for police misconduct. Yet most of the people who make this criticism do not argue that the misconduct should be condoned, or redefined as proper conduct; they merely advocate the substitution of other sanctions that would not involve excluding the fruits of the illegal search. But if the substitute sanctions were effective in deterring the misconduct, there wouldn't be any fruits, and so there would be no gain from the standpoint of accuracy in adjudication. What the critics *should* be advocating is either that the standard for determining whether a search is illegal should be redefined, and specifically that searches should be deemed illegal only if the evidentiary benefits do not equal or exceed the costs of the search to the victim, or that the only sanction for an illegal search should be a suit for compensatory damages. The latter approach would require the police, in effect, to "buy" the fruits of their "illegal" searches from the victims, which they presumably would do when the evidentiary benefits exceeded the costs to the victim of the search. So less evidence would be excluded than under the exclusionary rule.

The most controversial of the evidentiary privileges is the constitutional privilege against compulsory self-incrimination. Concerns with the use of torture to extract confessions are understandable but could be allayed by prohibiting torture (including its attenuated forms, such as relay questioning and the "third degree") and making punishment for contempt of court—whether by fine, imprisonment, or forfeiture of the right to defend—the sole sanction for a refusal to testify.

The privilege denies the court highly probative evidence, and its benefits are difficult to pin down. One argument is the "strong policy in favor of government's leaving people alone . . . The government should not disturb the peace of an individual by way of compulsory appearance and compulsory disclosure which may lead to his conviction unless sufficient evidence exists to establish probable cause. Obviously, if the individual's peace is to be preserved, the government must obtain its prima facie case from sources other than the individual."[29] But this argument, which parallels the one discussed earlier for placing the burden of producing evidence on plaintiffs rather than defendants, could

29. John Henry Wigmore, *Evidence in Trials at Common Law*, vol. 8, § 2251, p. 317 (John T. McNaughton revision 1961). McNaughton's entire discussion of the arguments for the privilege is exemplary. See id., pp. 295–318.

be deflected by cutting off the privilege as soon as the government has gathered enough evidence from independent sources to indict and by limiting the amount of time that the government could demand of the suspect for answering questions.[30]

One way to pose the issue of abolishing the privilege is to adopt an ex ante perspective and so ask whether, if the privilege protects only (or mainly) the guilty, people choosing behind the veil of ignorance, and so not knowing whether they will be victims of crime or criminals (or innocent people mistakenly prosecuted), would support or reject the privilege. Since only a modest fraction of the community will become criminals or even criminal suspects, and since the only cost to the criminal from the abrogation of the privilege would be to make it more difficult for him to avoid his just deserts, there might be an overwhelming vote in favor of abrogation.

The preceding paragraph began to relax the implicit assumption that the only people who make damaging admissions are guilty people. An innocent person can be suspected of crime and he may say things that can be used to weave the net of suspicion more tightly around him; or he may simply have a suspicious cast of countenance. The greater the danger that the abolition of the privilege would lead to some erroneous convictions, the stronger the case for the privilege. This point bears on an unraveling problem that the right to waive an evidentiary privilege creates. Suppose that only guilty people would make the kind of damaging admissions that the privilege against compulsory self-incrimination (and also the lawyer-client and marital privileges) enables defendants to avoid or conceal. Then the innocent would always waive privilege in order to signal their innocence.[31] Anyone who did not would properly be considered guilty. This is the basis on which jurors often infer guilt from the defendant's refusal to take the stand, even though they are told not to draw any inference of guilt from such a refusal. If, however, the innocent too bear a cost of waiving privilege, then the refusal to waive it cannot be reliably interpreted as a sign of guilt. Judges who want jurors to take seriously the principle that guilt should not be inferred from a refusal to waive the privilege against be-

30. I shall not examine the distinct problems presented by the assertion of the privilege in nonlitigation settings, such as hearings before congressional committees.

31. See generally Daniel R. Fischel, "Lawyers and Confidentiality," 65 *University of Chicago Law Review* 1 (1998).

ing compelled to incriminate oneself will have to come up with a credible explanation to give juries for why an innocent person might fear the consequences of testifying. I am not sure there *is* a credible explanation; the danger of an innocent person's making admissions that would make the jury think him guilty may be theoretical rather than real.

The criminal defendant's decision whether to testify, thus waiving his privilege against compulsory self-incrimination, can be modeled as

$$(3) \qquad p = p_1x_1 + (1 - t)p_2 + tp_3tx_2$$

where p is the probability that the defendant will be found guilty, p_1 the probability of guilt generated by the other evidence in the case (x_1), p_2 the probability of guilt that the jury will infer if he doesn't take the stand, p_3 the probability of guilt that the jury will infer if he takes the stand and testifies (with x_2 being the testimony that he will give), and t being the decision whether to testify, with t taking a value of 1 if he testifies and 0 if he does not. If he testifies, the middle term on the right-hand side of the equation is wiped out, but if his testimony is damaging to him then the third term (which becomes simply p_3x_2) will be positive, while if he declines to testify the third term disappears but the second term is positive. The decision to testify will depend, therefore, on a comparison of the middle term in the decline case with the third term in the testify case.

This approach can be used to model any case in which the absence of evidence gives rise to an inference, as in versions discussed in the preceding chapter of the *McDonnell Douglas* scenario and the hypothetical bus case, and in cases of statistical evidence with low significance levels. In the bus case, for example, p would be the probability that the owner of the bus that injured the plaintiff was Company A, the defendant; p_2 would be the (negative) contribution to p if the only evidence is the percentage of buses owned by A and if this implies that the plaintiff is withholding evidence that the bus in question was actually owned by B (that is, if $t = 0$); and p_3 would be the contribution to p if the plaintiff puts in additional evidence (x_2), beyond the bare statistic, concerning ownership.

Seidmann and Stein have made a fresh argument for the privilege against compulsory self-incrimination.[32] They point out that it gives

---

32. Daniel J. Seidmann and Alex Stein, "The Right to Silence Helps the Innocent: A Game-Theoretic Analysis of the Fifth Amendment Privilege" (forthcoming in *Harvard Law Review*).

the guilty defendant a choice between taking the stand and lying, on the one hand, or keeping silent, on the other. If the second option is removed by abolition of the privilege, guilty defendants will take the stand more often and lie more often. Since most criminal defendants are guilty, most criminal defendants who testify will lie, and this will make it more difficult for innocent defendants to be believed; triers of fact will expect defendants' testimony to be dishonest.

Articles VI and VII of the Federal Rules of Evidence contain a number of provisions relating to witnesses, especially expert witnesses (Article VII). The most important are Rule 602, which confines nonexpert witnesses to testifying from first-hand knowledge, and Rule 702, which permits an expert witness to testify about matters within his area of expertise "in the form of an opinion."[33] An opinion is an inference drawn from a combination of first-hand knowledge and background knowledge. If one sees dark clouds and offers an opinion that it is about to rain, the opinion represents the conjunction of the observation of the clouds with background knowledge about weather signs. The extensive background knowledge that denotes a person as being expert in some field enables him to offer opinions that would be irresponsibly speculative in the mouth of a lay person.

Because of the technical complexity of many of the issues that arise in modern lawsuits, heavy reliance on expert witnesses seems to be the only alternative to moving to a system of specialized rather than (largely) generalist courts—a movement that would have its own problems.[34] But there is considerable dissatisfaction with the use of expert witnesses. This dissatisfaction has two main sources, which are related. First, because the experts are paid by the respective parties, it is feared that they are partisans of whoever hired them ("hired guns") rather than being disinterested, and hence presumptively truthful, witnesses. This of course does not distinguish them sharply from a number of other types of witness, notably the parties themselves, who once were forbidden on this ground to testify at all. But, second, it is feared that expert witnesses can mislead judges and juries more readily than lay witnesses can because they are more difficult to pick apart on cross-examination; they can hide behind an impenetrable expertise expressed in

---

33. Rule 701 permits very limited opinion testimony by lay witnesses.

34. Discussed in Richard A. Posner, *The Federal Courts: Challenge and Reform*, ch. 8 (1996). But it is important to realize that specialized courts *are* a possible solution to the perceived problems with using expert witnesses.

an unintelligible jargon. Even if they are demolished on cross-examination by a lawyer who has been carefully prepped by his own expert, the jury may not understand the questions and answers in the cross-examination well enough to realize that the expert *has* been demolished. A subordinate concern, closely related to the concern with intelligibility, is that opposing experts often simply cancel each other out. The expected outcome is unaffected, and so the use of the experts creates costs without any benefits.

Neither concern seems especially grave, provided—a vital qualification to which I'll return—that the expert is testifying in an area in which there is a consensus on essential substantive and methodological premises.

Regarding the first concern, lack of disinterest, five points need to be made:

1. Because most expert witnesses, unlike most lay witnesses, are repeat players, they have a financial interest in creating and preserving a reputation for being honest and competent. Any public judicial criticism of a witness (in an opinion, whether or not formally published, or even in the transcript of a trial or other hearing) is apt to impair the expert's career as a witness, sometimes fatally, because the criticism is likely to be brought up in subsequent cross-examination of this expert.[35] Many expert witnesses, moreover, are employed by consulting firms, which have a corporate reputation that can be damaged by the errors of any of their employees. And professors may incur nonpecuniary costs in diminished academic reputation (something they value a lot, or else they probably would not be academics) if they are shown up as careless or dishonest witnesses.

This discussion does not provide a complete answer to the concern with partisanship, because it is also the repeat player who has an incentive to please his client, so that he'll be hired in the future. Because it is forbidden to pay expert witnesses on a contingent basis, the one-time expert witness has nothing to lose *or gain* from giving dishonest or slanted testimony.

35. "A favorable mention in a reported case is of real benefit to a forensic [that is, a testifying] economist, while an unfavorable mention is a major cost." Thomas R. Ireland, Walter D. Johnson, and Paul C. Taylor, "Economic Science and Hedonic Damage Analysis in Light of *Daubert v. Merrell Dow*," 10 *Journal of Forensic Economics* 139, 156 (1997). For an example of "unfavorable mention," see In re Brand Name Prescription Drugs Antitrust Litigation, 1996 WL 351178 (N.D. Ill. June 24, 1996).

2. The expert witness who has a record of academic publication will be "kept honest" by the fact that should he try to repudiate his academic work on the stand, he will be open to devastating cross-examination. This implies that a warning flag should go up whenever an expert witness either has no record of academic publication or is testifying about matters on which he has never published. Not only is such an expert less likely to testify truthfully; the lawyer's choice of him as an expert witness implies that the lawyer was unable to find a genuinely knowledgeable person who was willing to testify in support of the client's position.

3. Because of the adversary character of the American system of litigation, and the requirement that the expert disclose his evidence during the pretrial discovery process and thus before the trial begins, expert evidence is subject to intense critical scrutiny.[36] This should deter at least some irresponsible expert testimony. In the case of economics, where the tradition of replicating previous academic studies is relatively weak,[37] a study conducted for purposes of litigation is likely to receive closer scrutiny that an academic study, even one published in a refereed journal.

4. An expert witness's evidence is inadmissible if it does not satisfy the methodological standards of his field.[38] That is something easier for the judge to determine than whether the evidence is sound. This rule acts as a screen against "junk science." The mesh of the screen may actually be too fine for statistical evidence, as we saw earlier. Notice that the existence of the screen may not only exclude subprofessional expert testimony; it may also deter the preparation of such testimony because the expert will worry that his reputation may be impaired if his evidence is excluded as "junk science."

36. As an example of what awaits expert witnesses in cross-examination, see Stan V. Smith, "Pseudo-Economists—The New Junk Scientists," 47 *Federation of Insurance and Corporate Counsel Quarterly* 95 (1996).

37. This may be why academic researchers have adopted the 5 percent significance level rather than a 10 or 20 percent level. The less frequently studies are replicated, the more important it is to subject them to the internal discipline of a stiff significance test. See Lempert, note 8 above, at 1099.

38. See, for example, Kumho Tire Co. v. Carmichael, 119 S. Ct. 1167 (1999); Daubert v. Merrell Dow Pharmaceuticals, Inc., 509 U.S. 579 (1993); Navarro v. Fuji Heavy Industries, Ltd., 117 F.3d 1027, 1031 (7th Cir. 1997); People Who Care v. Rockford Board of Education, 111 F.3d 528, 537 (7th Cir. 1997); Rosen v. Ciba-Geigy Corp., 78 F.3d 316, 318–319 (7th Cir. 1996); David L. Faigman et al., *Modern Scientific Evidence: The Law and Science of Expert Testimony*, vol. 1, pp. 2–45 (1997).

5. As an extension of the preceding point, consider the fact that to-day, with almost all judicial rulings on line, any judicial criticism of an expert witness is likely to become common knowledge in the litigation community within a very short time and to be used to impeach any future testimony that the expert gives. This prospect gives expert witnesses a significant incentive to avoid error, overreaching, and excessive partisanship in their testimonial appearances. It should also serve to rehabilitate the often-derided "professional" expert witness. The more often he testifies (more precisely, the more often he anticipates testifying as an expert in the future), the greater his stake in maintaining an unblemished reputation by not provoking judicial criticism, and so the more credible his testimony is. A "professional" witness who has testified in dozens or hundreds of cases without drawing judicial criticism, and expects to testify in many more, is especially likely to be a reliable witness. For he has withstood the pummeling of his adversaries in his previous cases, thereby accumulating a considerable reputation capital that he would jeopardize by testifying dishonestly in the present case.

If market incentives kept experts fully honest, defendants' lawyers would often not introduce expert testimony at all, because they would find it difficult to locate a reputable expert who would contradict the plaintiff's expert.[39] So we should expect both sides in a case to present expert witnesses more often the "softer" the science related to the case.

The second concern with the use of expert witnesses—the concern with intelligibility once the evidence has been admitted—has undoubted merit, but not as much as intuition might suggest. For it ignores incentive effects. A witness who cannot make himself understood by the court is unlikely to be persuasive. This is a particularly important consideration in jury trials, because jurors often give less weight to credentials than to clarity.[40] If expert testimony is clearer in jury than in judge trials, juries may understand expert testimony as well as judges even if the average judge is brighter than the average juror.

This is not a complete answer to the criticism from unintelligibility.

39. See Deanne M. Short and Edward L. Sattler, "The Market for Expert Witnesses," 22 *Journal of Economics* 87, 89 (1996).

40. See Daniel W. Shuman, Anthony Champagne, and Elizabeth Whitaker, "Juror Assessments of the Believability of Expert Witnesses: A Literature Review," 36 *Jurimetrics Journal* 371, 379 (1996).

Many fields are so technical that it is unrealistic to expect the average juror *or judge* to be able to understand all the criticisms of a study conducted by an expert in the field. That is why increased technical complexity of evidence is not a powerful argument against the use of juries. A partial solution is suggested by a study that found that jurors give great weight to credentials when the expert testimony is very complex.[41] This is rational. The more credentialed expert has a larger potential reputation loss from giving evidence that falls below acceptable professional standards.

Another way to deal with the problem of intelligibility would be more frequent appointment of court-appointed experts. The power to make such appointments is explicitly conferred on federal judges by Rule 706, yet rarely exercised.[42] The usual objection to its exercise is that the judge can't know whether he is picking a genuine neutral to be the court's expert. This objection can be overcome by borrowing a leaf from a common method of selecting arbitrators: each party chooses an arbitrator and the two arbitrators choose a neutral arbitrator, who generally casts the deciding vote. The parties' experts could, similarly, agree on a neutral expert who would be appointed by the court and would testify either along with or instead of the parties' experts.[43] His neutrality would quite properly give his views decisive weight with the jury. It would not matter whether the jurors understood him; his conclusion would be credible because of his neutrality and expertise. Things can be rationally believed though not understood. People rationally believe that airline travel is safe without knowing what keeps the plane in the air.[44]

The third concern about expert testimony, that opposing experts of-

41. Joel Cooper, Elizabeth A. Bennett, and Holly L. Sukel, "Complex Scientific Testimony: How Do Jurors Make Decisions?" 20 *Law and Human Behavior* 379, 391–392 (1996).

42. See Joe S. Cecil and Thomas E. Willging, *Court-Appointed Experts: Defining the Role of Experts Appointed under Federal Rule of Evidence 706* (1993); Faigman et al., note 38 above, at 43–44. However, this may be changing. See Howard M. Erichson, "Mass Tort Litigation and Inquisitorial Justice," 87 *Georgetown Law Journal* 1983, 1988–1993 (1999).

43. This has been proposed, Daniel L. Rubinfeld, "Econometrics in the Courtroom," 85 *Columbia Law Review* 1048, 1096 (1985), and a variant of the procedure has been employed in at least one case, Leesona Corp. v. Varta Batteries, Inc., 522 F. Supp. 1304, 1312 (S.D.N.Y. 1981). See also American Bar Association, note 26 above, at 246.

44. This is an example of Coady's point that testimony can be a source of real knowledge. See Chapter 10.

ten cancel each other out, would be taken care of if the parties' experts selected a neutral expert to be the only expert witness. But is it a real concern? For it might seem that whenever the opposing experts canceled each other out, the parties would agree not to call them, in order to reduce the expense of litigation. This happens occasionally, but not often, maybe because a lawyer who suggested it would be understood to be signaling that he thought his expert less credible than the opponent's expert. Furthermore, there is selection bias at work; the canceling-out phenomenon is observed only in cases that go to trial, and many cases may settle (or not be brought in the first place) because the experts consulted by the parties have convinced them that there is no triable issue.

The use of expert witnesses is most problematic in areas in which there is insufficient common ground to keep the witness honest. This used to be, and to some extent still is, the situation with regard to antitrust economics. A perfectly respectable economist might be an antitrust "hawk," another equally respectable economist a "dove." Each might have a long list of reputable academic publications fully consistent with systematically pro-plaintiff (or pro-defendant) testimony. A judge or jury would have little basis for choosing between them, especially since each witness might be reasoning with impeccable logic from his premises—premises equally plausible to a lay audience. There might be no neutrals having relevant expertise, in which event a court-appointed expert would perforce be a partisan. I do not have a solution to this problem.

A major social cost of expert evidence is not discussed at all in the literature on expert witnesses: the deflection of academic researchers, especially those with tenure, from scholarly work to testifying. Although testifying, by giving academics access to data that they would not otherwise have, may occasionally pay academic dividends, it is unlikely that the net output of American universities (weighting quantity by quality) is greater as a result of professors' being in demand as expert witnesses. If academic salaries were equal to the social marginal product of academics, the deflection of academics from doing research to giving testimony would not reduce social welfare. But if academic research produces social gains not captured by the researcher, and if that surplus is less than the surplus created by academics' testifying, then the practice of hiring academics to testify does impose social costs.

The second "if" is particularly iffy. Accurate adjudication creates social benefits (in particular, enhanced deterrence of wrongful conduct) not wholly captured by the expert witnesses in the fees they charge, because the lawyers will not pay them for conferring benefits on the rest of the community. In addition, the opportunity to make extra income may draw able people into academia who would otherwise choose some other occupation. But this is a weaker point. The opportunity of professors to moonlight may enable universities to pay lower salaries to academics, and so may not affect the supply of academics. And since testimonial opportunities are randomly distributed across the academic spectrum in relation to value of research output, the principal effect of moonlighting income, even if it is not offset by lower academic salaries, may be to alter the distribution of academics across fields without regard to social product.

Supposing that expert testifying is here to stay, we should consider how it might be improved. I have suggested greater use of court-appointed experts selected by the method used to pick a neutral arbitrator. I have also mentioned judicial criticism as a method of bringing reputation costs to bear on the errant expert. Although there is a danger that such criticism may be uninformed, if so the damage to the expert's reputation will be less. The next time he testifies he will have an opportunity to try to rebut the criticism if it is thrown up at him on cross-examination. And his lawyer may be able to persuade the judge in the new case to prevent the use of the earlier judge's criticism on cross-examination, on the ground that its probative value is slight in relation to its prejudicial effect.

Two further measures for improving the quality of expert evidence are worth considering. The first is for each professional association from whose membership expert witnesses are drawn to maintain a roster of all testimonial appearances by members. The roster would contain abstracts of each member's testimony and any criticisms of the testimony by the judge in the case or by the lawyers or experts on the other side of the lawsuit. It would enable the profession to monitor its members' adherence to high standards of probity and care in their testimonial forays. Procedures could be established to enable members to challenge inaccuracies, and, having thus been validated, the roster could be made available to the courts.

I am not appealing to altruism in making this suggestion. Each association, which is to say the members (or rather the majority of them) of the association, would benefit from the maintenance of the roster. The effect of the roster in deterring the hiring as expert witnesses of disreputable members of the profession represented by the association would increase the association's prestige. It would also increase the consulting incomes of its reputable members by reducing the competition of the disreputable members of the profession. The incentive to maintain such a roster would thus be the same as that of any other form of professional self-policing: to reduce the external costs that the misbehavior of one member of a profession imposes on other members.

Second, lawyers who call an expert as a witness could be required to disclose the name of all the experts whom they had contacted as possible witnesses before settling on this one. This would alert the jury to the problem of "witness shopping." Suppose that the lawyer for the plaintiff hired the first economist, agronomist, physicist, physician, and so on whom he interviewed and the lawyer for the defendant hired the twentieth whom *he* interviewed. A reasonable inference from this pattern is that the defendant's case is weaker than the plaintiff's. The parallel is to conducting twenty statistical tests of a hypothesis and reporting (as significant at the 5 percent level) the only one that supported the hypothesis being tested.

~ V
EMPIRICISM

~ 13

Counting, Especially Citations

$\mathcal{A}$ DEARTH OF QUANTITATIVE scholarship has been a serious shortcoming of legal research, including economic analysis of law. When hypotheses cannot be tested by means of experiments, whether contrived or natural, and the results assessed rigorously by reference to the conventions of statistical inference, speculation is rampant and knowledge meager. This is not to say that nonquantitative empirical research on the legal system is valueless; much valuable work in that vein has been done in recent years.[1] Much of the study of legal rules by economic analysts of law is empirical in spirit yet nonquantitative.[2] There is a certain amount of quantitative study as well of law, much of it based on what are now abundant data concerning cases filed and decided; I have done some of this work myself.[3] In Chapter 3, I presented a quantitative study of the relation between economic equality and political and legal justice. There is also an extensive literature testing the Bentham-Becker model of crime (see Chapter 1) on statisti-

1. An example is Robert Ellickson's justly celebrated field study of norm-guided behavior, *Order without Law: How Neighbors Settle Disputes* (1991), which I cited in Chapter 9.

2. See, for example, William M. Landes and Richard A. Posner, *The Economic Structure of Tort Law* (1987).

3. See, for example, Richard A. Posner, *The Federal Courts: Challenge and Reform*, pts. 2–3 (1996); Posner, "Explaining the Variance in the Number of Tort Suits across U.S. States and between the United States and England," 26 *Journal of Legal Studies* 477 (1997).

cal data.[4] Behavioral law and economics is notably empirical in its emphasis—a mark in its favor even if one questions, as I did in Chapter 8, some of its methods and results. Legal sociologists have done a lot of valuable empirical work as well, much of it quantitative.[5] But the amount of quantitative empirical research in law remains slight in proportion not only to the amount of other legal research but also to the opportunities that a quantitative approach offers for illuminating hitherto intractable issues. Let me give an example.

The U.S. Court of Appeals for the Ninth Circuit is by far the largest federal court of appeals in terms both of population served and number of judgeships—twenty-eight, compared to seventeen for the next-largest circuit (the Fifth). It is also highly controversial, in some quarters considered the most erratic of the federal courts of appeals. Its critics often attribute its problems to size, and there is now a movement afoot in Congress to split the circuit in two, perhaps as part of a larger realignment of circuit boundaries. Congress created a Commission on Structural Alternatives for the Federal Courts of Appeals to study the issue of splitting and realignment and related issues, and although the Commission recommended against a split[6] the issue continues to fester.

There are two theoretical reasons for expecting a court as large as the Ninth Circuit to perform less well than a smaller court, other things being equal. The first is that federal judges, protected as they are from the usual incentives to work hard and well by life tenure and the structure of judicial compensation, are "kept in line" if at all mainly by informal norms of judicial propriety and restraint; and informal norms, we know from Chapter 9, are more effective the smaller the group in which they are operative. Second, the large size of the Ninth Circuit has led that court, with Congress's authorization, to adopt a bobtailed en banc procedure. Cases accepted for rehearing en banc are assigned to an eleven-judge panel consisting of the circuit's chief judge plus a randomly selected ten of the remaining judges in active service. Be-

---

4. For summaries of this literature, see Isaac Ehrlich, "Crime, Punishment, and the Market for Offenses," *Journal of Economic Perspectives*, Winter 1996, pp. 43, 55–63; D. J. Pyle, "The Economic Approach to Crime and Punishment," 6 *Journal of Interdisciplinary Studies* 1, 4–8 (1995).

5. I review this literature briefly in my book *The Problematics of Moral and Legal Theory* 213–215 (1999).

6. Commission on Structural Alternatives for the Federal Courts of Appeals, *Final Report* (Dec. 1998).

cause of the random assignment of just a fraction of the court's full complement of judges to the en banc panel, a three-judge panel that decides to defy circuit precedent or otherwise go out on a thin limb has a reasonable prospect of getting away with it. For even if rehearing en banc is sought and granted, the luck of the draw may result in the en banc panel's being dominated by the original panel's members or their allies.

Whether these factors predisposing to judicial irresponsibility have impaired the quality of the Ninth Circuit is an empirical question, and recently a judge of that court tried to answer it.[7] After acknowledging that in 1995 through 1997 the Supreme Court had reversed forty-eight decisions of the Ninth Circuit and affirmed only seven, and that this was a higher reversal rate than experienced by any other federal court of appeals during this period,[8] Judge Farris points out that the Supreme Court "let stand as final 99.7 percent of the Ninth Circuit's 1996 cases."[9] Both sets of statistics are meaningless from the standpoint of evaluating the Ninth Circuit, the first because, as Judge Farris points out, reversals by the Supreme Court often involve disagreement rather than the correction of error, and the second (which is related to the first) because the Supreme Court has neither the capacity nor the incentive to review any but a tiny percentage of federal court of appeals decisions. So Judge Farris has said nothing either pro or con his court and later in his article he undermines his conclusion that the Ninth Circuit is doing a fine job by denying that the reason it is reversed so often is that it is more liberal than the Supreme Court.[10] If that were the reason, it would strengthen the hypothesis that the rate of reversal by the Supreme Court is irrelevant to judgments of judicial quality; the reason for different rates of reversal would be differences in political congruence with the Supreme Court.

So the judge's empirics lead nowhere, but still the issue he discusses is an important one. Let me try an alternative empirical approach based

7. See Jerome Farris, "The Ninth Circuit—Most Maligned Circuit in the Country—Fact or Fiction?" 58 *Ohio State Law Journal* 1465 (1997). See also Marybeth Herald, "Reversed, Vacated, and Split: The Supreme Court, the Ninth Circuit, and Congress," 77 *Oregon Law Review* 405 (1998).

8. Farris, note 7 above, at 1465 and n. 2.

9. Id. at 1465. The judge does not explain why he limited the comparison to 1996.

10. Id. at 1471.

on the fact that there are two types of Supreme Court reversal. The more common one is where the Court grants certiorari and sets the case for full briefing and oral argument, followed eventually by a decision. Less commonly, the Court grants certiorari and reverses summarily, without briefing and argument. This second type of reversal can fairly be described as a rebuke to the lower court: the latter got the issue so clearly wrong that there is no need for the illumination of the issue that briefing and argument would afford.

So let us ask how the Ninth Circuit fares in comparison to the other federal courts of appeals if consideration is limited to rates of summary reversal. The denominator in the comparison is the total number of terminations in the preceding year classified as "on the merits" by the Administrative Office of the U.S. Courts, for this is the population from which most cases eligible for further review are drawn (most of the rest are settled, abandoned, dismissed as frivolous, or consolidated with other cases). Data for 1985 through 1997 are presented in Table 13.1.

As the critics of the Ninth Circuit would expect, and as the simple theoretical points noted at the outset of my discussion suggest, the Ninth Circuit has the highest rate of summary reversal by the Supreme Court. This is also true if we use as the denominator not the total number of merits terminations but the total number of cases in which the

Table 13.1 Supreme Court summary reversals, by circuit, 1985–1997

Circuit	Reversals	Merits terminations	% Reversals
9th	15	48,669	0.030820
6th	7	28,714	0.024378
10th	4	16,712	0.023935
8th	4	22,957	0.017424
11th	4	33,400	0.011976
5th	2	39,278	0.005092
2nd	1	19,732	0.005068
3rd	1	21,869	0.004573
4th	1	29,218	0.003423
7th	0	18,662	0
D.C.	0	9,748	0
1st	0	9,425	0
Total	39	298,384	

Supreme Court grants certiorari. The percentage summarily reversed is then 4.98 percent for the Ninth Circuit and 4.05 percent for the next highest, the Sixth. But how much confidence to place in these statistics depends in part on whether the difference between the Ninth Circuit's rate of being summarily reversed and that of the other circuits is statistically significant. The answer is given in Table 13.2, where the figures in boldface are those that are statistically significant at the conventional 5 percent level.

Table 13.2 reveals that with the exception of the Sixth, Tenth, Eighth, and Eleventh Circuits, the difference between the Ninth Circuit's summary reversal rate and that of the other circuits is statistically significant, while the Sixth's summary reversal rate is statistically significantly higher than all but three of the other circuits. So while the Ninth has the worst summary reversal record, it is impossible, using the conventional test for statistical significance (see Chapter 11), to reject the inference that its "worseness" than the three runner-up circuits is due to chance. When the alternative denominator (number of petitions for certiorari granted) is substituted, the difference between the Ninth Circuit's summary reversal rate and that of all but the Eighth, Tenth, and Eleventh Circuits is statistically significant, so again the Ninth Circuit is not clearly separate from the pack.

But let us now expand the analysis to consider the other reversals,

Table 13.2 Significance levels for differences in Supreme Court summary reversal rates across circuits, 1985–1997

Circuit	9th	6th	10th	8th	11th
9th					
6th	0.403				
10th	0.368	0.023			
8th	0.744	0.417	0.340		
11th	0.942	0.741	0.629	0.304	
5th	**0.997**	**0.949**	0.868	0.809	0.676
2nd	**0.994**	**0.934**	0.854	0.780	0.622
3rd	**0.996**	**0.946**	0.869	0.809	0.674
4th	**0.998**	**0.967**	0.864	0.865	0.785
7th	**0.999**	**0.989**	0.947	0.943	0.934
D.C	**0.999**	**0.983**	0.935	0.922	0.892
1st	**0.999**	**0.983**	0.934	0.920	0.889

that is, the nonsummary ones. As explained earlier, nonsummary reversal is not a powerful quality variable, but it may have some quality dimension. The statistics are presented in Table 13.3.

Here the Ninth Circuit falls to second place after the District of Columbia Circuit. But the high reversal rate of the latter doubtless reflects that court's dense menu of cases of national importance; the Ninth Circuit has no similar excuse for its high reversal rate. Statistically, however, that rate is not significantly different from that of the Second, Eighth, and Tenth Circuits, so again the evidence in support of the critics of the Ninth Circuit is inconclusive.

Now suppose we look at just those nonsummary reversals that are unanimous, thus eliminating cases in which ideology is likely to figure significantly in the Supreme Court's decision to reverse. A lower-court decision that the Court reverses unanimously, even if after full briefing and argument, is more likely to be just plain incorrect, rather than merely the reflection of political difference. The figures for the different courts of appeals are given in Table 13.4. And again the Ninth Circuit is at the top, and this time by a margin over all the other circuits that is statistically significant.

Tables 13.1 through 13.4 are not conclusive, but they provide sub-

Table 13.3 Supreme Court nonsummary reversals, by circuit, 1985–1997

Circuit	Reversals[a]	Merits terminations	% Reversals
D.C.	42	9,748	0.430858
9th	142	48,669	0.291767
2nd	51	19,732	0.258463
8th	53	22,957	0.230866
10th	36	16,712	0.215414
7th	38	18,662	0.203622
6th	54	28,714	0.188062
3rd	40	21,869	0.182907
1st	16	9,425	0.169761
4th	49	29,218	0.167705
5th	61	39,278	0.155303
11th	42	33,400	0.125749
Total	624	298,384	

a. Includes reversals in part

Table 13.4 Unanimous nonsummary Supreme Court reversals, by circuit, 1985–1997

Circuit	Reversals	Merits terminations	% Reversals
9th	38	48,669	0.078078
10th	11	16,712	0.065821
D.C.	6	9,748	0.061551
7th	11	18,662	0.058943
6th	15	28,714	0.052239
8th	11	22,957	0.047916
3rd	10	21,869	0.045727
5th	14	39,278	0.035643
4th	10	29,218	0.034225
1st	3	9,425	0.031830
2nd	6	19,732	0.030407
11th	10	33,400	0.029940
Total	145	298,384	0.048595

stantial grounds for believing that the critics of the Ninth Circuit are on to something.[11]

Of more general interest is the relation that the data suggest between summary reversals and circuit size. When the percentage of summary reversals in Table 13.1 is regressed on the number of judgeships per circuit, the correlation is positive and is significant at the 5 percent level (t value of 2.23), with an adjusted R^2 of 0.27. The coefficient on the judgeship variable implies that increasing the number of judgeships in a court of appeals by one increases the summary-reversal percentage by 0.00168 percent, which although small is not trivial, considering that the Fourth Circuit's summary-reversal percentage is only 0.0034 percent and that three circuits have zero percentages. The implication is that problems of quality control indeed increase with the size of a circuit, as theory predicts. The implication persists if we vary

11. Additional statistical evidence bearing on this question can be found in a recent survey of lawyers who litigate cases in the various federal courts of appeals. Among experienced litigators, 25 percent reported that they often had trouble predicting the outcome of an appeal in the Ninth Circuit, and this was higher than for any other circuit. "Survey of Appellate Counsel," in *Working Papers of the Commission on Structural Alternatives for the Federal Courts of Appeals* 79 (Federal Judicial Center, July 1998).

the test by comparing summary reversals with the number of cases in which certiorari is granted, as opposed to the total number of merits terminations, per circuit. The percentage of summary reversals remains positively correlated with the number of judgeships; the correlation is statistically significant at the 4 percent level ($t = 2.33$) and the adjusted R^2 is 0.29. Finally, if the percentage of unanimous nonsummary reversals (Table 13.4) is regressed on the number of judges, there is again a positive correlation, which is significant at the 7 percent level ($t = 2.07$, with an adjusted R^2 of 0.23); if the independent variable is judgeships squared, on the theory that the effects of size on performance are likely to be increasing in size, then the significance level rises to 4 percent ($t = 2.33$, with an adjusted R^2 of 0.29).

A "natural" experiment provides further evidence that an increase in number of judgeships is correlated with a reduction in quality as proxied by the number of summary reversals by the Supreme Court. In 1981 the Fifth Circuit, which then had twenty-six judgeships—almost as many as the Ninth Circuit today—was split into two courts (the Fifth and Eleventh Circuits) of roughly equal size. The combined rate of summary reversal of the split courts through 1997 is 0.000146; the Fifth Circuit's rate for the five years before the split was 0.000597. The difference is statistically significant.

Further light can be cast on the issues of circuit size in general and the Ninth Circuit's performance in particular by using citations analysis, specifically in the form of counting "other court" citations. I discuss citations analysis at greater length in the second part of this chapter; suffice it for now to say that one measure of the quality of a judge's or a court's decisions is the frequency with which his or its decisions are cited by courts that are not obligated as a matter of stare decisis to follow them. In the federal courts of appeals, this method of evaluation is most readily implemented by examining citations to the judge or court of appeals in question by the other federal courts of appeals, correcting for the fact that the larger a court is, the fewer "other court" judges there are to cite the decisions of the court. Using this method, William Landes, Lawrence Lessig, and Michael Solimine ranked the Ninth Circuit eleventh out of thirteen in the quality of its decisions; and the lowest-ranking position of the Federal Circuit is probably due to its highly specialized jurisdiction. Among the regional circuits, the Ninth ranks eleventh out of twelve (the twelfth being the Sixth Circuit). Even the D.C. Circuit (ranked tenth), which is also specialized, though less so than the Federal Circuit, outranks the Ninth Circuit.[12]

Still using citations analysis, let me return to the more general question of the effect of the number of judges of a court on the quality of the court's output. An earlier study of the federal courts of appeals found that output weighted by other-court citations fell as the number of judges on the court rose.[13] And regressing the other-court citations data in the LLS study on the number of judgeships per circuit yields a negative correlation that barely misses statistical significance at the 95 percent confidence level.[14] This is additional evidence that increasing the number of judges of an appellate court reduces the quality of the court's decisions, which in turns suggests that the Ninth Circuit's problems may be systemic rather than due to accidents of the appointing process.

A more systematic attempt to distinguish between the two hypotheses—that the Ninth Circuit's poor performance relative to the other circuits is due to its size, and that it is due rather to unrelated factors, such as the quality of appointments to it—is attempted in Table 13.5. The rate of summary reversal by the Supreme Court is regressed on several potential explanatory variables (not just number of judgeships and number of judgeships squared, the particular variables of interest to us), and on dummy variables for each circuit, which identify quality effects that are due to other characteristics of a circuit.[15]

The coefficients on the judgeship variables are not significant at the 95 percent confidence level, but they are significant at (or very near) the 90 percent confidence level.[16] They imply, however, that the positive effect of size on the summary-reversal rate peaks at 12.98, suggest-

12. William M. Landes, Lawrence Lessig, and Michael E. Solimine, "Judicial Influence: A Citation Analysis of Federal Courts of Appeals Judges," 27 *Journal of Legal Studies* 271, 318 (table 5) (1998). See also id. at 277 (table 1), 332. Using a somewhat different sample, however, the study has the Ninth Circuit receiving an average number of other-court citations. See id. at 331 (table A4). In the rest of this chapter I refer to this study as "LLS."

13. *The Federal Courts: Challenge and Reform*, note 3 above, at 235–236 and table 7.7.

14. The t statistic is -2.091 and the adjusted R^2 is 0.25.

15. The circuit dummies for the circuits that had no summary reversals are omitted. The failure to report the standard error on the dummy variable for the Second Circuit results from an unexplained glitch in the statistical program (Stata version 5). Each year is treated as a separate observation for each circuit, so that the total number of observations is 156.

16. An F-test of the hypothesis that both judgeship variables are zero rejected the hypothesis at only the 80 percent confidence level.

Table 13.5 Probit regression of Supreme Court summary reversals per merit termination on number of judgeships, circuit dummies, and other variables, 1985–1997

Variable	Coeff.	St. error	P-value
Judgeships	4.9040	3.0353	0.106
Judgeships Squared	−0.1888	0.1126	0.094
2d Cir. Dummy	4.5805		
3d Cir. Dummy	4.2690	0.2984	0.000
4th Cir. Dummy	4.7963	0.4858	0.000
5th Cir. Dummy	5.8646	1.3437	0.000
6th Cir. Dummy	6.2084	0.7008	0.000
8th Cir. Dummy	5.7619	1.0033	0.000
9th Cir. Dummy	46.4215	23.8682	0.052
10th Cir. Dummy	5.9558	0.5556	0.000
11th Cir. Dummy	4.6442	0.6972	0.000
Merit Terminations	0.0009	0.0007	0.197
Cert. Pets. Filed	−0.0015	0.0018	0.399
Cert. Pets. Granted	0.0963	0.0372	0.010
Constant	−40.0116	20.7634	0.054
No. Observations	156		
Log Likelihood	−51.1906		
Pseudo R^2	0.375		

ing that the Ninth Circuit's uniquely high summary-reversal rate is not a product of its uniquely large size. I conclude, though tentatively, that (1) adding judgeships tends to reduce the quality of a court's output; and (2) the Ninth Circuit's uniquely high rate of being summarily reversed by the Supreme Court (a) is probably not a statistical fluke and (b) may not be a product simply of that circuit's large number of judges.

⌒ BOTH ADJUDICATION, a central practical activity of the legal system, and legal research are citation-heavy activities. I hope to show in the remaining part of this chapter that by exploiting the rich data contained in citations indexes, we can test economic hypotheses about the legal system, improve our knowledge of adjudication and legal scholarship, and eventually bring about improvements in both these aspects of the legal enterprise. We have already seen how citations analysis can help answer the question of the relation between the size of a court and the quality of its output.

Counting citations—mainly citations in legal cases of other legal cases, and citations in scholarly journals of scholarly works—has become a significant method of empirical research in law, economics, sociology (especially the sociology of science), and academic administration. It has been greatly facilitated by advances in computerization.[17] But of course the fact that a particular kind of research is easy to do cannot explain why anyone *wants* to do it. Low cost is not enough; there have to be benefits—and anyway the *opportunity* costs of adopting one research method over another are not low. Citations analysis is growing mainly because it a method of quantitative analysis of phenomena that are very difficult to study quantitatively, such as reputation, influence, prestige, celebrity, decision according to precedent, the quality of scholarly output, the quality of journals, and the productivity of scholars, judges, courts, and university departments.[18]

Citations analysis is not inherently economic. It is an empirical methodology usable by a range of disciplines. But we shall see that an economic framework fosters precision in its use. Indeed, the human capital model developed by economists may be indispensable to the use of

17. Computerized databases for the natural sciences (*Science Citation Index*), social sciences (*Social Sciences Citation Index*), and the arts and humanities (*Arts and Humanities Citation Index*) published by the Institute for Scientific Information (ISI). For law, in addition, West Publishing Company has excellent computerized databases of both judicial opinions and legal articles. The original legal citations service, *Shepard's Citations*, was in fact the inspiration for the ISI indexes. Laura M. Baird and Charles Oppenheim, "Do Citations Matter?" 20 *Journal of Information Science* 2, 3 (1994); see also Fred R. Shapiro, "Origins of Bibliometrics, Citation Indexing, and Citation Analysis: The Neglected Legal Literature," 43 *Journal of the American Society for Information Science* 337 (1992). The Web is also a potential data source for citations analysis; search engines such as AltaVista and Google can be used to count "hits" to named individuals, books, or articles. See William M. Landes and Richard A. Posner, "Citations, Age, Fame, and the Web," 29 *Journal of Legal Studies* 319 (2000); Marcy Neth, "Citation Analysis and the Web," 17 *Art Documentation* 29 (1998).

18. The literature of citations analysis is by now vast, and I will not attempt exhaustive citation. The pioneers were sociologists of science. See, for example, Robert K. Merton, *The Sociology of Science: Theoretical and Empirical Investigations*, pt. 5 (Norman W. Storer ed. 1973). For a book-length discussion, now unfortunately rather out of date, see Eugene Garfield, *Citation Indexing—Its Theory and Application in Science, Technology, and Humanities* (1979), somewhat updated, however, in Garfield, "From Citation Indexes to Informetrics: Is the Tail Now Wagging the Dog?" 48 *Libri* 67 (1998). Baird and Oppenheim's article, cited in the preceding footnote, gives a good overview of the field; with reference to science citations, see Dirk Schoonbaert and Gilbert Roelants, "Citation Analysis for Measuring the Value of Scientific Publications: Quality Assessment Tool or Comedy of Errors?" 1 *Tropical Medicine and International Health* 739 (1996).

citations analysis to compare and evaluate individual performance whether of judges or scholars.

Citations are mentions of a previous work, published or unpublished, or simply of an author's or other person's name. They figure prominently in many forms of documentation (electronic as well as printed), including patents, newspaper and magazine articles, scholarly journals and books, and—in case-law systems, such as those of the United States and England—judicial opinions. If citations were random, there would be no point in studying citation practice; indeed, there would be no *practice* of citations. But if only because citing is not costless—there is the bother of finding the citation, and the possibility of being criticized for misciting or failing to cite—it would be surprising if citations were random, and there is evidence they are not. Notably, citations counts have been consistent predictors of the recipients of high academic honors, such as the Nobel prizes in the natural sciences.[19]

Several reasons for citing come to mind. The first, which is dominant in historiography, is simply to identify a source of information so that the reader of the citing work can verify the accuracy of statements of fact made in it.[20] The second reason, which is closely related, is to incorporate a body of information by reference, that is, to guide the reader to a place where he can find the information if interested in it. Let me merge these two reasons for citing into one: "information." I emphasize that "information" is to be understood broadly, as taking in ideas and arguments as well as facts. The motive for the informational citation is simply to respond to a demand for information.

19. See references in Gregory J. Feist, "Quantity, Quality, and Depth of Research as Influences on Scientific Eminence: Is Quantity Most Important?" 10 *Creativity Research Journal* 325, 326 (1997), and in Blaise Cronin and Taylor Graham, *The Citation Process: The Role and Significance of Citations in Scientific Communication* 27 (1984); cf. C. Y. K. So, "Citation Ranking versus Expert Judgment in Evaluating Communication Scholars: Effects of Research Specialty Size and Individual Prominence," 41 *Scientometrics* 325 (1998); Paul R. McAllister, Richard C. Anderson, and Francis Narin, "Comparison of Peer and Citation Assessment of the Influence of Scientific Journals," 31 *Journal of the American Society for Information Science* 147 (1980). As pointed out later in this chapter, citation studies of eminent judges yield results consistent with the more common, qualitative indicia of judicial distinction.

20. "Historical footnotes list not the great writers who sanction a given statement or whose words an author has creatively adapted, but the documents, many or most of them not literary texts at all, which provided its substantive ingredients." Anthony Grafton, *The Footnote: A Curious History* 33 (1997).

The next reason for citing, which I'll call "priority," is to demonstrate compliance with any applicable norm against plagiarism by acknowledging the authorship of ideas, arguments, or (in the case of citations to "prior art" in patent applications) technology used in the citing work. In scientific and social scientific fields, with the partial exception of law, most citations are "priority" citations. Strictly, priority citations are a subset of informational citations; the priority is in making an argument, discovering an idea, inventing a product or process. But whereas a writer will make informational citations without prodding, simply in order to make his work more valuable to the reader, he will make priority citations (except to himself!) reluctantly, under the constraint of the antiplagiarism norm.

Most *self*-citations are designed either to incorporate by reference information contained in other works by the citer or to establish the priority of some earlier work of his over subsequent work done by others. One of the worries about citations analysis is that as it becomes more familiar, citation practices will become strategic, and authors thus will cite themselves more in order to increase their citations count. But this gambit is unlikely to succeed, because it is easy to subtract out self-citations in counting citations to a person's work. Reciprocal citing is a greater problem. One can imagine informal deals between academic allies to jack up each other's reputations by citing each other heavily. And there is some evidence that journal editors receive citations in the journals they edit that they would not receive if they were not editors—citations designed to increase the likelihood of publication.[21]

Another common reason for citing is to identify works or persons with which or with whom the author of the citing work disagrees. These citations ("negative citations") are motivated not by antiplagiarism norms but by the need to establish the context of the citer's work. Not to cite one's opponent would be like reviewing a book without naming the book or its author.

Still another reason for citing, one particularly important in law and other "authoritarian" institutions such as hierarchical churches and totalitarian states (consider the reason for citations to *Mein Kampf* in

21. See Lydia L. Lange and P. A. Frensch, "Gaining Scientific Recognition by Position: Does Editorship Increase Citation Rates?" 44 *Scientometrics* 459 (1999); Richard A. Wright, "The Effect of Editorial Appointments on the Citations of Sociology Journal Editors, 1970–1989," 25 *American Sociologist* 40 (1994).

Nazi Germany or for citations to the works of Marx and Engels in communist societies), is to provide an authoritative basis for a statement in the citing work. I'll call this "authority" citing. In a system of case law, previously decided cases provide a reason independent of analytical power for reaching a particular outcome in the current case, and the citation of such a case is an invocation of that authority. This is true even when the citation seeks to distinguish or overrule the previous case. The citation is motivated by the authority of the previous case, which may have to be deflected or destroyed in order to enable the desired outcome of the current case. But many judicial decisions have an informational rather than an authority-related role; they are cited as shorthand for legal doctrines, cogent arguments, or forceful articulations of relevant ideas or policies. Few judicial citations are priority citations, because there is no antiplagiarism norm in adjudication. In this respect the situation in law resembles that in literature before creativity became defined as originality.[22]

A final reason for citing, call it the "celebratory," is midway between informational citing and authority citing. The feature of the cited work that induces the citation is the work's prestige or reputation.[23] By associating it with his own work, the citer enhances the credibility of his work. (Notice the relation between this form of citation and persuasion by "testimony," discussed in Chapter 10.)

Thus, citations can signify an acknowledgement of priority or influence, a useful source of information, a focus of disagreement, an acknowledgment of controlling authority, or the prestige of the cited work or its author. The heterogeneity of the reasons for citing problematizes the use of citations to measure either influence or quality. To see this, distinguish between a *reason* for citing and a *motive* for citing.[24] Many self-citations are motivated by a desire for self-aggrandizement, or by sheer laziness—the cost of finding one's own work to cite is less than the cost of finding someone else's. Some citations to work of oth-

22. See Richard A. Posner, *Law and Literature* 389–405 (revised and enlarged ed. 1998).

23. There is an analogy to celebrity endorsements of products. See Jagdish Agrawal and Wagner A. Kamakura, "The Economic Worth of Celebrity Endorsers: An Event Study Analysis," 59 *Journal of Marketing* 56 (1995).

24. For a rare study of the motives for citing, see Peiling Wang and Marilyn Domas White, "A Qualitative Study of Scholars' Citation Behavior," 33 *Proceedings of the 59th ASIS Annual Meeting* 255 (1995).

ers are motivated by a desire to flatter the author of the cited work, who may be in a position to assist the citer's career or may be a likely journal referee of the cited work. Some are motivated by piety or gratitude, or by a desire to make a display of erudition. I mentioned the possibility of reciprocal citing. It is even conceivable that in highly competitive fields of scholarship, young scholars especially might be reluctant to cite their peers, and prefer to cite the dead, who are no longer competitors. Because the cost of inaccurate citing usually is low (primarily the cost in being subjected to criticism for miscitation or for failing to find the most apt work to cite), there is much careless citing; and so quantitative studies of citations are bound to contain a lot of "noise." But imperfection of data is nothing new; it need not (as we shall see) disable useful statistical analysis; and there is some competitive constraint on irresponsible citing because rival scholars have an incentive to expose such practices.

Even if all citers were scrupulous and accurate, the heterogeneity of citations would make simple aggregation prone to mislead, even after such obvious sources of distortion as self-citations were removed. Suppose, for example, that an academic department relied on the number of citations to an academic's scholarly writing as a factor in deciding whether to give him tenure. Suppose further that the principal criterion for tenure was originality. The individual under consideration might have a great many citations to his work, but if they were mostly informational in character (perhaps he had written a series of review articles that provided convenient summaries of previous work), the count of his citations would give a misleading impression of his suitability to be awarded tenure.

This is a greater source of distortion than the possibility that many of the citations to the individual's work are negative. Negligible work is more likely to be ignored than to be cited. A negative citation often indicates that a work has gotten under the skin of the critic, perhaps because it mounts a powerful challenge to established ways of thinking.

Citations are heterogeneous in quality as well as in kind. A newspaper citation to a scholar's work is a better indication of the popular appeal of his work than a citation in a scholarly citation to that work is, but the latter is a better indication of the work's scholarly character. A citation made by a distinguished scholar or appearing in a high-quality journal is a better indication of quality than a citation by an undistinguished scholar or in an undistinguished journal. A citation by the same or a lower court, for which the cited case is authoritative, is a weaker signal of respect or regard for the cited case or its author than a citation by a higher or coequal court, which is not required as a matter of stare decisis to follow, distinguish, or otherwise refer to the cited case.

The number of citations to a scholarly work or a judicial opinion may, moreover, reflect completely adventitious factors—in particular the size of the population of potential citers and the citation conventions of particular disciplines[25]—that may make comparisons across fields and, because of growth in the number of journals, across time meaningless. Even within a single field, differences in the extent of specialization can confound citation comparisons; other things being equal, more specialized work is cited less often than more general work (such as a survey article)—the potential audience is smaller. Similarly, methodological articles, and judicial opinions dealing with procedural issues, tend to be cited more frequently than substantive works because they have a broader domain of applicability.

Differences in the vintages of cited works also bedevil comparison. The older the work, the more time it has had to accumulate citations, but the number of citations is apt to be depressed by shifts in interest away from the topic of the cited work or by the appearance of up-to-date substitutes for it. For just like a stock of physical capital, a stock of knowledge capital created by scholarly or judicial activity both is durable and depreciates. A further problem in interpreting the number of citations to a work is that it may be difficult to distinguish empirically between a work that is no longer cited because it has been totally depreciated and a work that has been so influential that the ideas in it are now referred to without citation to the works in which they first appeared, and often without mention of the author's name (the theory of relativity, or the theory of evolution, or the concept of consumer surplus).[26] Counting citations to the writings of Adam Smith or Jeremy

25. "The erudite scholar (rightly or wrongly associated with an older Germanic tradition) who displays his learning in his footnotes is hardly recording the strong intellectual influences which have acted upon him. The ostensibly casual scholar (surely trained at Oxbridge) considers citation beyond a name, preferably misspelled, to be a pedantical display." George J. Stigler and Claire Friedland, "The Citation Practices of Doctorates in Economics," 83 *Journal of Political Economy* 477, 485 (1975).

26. "An innovator's work is accepted and used by others. The influence may be most powerful when we simply do not cite at all." Id. at 486.

Bentham would be certain to produce an underestimation of their influence—and in Bentham's case for the additional reason that he published little during his lifetime and much of his influence was through personal contact with people who became his followers and transmitted his influence through their own writings.[27] Citations analysis will thus, alas, not answer the difficult question of Bentham's influence, discussed in the first chapter of this book.

A related point is that differences in citation rates may be magnified because of the information costs of citers, which may fall with the number of times a work is cited.[28] The more often the work is cited, the more familiar it becomes, reducing the cost of recalling and locating the work in comparison to the cost of recalling and locating a less cited and hence less familiar work. This is a kind of network externality, akin to that which makes telephone service more valuable the more subscribers it has or a new word more valuable the more people know its meaning.

Another way to see this is to think of the citer as a shopper among competing "brands," and, since no citation royalty is paid to the author of the cited work, the more familiar the brand the cheaper it is to cite it rather than a substitute. John Rawls is thus the standard citation for the concepts of the original position and the veil of ignorance, even though those concepts were explained earlier by John Harsanyi.[29] Harsanyi is less well known than Rawls and so it is "costlier" to cite him. The cost of citing the better-known work is lower not only to the citer but also to his audience, to which a citation to a familiar work may convey more information. A raw comparison of the number of citations to Rawls and to Harsanyi would thus exaggerate the relative quality, originality, and even influence of the two theorists.

For all these reasons and others,[30] it would be absurd to make lists of

27. The problems of using citations analysis to gauge intellectual influence are well discussed in Harriet Zuckerman, "Citation Analysis and the Complex Problem of Intellectual Influence," 12 *Scientometrics* 329 (1987).

28. Cf. Moshe Adler, "Stardom and Talent," 75 *American Economic Review* 208 (1985).

29. As acknowledged, somewhat grudgingly as it seems to me, in John Rawls, *A Theory of Justice* 118 n. 11 (rev. ed. 1999), citing J. C. Harsanyi, "Cardinal Utility in Welfare Economics and in the Theory of Risk-Taking, 61 *Journal of Political Economy* 434 (1953).

30. Anthony J. Chapman, "Assessing Research: Citation-Count Shortcomings," *The Psychologist: Bulletin of the British Psychological Society* 336, 339–341 (1989), lists twenty-five problems with using citation data published by the ISI (see note 17 above) to estimate the quality or impact of research. I discuss the principal ones in the text, but it may be useful to list all twenty-

the most-cited judges or most-cited scholars and think that one had generated meaningful data. But this does not make citations analysis absurd. What critics of citations analysis often fail to note is that if errors in data are randomly distributed with respect to the variable of interest (such as research quality or impact), they are unlikely to invalidate the conclusions of the study, provided that the data sample is large.[31] A related point is that errors that bias equally both sets of data being compared do not bias the comparison.[32] If, for example, the question is whether a particular scholar or journal was cited more heavily in 1999 than in 1989, many of the errors that might distort the number in each year can be ignored as not affecting the comparison. All this is not to deny the importance of care in methods of aggregation, correction, and interpretation of citations. I shall give illustrations of the key adjustments in the course of explaining the two main uses of citations analysis that have emerged to date—as a tool of management and as a means of hypothesis testing.[33]

When an enterprise produces goods that are sold in an explicit market, the valuation of the enterprise's output is straightforward, and generally the contribution of the enterprise's employees and other suppli-

---

five, in Chapman's words: "Some journals not considered"; "Exclusion of citations in books"; "Bias toward applied research"; "Psychology is in [both] the SCI [*Science Citation Index*] and SSCI [*Social Sciences Citation Index*]"; "Referencing [i.e., citing] conventions"; "Inclusion of letters, abstracts, book reviews"; "Prestige of publication outlets"; "One 'citation' even if there is repeated reference to the work"; "First-authors only [i.e., only the name of the first-listed author of a coauthored work is indexed]"; "Cross-disciplinary comparisons; and psychology's multi-dimensionality"; "Comparisons of individuals; and 'straight' *versus* 'complete' counts"; "Social factors influence choice"; "'Stars' are overwhelming"; "Name-initial homographs"; "Bias against some married women [if they have published under more than one name]"; "Bias against newcomers"; "Few to cite in a narrow speciality; and self-citations"; "One person—several alphabetical entries"; "Human errors at ISI"; "Obliteration by incorporation"; "Methods/recipe papers—spuriously inflated citations?"; "Citation does not necessarily denote approval"; "Citation without knowledge"; "Quantity is not quality"; "Citations reflect existing recognition." See also Cronin and Graham, note 19 above, at 63–73; Michael H. MacRoberts and Barbara R. MacRoberts, "Quantitative Measures of Communication in Science: A Study of the Formal Level," 16 *Social Studies of Science* 151 (1986). Chapman, above, at 342, acknowledges that some of the criticism of citations analysis may be due to sour grapes on the part of scholars who discover that they are not heavily cited.

31. Stephen M. Stigler, "Precise Measurement in the Face of Error: A Comment," 17 *Social Studies of Science* 332 (1987).

32. Id. at 333.

33. I do not discuss efforts to develop objective measures of citation *content* analysis. See, for example, John Swales, "Citation Analysis and Discourse Analysis," 7 *Applied Linguistics* 39 (1993).

ers to that output can also be determined. But not all enterprises are like that. Two notable exceptions are research universities and appellate courts. A principal output of both types of enterprise is published work that is not sold. This has been thought in some quarters to preclude analyzing the outputs of these institutions in market terms.[34] An economist would be inclined to disagree. Academics and judges, economists are prone to believe, are not much different in basic tastes and drives from other people, and universities and courts are subject to budget constraints that require economizing activity. Academic and judicial productivity is much discussed and comparisons across academics, academic departments, courts, and judges are attempted, as we saw at the outset of this chapter. The problem is one of measurement rather than of fundamental incentives and constraints. If that problem can be solved, the market for professors and judges can be assimilated to normal labor markets. Citations analysis can make a significant contribution to the solution, and this is important for effective maneuvering in these markets as well as for understanding their operation.

The federal government has for the last fifteen years been encouraging its research laboratories to focus more on research having commercial applications. Has the change in policy been effective? A study of government patents found that government research is indeed being cited more frequently in private patents.[35] The Patent Office has strict requirements about citing the "prior art," as it is called, and this provides a basis for believing that counting citations in patents provides meaningful, though not wholly reliable, information about the utility of the cited inventions.[36] The application of this methodology to the evaluation of research programs, academic or otherwise, is straightforward.[37]

---

34. For a forceful statement of this position, see John O'Neill, *The Market: Ethics, Knowledge and Politics* 155–157 (1998).

35. See Adam B. Jaffe, Michael S. Fogarty, and Bruce A. Banks, "Evidence from Patents and Patent Citations on the Impact of NASA and Other Federal Labs on Commercial Innovation," 46 *Journal of Industrial Economics* 183 (1998). The authors cite several previous studies of patent citations. Id. at 185.

36. The authors tried to verify the accuracy of the citations, and found that 75 percent were meaningful, the rest essentially noise. Id. at 202. Baird and Oppenheim, note 17 above, at 7, estimate that at least 20 percent of citations are erroneous.

37. See, for example, Lawrence D. Brown, "Influential Accounting Articles, Individuals, Ph.D. Granting Institutions and Faculties: A Citational Analysis," 21 *Accounting, Organizations and Society* 723 (1996); Charles Oppenheim, "The Correlation between Citation Counts

Weighting the number of decisions of a federal court of appeals by the number of citations to those decisions by other courts of appeals yields a measure of judicial output that, as we've glimpsed already, can be used to compare the productivity of the different courts.[38] It can't be the complete measure, if only because it implicitly weights unpublished decisions, which are not citable as precedents, at zero, even though they are an important part of the output of modern appellate courts. An unpublished decision resolves a dispute, which is a useful thing to do even though it doesn't create a citable precedent. Some adjustment should be feasible, however, to yield a total productivity figure. And when productivity is regressed on the different production functions of the different courts, it becomes possible to suggest improvements, as I suggest later.

An even more audacious use of citations as a judicial management tool is to "grade" appellate judges by the number of other-court citations to their opinions. The LLS study ranks federal appellate judges in just this way.[39] There are comparability problems; the judges are appointed at different times and to courts that have different caseloads, and the number of judges as well as the number of cases is changing over time. The study seeks to overcome these problems by regressing other-court citations on variables that include—besides the judge himself—the judge's length of service, his court's caseload, the date he was appointed, and other factors that are expected to influence the number of citations that the judge would receive if he were of average quality. The coefficient on the judge variable thus indicates how many other-court citations are due to his personal characteristics rather than to the factors that are not judge-specific that influence citations.

Since those factors cannot be controlled for perfectly (in particular, differences in the composition of a court's caseload will affect the potential number of citations, since number of cases is not constant across

---

and the 1992 Research Assessment Exercise Ratings for British Research in Genetics, Anatomy and Archeology," 53 *Journal of Documentation* 477 (1997).

38. See also *The Federal Courts: Challenge and Reform*, note 3 above, at 234; Mitu Gulati and C. M. A. McCauliff, "On *Not* Making Law," *Law and Contemporary Problems*, Summer 1998, pp. 157, 198–200, 202.

39. See note 12 above. For a somewhat similar study, but of Supreme Court Justices, see Montgomery N. Kosma, "Measuring the Influence of Supreme Court Justices," 27 *Journal of Legal Studies* 333 (1998).

subject-matter classes of case), the ranking that the study produced is at best a rough guide to the relative quality (or influence, or reputation—it is not altogether clear which is being measured) of the judges in the sample. Still, it may well be an improvement over purely qualitative efforts to evaluate appellate judges. Entire courts can be evaluated similarly, as I suggested earlier in reference to the Ninth Circuit.

Citation analysis is more commonly used to rank scholars than judges[40] and as such is now a fairly widely used management tool in connection with the hiring and promotion of faculty in research universities.[41] This is a natural use of citation analysis because the principal output of the faculty of such universities is published research and the more heavily a research paper is cited the more influential and important it is likely to be. Again, comparability problems must be overcome; it would be ridiculous to count citations of rival candidates of very different length of service and think that one had made a meaningful comparison, unless perhaps the younger (not necessarily in age, but in length of time in academia) had more citations than the older. But adjustments similar to those that have to be made in comparing the output of different judges should be feasible and with these adjustments citations analysis becomes a reasonably objective basis for making decisions on hiring, promotion, and salary. The need for an objective basis for such decisions is particularly important in an era in which academic administrators can be forced to defend their personnel decisions in the courts against charges of racial, sexual, or other invidious discrimination.

Citations analysis can similarly be used to evaluate the impact (and so presumably the quality) of scholarly journals and academic presses.[42]

40. See, for example, Fred R. Shapiro, "The Most-Cited Legal Scholars," 29 *Journal of Legal Studies* 409 (2000); B. K. Sen, T. A. Pandalai, and A. Karanjai, "Ranking of Scientists—A New Approach," 54 *Journal of Documentation* 622 (1998); Michael E. Gordon and Julia E. Purvis, "Journal Publication Records as a Measure of Research Performance in Industrial Relations," 45 *Industrial and Labor Relations Review* 194 (1991); Marshall H. Medoff, "The Ranking of Economists," 20 *Journal of Economic Education* 405 (1989).

41. See, for example, Philip Howard Gray, "Using Science Citation Analysis to Evaluate Administrative Accountability for Salary Variance," 38 *American Psychologist* 116 (1983).

42. See, for example, Geoffrey M. Hodgson and Harry Rothman, "The Editors and Authors of Economics Journals: A Case of Institutional Oligopoly?" 109 *Economic Journal* F165 (1999); Alireza Tahai and G. Wayne Kelly, "An Alternative View of Citation Patterns of Quantitative Literature Cited by Business and Economic Researchers," 27 *Journal of Economic Education* 263 (1996); S. J. Leibowitz and J. P. Palmer, "Assessing the Relative Impacts of Eco-

A journal's "impact factor" (conventionally, the number of citations in year t to articles published in the journal in years $t-1$ and $t-2$ divided by the number of those articles) can be used to weight a scholar's citations by multiplying the number of citations to his work by the impact factor of the journals in which those citations appear.[43] The aim is to correct objectively for differences in journal, and hence citation, quality. Impact-adjusted citations can be used to rank not only individual scholars but also departments.[44]

The practical utility of citations ranking of scholars is not limited to academic administration. As I have already intimated, in cases in which academics claim to have been discriminated against by the university that employs them citations analysis can be used to help determine whether the alleged discrimination was invidious or was instead based on the plaintiff's lack of scholarly distinction.[45]

The use of citations analysis in academic research is conceptually distinct from its use in academic or judicial administration but overlaps

---

nomics Journals," 22 *Journal of Economic Literature* 77 (1984). The use of the impact factor to weight citations might seem to be double counting, since citations are used to weight the journal, and if it is heavily cited this might be thought to imply that articles cited in it will be cited by later journals as well. But this is not necessarily so. Suppose an article by A is cited in an article by B published in heavily cited (hence imputed to be high-quality) journal X. B's article can be expected to be cited more frequently than if it had been published in a lower-quality journal, but articles citing B's article will not necessarily cite articles cited by B. Nevertheless the fact that B cited A is, given that B's article appeared in a high-quality journal, a mark in A's favor. It should be noted, however, that the impact-factor measure has been criticized as "entirely miss[ing] the archival impact of the journals and giv[ing] much greater weight to those publications of a more ephemeral nature or to those publications more concerned with debates about current issues than with research." Stephen M. Stigler, "Citation Patterns in the Journals of Statistics and Probability," 9 *Statistical Science* 94, 98 (1994). For a striking example, see John P. Perdew and Frank J. Tipler, "Ranking the Physics Departments: Use Citation Analysis," *Physics Today*, Oct. 1996, pp. 15, 97.

43. See, for a critical discussion of this procedure, Editorial, "Citation Data: The Wrong Impact?" 1 *Nature Neuroscience* 641 (1998).

44. See, for example, Raymond P. H. Fishe, "What Are the Research Standards for Full Professor of Finance?" 53 *Journal of Finance* 1053, 1057 (1998); Richard Dusansky and Clayton J. Vernon, "Rankings of U.S. Economics Departments," *Journal of Economic Perspectives*, Winter 1998, p. 157.

45. Cases in which citations analysis has been used for this purpose include Tagatz v. Marquette University, 861 F.2d 1040, 1043 (7th Cir. 1988); Weinstein v. University of Illinois, 811 F.2d 1091, 1093 (7th Cir. 1987); Demuren v. Old Dominion University, 33 F. Supp. 2d 469, 481 (E.D. Va. 1999); and Fisher v. Vassar College, 852 F. Supp. 1193, 1198–2000 (S.D.N.Y. 1992), reversed on other grounds, 70 F.3d 1420 (2d Cir. 1994), reversed, 114 F.3d 1332 (2d Cir. 1997) (en banc).

as a matter of practice. The patent study I cited earlier can be used to evaluate the government's research policy but also to test hypotheses about the economics of technology transfer.[46] Studies of judicial citation practices can be used both to evaluate courts and judges and to test hypotheses about judicial behavior and explain differences in productivity.

We need models to orient research that employs citation analysis, and I'll suggest three: a human capital model, a reputation model, and an information model. The first is the most useful, for reasons that will become clear, and I'll discuss the other two very briefly. In a reputation model,[47] emphasis is laid on the fact that reputation is something accorded by the "reputers" to advance their own self-interest, for example their interest in economizing on information costs. This can produce, as I hinted earlier, a "superstar" effect, in which small differences in quality generate huge differences in income, or, in this case, in citations.[48] Comparing Web "hits" and newspaper citations to leading legal scholars with citations to these scholars in scholarly journals,[49] Landes and I found a greater superstar effect for celebrities than for scholars. We conjectured that this is a function of the extent of the market. The general public's interest in law is quite limited, and the public demand for the output of legal scholars is therefore easily satisfied by a handful of high-profile figures. The scholarly community has a much broader interest in legal scholarship and therefore values the output of a much larger number of scholars.

In the information model, citations are conceived of as creating a

46. See Jaffe, Fogarty, and Banks, note 35 above, at 202–203; also Adam B. Jaffe, Manuel Trajtenberg, and Rebecca Henderson, "Geographic Localization of Knowledge Spillovers as Evidenced by Patent Citations," 108 *Quarterly Journal of Economics* 577 (1993).

47. See, for example, Richard A. Posner, *Cardozo: A Study in Reputation*, ch. 4 (1990).

48. Cf. Sherwin Rosen, "The Economics of Superstars," 71 *American Economic Review* 845 (1981). Robert K. Merton described essentially this effect, which he dubbed the "Matthew Effect." Merton, "The Matthew Effect in Science," 159 *Science* 56 (1968). He argued that scholars would use an author's reputation as a screening device, and hence tend to cite better-known authors more frequently than warranted by any actual difference between the quality of their work and that of less well-known authors. A related finding is that journals that use "blind" refereeing (that is, that do not disclose the author's name to the referee) are cited more frequently, after correction for other differences, than non-blind-refereed journals. David N. Laband and M. J. Piette, "A Citation Analysis of the Impact of Blinded Peer Review," 272 *JAMA (Journal of the American Medical Association)* 147 (1994).

49. Landes and Posner, note 17 above.

stock of information. The analyst can use the model to illuminate such issues as the geographic diffusion of information, as in the patent study that I cited earlier, and the rate at which the stock depreciates, for example as a function of the generality, and hence adaptability to changing circumstances, of the cited work. A related approach, sociological rather than economic in character, seeks to demarcate schools of thought by identifying patterns of cross-citation.[50]

In the standard human capital model used in labor economics, earnings are modeled as a function of the investment in the worker's human capital (that is, his earning capacity). His stock of human capital grows in the initial stages of his working career as a result of on-the-job training and experience. But like other capital, human capital depreciates. Eventually the worker's total stock of human capital declines when new investment falls below the replacement level as the worker approaches retirement, since the shorter the worker's remaining working life, the less time he and his employer have to recover the cost of any new investment.

Earnings (E) and years worked (time, t) are thus related as in $E(t) = a + b_1 t - b_2 t^2$, where $E(t)$ is annual earnings as a function of time (years worked from first job to retirement), a is an earnings component that is independent of investment in human capital and is assumed to be constant over time, b_1 represents an annual increase in earnings brought about by investments in human capital, and $-b_2$ represents an annual reduction in earnings caused by depreciation of the individual's stock of human capital. The peak year of earnings (t^*) is found by differentiating $E(t)$ with respect to t and setting the result equal to zero (satisfaction of the other conditions for a maximum can be assumed). This procedure yields $t^* = b_1/b_2$. An individual reaches his peak year of earnings later the more his earnings are raised by investments in human capital (b_1) and the smaller the effect of length of service (hence imminence of retirement) in reducing his earnings by causing him to invest less in replacing human capital as it depreciates (b_2). If $E(t)$ is replaced by the natural log of $E(t)$, then the coefficients (b_1 and b_2) can be interpreted as rates of growth.

The twist that human capital citations analysis gives to the standard model is to replace earnings with citations. This is an appropriate ad-

---

50. See, for example, Stigler and Friedland, note 25 above.

justment in the case of activities in which earnings are not well correlated with output. The federal judiciary provides an excellent example. All judges of the same rank (district judges, circuit judges, and
so forth) are paid the same salary, regardless of years of service, reversal rate, number of opinions published, or any other factor that
might be used by a private employer to determine a worker's marginal
product.

In many universities, too, faculty compensation is on a lockstep basis, and even when it is not, salary differentials are invariably far smaller
than any reasonable estimate of differences in the academic output of
different members of the faculty.[51] A possible explanation is that an academic's full income includes fame[52] and so varies across academics in
accordance with differences in the quality or their work. This point has
been made in distinguishing between science and technology. "Science
aims at increasing the stock of knowledge, while the goal of technology
is to obtain the private rents that can be earned from this knowledge."[53]
Because the achievement of the scientist's goal depends on complete
disclosure, and complete disclosure impedes the obtaining of rents, science must devise an alternative method of compensation. "The rule of
priority is a particular form of payment to scientists."[54] This can help us
understand why the acknowledgment of priority is a norm of scholarship—and the usual form of acknowledgment of priority is citation,
although citations acknowledge other forms of scholarly contribution
as well.

The economic model of citations as an earnings substitute recognizes that variance in earnings is not a function just of length of service

51. Nevertheless, there is evidence that number of citations to an academic's work is a significant predictor of his salary. See, for example, Raymond D. Sauer, "Estimates of the Returns to Quality and Coauthorship in Economic Academia," 96 *Journal of Political Economy*
855 (1988); Arthur M. Diamond, Jr., "What Is a Citation Worth?" 21 *Journal of Human Resources* 200 (1986). This is presumably because scholarly fame is positively correlated with the
value of the scholar's output.

52. See Paula E. Stephan, "The Economics of Science," 34 *Journal of Economic Literature*
1199, 1206 (1996). Empirical evidence for this conjecture in the case of economists is presented in David M. Levy, "The Market for Fame and Fortune," 20 *History of Political Economy*
615 (1988).

53. Partha Dasgupta and Paul A. David, "Information Disclosure and the Economics of
Science and Technology," in *Arrow and the Ascent of Modern Economic Theory* 519, 529 (George
R. Feiwel ed. 1987) (footnote omitted).

54. Id. at 531.

and investments in human capital. The variable that I labeled *a* represents the other factors that influence output, including quality variables such as intelligence, judgment, and writing skill that are only loosely (and sometimes not at all) related to training or other forms of investment in human capital. Recall that in the LLS study of cross-circuit judicial citations the human capital model was used to predict differences in the output of judges and the residual (unexplained) differences were then used to rank the judges, that is, to determine their relative endowments of *a*.

An alternative method of getting at *a* is to confine the comparison of citations to judges serving on the same court in the same period of time, thus obviating the need to make adjustments for differences in caseload composition and in the dates of the cited works, or to scholars of the same approximate age or length of service. I have used this cruder method of adjustment to verify the superior quality or influence of Benjamin Cardozo and Learned Hand relative to their colleagues on the New York Court of Appeals and U.S. Supreme Court (for Cardozo) and the U.S. Court of Appeals for the Second Circuit (for Hand).[55] But for broader comparisons, the human capital model is indispensable, as it enables correction for differences in the location of a judge or scholar in the life cycle.

We need not view *a* as a black box; LLS sought to explain the rankings of federal court of appeals judges by such factors as self-citation, the degree to which the judge's court has a specialized jurisdiction (which would tend to reduce the number of citations by other courts), and whether the judge had attended an elite law school, received a good rating from the American Bar Association when he was evaluated for appointment, or had previous judicial experience.[56] All the factors but the last were found to have a statistically significant relation to the judge's rank, and in the predicted direction.

A finding of the LLS study that is likely to raise eyebrows is that self-citations increase the number of other-court citations to the self-citing judge. The authors explained, however, that self-citing indicates a greater judicial involvement in the opinion-writing process; a judge

55. Posner, note 47 above, at 83–90; Richard A. Posner, *Aging and Old Age* 188–192 (1995). See also Henry T. Greely, "Quantitative Analysis of a Judicial Career: A Case Study of Judge John Minor Wisdom," 53 *Washington and Lee Law Review* 99, 133–150 (1996).

56. Landes, Lessig, and Solimine, note 12 above, at 320–324.

who remembers and cites his previous opinions will generally be more engaged in the opinion-writing process than a judge who leaves citations to his law clerks.

The study did not find any effect of race or sex on the number of judicial citations. In contrast, a study of citations in scholarly journals to legal academics finds that being female or a member of a minority is associated with being cited less frequently after correction for other factors, such as field and length of service. The implication is that affirmative action, which is common in law schools' faculty hiring, leads, as opponents contend, to the hiring of less-qualified minority and female candidates, as measured by their scholarly output once hired. Indeed, the study finds significant discrimination against Jewish males, who other things being equal are cited much more frequently than other legal academics.[57] Of course, the Jewish males might just be better than the other groups. The acid test for discrimination would be to compare the number of citations to marginal Jewish males to the number of citations to the marginal members of other groups; if the first number were higher, implying that the hiring of more Jews would raise the total number of citations to the faculty, this would be evidence of discrimination.

Another study of the legal academy finds a negative relation between research output as measured by citations and hiring one's own graduates in preference to those of other law schools.[58] Still another study contributes to our knowledge of the legal-academic production function by finding (though on the basis of a very small sample) that scholarship and teaching are net complements rather than substitutes in the production of scholarship.[59] A study of the citations output of the fed-

---

57. Deborah Jones Merritt, "Scholarly Influence in a Diverse Legal Academy: Race, Sex, and Citation Counts," 29 *Journal of Legal Studies* 345 (2000). That is not, however, Merritt's interpretation of her data. A different study, also employing citations as a proxy for quality, finds discrimination against women by economics departments. Van W. Kolpin and Larry D. Singell, Jr., "The Gender Composition and Scholarly Performance of Economics Departments: A Test for Employment Discrimination," 49 *Industrial and Labor Relations Review* 408 (1996).

58. Theodore Eisenberg and Martin T. Wells, "Inbreeding in Law School Hiring: Assessing the Performance of Faculty Hired from Within," 29 *Journal of Legal Studies* 369 (2000).

59. James Lindgren and Allison Nagelberg, "The False Conflict between Scholarship and Teaching" (Northwestern University Law School, unpublished, n.d.).

eral courts of appeals[60] that inquires into the production function of appellate courts finds among other things that the greater the number and length of a court's majority opinions, and the fewer the number of footnotes and of dissenting opinions, the greater will be the number of citations to that court by other courts. Footnotes in judicial opinions tend to confuse the reader, and a dissenting opinion undermines the majority opinion not only by indicating a lack of unanimity but also by expressing criticisms of the outcome that the majority would have preferred to pass over in silence. The study also found that citation-weighted output fell as the number of judges on the court rose, which is consistent with other evidence presented in this chapter.

The LLS study was limited to judges of the same court system (allowing for some differences in specialization), and my studies have been limited to judges of the same court or to courts of the same system (the federal courts of appeals, again). When citations to heterogeneous courts are aggregated, citation totals may still be meaningful as measures of influence, but they cease to be meaningful as measures of quality. The same is true with regard to studies of scholarly citations. Comparing total scholarly citations across all legal scholars[61] may be a valid measure of influence, but it cannot be a valid measure of quality, since differences in citations across fields may reflect differences in the size of fields and in the number of journals in different fields, and even citation conventions, rather than differences in perceived quality. But aggregating scholarly citations by field *over time* is a valid method of charting the rise and fall of different fields, for example (in law) economic analysis, feminist jurisprudence, and doctrinal analysis.[62] For that matter, comparison of citations across fields is meaningful if what one is interested in is the relative size of different fields.

Treating a body of judicial opinions as a capital stock invites atten-

---

60. *The Federal Courts: Challenge and Reform*, note 3 above, at 234–236.

61. As in Shapiro, note 40 above.

62. See William M. Landes and Richard A. Posner, "The Influence of Economics on Law: A Quantitative Study," 36 *Journal of Law and Economics* 385 (1993). We concluded in that study that "the influence of economics on law was growing at least through the 1980s (it is too early to speak about the 1990s), though the rate of growth may have slowed beginning in the mid-1980s; that the growth in the influence of economics on law exceeded that of any other interdisciplinary or untraditional approach to law; and that the traditional approach [of legal scholarship]—what we call 'doctrinal analysis'"—was in decline over this period relative to interdisciplinary approaches in general and the economic approach in particular." Id. at 424.

tion to the depreciation of precedent, a topic that Landes and I addressed in the first economic study of legal citations.[63] The analogy to physical capital is here quite close. A specialized machine can be expected to obsolesce more quickly than one that can be adapted to different tasks, since the former is less adaptable to change. Similarly, the more general a precedent is, the less rapidly it is likely to depreciate. And just as a sturdy machine can be expected to depreciate less rapidly (other things being equal) than a fragile one, so the more authoritative the court (for example, the Supreme Court relative to a lower federal court), the more slowly the precedents it produces are likely to depreciate.[64] We can also expect the depreciation rate to be higher the greater the rate of legal change—and so I found in a comparison of English and American cases.[65] And a big change in law, such as the abolition of the general federal common law by the *Erie* decision,[66] can have a dramatic effect in obsoleting precedent.[67]

The age profile of citations is relevant to the study of scholarship, including legal scholarship, as well as judicial behavior. Other things being equal, the half-life (or other measure of decay) of citations to scholarly work and scholarly journals is shorter the more progressive the discipline (or subdiscipline, such as economic analysis of law, critical legal studies, or feminist jurisprudence) in the sense that it is continuously generating new research that yields findings that supersede earlier findings, but longer the more rapidly the number and size of the discipline's publication outlets are growing. The reason for the latter, less obvious effect is that a rapid expansion of outlets creates more opportunities for older articles to be cited, assuming there is some citation lag (in part because of the "Matthew Effect"[68]—the new journal is not as heavily cited as the old until it accrues a reputation) so that the articles in the new outlets will not be cited immediately.[69]

63. William M. Landes and Richard A. Posner, "Legal Precedent: A Theoretical and Empirical Analysis," 19 *Journal of Law and Economics* 249 (1976).

64. Both hypotheses are supported by the study cited in the previous footnote.

65. Richard A. Posner, *Law and Legal Theory in England and America* 84–87 (1996).

66. Erie R.R. v. Tompkins, 304 U.S. 64 (1938).

67. See William M. Landes and Richard A. Posner, "Legal Change, Judicial Behavior, and the Diversity Jurisdiction," 9 *Journal of Legal Studies* 367 (1980).

68. See note 48 above.

69. Helmut A. Abt, "Why Some Papers Have Long Citation Lifetimes," 395 *Nature* 756 (1998).

The net depreciation of human capital is a function not only of the depreciation rate but also of the rate of new investment. That rate falls off not only because the expected return is truncated by retirement but also because of the aging process. We recall from Chapter 4 that judging is a famously geriatric profession in the common law countries, such as England and the United States. In part this is an artifact of the lateral-entry method of filling judgeships in these countries: the older the average age of entry, the older the average age of the profession is bound to be. But another possibility is that in a judicial system that relies heavily on precedent—a backward-looking mode of decisionmaking—aging will take a lesser toll on ability than in a profession such as mathematics that emphasizes the manipulation of abstract models.[70] This hypothesis can be tested by relating citations to the age of the judge whose decision is being cited; I have done this and found little evidence of an aging effect before the age of 80.[71]

70. Psychologists distinguish between "fluid intelligence," the ability to manipulate abstract symbols, and "crystallized intelligence," the ability to work from a long-established knowledge base, such as knowledge of one's language.

71. Posner, *Aging and Old Age*, note 55 above, at 182–192.

Acknowledgments

I thank Susan Burgess, Paul Choi, Schan Duff, France Jaffe, Eugene Kontorovich, Gene Lee, Bruce McKee, and Anup Malani for their very helpful research assistance. For helpful comments on earlier drafts of most of the papers from which I have drawn in composing this book, I am greatly indebted to Lawrence Lessig, Martha Nussbaum, Eric Posner, and Cass Sunstein. I also received a number of very helpful comments on particular papers from Ronald Allen, Albert Alschuler, Jack Balkin, Susan Bandes, Gary Becker, Andrew Daughety, Neil Duxbury, Robert Ellickson, Richard Epstein, Stanley Fish, Gertrud Fremling, Richard Friedman, Joseph Gastwirth, Richard Helmholz, Laura Kalman, Bruce Kobyashi, Larry Kramer, William Landes, Brian Leiter, Frank Michelman, Peter Newman, Eric Rasmusen, Jennifer Reinganum, Richard Rorty, Carol Rose, Michael Saks, Erich Schanze, Steven Shavell, Stephen Stigler, Geoffrey Stone, David Strauss, and David Wilson. I owe a special acknowledgment to Gertrud Fremling and Eric Rasmusen, with each of whom I coauthored a paper on which I have drawn (in places verbatim) in Chapters 8 and 10 respectively; they are not to be held responsible for the revisions that I have made in adapting these papers for the present volume.

Let me indicate the provenance of the various chapters. The Introduction draws in part from an essay on "Legal Theory" prepared for the *Encyclopedia Britannica;* in part from a review of Mark Tushnet,

Taking the Constitution away from the Courts (1999), published under the title "Appeal and Consent" in the *New Republic*, August 16, 1999, p. 36; and in part from my review of Jeremy Waldron, *Law and Disagreement* (1999), 100 *Columbia Law Review* 582 (2000). Chapter 1 is based on a Coase Lecture delivered at the University of Chicago Law School on January 6, 1998 and published under the title "Values and Conse- quences: An Introduction to Economic Analysis of Law," in *Chicago Lectures in Law and Economics* 189 (Eric A. Posner ed. 2000); in part on my Presidential Address to the Bentham Club of University Col- lege London on March 2, 1998, published under the title "Bentham's Influence on the Law and Economics Movement," 51 *Current Legal Problems* 425 (1998); and in part on a lecture in the Distinguished Lec- ture Series on Economics and the Law that I delivered at George Mason University School of Law on September 14, 1999. Chapter 2 is based on an essay prepared for a collection (not yet published), ed- ited by Lee Bollinger and Geoffrey Stone, of essays commemorat- ing the Supreme Court's first great free-speech decision, *Schenck v. United States*, 249 U.S. 47 (1919). Chapter 3 draws heavily on my arti- cle "Equality, Wealth, and Political Stability," 13 *Journal of Law, Eco- nomics, and Organization* 344 (1997), which in turn is based on an ad- dress that I gave on March 27, 1996, at a UNESCO conference in Paris on the subject *"Qui Sommes-Nous?"* ("Who Are We?"); and also on my article "Cost-Benefit Analysis: Definition, Justification, and Comment on Conference Papers," 29 *Journal of Legal Studies* 1153 (2000).

Chapter 4 is based on my paper "Past-Dependency, Pragmatism, and Critique of History in Adjudication and Legal Scholarship," which was prepared for a conference on Past Dependencies to be held at Stanford University on November 5 and 6, 1999, and published in 67 *University of Chicago Law Review* 573 (2000). Chapter 5 is based in part on that pa- per; in part on my review of Bruce Ackerman, *We the People*, vol. 2: *Transformations* (1998), published under the title "This Magic Mo- ment," *New Republic*, April 6, 1998, p. 32; and in part on my review of Paul W. Kahn, *The Cultural Study of Law: Reconstructing Legal Scholar- ship* (1999), published under the title "Cultural Studies and the Law" in *Raritan*, Fall 1999, p. 42. Chapter 6 is based on my lecture "Savigny, Holmes, and the Law and Economics of Possession," the inaugural Savigny Memorial Lecture at Philips-Universität Marburg, delivered on June 25, 1999, and published in 86 *Virginia Law Review* 535 (2000).

Chapter 7 draws mainly on a paper entitled "Emotion versus Emotionalism in Law" which was delivered on May 23, 1998, at a Conference on Emotions and the Law sponsored by the University of Chicago and DePaul University and which is published in *The Passions of Law* 309 (Susan Bandes ed. 2000); Chapter 7 also draws on "Social Norms, Social Meaning, and Economic Analysis of Law: A Comment," 27 *Journal of Legal Studies* 553 (1998). Chapter 8 draws on that comment as well but is mainly based on my article "Rational Choice, Behavioral Economics, and the Law," 50 *Stanford Law Review* 551 (1998), and on my as yet unpublished paper with Gertrud M. Fremling, "Market Signaling of Personal Characteristics" (November 2000). Chapter 9 is based on my article "Social Norms and the Law: An Economic Approach," 87 *American Economic Review Papers and Proceedings* 365 (May 1997); on an article coauthored with Eric B. Rasmusen, "Creating and Enforcing Norms, with Special Reference to Sanctions," 19 *International Review of Law and Economics* 369 (1999); and on my "Comment on Laurence R. Iannaccone, 'Religion, Values, and Behavioral Constraint,'" which was delivered at a Symposium on the Economic Analysis of Social Behaviour sponsored by the Fraser Institute and held on December 1 and 2, 1995, to celebrate Gary Becker's 65th birthday.

Chapter 10 is based in major part on "In the Fraud Archives," my review of Janet Malcolm, *The Crime of Sheila McGough* (1999), published in the *New Republic*, April 19, 1999, p. 29. Chapters 11 and 12 are based on my article "An Economic Approach to the Law of Evidence," 51 *Stanford Law Review* 1477 (1999). Chapter 13 is based on my survey article "A Economic Analysis of the Use of Citations Analysis in the Law," 2 *American Law and Economics Review*, 381 (2000), and on my paper "Is the Ninth Circuit Too Large? A Statistical Study of Judicial Quality," 29 *Journal of Legal Studies* 711 (2000).

All previously published material has been revised, often extensively, for this volume.

Index